k16.00

GOOD NEWS F
THE EAST MIDLA

An account of the background to, and the story of, the Diocese of Nottingham

Compiled by
Anthony P. Dolan
Priest of the Diocese of Nottingham

Dedication

This work is respectfully dedicated to
all those who
by their words and lives
have witnessed to Jesus Christ
since the Christian Faith first arrived
in the English East Midlands

GOOD NEWS FOR THE EAST MIDLANDS

An account of the background to, and the story of, the Diocese of Nottingham

Anthony P. Dolan

INTRODUCTION

To mark the centenary, in 1950, of the Restoration of the Catholic Hierarchy in England and Wales, Canon Garrett D. Sweeney, at that time Archivist of the Diocese of Nottingham, wrote, anonymously, the 'Centenary Book', a brief history of the diocese or, to be more precise, of Catholic Christianity in the English East Midlands. A previous archivist, Monsignor William Croft, had, in the years immediately prior to the First World War, gathered material with a similar end in mind, but his work had never been published.

In more recent years, it has been felt by a number of people that it would be useful if laity, religious and clergy of the diocese, and others, could be made more aware of the rich but often unknown spiritual tradition we have inherited in this part of England. Such an awareness could, it has been suggested, be a powerful aid in spreading the Good News of Jesus Christ in the twenty-first century. *That is the principal aim of this book.*

It must be clearly understood that this is not an academic work, nor is it by any means original. The earlier section (until 1850) is little more than an abbreviated and modified copy of Canon Sweeney's Centenary Book; and a lot of the material on the parishes of the diocese is based on his typescript accounts of them. These latter go only as far as the mid1950s and have been brought up to date with the help of various individuals including the present diocesan archivist, Fr. Philip McBrien (who has also provided maps), and the assistant archivist, Dr. Graham Foster.

Many sources, too many to list individually, have been consulted. Among the most important of these has been the Nottingham Diocesan Year Book of which the first issue appeared in 1921. The present publication would have taken several years longer had it not been for the thorough index of the year books compiled by Dr. Foster. To him perhaps more than to any other person is owed a deep debt of gratitude, and this is gladly given.

Other individuals and organisations, too, have played a part in this production. Sister Susan Richert PBVM, Episcopal Vicar for Religious in the Diocese of Nottingham, has spent a great deal of time helping to obtain and collate information about the more than fifty Religious Congregations who have worked in the diocese. The Patrimony Committee of the Bishops' Conference and English Heritage have kindly given permission to use material from the 'Taking Stock' survey. The writers of specific articles and appendices as well as the many schools, religious communities, parishes and individuals who have responded to questionnaires, telephone calls and emails are sincerely thanked for their contributions to this publication.

Special gratitude goes to the staff of Tucann Design & Print, the publishers of this book, for their constant friendly and helpful advice and support.

Monsignor Brian Dazeley, who suggested the project as one way of filling in the time allegedly available to a retired archivist and parish priest, has firmly and gently guided it throughout its period of gestation.

Although (almost) every effort has been made to ensure accuracy, this work is not free from errors. For these, and for any omissions, the present author takes full responsibility and offers sincere apologies not least to those who may feel that their parish or community has not been adequately, if at all, represented.

If even a few people come to appreciate something about the wonders God has worked through Christians in the East Midlands over the past millennium and a half, and are perhaps led to a knowledge and love of Him, the time and energy which has gone into the compilation of this story will be, for the author, a more than sufficient reward.

Anthony P. Dolan
Easter, 2018.

FOREWORD

"Sensitivity to the past contributes to our lives in a necessary and salutary way. It is not just a temperamental or intellectual accident, like a talent for chess or a passion for whiskey, but a foundational human gift that is potentially as life-enhancing and civilising as our gift for love."

Seamus Heaney

I warmly commend to you this diocesan project which sets out to bring up to date the rich and interesting, but perhaps still largely unknown, story of Catholic Christianity in the East Midlands, the area broadly covered by the Diocese of Nottingham. As someone who has been bishop for little more than two years, and who did not have much acquaintance with the diocese before then, this 'history' will certainly be invaluable in enabling me to learn more of its fascinating past. I hope that you too will find it helpful.

It is always instructive to root ourselves as a diocese in our history, not simply to be nostalgic but to draw on and learn from the past so as to equip ourselves for the future. This is especially so at a time when so much in our society and in our Church seems to be constantly changing, and what lies ahead can appear far from clear.

This publication builds upon work produced in 1950 to celebrate the Centenary of the Restoration of the Catholic Hierarchy in England and Wales, and it is the fruit of the contributions of many men and women, lay, religious and clergy, from across the diocese.

This is as it should be, because Vatican II gave us a vision of the Church in which all of us are invited to be actively involved in its missionary work of serving the needs of all, especially those who are in most need, and of sharing with everyone the Good News of Christ Jesus.

I am most grateful to Canon Dolan, who has edited this work, and to all who have contributed in any way to its production. The years since Vatican II have certainly taught us that, while we are indeed a pilgrim people, there is still a long and uncertain way to go. I pray that, as we reflect upon the eventful and exciting history of our diocese, and read the story of those who have generously walked this way before us, we will all wish to pray for the grace to follow the Lord forward, wherever he may be leading us.

'Unless the Lord build the house, in vain do its builders labour.' (Psalm 127)

† Patrick
Right Rev Patrick McKinney
Bishop of Nottingham July 2017

From the Fourth Century to the Reformation

Conversion of the Romano-Britons and Anglo-Saxons

Through a mist of uncertainty, Lincoln emerges dimly as the earliest known centre of Christianity in the present Diocese of Nottingham. There is evidence that there were Christians in the town early in the fourth century, and that they may have had a bishop of their own, named Adelphius, who was one of the three British bishops present at the Council of Arles in 314 AD.

The rest is conjecture. It has been suggested that one-tenth of the population of Britain, living to the east and south of the Fosse Way, had received baptism before the age of persecutions came to an end with the Edict of Milan in 313. And the Fosse Way cuts through the diocese diagonally from Lincoln in the north-east to Hinckley in the south-west. It has likewise been suggested that in the fourth century there were twenty-four bishops in Britain. If so, one of these would almost certainly have been resident at Leicester, which was a centre of the imperial administration. But this is a guess.

After 410 Roman rule disintegrated. Roman Britain developed gradually into Anglo-Saxon England. The incomers, entering from the North Sea into the Humber and the Wash, settled in the river valleys that penetrate this diocese. They undoubtedly destroyed the organisation of the Church. Did they also destroy the tradition of the Faith? Many of the Romano-Britons survived. And the ease with which the populations received Baptism from the sixth-century missionary priests suggests that there must also have been some survival of the Faith.

St. Paulinus came to England in 601 to join the missionary band of St. Augustine. He may be regarded as the Father of the Church in our diocese: the flame he lit has never been extinguished. Sometime between 627 and 631 he converted the governor of Lincoln, built a stone church there, and carried out a mass-baptism on the Trent at a place called "Teolfinga Ceastre" which most probably is Littleborough, four miles south of Gainsborough.-

In the southern parts of the diocese, the early memories of the Faith centre round Repton. This was the principal residence of Peada, King of the Middle Angles, who was baptised in 653.

In 680 the Saxons gave Leicester its first Bishop, Cuthwine.

Christianity in AD 650

Two hundred years later, the last Saxon bishop fled south from the invading Danes. In 870 the Midlands were invaded by the Danes, and Leicester ceased to be a separate diocese. Thenceforth the people of Leicestershire were looked after by the Bishops of Lincoln.

The organisation of the Anglo-Saxon Church followed the civil organisation of the country. Lincolnshire at first came under the jurisdiction of Paulinus, Bishop of York, because it then formed part of the Kingdom of Deira, of which York was the capital. In 655 a bishop was appointed for the whole of the dominions of Peada. His name was Diuma, an Irish monk who had come to the area in 653. He established his see first at Repton, the king's residence, but moved it to Lichfield in the following year. This bishopric served both the Mercians and the Middle Angles.

Until the Norman Conquest, the boundaries of bishoprics tended to vary; at first with the changing boundaries of the kingdoms into which Britain was divided, then under the pressure of the Danish raids. Nottinghamshire emerged, by 1066, as a part of the Archdiocese of York. Derbyshire remained in the Diocese of Lichfield throughout – although the episcopal see of this diocese had a tendency to wander from Lichfield to Chester and Coventry and back again. Leicester had its own bishop from 680 to 874, when it was amalgamated with Dorchester-on-Thames – an arrangement which endured up to the Norman Conquest. The foundation of Leicester was the work of Archbishop Theodore, a native of Tarsus in Cilicia, who ruled Canterbury from 668 to 690 and did so much to reduce the chaotic Anglo-Saxon Church to some sort of order and to revive learning in the country. Another episcopal see founded by Theodore, in 680, was that of Stow in Lincolnshire, and this also was subsequently amalgamated with Dorchester. By the end of this period, the counties of the present Diocese of Nottingham were divided as follows: Lincolnshire, Leicestershire and Rutland under Dorchester-on-Thames, Nottinghamshire under York, and Derbyshire under Lichfield-and-Coventry.

Monasteries arose, centres both of contemplation and of learning. That at Repton was said to have been founded by King Wulfhere of Mercia (658-675). One of the monks, intending to devote himself to a hermit's life, became St. Guthlac, who died at Croyland in the Lincolnshire Fens in 714 and who may be considered as the earliest saint of the diocese. His last home became a shrine and the site of a Benedictine monastery. Repton church was later to be the last resting-place of St. Wystan, a member of the Mercian royal house, who died a martyr's death in 850. When the Danes sacked this monastery in 874 his body was carried to Evesham. In Lincolnshire, Bardney Abbey was founded shortly after 679, and from this time to 909 was the centre of the cult of St. Oswald who died in 642 after ruling Northumbria for nine years and whose body had been translated to the abbey church.

The present diocese has connections with two other Saxon saints. Lincolnshire formed part of the territory under the jurisdiction of St. Aidan, Bishop of Lindisfarne from 635 to 651. Derbyshire, and possibly the two counties to the east, were similarly ruled at one time by St. Chad, Bishop of Lichfield from 669 to 672.

The Church in the Middle Ages

The coming of the Normans brought organisation and discipline to the Church. The Anglo-Saxons had been very different from their efficient descendants in modern England. Immediately prior to the Norman Conquest, the diocesan structure of England was as follows.

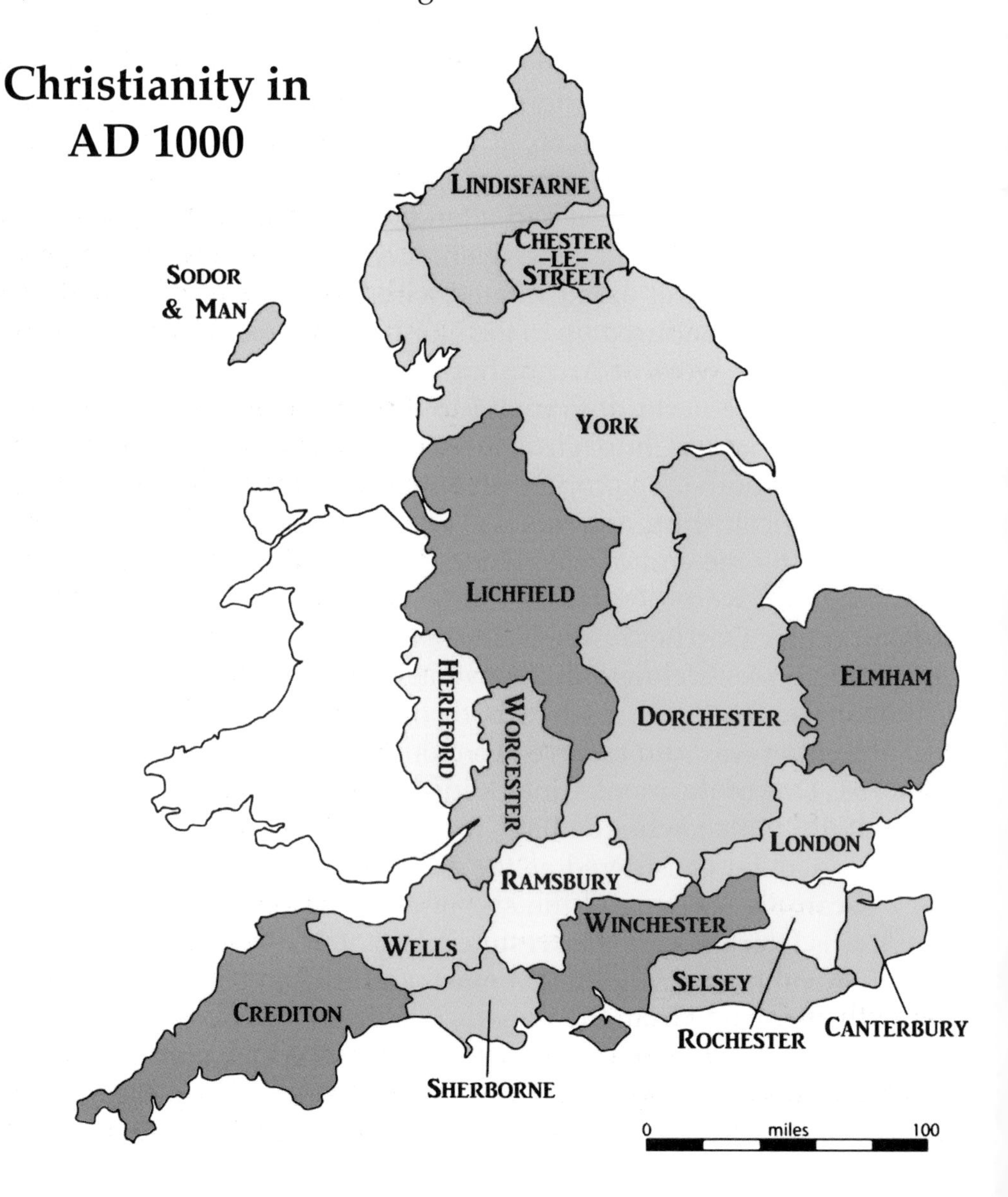

William the Conqueror changed this so that, whereas bishops were sometimes based in villages, they now moved to the large towns. Thus, for example, Dorchester gave place to Lincoln, which became the centre of an enormous diocese stretching from the Thames to the Humber.

Early in the twelfth century the dioceses were divided into archdeaconries. These were usually coterminous with the counties: Derbyshire, Leicestershire and Nottinghamshire each had its own archdeacon. Lincolnshire was divided into the Archdeaconries of Stow and Lincoln. Shortly after this there was a further sub-division into deaneries, each averaging about twenty parishes. Some idea of the contrast between the thirteenth century may be obtained from Lincolnshire, where there were twenty-four of these deaneries – and there are now twenty-two parishes!

It is impossible in this short space to deal with all the variations in the four hundred and fifty years between the Conquest and the Reformation. But it may be asserted that diocesan administration was careful and extremely healthy so long as it was free from governmental interference. The bishops were constantly on the move in a round of visitations; the clergy were under the close supervision of their archdeacons. The parishes were filled by priests who had been at least competently educated and properly examined before being given the care of souls. The number and beauty of the churches erected during these centuries are sufficient witness of the devotion of the people.

There was one flaw in the organisation of the medieval Church: control of the higher appointments passed practically into the hands of the king, and of the lower appointments into the hands of the local gentry. At the lower levels, the bishop actually appointed the parish priests – but he could usually only appoint a nominee "presented" by the lay patron of the parish. His choice was, therefore, very limited. At the higher levels, the bishops were, in theory, elected by the Cathedral Chapters. But, in practice, towards the end of the Middle Ages, the canons grew more and more accustomed to electing a candidate suggested by the king. Thus it happened that the character of the bishops steadily deteriorated. Lincoln had a succession of great bishops from the twelfth to the fourteenth centuries: one, St. Hugh of Lincoln (1186-1200) was canonised; two others - Robert Grosseteste (1235-53) and John Dalderby (1280-1300) – were honoured locally after their death as saints, although they were never raised to the altars of the Church. In the fifteenth century things went from bad to worse, the bishops being little more than statesmen and civil servants provided by the king with an income from the Church as a cheap way of paying them.

In the years immediately before the breach with Rome, the five counties of the diocese were practically without any episcopal government. Bishop Smythe of Lincoln (1496-1514) was taken up with his duties as President of the Council of Wales, and the same may be said of Bishop Blythe of Lichfield (1503-33) who succeeded him in the Presidency. Cardinal Wolsey never set foot in his Archdiocese of York until his fall in 1529. The stage was set for the next generation of bishops who, under Henry VIII, were to lead the Church in England away from its allegiance to the Successor of St. Peter.

The Church in England & Wales prior to The Reformation

From the Reformation to the Restoration of the Catholic Hierarchy

Henry VIII

The apostasy of the nation began at the top; only in London and the south-east was there any movement of the people away from the ancient Faith.

In 1534 it became necessary for all the leaders of the Church to repudiate the authority of the Holy See or to suffer the extreme penalty for treason. With very few exceptions, this repudiation (it took the form of an oath accepting the Act of Succession) was made by all the bishops, the canons of the cathedral chapters, the universities, the heads of religious houses, and those of the clergy who sat as members of Convocation – the clerical "Parliaments" of Canterbury and York. The pass was sold by the three bishops who then ruled the five counties of the present Diocese of Nottingham: Edward Lee of York, John Longland of Lincoln and Rowland Lee of Lichfield. The canons of the cathedrals and the archdeacons followed the example of their superiors – but one must not forget the extenuating circumstances: the penalty for refusal was torture and death.

Among the few exceptions to the general submission were the Carthusians Robert Lawrence, Prior of Beauvale; John Houghton, his predecessor in that role, and Augustine Webster, Prior of Axholme. On 4 May 1535 they, along with two other priests, were hung, drawn and quartered at Tyburn. They were the first Reformation martyrs of the present diocese and, indeed, of the Reformation as a whole.

From this time until the death of Henry VIII in 1547 the situation was as follows. The common people of the Midlands remained Catholic, attending Mass said by Catholic priests and receiving the sacraments. The higher clergy were schismatic – having repudiated the authority of the Holy See but not yet the dogmatic and moral teaching of the Universal Church.

At the same time the chances of the Catholic Faith surviving any length of time grew less and less. In 1535-36 the smaller monasteries and religious houses were suppressed and their property sold for a song to the landed gentry and wealthier townsfolk. There can be no doubt as to the high value that the people of Lincolnshire set on the monasteries. Popular risings broke out at Louth and Horncastle, spread throughout Lincolnshire and thence to Yorkshire and the north. Soon there were 30,000 peasants under arms against the king. He was at their mercy, promised not to molest the monasteries, waited for them to disperse, then collected troops and hanged the leaders. The Pilgrimage of Grace of 1536 was thus followed by the complete suppression of the monasteries in 1537.

Among those who were executed for their part in this rising were the abbot and monks of Barlings in Lincolnshire – they had armed and taken the field in person - and the prior and monks of Lenton then outside Nottingham. The effect of the suppression of the monasteries was twofold: the common people lost the benefit of the stream of spiritual life and material assistance that had flowed from the religious houses; and the landed gentry had now a vested interest in the king's Church. If the Pope's authority were now restored, they stood to lose the monastic lands they had picked up at the suppression. Thus the matter rested for the remaining years of Henry's life.

His successor, Edward VI, was a minor. The government of the country passed to Protector Somerset and the class of landed proprietors who stood to gain from the extinction of Catholicism. Protestant preachers from the continent were imported, and although they had considerable success in London and the south-east, their influence in the Midlands and North was small.

In 1549 the first attempt was made to change the religion of the common people. From Whitsunday of this year their priests were bound by law to use a form of service set out in the first Book of Common Prayer. It seems that the law was pretty well obeyed throughout the country. There was, indeed, an immediate rising of the peasantry of Cornwall and Devon against a form of service which they described as "like a Christmas game." But this was soon suppressed by the German and Italian troops sent down by the government. The new service had, in fact, been carefully worded to suit all parties. It was little more than an English translation of the Roman Mass, and when used by a validly ordained priest could be a truly Eucharistic Sacrifice. Unfortunately, from 1550, the stream of validly ordained priests dried up. In that year, the Ordination Service was changed, and those clergy who were "ordained" under this form were not true priests. The Apostolic Succession came to a sudden end. The final step was taken in 1552, when a second Book of Common Prayer was imposed upon the clergy, and the form of service it contained could not possibly have the efficacy of the Mass. At the same time a destruction of altars and sacred vessels was carried out to make sure that Mass could no longer be said.

It is difficult to obtain an exact picture of the religious state of England in 1552-53. Some parishes had validly-ordained priests; others were in the care of ministers of the new non-priestly type. In all parishes it seems that the new service in English was read; in many it seems that Mass was also said as well, and that the people continued to receive the sacraments. The situation was confused, and the only thing that can safely be asserted is that the common people of the Midlands had not apostatised from the true Church, but were being slowly starved out of it.

Elizabeth I

The reign of Mary (1553-58) gave back the Mass and communion with Rome to the people of England. The pseudo-priests of Edward VI were ejected. New bishops were appointed. Cardinal Pole in 1554 formally absolved the country from a schism in which the people had never participated. Unfortunately, Mary's reign marked the beginning of an irreconcilable hatred for the Faith in a certain section of the population. Her revival of the medieval heresy laws and three hundred executions left a lasting resentment; her Spanish marriage gave the impression that Catholicism meant subservience to Spain. The Protestant minority grew hard and determined.

Elizabeth I (1558-1603) came to the throne with a set determination to uproot the old Faith. Her policy was at first tactful – to cut the thread of the Apostolic Succession and leave the old religion to die out of the hearts of the people for want of instruction and of the sacraments. Violence was to come later.

In 1559 the bishops were called upon to take an oath repudiating the authority of the Pope. This time there was only one submission; they were men of a very different stamp from Henry's bishops. Nicholas Heath, Archbishop of York, had shown immense courage from the moment of Elizabeth's accession. On his refusal of the oath he was ejected from his see, underwent a short imprisonment, and finally died in 1579 at Cobham in Kent. The Bishop of Lichfield, Ralph Bayne, was likewise deprived and died at Islington 18 November 1559. Thomas Watson, Bishop of Lincoln, suffered the most. He had preached the panegyric at the funeral of Queen Mary and had made no secret of his opposition to the schemes of her successor. He was imprisoned successively in the Tower and the Marshalsea and died finally in Wisbech Castle on 27 September 1584. These three must surely be honoured as Confessors for the Faith, and with their death the Catholics of the five counties were left without a lawful spiritual head. Watson's death also marked the end of the old Catholic hierarchy of England, for no other bishop survived him.

The lesser clergy were not called upon to take the same oath as the bishops. Instead, they were called together at various centres throughout the country and ordered to sign a statement that they believed the queen's supremacy over the Church, and the order of service as set out in the Book of Common Prayer, "to be according to the true word of God." It has been shown that almost all the clergy were reluctant to sign – but that most of them did. Among those who refused were the two Lincolnshire Archdeacons and the Archdeacons of Derby and Nottingham.

To understand this submission of the clergy it must be remembered that few men as yet were able to realise that they could not both obey the queen and remain inside the Catholic Church. Her claim to supremacy could be understood, with some quibbling, in a way that did not conflict with the claims of the Holy See. The new service contained in the Book of Common Prayer bore some resemblance to the Mass. And Rome had not yet spoken to point out the clear path of duty. Another thirty years were to pass before the confusion was cleared away, and men could no longer claim to be Catholics while attending the Established Church.

As yet, the death penalty was threatened only against those who persistently spoke in favour of Papal Supremacy. But there was outspoken comment on the new religion all over the country. The situation changed abruptly in 1570 when Pope Pius V excommunicated Queen Elizabeth and called upon the princes of Christendom to depose her. To the Catholics of England this brought persecution and death.

In 1568 the foundation of Cardinal William Allen's college at Douai in the Netherlands brought to them the hope of once more receiving the true priesthood into their midst. And in 1569 the rising of the Northern Earls – the last armed protest of Catholic England against the new state of things – threatened to put the Queen of Scots upon the English throne and to restore the old religion. Elizabeth was alarmed; she clamped down upon the whole missionary effort of such priests as continued their administrations in the country. A priest who reconciled one of the queen's subjects, was, from 1571, to be hung, drawn and quartered.

The coming of the first Jesuits in 1580 crystallised the Catholic opposition. They made it clear that there could be no longer any compromise, and that men must stand out either as Catholics or Protestants. At the beginning of the reign it had been estimated that only one-third of the country had any Protestant sympathies – and that these were mainly concentrated around London and the south-east. When, after 1580, the wheat was winnowed from the chaff, it was found that some 100,000 out of a population of three to four million were ready to pay the price and to refuse attendance at the Anglican services. These were the hard core, the "recusants" (i.e. "refusers") whose numbers were to grow to 200,000 in the next century.

From this time, we may date the beginning of the Catholic counter-attack, which was made by a close-knit spiritual army of 100,000 under some two hundred and fifty missionary priests, working underground at the risk of their lives. Elizabeth replied with the laws of 1581-82. These made it high treason for a priest even to set foot on the soil of England or for a layman to give him shelter. The penalty for absence from the Sunday service in the Church of England was raised from one shilling per time to twenty shillings per month. These fines were not levied continuously, but there was no relaxation in the hunting of priests. By the end of the reign of Elizabeth, 128 priests, 58 laymen and 3 women had given their lives for the Faith.

James I

Continual, violent persecution ceased with the death of Elizabeth in 1603. Executions took place sporadically throughout the next eighty-two years, for the Penal Laws remained on the statute book; but the daily burden of fear was somewhat dispelled. The House of Commons, representing the landed interest which had done so well out of the dissolution of the monasteries, kept up the pressure against the old Faith. The Stuart kings, on the other hand, were always a centre of hope; the fourth, James II, reigned as a Catholic, the third, Charles II, was a deathbed convert, each of the last three had a Catholic queen, and the first, James I, began his reign by announcing that he would not molest the Catholics so long as they did not waver in their loyalty.

James I's promise of non-molestation brought in its train a revelation of the true religious feeling of the country. Reliable estimates of the time show that perhaps a third of the population was in sympathy with the old religion. His promise was soon withdrawn, and the consequent disappointment prompted a small band of desperadoes to the folly of the Gunpowder Plot in 1605. This did immeasurable damage to the Catholic cause. It was used by the government for all it was worth – as most effective propaganda against the loyalty of the Catholic body. Executions were resumed: eight laymen and twenty priests suffered for their faith during this reign.

This was, however, the classic period of the overseas province of English Catholicism which was being formed in the Low Countries. Here it was possible to establish in security the institutions needed to feed the

Catholic Faith in England. It became a matter of course for the sons of the gentry to go for their education to the colleges at Douai and St. Omer which had been founded as a temporary expedient in the reign of Elizabeth. Now, in the reign of James I, began the foundation of monasteries and convents in the Low Countries and Northern France. The English Benedictines had their houses at Douai, Paris and Dieulouard; the Dominicans at Bornhem. Communities of English nuns appeared at Louvain, Liège, Bruges, Brussels, Antwerp, Gravelines and Neuilly. These institutions flourished, and a steady flow of Catholic life flowed back into the persecuted island.

Towards the close of this reign, James was negotiating a marriage for his son with a Catholic princess. He was prepared, as part of the marriage settlement, to promise toleration. This paved the way for a restoration of some form of episcopal government in England. From 1598 until 1621 the Catholic Church in England had been governed by 'archpriests', but when the third and last of these died, he was not replaced. Instead, two years later, Dr. William Bishop was sent to England as Vicar-Apostolic for the whole country, the first Catholic bishop since the death of Dr. Watson of Lincoln in 1584. In his short episcopate of one year (he died in 1624) Bishop gave the Church some form of organisation. The country was divided into seven vicariates, each under a Vicar General; and these vicariates were subdivided into nineteen archdeaconries. The Vicars General, Archdeacons and ten other priests formed a Chapter of twenty-six canons which became the effective government of the English Catholic body after 1631, when the second Vicar-Apostolic, Bishop Richard Smith, was compelled to leave the country.

It is hardly possible to form an accurate estimate of numerical strength at this time in the five counties of the present diocese. But seventeen Jesuits were at work in the area in 1625 and this would imply that the total number of priests, secular and regular, amounted to about fifty and that the number of known practising Catholics was in the region of 7500.

Charles I

Up to the outbreak of the Civil War in 1642 they were only two executions of priests during this reign. Toleration (in the limited sense of non-violence - for penal disabilities still continued) became an accomplished fact especially during the eleven years after 1629, when the king ruled without the assistance of his disgruntled Parliament. Moreover, the Church of England, guided by Archbishop Laud, swung over to Anglo-Catholicism. There was some hope of corporate re union, and one Anglican bishop (Gloucester) did in fact die a Catholic.

It was against the general trend of the times that, in 1635, a raid was carried out on the Jesuits' secret school for boys at Stanley Grange near Ilkeston. This school had been in existence for some fifteen years and then accommodated about a dozen sons of the gentry. The raid was unsuccessful, for warning had been received and the school was moved, probably to the house of the Pole family at Spinkhill.

Civil War broke out in 1642. The Catholic gentry and peasantry stood by Charles to a man, thereby inflaming the passions of the Parliamentarians against the Church. Twenty-one priests were executed in the five years preceding the king's surrender at Newark. The laity suffered heavily, losing their lives in the unexpected struggle and their property in the confiscations that followed the defeat of their cause. The Venerable Robert Price, a Huntingdonshire gentleman, was captured after the fall of Lincoln and was shot out of hand on 7 May 1644. The Jesuits also suffered heavily at Lincoln, where three of their number died.

Although the end of hostilities brought some relief, the Catholic gentry emerged from these years diminished in numbers and impoverished. By contrast, there was a considerable increase in the numbers of convinced Protestants. Many of those for whom the Established Church had no attraction, were impressed by the success of Cromwell's deeply religious New Model Army; and a Puritan Parliament had been the champion of civil liberties. From this time dates the conviction that a liberty-loving British democrat must be of necessity an Evangelical Protestant.

Charles II

From 1660 England was once more ruled by a king. Hope rose again among the Catholic minority. If Charles II had any settled religious convictions, they tended vaguely to the Church of Rome. After the battle of Worcester, he had been saved by a Benedictine priest; and before the Restoration he had expressed a desire for tolerance. Unfortunately, his need for money forced him to consider the wishes of his Parliaments, the temper of which was now Anglican, intent on maintaining the privileges of that group of the gentry which had accepted the Established Church. New legislation found its way onto the statute book, confining the Catholics to their country estates, and thus isolating them from professional life and the work of local government.

The five counties of the present diocese have not hitherto appeared prominently in the Catholic life of the country. When active persecution took place, it had been confined mainly to London and the south-east. During the Civil Wars the Lincolnshire squires rallied to the king, and Lord

Widdrington of Blankney had risen to high command. Impoverishment followed, but there is no indication of any considerable rise or fall in numbers. The priests seem to have gone about their work from house to house and village to village – always cautiously and never secure, but practically unmolested. After 1649 there is no mention of any priest being taken up in this area until the Oates Plot of 1678-79 gave the signal for an outbreak of persecution throughout the country.

Oates' informers declared that the Jesuits were conspiring with some of the Catholic peers for a military invasion and for the assassination of the king and the leaders of the Anglican nobility. Oates carried the day by the sheer force of hard lying. Parliament took it all in and orders were issued for the arrest of priests all over the country. Before Oates could be unmasked, six priests were executed in London and eight in the provinces.

Among the London victims were two Jesuits, natives of the present Diocese of Nottingham. Blessed William Ireland was a native of Lincolnshire; he suffered at Tyburn on 24 January 1679. On 20 June of that same year, Blessed Anthony Turner, a native of Dalby Parva in Leicestershire, was also executed at Tyburn. At the close of 1679 the Jesuit, Father Francis Blackiston, was in Nottingham Gaol; and on 16 March 1681, the Jesuit, Father George Busby, was arrested at the house of Mr. Powtrell at West Hallam in the present Parish of Ilkeston. He was imprisoned in Derby Gaol, and at the Derby Summer Assizes on 25 July 1681, was condemned to be hung, drawn and quartered. The sentence was, never, however, carried out, and after a long imprisonment he was allowed to go into exile in Belgium. In Leicestershire, another Jesuit, Father William Bentney, was arrested at about the same time. An apostate Catholic gave evidence that this priest had said Mass at West Hallam, and he also received the sentence for high treason. For Father Bentney there was no release. He died of gaol-fever in Leicester Gaol, aged eighty-four, on 30 October 1692. A plaque to his memory was erected adjacent to the Leicester Royal Infirmary in 1998. It seems that he was the last priest to lay down his life for the Catholic Faith in this diocese.

The scare of the Popish Plot died down. Even so there was a round-up of the recusant laity in 1682, followed by persecutions and fines.

James II

The year 1685 brought a Catholic king to the throne of England and a Catholic bishop to the country for the first time since 1631. This was the Vicar-Apostolic, John Leyburn. There was to be no repeal of the Penal Laws, but their operation was suspended. It became possible for

Catholics to practise their religion without concealment.

Perhaps the most notable development of the time was the opening of a network of Jesuit schools. These were situated in the principal Catholic centres of England: two in London, and the others at Wigan, Wolverhampton, Bury St. Edmunds's, Lincoln and Pontefract. The choice of Lincoln for a school is an indication of its importance in the Catholic life of the period. It is not known how many boys attended this school. A public chapel was also opened at Lincoln.-

James II, sincerely and ostentatiously Catholic and utterly tactless, was successful only in alienating the Protestant majority of his subjects. Both parties, Whigs and Tories, saw their privileges threatened; Catholics were being given commissions in the army, appointed to governorships, imposed on the Oxford colleges, admitted to the Privy Council – one of its members being the Jesuit Father Petre. The parties united to sell the kingdom to the Dutch, and when, in the last days of 1688, the Dutch forces landed at Torbay, James found himself deserted and fled the country. Local rioting broke out all over the country. Mobs destroyed the Jesuit school and chapel at Lincoln. There was some imprisonment and banishment of priests, but there were no executions.

The accession of William III in 1689 marked the end of the Catholic resistance in England. Hitherto the morale of the Catholic minority had been high, buoyed up by the eternal hope that a Catholic king might restore civil liberty and open the way for a return of the country to the Catholic Faith. Hope had now departed. In the grey years of the eighteenth century the Catholics were content to hold what they had, preserving their legacy but not fighting back, depressed and sinking by the middle of the century to a new low-water mark.

The Church underground: from the flight of James II to the First

Catholic Relief Act

After the flight of James II in 1689 the Catholics of this country seemed to lose the spirit of resistance. For roughly the next hundred years they became the Church of the Underground.

The Penal Laws were changed, and became less violent but more soul-deadening. Priests who exercised their ministry in England were no longer liable to the death penalty, but could be condemned to life-imprisonment. Common informers were offered a reward of £100 for securing the conviction of a priest. In the first part of the century there were sporadic outbursts of priest-hunting. But the feeling of the country gradually became more humane, and the last priest to be sentenced to life-imprisonment was convicted in 1767.

The laity suffered by new laws preventing them from buying new land to add to their estates, and making it possible for a Catholic heir to be disinherited if he did not give up the Faith when he came of age. The medical and legal professions were closed to them, and as they were already barred from the army and the universities, there was nothing left for them to do but to vegetate in the country – where even their sports were restricted by a law forbidding them to possess a horse worth more than five pounds.

It was not until 1778 that Lord North, needing the fighting Catholic clans of Scotland for his war against the American colonies and France, secured the passage of the First Catholic Relief Act. This removed all penalties on priests for exercising their functions and allowed Catholics once more to purchase and inherit land. The black cloud of depression was beginning to lift.

The whole organisation of the Church at this time (with few exceptions) was built around the estates of the Catholic gentry. They maintained the priest, provided the half-secret chapel, sent their sons across the English Channel regularly to be educated at Douai, and their daughters to be educated in the English convents of the Low Countries; above all they gave their sons to the priesthood.

Town Missions were almost non-existent. Lincoln, however, never lacked its priest and always had about half a dozen Catholic families. Derby also and Grantham had their small, persistent groups of Catholics, never without the Mass, although their priests sometimes had to live outside the town. Louth, and almost certainly Nottingham, were never without a faithful few, although they had no priest of their own. In other towns such as Boston, Gainsborough, Stamford and possibly Leicester, there seems to be no evidence of any continuous Catholic life.

In 1773 there were resident priests in three places in Nottinghamshire; six in Derbyshire; two in Leicestershire; seven in Lincolnshire and one in Rutland.

The Governance of the Church during Penal Times

The Jesuit Mission 1580 – 1773

A curious feature of the Catholic life of Penal days was its division between two completely independent organisations. On the one hand were the secular priests, mainly from Douai, together with a mixture from the older religious orders; they were loosely organised, governed – in so far as they were governed at all – successively by Archpriests, Vicars-Apostolic, the Chapter, and Vicars-Apostolic once more. There was no central direction behind their missionary work, and they tended to go wherever they might be invited by the recusant gentry. On the other hand were the Jesuits, in numbers averaging between a third and a quarter of the priests serving in England, tightly organised, with strong central direction, intensively trained, and almost completely independent of any authority except that of their own superiors. After the Elizabethan Age they were to be the spearhead of the Catholic resistance, and bore the brunt of the sporadic attacks that were made upon the clergy.

The first two Jesuits – Edmund Campion and Robert Persons – came to England in 1580. Characteristically, they divided up the country between them. Derbyshire fell to Fr. Persons, and he appears to have made Spinkhill his headquarters for the county. Campion, among the most glorious of the English martyrs (hung, drawn and quartered at Tyburn, 1 December 1581) visited Nottinghamshire, spending Christmas with Henry Pierrepont of Holme Pierrepoint. Reinforcements followed. The special work of the Jesuits was to end the spirit of compromise among the Catholics and convince them that acceptance of the Queen's oaths and attendance at the Anglican services were incompatible with the Catholic Faith.

By 1619 the Jesuits were strong enough to establish a "Vice-Province" divided up into "Missions." Lincolnshire formed one of these, and the three counties of Derby, Nottingham and Leicester formed another. This was entitled the "Leicestershire Mission" indicating that there was still an important group of Catholics in the county at that time. Four years later, in 1623, a full "Province" was erected. The group of Jesuits working in Lincolnshire were known as the "Residence of St. Dominic" until 1676, when the county was given higher status and became known as the "College of St. Hugh." Derbyshire, Nottinghamshire, Leicestershire and Rutland formed the "College of the Immaculate Conception." (It may be noted that the word "College" does not here bear a scholastic meaning; it merely denotes the corporate body of priests working in the area.) This scheme of organisation cut across the secular scheme, in which Lincolnshire was joined with Nottingham to form a single archdeaconry. The boundaries of the Nottingham Diocese were - until 1980, when sixteen parishes in Derbyshire and Nottinghamshire were cut off to form part of the new Diocese of Hallam – exactly coterminous with those of the old Jesuit Colleges of St. Hugh and the Immaculate Conception and under the same two patronal dedications.

Some indication has already been given of the work of the Jesuits under the Stuarts. Their school at Stanley Grange near Ilkeston, begun about 1620 and raided in 1635, was certainly renewed elsewhere in the Derbyshire district; it is heard of from 1641 to 1648 although its location is not stated. Lincolnshire proved a good recruiting ground for the Society, providing some forty of its priests up to the time of the suppression of the Society in 1773. Derbyshire was not far behind. Three Jesuits died of their sufferings in Lincoln Gaol after the capture of that city in 1644; and one in Leicester Gaol in 1692 (W. Bentney), a forgotten victim of the Oates Plot.

Some measure of the Jesuit effort may be obtained from the returns of their numbers through the seventeenth century. In the five counties, there were seventeen of them in 1625; twenty-three in 1632; and then began a steady decline to twelve in 1700. When the Society was dissolved in 1773, the two Colleges were a shadow of their former selves, numbering only seven priests between them.

The Vicars-Apostolic 1685 - 1850

For many years there was no Catholic bishop in England. The Holy See thought it better not to send one, fearing lest the government might intensify the persecution. The danger passed with the accession of the Catholic King James II in 1685. On his petition, in 1685, the Holy See sent John Leyburn as bishop for the whole of Britain. He had the title 'Vicar-Apostolic', which meant that, while the Pope was technically the bishop, he delegated some of his powers to the Vicar-Apostolic. In 1688 Bishop Leyburn made a visitation of, among other places, Lincolnshire where he confirmed 105 at Irnham (near Grantham), 149 at Lincoln, and 115 at Hainton (near Market Rasen.)

In 1688 England and Wales were divided into four Districts – London, Midland, Northern and Western – each governed by a Vicar-Apostolic. The whole of the present Diocese of Nottingham belonged to the Midland District.

Map of the English Mission
1688 to 1840

The first seven of the Vicars-Apostolic of the Midland District came from the highest level of the Catholic peerage and landed gentry; they left behind them a tradition of solid piety and conscientious devotion to duty; they did little that was notable. Their lives were spent largely in the saddle, making their way from one isolated Mission to the other. Of the stories that can be related about them with reference to the Diocese of Nottingham, one may be of particular interest. John Hornyold, the third of the Vicars-Apostolic was, as a young priest in the 1730s, stationed at Grantham. One day he was saying Mass in a room next to the - still existent - Beehive Inn when the constable came to arrest him. He escaped arrest by throwing an old woman's cloak over himself and kneeling in the room in an attitude of prayer.

The Second Catholic Relief Act of 1791 legalised the erection of Catholic chapels – without steeples or bells. The first of these chapels in the Diocese of Nottingham, at Osgodby near Market Rasen, built in 1793, is still in use in 2018.

John Milner, son of a Lancashire tailor, was appointed eighth Vicar-Apostolic of the Midland District in 1803. He was very different in background and style from his predecessors, and part of his mission as he saw it was to bring Catholicism into the towns; this was, after all, the age of the Industrial Revolution. During the twenty-three years of his ministry in the Midlands, among the significant factors in the development of Catholicism in what was later to become the Diocese of Nottingham was the number of French priests in exile after the Revolution. In 1826, the year of Bishop Milner's death, nine of the twenty-five priests working in the territory at the later Diocese of Nottingham were French émigrés. Bishop Milner was also responsible for sending to minister to the Catholics of Nottingham early in 1825 one Robert William Willson about whose work much could be said. In addition to building the church or "Popish Chapel" as it was then called (since 1850 it has been known as St. Barnabas' Cathedral,) Fr. Willson became, in 1842, first Bishop of Hobart Town, Tasmania.

Bishop Milner was succeeded by Bishop Thomas Walsh, the ninth and last of the Vicars-Apostolic. A significant further development, in 1840, which would lead to the Restoration of the Catholic Hierarchy ten years later, was the subdivision of the four Districts established in 1688 into eight. The territory of the future Diocese of Nottingham was now split between the Eastern District to which Lincolnshire and Rutland were assigned, and the Central District which got Nottinghamshire, Derbyshire and Leicestershire. Bishop Walsh became the first Vicar-Apostolic of the Central District, moving his residence to Nottingham in 1844, the year of the consecration of St. Barnabas' Church. Transferred to the London District in 1848, Bishop Walsh died the following year.

The Restoration of the Hierarchy

On 29 September 1850 the normal system of governance in the Catholic Church was restored with the creation, in England and Wales, of an archdiocese (Westminster) and twelve dioceses. One of these was the Diocese of Nottingham.

Dioceses of England and Wales 1850

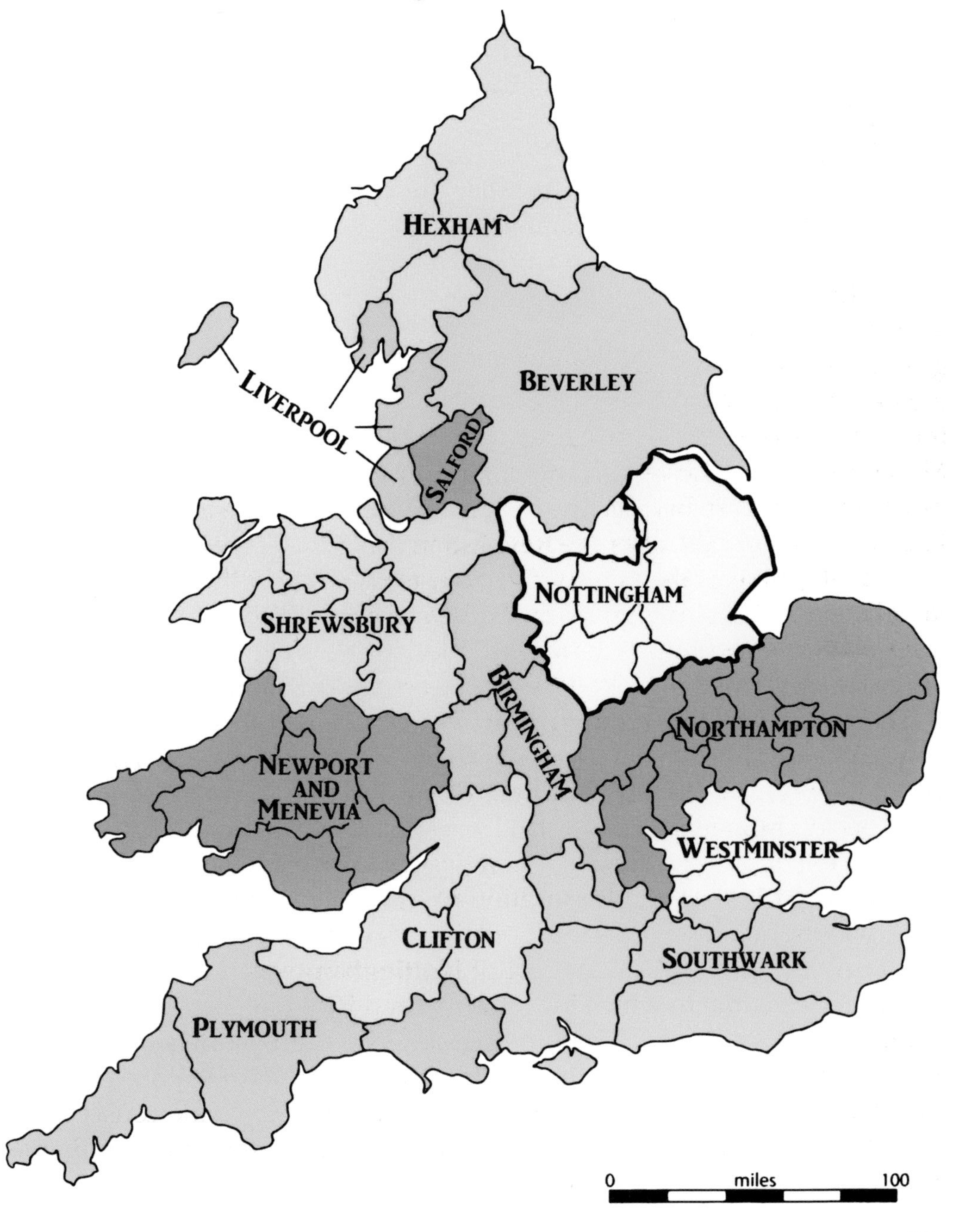

Whereas in 1773 it was estimated that there were some 2,160 Catholics in the five counties which were to make up the Nottingham Diocese, by 1850, there were (again an estimate) roughly twenty thousand. Of these, about half were immigrants from Ireland, three-eighths came from old Catholic stock, and one eighth were converts.

In 1850, twenty-seven 'Missions' (later to be known as 'parishes') had a resident priest. Of these, three were in Nottinghamshire, six in Derbyshire, seven in Leicestershire, eleven in Lincolnshire. There were none in Rutland. In 2016 there were one hundred and eight parishes in the diocese.

The Bishops of Nottingham

Since the bishops are the successors of the Apostles, it is appropriate at this point in our story to give a brief account of the Bishops of Nottingham. We begin with one who was never Bishop of Nottingham but fulfilled the role of 'Apostolic Administrator' of the diocese until its first bishop was appointed. This is

William Bernard Ullathorne

Born 1806 in Yorkshire, William Bernard Ullathorne became a Benedictine of Downside and was ordained priest in 1831. Two years later he went to Australia. On his return to England in 1841, he served in Coventry and was consecrated Vicar-Apostolic of the Western District in 1847. The following year he was transferred to the Central District, and in 1850 became first Bishop of Birmingham. Bishop Ullathorne was appointed Apostolic Administrator of the Diocese of Nottingham for the first nine months of its existence. He died in 1889 and is rightly remembered as one of the most influential figures in nineteenth century English Catholicism.

Joseph William Hendren (22 June 1851 - 23 February 1853)

Joseph William Hendren was born in Birmingham in 1791 and entered the Franciscan Order in 1806. He was ordained priest on 28 September 1815 by Bishop Milner. He taught in various Franciscan houses, and worked in Abergavenny for thirteen years. He was confessor and spiritual director to the Franciscan Sisters at Taunton, Somerset. In 1848 he succeeded Bishop Ullathorne as Vicar-Apostolic of the Western District and became the first Bishop of Clifton in 1850. The following year he was appointed first Bishop of Nottingham on 22 June 1851 and enthroned in the Cathedral Church of St. Barnabas on 2 December 1851.

The new diocese was a great challenge for its first bishop, who was already unwell, and Bishop Hendren was soon to retire on health grounds. He established the Cathedral Chapter on 2 July 1852 and began to organise the diocese, despite the shortage of priests and the large area to cover. He attended the first meeting of the Hierarchy at Oscott College in July 1852, when Fr. John Henry Newman preached his memorable 'Second Spring' sermon. In August 1852 Bishop Hendren decided that the challenge of the diocese was too formidable for his years and illness and submitted his resignation. This was accepted 23 February 1853.

Bishop Hendren was appointed Titular Bishop of Martyropolis in May 1853 and left Nottingham for Birmingham - and eventually Taunton - where he died on 14 November 1866. He was buried initially in the grounds of the Franciscan Convent, Taunton. In October 1997 his remains were transferred to the grounds of St. George's Catholic Church, Taunton.

Richard Roskell (21 September 1853 - 10 October 1874)

Richard Roskell was born in Gateacre, Liverpool, on 15 August 1817 and educated at Ushaw and the Venerable English College, Rome. After ordination, he served at St. Patrick's, Manchester, becoming Provost of the Salford Cathedr.al Chapter and Vicar General of the Salford Diocese. On 29 July 1853 Provost Roskell was appointed second Bishop of Nottingham and was consecrated by Cardinal Wiseman on 21 September 1853 in St. Barnabas' Cathedral.

During the next twenty-one years the diocese expanded slowly but surely, as the bishop set up parishes and Mass centres with the help of religious orders and the expanding numbers of secular clergy in the diocese.

Bishop Roskell attended the First Vatican Council (1869-1870), although he was suffering from cataracts in both eyes which made it impossible for him to read. In 1873 Bishop Roskell offered his resignation as Bishop, but the Pope persuaded him to remain, with the promise of a Coadjutor Bishop. After Fr. Bagshawe had been appointed in 1874, Bishop Roskell offered to resign once more, and this time it was accepted. He retired as Titular Bishop of Abdera to Glascoed in North Wales, and later to the Vale of Whitewell. He died on 27 January 1883 and was buried in the churchyard of St. Hubert's, Dunsop Bridge.

Edward Gilpin Bagshawe (12 November 1874 - 6 December 1901)

Edward Gilpin Bagshawe was born 12 January 1829 and educated at Oscott. He went to London University intending to study for the Bar, but in 1849 entered Brompton Oratory and was ordained priest in 1852. He was appointed third Bishop of Nottingham on 1 October 1874 and consecrated at the Brompton Oratory on 12 November that year by Archbishop Manning.

Bishop Bagshawe continued the work of his predecessor and all areas of the diocese benefited from his attention. Numerous houses of religious women were opened, including Nazareth House Nottingham, and two Congregations were founded, viz., the Little Company of Mary and the Sisters of St. Joseph of Peace. Bishop Bagshawe also established a major seminary next to the cathedral in 1883; this continued until 1902.

In 1901 Bishop Bagshawe's health was failing, and while in Rome in May that year he was encouraged to offer his resignation. As Titular Bishop of Hypoepa, Bishop Bagshawe went to live in the Little Company of Mary's House at Hounslow. In 1904 he was named Titular Archbishop of Seleucia. He died 6 February 1915 at Isleworth and was buried at Isleworth Cemetery. Some years later, Bishop Dunn decided to bury his predecessors in the cathedral crypt, and Archbishop Bagshawe's body was removed from Isleworth and laid to rest in the crypt of St. Barnabas' Cathedral on 16 December 1921.

Robert Brindle DSO (6 December 1901 - 1 June 1915)

Robert Brindle, born in Liverpool 4 November 1837 and educated at Lisbon for the Diocese of Plymouth, was ordained priest in 1862. He worked first at the cathedral in Plymouth and in 1874 became a Chaplain to the Forces, stationed at Woolwich, Aldershot and at Halifax (Nova Scotia). He went to the Egyptian War in 1882 where he was award the DSO for his conduct. On his return to England, Fr. Brindle was nominated Auxiliary Bishop of Westminster, and consecrated Titular Bishop of Hermopolis on 12 March 1899. Bishop Brindle succeeded Bishop Bagshawe as fourth Bishop of Nottingham 6 December 1901, and was enthroned in the Cathedral 2 January 1902. His time as bishop was marked by steady consolidation on the work of his three predecessors

By 1913 the bishop's health was failing and he offered his resignation, which was accepted 1 June 1915, when he was appointed Titular Bishop of Tacape. Bishop Brindle spent his last weeks of his life at Mount St. Mary's College, Spinkhill, where he died 27 June 1916. After his funeral in the cathedral, his body was buried in the cathedral crypt.

Thomas Dunn (25 February 1916 - 21 September 1931)

Thomas Dunn was born 25 July 1870 in London and educated at Beaumont College, Hammersmith Seminary, and, in Rome, at the Academia dei Nobili Ecclesiastici. He was ordained priest 2 February 1892 and appointed secretary to Cardinal Vaughan 1893-1903. In 1902 he was appointed a canon, and in 1906 he was put in charge of the Mission of Staines. Canon Dunn was appointed fifth Bishop of Nottingham in 1915 and consecrated by Cardinal Bourne at Westminster 25 February 1916. He came to Nottingham 20 March 1916.

Bishop Dunn found a rapidly growing diocese and encouraged church building on an unprecedented scale. The work of religious orders was given fresh impetus – for example, the Assumptionists who opened the Becket

School, Nottingham, in 1931; and new parishes were established all over the diocese. Bishop Dunn paid particular attention to his cathedral, seeking to "restore all things in Pugin," and made efforts to restore Gregorian Chant (Plainsong) to the cathedral's Sacred Liturgy, after the inspiration of Pope St. Pius X (1903-1914).

During Bishop Dunn's time in Nottingham there was a notable increase in vocations and thirty-four priests were ordained for the diocese.

Early in autumn 1931 Bishop Dunn's health began to deteriorate. He died 21 September 1931 and was buried in the cathedral crypt.

John Francis McNulty (11 June 1932 - 8 June 1943)

John Francis McNulty was born in Manchester in 1879 and educated at St. Bede's College, Manchester, before joining a local shipping office as a clerk. He began his studies for the priesthood at Douai, and in 1901 moved to Ushaw. He was ordained priest in 1911. Following ordination Fr.McNulty returned to St. Bede's College as College Prefect and remained in that post until 1921 when he was appointed Master of St Edmund's House, Cambridge. In 1930 F. McNulty was recalled to the Salford Diocese to take up the post of Parish Priest of St. Anne's, Ancoats.

In 1932 he was appointed sixth Bishop of Nottingham and was consecrated 11 June of that year. His eleven years as bishop might be singled out for the vigorous activity of the laity in the diocese. Pope Pius XI (1922-39) had frequently emphasised the need for a generous lay apostolate, and Bishop McNulty fostered this. The later part of his episcopate was darkened by the Second World War, but this brought fresh impetus to the growth of the diocese by the arrival of many refugee Catholics from various parts of Europe. The clergy of the diocese increased in numbers; in Bishop McNulty's eleven year episcopate sixty priests were ordained.

One local change in the administration of the diocese, thought of by Bishop Dunn, but brought about by Bishop McNulty, was the establishing of a separate residence for the bishop. Until 1933 the Bishops of Nottingham had lived at Cathedral House, but then Bishop McNulty leased a house in The Park, five minutes' walk from the cathedral, where his successors have continued to live.

Just four years after his appointment, Bishop McNulty suffered the first symptoms of the illness that would prove fatal. On 9 December 1942 he suffered a serious haemorrhage and spent six months in nursing care before a serious operation on 6 June 1943. He died two days later and was buried in the cathedral crypt.

Edward Ellis (1 May 1944 - 31 October 1974)

Edward Ellis was born in Radford, Nottingham, 30 June 1899 and educated at St. Mary's School next to the cathedral and at Ratcliffe College, Leicestershire. He went to the Venerable English College in Rome in 1916 and was ordained priest 15 October 1922 in St. Barnabas' Cathedral by Bishop Dunn. He was curate at Hadfield and then at St. Augustine's, Nottingham before becoming Cathedral Administrator in 1930. Three years later he was appointed Parish Priest of Hadfield, a post he held for six years. He returned to the cathedral as Administrator in 1939.

Following the death of Bishop McNulty, Fr. Ellis was appointed seventh Bishop of Nottingham 25 March 1944 and consecrated by Archbishop Godfrey 1 May 1944 in St. Barnabas' Cathedral. With the appointment of Bishop Ellis, the Diocese of Nottingham produced its first and, so far, only, native bishop. Bishop Ellis' episcopate of thirty years was marked by tremendous growth and a rise in the Catholic population from 67,715 in 1944 to 150,812 in 1974. Forty new parishes were established and sixty-four new churches built. Bishop Ellis' special interest in education was shown by his now-famous remark: "I would rather open a school than a church any day". During his episcopate, the number of schools in the Diocese of Nottingham rose from 69 to 116.

Other great initiatives from Bishop Ellis' time as bishop include the foundation of the Catholic Children's Society and a Junior Seminary at Tollerton, near Nottingham. The Junior Seminary was named St. Hugh's College, like its predecessor of the previous century. The Briars Residential Centre for young people was opened in 1970 and continues to this day serving young people in the diocese and beyond.

Bishop Ellis attended the Second Vatican Council (1962-65) and oversaw the implementation of the decrees of the Council, especially the reforms of the Liturgy. He suffered some ill health during his life and in 1972 was able to consecrate Monsignor James McGuinness as coadjutor bishop with right of succession. Bishop Ellis retired 31 October 1974 and became chaplain to Nazareth House, Nottingham, although he continued to play an active part in the life of the diocese. In 1976 the City of Nottingham granted him the Freedom of the City in recognition of his contribution to the life of the city.

Shortly before his eightieth birthday, Bishop Ellis suffered a serious recurrence of his illness and died 6 July 1979. He was buried in the cathedral crypt.

James Joseph McGuinness (31 October 1974 - 8 December 2000)

James Joseph McGuinness was born 2 October 1925 in Derry, Northern Ireland. He was educated at St. Columb's, Derry, and attended the seminaries of St. Patrick's, Carlow and St. Mary's, Oscott. He was ordained priest by Bishop Ellis in St. Barnabas' Cathedral on 3 June 1950. After spending three years as a curate at St. Mary's, Derby, he was appointed Bishop's Secretary, and in 1956 he became the first Parish Priest of Corpus Christi, Clifton. In 1969 Fr. McGuinness was appointed Vicar General to assist Monsignor E. H. Atkinson, with responsibility for Nottinghamshire and Derbyshire, and on 2 February 1972 was nominated coadjutor bishop with right of succession. He was ordained Titular Bishop of St. German's by Bishop Ellis in St. Barnabas' Cathedral 23 March 1972. For the next two and a half years he was based in the Mother of God Parish, Leicester.

Upon the retirement of Bishop Ellis on 31 October 1974, Bishop McGuinness became Bishop of Nottingham. He set about building on the work of his predecessor. For example, the lay apostolate saw great advances, not least of which was the introduction of Extraordinary Ministers of the Eucharist in 1978. Lay involvement was at the heart of the many diocesan commissions and other bodies which grew to help Bishop McGuinness care for his diocese. Bishop McGuinness was Chairman of the Catholic Youth Services Commission for twenty years and played a significant part in the visit of Pope John Paul II to Great Britain in 1982. When the Diocese of Hallam was established in 1980, the Diocese of Nottingham contributed sixteen parishes in north Nottinghamshire and Derbyshire to the new diocese.

In 1986 the decision was taken to close St. Hugh's College, where over almost forty years, many priests had been educated for the Nottingham Diocese and beyond. Some years earlier, in 1981, Peter Skoyles was ordained a permanent deacon, the first of many men to be ordained for this ministry in the Diocese of Nottingham.

In 1997 the diocese gathered in the cathedral to celebrate the Silver Jubilee of Bishop McGuinness's episcopal ordination, in the presence of Cardinals Hume, Daly and Winning, the Papal Nuncio, Archbishop Barbarito, and many other bishops, with members of the bishop's family and friends from far and wide. Later that year, Bishop McGuinness had to undergo serious heart surgery and spent some months convalescing. He continued working until his seventy-fifth birthday, celebrating the Golden Jubilee of his priestly ordination in June 2000.

On his birthday, Bishop McGuinness offered his resignation to the Holy Father, and this was accepted shortly after with the announcement of the appointment of his successor. On 8 December 2000 Bishop McGuinness ordained Fr. Malcolm McMahon OP as the ninth Bishop of Nottingham.

Bishop McGuinness retired to Nazareth House, Nottingham, and just over a year later he moved to St. Mary's Nursing Home, Ednaston, where he died on Good Friday, 6 April 2007. He was buried in the cathedral crypt.

Malcolm Patrick McMahon OP (8 December 2000 - 1 May 2014)

Malcolm Patrick McMahon was born in London 14 June 1949 and educated at St. Dominic's Primary School. He moved to St. Aloysius College, Highgate, before studying Mechanical Engineering at the University of Manchester Institute of Science and Technology (UMIST). After graduating he worked for the Daimler Motor Company in Coventry and then for London Transport.

In 1976 Malcolm McMahon joined the Dominican Order, beginning his novitiate and philosophical studies at Blackfriars, Oxford, before being professed in December 1977. He began his studies in theology at Heythrop College in 1979 and was ordained priest in 1982. He continued his studies at Heythrop and Blackfriars after ordination and was appointed Chaplain to the students at Leicester Polytechnic in 1984-5. From 1985 to 1989 Fr Malcolm was a curate in London until his appointment as Parish Priest of St. Dominic's, Newcastle-upon-Tyne. In 1989 Fr. Malcolm was appointed Parish Priest of St. Dominic's, Haverstock Hill, London. Three years later, the members of the English Province of Dominicans elected Fr. Malcolm as their Prior Provincial, and re-elected him in 1996. Early in 2000, Fr. Malcolm was appointed Prior of Blackfriars in Oxford at the end of his second term as Prior Provincial.

On 7 November 2000 Fr. Malcolm McMahon OP was appointed ninth Bishop of Nottingham and was ordained bishop by Bishop McGuinness in St. Barnabas' Cathedral on 8 December 2000.

Among Bishop McMahon's many achievements were: the establishment of the Bishop's Council - this took on the role of the College of Consultors; the separation of the hitherto linked functions of Parish Visitation and Confirmation; the thoroughly prepared Diocesan Assembly of 2003 with the Diocesan Pastoral Plan which resulted from it; the 'Living Stones' project the aim of which was to develop a strategy for responding more effectively to pastoral needs across the diocese. Bishop McMahon also opened up to lay involvement various areas of diocesan management which had previously been run almost exclusively by clergy; and he strengthened the role of the diocesan education service and promoted the setting up of academies.

Bishop McMahon was translated to Liverpool as its ninth Archbishop and was installed in the Metropolitan Cathedral of Christ the King on 1 May 2014.

Patrick Joseph McKinney (3 July 2015 -)

Patrick Joseph McKinney was born in Birmingham 30 April 1954, the eldest son of Patrick and Bridget McKinney, originally from Ireland. His family moved to Buncrana, County Donegal, Ireland, when he was still very young, but eventually returned to Birmingham.

Patrick began his studies for the priesthood at St. Mary's College, Oscott, in 1972, and was ordained priest on 29 July 1978 in St. Mary's Church, Buncrana, by Bishop Joseph Cleary, Auxiliary of the Archdiocese of Birmingham.

After his ordination, Father McKinney was appointed assistant priest in the Parish of Our Lady of Lourdes, Yardley Wood, Birmingham, and chaplain to St. Thomas Aquinas Secondary School, Kings Norton, Birmingham. From 1982 to 1984 he was a student at the Pontifical Gregorian University, where he gained a Licentiate in Sacred Theology.

Returning from Rome, he taught fundamental theology at St. Mary's College, Oscott, until 1989, when he was appointed Rector, a post he held for nine years, during which period he was also a lecturer in ecclesiology. He was made a Prelate of Honour in 1990 and a member of the Metropolitan Chapter of St. Chad in 1992.

Monsignor McKinney left Oscott in 1998, becoming Parish Priest of St. John, Great Haywood, and Episcopal Vicar for the north of the Archdiocese of Birmingham. Three years later he was asked to become full time Episcopal Vicar for the northern area and was moved to Tean, near Stoke-on -Trent. In 2006 he was appointed Parish Priest of Our Lady and All Saints, Stourbridge, and Dean of the Dudley Deanery. He also served for a time as Chair of the Birmingham Archdiocesan Ecumenical ComMission.

Monsignor McKinney was appointed tenth Bishop of Nottingham on 14 May 2015. He was ordained bishop by Cardinal Vincent Nichols in St. Barnabas' Cathedral on 3 July 2015.

NOTTINGHAM

St. Barnabas' Cathedral

Father Robert William Willson arrived in Nottingham early in 1825. At that time the Catholics of the town worshipped in a small chapel in King's Place in the Lace Market; this had been opened in 1789. Under Fr. Willson's dynamic leadership, the congregation soon outgrew the King's Place chapel, and a larger building, dedicated to St. John the Evangelist, was erected on George Street in 1828. But the population of Nottingham, including the Catholic population, continued to increase. Father Willson had, therefore, to find a site on which to build an even larger church. He acquired ten thousand square yards of land on Toll House Hill, just beyond the city boundary. Part of this land was set aside for a Convent of Mercy and most of it for the new church and priests' house. Roughly eighty per cent of the total cost was for the building of the church. A major benefactor was the Earl of Shrewsbury, and the architect was Augustus Welby Northmore Pugin.

The building began discretely to avoid unwanted attention from those opposed to its erection. The first stone of the church was laid on 10 May 1841. In November of the following year, assisted by, among others, Fr. Willson, Bishop Wiseman laid the foundation stone. In 1842 Fr. Willson was appointed first Bishop of Hobart in Tasmania, and one of his last acts prior to leaving for Australia early in 1844 was to bless the cross on the one hundred and seventy-three feet high spire of the church. The consecration of the church took place in August 1844 and not – as had originally been hoped - on 11 June, the feast of St. Barnabas to whom the church was dedicated. The celebrant once again was Bishop Wiseman, who personally brought relics of the patron saint from Rome for the celebration. (No satisfactory explanation has ever been given as to why St. Barnabas was chosen as patron.)

Bishop Willson left for Hobart in February 1844. This is not the place to recount the great work he did there. Suffice it to say that, on the basis of that work, he is justly regarded as 'the apostle of Tasmania.' In the course of the next twenty years Bishop Willson twice returned to England. In February 1865 he set out on a farewell visit to his native land with the intention of returning to Hobart where he had already made arrangements for his retirement. Soon after leaving Hobart he suffered a stroke from which he never recovered. The bishop spent the last months of his life in Nottingham, where he died on 30 June 1866 and was buried in the cathedral crypt several days later. His wish to return to Hobart was eventually fulfilled when, in February 2017, at the request of his successor as Archbishop of Hobart, and with the consent of the Bishop of Nottingham, his remains were exhumed from the original burial place and taken back to Hobart.

Father Francis Cheadle took Bishop Willson's place as leader of the Catholic community in Nottingham and was assisted by Fathers Joseph Mulligan and James Griffin. Circumstances changed radically in September 1850 when Pope Pius IX restored the hierarchy in England and Wales. Overnight the eight Vicars-Apostolic became bishops with dioceses. Nottingham had been chosen as the seat of one of the thirteen new Sees, but for the first nine months of its existence, it did not have its own bishop. Instead, Bishop Ullathorne of Birmingham ruled the diocese as Apostolic Administrator until the Franciscan, Joseph William Hendren, Bishop of Clifton, was appointed first Bishop of Nottingham. He and his four immediate successors resided at Cathedral House. Since 1933 the bishops have lived in The Park, a few minutes' walk from the Cathedral.

In the course of its history, St. Barnabas has, like most other places, seen a number of alterations to the sanctuary, the ambulatory and the body of the church, particularly under Bishops Dunn, Ellis and McGuinness.

In the early 1980s the exterior of the building was restored to its original warm stone colour by a process of sand-blasting. Nottingham City Council assisted with the cost of this work on the condition that the building be floodlit up until midnight, as part of a programme of lighting up a series of prominent buildings around the city.

As part of the preparation for the one hundred and fiftieth anniversary of the consecration of the cathedral, an extensive programme of decoration to the interior was undertaken. This included the careful stripping away of layers of paint to reveal the roundels in the nave as well as the names of diocesan martyrs on the rear wall of one of the ambulatory chapels. (These names had been inserted in the early 1930s.)

The Blessed Sacrament Chapel is considered by many to be the 'jewel in the crown' of St. Barnabas' Cathedral. It is richly decorated as Pugin had originally intended, and is the very heart of the cathedral. In addition to being used for private prayer, the Chapel also provides a space for more organised group prayer, such as that for Vocations on a Saturday morning.

There has been a choir at the cathedral church since the time of its consecration. The first Director of Music, was Edmund Hart-Turpin, who was also Organist of St. Bride's Church, Fleet Street.

A distinguished tradition of plainsong was maintained during the twentieth century, not least by Peter Smedley who reformed the boys' choir in 1955, directing an all-male choir, until 1979 when the choir once again became an adult ensemble. The introduction of Choral Scholars by Neil Page in 2003 transformed the capabilities of the main Cathedral Choir. Today, the Sunday choral services at the cathedral are led by various groups which offer opportunities for musicians of all abilities to contribute to the liturgy.

The cathedral is open all day, every day, and provides a place where people can spend time quietly with God in the heart of a very busy city.

A very significant event in the history of the cathedral was the reburial in the ambulatory, in 1997, of the Venerable Mary Potter, Foundress of the Little Company of Mary. She had come to Nottingham in 1877 to meet Bishop Bagshawe and was received by him in what is now the priests' sitting-room in Cathedral House.

In 1846 the Sisters of Mercy established St. Mary's Elementary School and St. Catherine's, a day and boarding school. (St .Catherine's was eventually recognised as a grammar school in 1951 and was relocated to Aspley in 1962.) St. Mary's, which had become a Voluntary Aided Primary School, closed in 1986. From 1846 until 1900 the Sisters of Mercy also ran an Industrial School in the old St. John's Church, George Street, where they taught domestic skills mainly to girls. St. Joseph's Preparatory School opened in 1931 - originally in the Convent of Mercy and shortly afterwards moved to Derby Road, where it is still housed although no longer served by the Sisters.

In 1881 the diocese purchased numbers 25, 27 and 29 Derby Road. These housed the Nottingham Boys' Catholic Grammar School which served as a minor seminary, and the major seminary of Our Lady and St. Hugh. Some ninety pupils passed through the grammar school which closed in 1895, and around forty men from the major seminary were ordained priests. The last of these, the Belgian Maurice Parmentier, died in 1962, sixty years after the closure of the major seminary.

The original Cathedral Hall was built in 1898, and served its purposes including that of a youth club for more than sixty years. In the 1970s it was replaced by a more spacious building which provides a venue for many diocesan celebrations and other functions. In the mid-1990s the Cathedral Hall was used for all the Masses while the Cathedral was being refurbished in preparation for the celebration, in 1994, of the one hundred and fiftieth anniversary of its consecration.

With the diminishing numbers of clergy in the diocese towards the end of the twentieth century and the first decade of the twenty-first, it became necessary for a number of parishes to be looked after by one priest. In some cases, a group of priests have looked after a number of parishes. In 2000 St. Augustine's returned to the care of the Cathedral clergy, and in 2002, Our Lady and St Patrick's was also added to their responsibilities. The latter was given to the care of the Parish Priest of Corpus Christi, Clifton, in 2014, while St. Augustine's remains joined to the cathedral parish.

NOTTINGHAM, *St. Barnabas' Cathedral – Convents*

Sisters of Mercy first came to Nottingham in 1844 and, two years later, moved to the purpose-built convent adjacent to the cathedral. The convent was designed mainly by Augustus Welby Northmore Pugin. St Catherine's Care and Nursing Home opened in the convent in 1991, but with the increasing demands of government regulations on care homes, it closed eight years later.

In addition to their work in education and nursing, the Sisters of Mercy were involved in many other aspects of the life of the cathedral and diocese, not least in the liturgy. For almost a decade, the Convent of Mercy provided a home for the diocesan archives. Due to a decline in vocations, the Sisters of Mercy subsequently sold the convent where they had been for more than a hundred and fifty years.

In recent decades, several communities of Religious Sisters have served in Cathedral House where they have made a home for the clergy and for the many visitors to the cathedral. They have also assisted with the liturgical life of the Cathedral. The Congregations were:

Daughters of Divine Charity: 1968 to 1984.

Sisters of the Holy Family of Nazareth: 1984 to 1990.

Sisters of St. Clothilde: 1991 to 1994.

Sisters of St. Clare: 1995 until 2004.

In 2004 members of the **Little Company of Mary** took up residence in Cathedral House. Members of this Congregation are also responsible for the Little Company of Mary Heritage Centre on Regent Street.

ALFRETON

Christ the King

The foundation of this Mission can be dated to 1877. At the time barely a dozen Catholics could be found out of a civil population exceeding twelve thousand. Nevertheless, Fr. Michael Ivers of Clay Cross (founded in 1862 from Ilkeston) opened a Mass centre, where Mass was at first said only on alternate Sundays.

A site for a church on Park Street was bought in 1879. A building was erected which was described as 'a plain brick structure faced with cement'. This held one hundred and twenty people, was dedicated to St Mary, and was opened on 3 June 1883, by the Vicar General, Monsignor McKenna. From 1894 Mass was celebrated every Sunday. The Mission passed through a period of great difficulty during the First World War. From 1915 to 1918 there was no resident priest at the parent church of Clay Cross; and for two more years, Alfreton had to be content with Mass once a fortnight. There was a decline in the spiritual life of the Mission, and its little church fell into a state of extreme dilapidation.

From 1920 its fortunes began to revive. Alfreton was cut off from Clay Cross and given its own priest. Its position was strengthened by the addition of the Ripley district, whose Catholics were at the time able to attend Mass in the private chapel of the Wright family at Butterley Grange.

When, in September 1922, Fr. Sydney Heald was appointed to the parish, the Mission of Clay Cross was added to his responsibilities. Until this time, probably quite half the inhabitants were unaware of the existence of a Catholic church in their midst. On one occasion, a policeman was asked the whereabouts of the Catholic chapel, and declared that there was no such place in Alfreton. People who lived in the street where the tiny building was situated thought it was a Sunday school belonging to a Dissenting chapel nearby! This is perhaps understandable, since it was only on Sunday mornings when Mass was said by a visiting priest that the church was open; it was locked up for the rest of the week. The neighbours grew vegetables on the little patch of church land, and used it on washing days as a drying-ground for clothes.

Under Fr. Heald's ministry (1922-1928) the parish got a burst of new life. The congregation increased to such an extent that the old chapel, although renovated, became inadequate. The number of Easter Duties made in the church almost doubled. The church was crowded each Sunday for Sung Mass and Benediction. All the liturgical and quasi-liturgical music was sung by the congregation to plainchant. For the first time in the history of the parish the people were introduced to the ceremonies and music of Candlemas, Ash Wednesday, Palm Sunday and Holy Week, and the first Sunday in May 1923 was celebrated by a dignified procession through the main streets of the town. The Protestant inhabitants, who were extremely well disposed towards the little Catholic community, lined the streets in hundreds, and the spectacle of a Catholic procession, carrying banners and a decorated statue of Our Lady, undoubtedly gave them genuine pleasure, as well as food for serious thought.

On 16 February 1927 Bishop Dunn laid the foundation stone of a new church. It was opened on 20 August of the same year and dedicated to Christ the King, and is said to have been the first church in England to bear this title. This church is a simple and dignified, but fragile, edifice in the Romanesque Style. Its simple stone altar was described at the time as being "a perfect example of all liturgical requirements without any of those unnecessary embellishments, such as reredos, gradines, a permanent Throne for Exposition, etc. with which architects and others are wont to overburden the altars they design and erect." This probably explains why Bishop Dunn "had no hesitation about consecrating [it]"!

In the early 1950s the Sheehy Brothers (Civil Engineering Contractors) donated to the parish materials for a small hall, which the parishioners then helped to build. It was envisaged that this hall would be able to be used not only for fundraising and social activities but also for meetings of groups such as the Legion of Mary and the Guild of the Blessed Sacrament.

Christ the King Primary School was opened in 1964 as a one-form entry school. As well as the more formal aspects of education, the school has always been involved in outreach to the wider community. For instance, as a result of the harvest festival of 1986, more than one hundred parcels were prepared by pupils and staff and given to local people who were in need, and other produce was given to various local charities. In learning to care for the environment, the children established a wildlife garden, and continued to care for it in spite of several outbursts of vandalism.

The school was staffed initially by Franciscan Minoresses who travelled each day from Clay Cross where they had a small house. Currently (2017) one Sister is on the staff of the school, and another is on the board of governors.

The Ripley district was cut off and assigned to Belper in 1927. But Alfreton still serves Clay Cross as a chapel-of-ease.

ALFRETON, *Christ the King – Convent*

A convent of **Franciscan Minoresses**, 'San Damiano', was established in Alfreton in 1993 to mark the eight-hundredth anniversary of the birth of St. Clare. From this base, they are involved in many aspects of the life of the parish.

ASHBOURNE

All Saints

A small group of Catholics, in and around Ashbourne, survived throughout Penal Times up to the first measure of Emancipation in 1778. The whole valley of the Dove had been notable for its large number of recusants in the seventeenth century and a chaplain had resided at Yeldersley Hall up to the middle of the eighteenth century. Ashbourne was one of the stations served 'occasionally' by Fr Thomas Bloodworth, priest of the Derby Mission from 1783/4 to 1815.

The first known Mass centre since the Reformation was at Hollyoak's Hotel, Ashbourne, registered as such with the justices of the peace in 1804. The registration was effected by the Rev. Paul Royer, a French émigré priest who was apparently resident at Ashbourne at that time. It is possible that this Mass centre was intended partly to serve the needs of some three hundred French officers, prisoners of war, who had been billeted in the town on parole the previous year. Bishop Milner visited Ashbourne in August 1806, but as he omitted the town from his visitation of Derbyshire in 1809 and from all subsequent visitations, it may be gathered that Fr. Royer left the Mission before the latter date.

In 1837 a Dr. Mulholland was resident priest at Ashbourne, and he had apparently been there for some time before that date. He maintained himself partly by means of a small private income, and partly by grants from the Earl of Shrewsbury. He was still there in December 1847, and in the course of the following year handed the Mission over to the care of the Oblates of Mary Immaculate. This community left Ashbourne for Maryvale, Oscott, in 1849 but continued to serve the Mission until 1852. For one year after this it was served by Passionists from Oakamoor. Then, in 1853, Yorkshireman Fr. Richard Raby, a former Jesuit, came to Ashbourne as the first of the long series of diocesan priests which has continued to the present day.

The date of erection of the first chapel is not known. When it was replaced in 1888 by the present church, its predecessor was described in the 'Derby Mercury' as a "dingy old edifice which was the more painfully remarkable by the fact that it occupied a lofty position .. on the ridge of a hill overlooking the town and the neighbourhood." This suggests that it was on Belle Vue Road near the site on which the present church and house now stand. This land was given to Bishop Bagshawe in 1877 by Mr. Joseph Shuttleworth of Bath. It already contained a house and some stables. These were converted into a school-chapel since, for six years from 1881, Ashbourne had its own Catholic school.

The new church, a neat, diminutive brick Gothic building, was opened on 26 August 1888. Funds for its erection were obtained by Fr. James O'Haire, a former missionary in South Africa. He came to Ashbourne in 1887 and remained there for about four years. In order to obtain money to pay off the debt on the church, he toured England preaching charity sermons! The church was altered in the 1960s by removing the north wall and building an extension there which became the sanctuary, although the porch is still in its original position and parts of the original altar, including the reredos, have been retained.

In 1931 a beautiful oak carved statue of local martyr Ralph Sherwin, born at Rodsley near Ashbourne about 1550 and martyred at Tyburn in 1581, was given to the church. The Sherwin Society was established in 1976 to honour St. Ralph Sherwin, who was one of the 40 martyrs canonised by Pope Paul VI in 1970. A diocesan pilgrimage to Rodsley takes place each June.

A parish room was opened in December 2006.

ASHBOURNE – *Convents*

A **Carmelite** Monastery at Offcote Hurst opened on 1 March 1948 when it was relocated from Mansfield where it had been since 1926. It closed around 1960.

The **Sisters of Mercy** purchased Ednaston Lodge in 1948 with a view to opening a nursing home, which they did later that year. It was called St. Mary's Nursing Home. In 1952 an operating theatre was opened for major and minor operations. On the occasion of the Golden Jubilee of St. Mary's, Bishop McGuinness blessed an extension.

At this time, owing to retirements and the ageing process, the decision was taken to withdraw the Sisters from the management and nursing care in the Home, and St. Mary's began to operate under carefully appointed lay management. One Sister, however, continued to live at St. Mary's offering pastoral care to the patients. Lay management worked very well for many years; but following a review of the Sisters' current ministries by the Institute Trustees, the decision was made to close the Home completely in November 2016.

During the almost seventy years of St. Mary's existence, the Sisters of Mercy cared not only for laypeople but also provided a place of rest and healing for priests and bishops.

ASHBY-DE-LA-ZOUCH

Our Lady of Lourdes

The first Mission at Ashby dates from the early days of the Rosminian missionary effort in Leicestershire. The Fathers of the Institute of Charity (Rosminians) took over the Mission at Whitwick in 1850, and from here, in the same year, they opened a Mass centre at Ashby. After their departure, the centre was continued by their successors at Whitwick (at first the Cistercians, and later the diocesan clergy) until 1870. The centre was then closed.

Its revival, after an interval of twenty-three years, was due principally to the Countess of Loudoun. Her residence at Willesley Hall, to the south of Ashby, was, in fact, the cradle from which three of the present Missions of this district were to spring. It is recorded that her chaplain (Fr. Otty, resident at Measham) said Mass at Ashby on December 24 1893. It is not clear that this was the beginning of a regular Mass centre, but from 1896 Mass was certainly said on one Sunday in each month.

The records speak of a 'temporary chapel' in South Street from at least 1905. This appears to have been superseded by another temporary chapel in 1908. By 1911 this bore a dedication to 'Our Lady of Perpetual Succour' and Mass was being said every Sunday. Until 192 the Mission was served from Measham. In that year, Ashby was erected as a parish, and Fr. John A. Wenham, was appointed the first parish priest and took up residence at the presbytery, Ashby-de-la-Zouch. Much needed repairs such as painting the doors and ironwork of windows, palings, gates, etc., were made possible thanks to the generosity of the Duchess of Norfolk who provided financial assistance for this undertaking.

Ashby had for some years prior to its erection as a parish possessed a church of unusual grandeur for so small a congregation. It is said that the erection was made possible by the generosity of Flora Hetty Paulina Barbara, Duchess of Norfolk and daughter of the Countess of Loudoun. Before her death in 1887 she left her jewellery to be sold for the purpose of erecting a church in Ashby. Her wishes were carried out by her husband, Henry, fifteenth Duke of Norfolk. His devotion to Our Lady of Lourdes is reflected in the current dedication. The site for the church was purchased in 1910. The new church was designed by Frederick Walter, a distinguished Catholic architect, and is considered to be a not unsuccessful experiment of the Norman style. The stained-glass windows in the sanctuary were made by Patrick Feeny of Hardmans. Most of the windows in the church are clear glazed. The oak benches in the nave are presumably original.

The foundation stone was laid in August 1913, but building was interrupted by the First World War and by the death of the fifteenth Duke in 1917. The church was finished and in use by 1920. The presbytery was built in 1956.

Due, among other things, to the delay in conveying the building into diocesan possession, the consecration of the church was overlooked. This eventually took place on 11 February 1998, the patronal feast. At that time, the opportunity was taken to re order the east end of the church in a more appropriate way than had been done in the immediate aftermath of the Second Vatican Council. The original high altar, to be used only for the reservation of the Blessed Sacrament, was restored; and the fine original gilded baldacchino painted with the arms of the Norfolk and Hastings families was brought forward to stand over the new smaller altar constructed on the first step of the sanctuary. The effective use of lighting emphasises the primacy of the new altar for the Eucharistic celebration.

BAKEWELL

The English Martyrs – served from Hassop

Bakewell is mentioned in the Domesday Book, and its market charter originated in the thirteenth century. There is a medieval parish church and the place was an important market town. It later became a minor spa promoted by the Duke of Rutland who partly rebuilt the centre of the town around 1800. The character of a stone-built market town has largely been preserved, and the place is a popular tourist destination and the administrative centre of the Peak District National Park.

The Mass, driven out of Bakewell in Elizabethan times, had found refuge in nearby Hassop Hall. It was fittingly brought back in 1888 by Fr. Arthur McKey, then Missionary Rector of Hassop. In this year he opened a Mass centre in Bakewell in a stable-loft at what was then known as the Rutland Mews.

Fr. McKey survived his new foundation no more than a year. His successor, Fr. James William Browne, was able, in 1890, to lease a plot of land on Granby Road from the Duke of Rutland at a nominal rent and to erect a tin chapel which served Bakewell for nearly sixty years. In 1892 the land was bought outright.

So matters rested until 1948 when a disused Congregational church, a substantial stone building with a parish hall underneath, built in 1849, was put up for auction and was bought by Monsignor Hargreaves on behalf of the diocese. The building was blessed by Bishop Ellis on 1 December 1948. From its first foundation Bakewell has been a chapel-of-ease within the Parish of Hassop, and retains this status up to the present day.

BARDNEY

St. Francis – served from St. Hugh's, Lincoln

At Bardney, which lies about half-way between Lincoln and Woodhall Spa, an abbey, one of the many in the valley of the River Witham, was founded in the seventh century; and in spite of invasions and depredations, it survived until the time of Henry VIII.

In the late 1920s a Miss Gladys Peet was received into the Catholic Church. At that time and for several years afterwards, she was the only Catholic in Bardney. During the latter part of the Second World War, services were held – it appears on an irregular basis - on Bardney Airfield and at the Angel Inn, and these were attended by local Catholics as well as German or Italian prisoners of war who were working on local farms. When the airfield closed, there was no longer a chaplain to help with the services, so Miss Peet persuaded the diocesan authorities to agree to open a Mass centre at Bardney. Land was bought and an old poultry shed was converted into a chapel – the first regular Catholic place of worship at Bardney since the dissolution of Bardney Abbey in 1538. A bungalow was built on the church land to ensure that a tenant could live near the chapel. From the opening of the chapel it was served from St. Hugh's, Lincoln. Petrol rationing in the period after the Second World War meant that coupons were hard to come by, and sometimes the priest coming out from Lincoln to say Mass at Bardney was given petrol coupons by his parishioners. It is said that when the priest presented his coupons at a local petrol station, these didn't always – as they should have done - match the registration of his car. However, a blind eye was turned to this!

Mass was said at first at irregular intervals, but for many years there has been a Mass every Sunday. The chapel proved especially useful for temporary labourers during the sugar beet season when sometimes two Sunday Masses were necessary.

The Pop Festival held at Bardney in May 1972 attracted some 40,000 young people from all over England and abroad. Along with Christians of other traditions, Catholic laity, religious and clergy made a significant contribution in helping to make Christ present to the young people who attended it.

In 1979 Fr. Joseph Wakefield retired to live at Bardney and had pastoral care of the Mass centre until his death four years later.

BARTON-UPON-HUMBER

(Our Lady & St. Augustine, Apostle of England) St. Augustine Webster – served from Brigg

Although at the very beginning of the eighteenth century, Fr. Jean Toussaint Froment, a former confessor to King Louis XVI, one of the many French clergy who came to England in the aftermath of the French Revolution, was ministering in the Barton area, it was not until 1841 that Mr. Astrop, a convert gentleman with business interests in Hull, asked Bishop Wareing, Vicar-Apostolic of the Eastern District, to send a priest to Barton. The bishop was unable at that time to spare a priest for a new Mission, but he compromised by combining the existing Mission at Brigg, ten miles to the south, with a new foundation, and instructing the priest to reside at Barton. For twelve months the priest divided his time between the two Missions, serving each on alternate Sundays. At the end of twelve months, the position had improved and the bishop was able to provide a priest for each of the two Missions.

It was never easy, however, for a bishop to find secular priests to spare for these northernmost parts of Lincolnshire. He therefore attempted to solve the difficulty, in 1848, by handing both Brigg and Barton over to the regular clergy. The Oblates of Mary Immaculate remained at Brigg for seven years, while Barton was served by Benedictines for just over a hundred years.

The first church was a converted cottage in Priestgate. The conversion was probably carried out in 1842. The sanctuary and rood-screen were added in 1854. This improvised church endured for nearly a century!

From about 1925 a serious attempt was made to collect money for a new church more worthy of the town. Building operations began in 1937, and on 10 July of the following year the new church was opened by Bishop McNulty in the presence of the Archbishop of Liverpool.

The second church comprised a spacious sanctuary, transepts, two sacristies and the first bay of the nave - later extended to four bays. There was a massive tower with a distinctly short spire, and the whole stood in a commanding position on rising ground south of the town. The architect was Mr. J. Beard Foss of London. "Wisely refraining from drawing on pre-Saxon work [in view of the two splendid pre-Reformation churches in the town], he gave a general Gothic appearance to the whole building", and he chose to blend in a single design the various styles of church-building in the locality. The new presbytery was built at the same time as the church. It has been said that the scale of the building was more suited to an abbey church rather than a market-town the size of Barton. Since the parish priest was a Benedictine, this is perhaps not surprising. It might also be said that there might have been competition with the two splendid pre-Reformation churches in the town, St. Peter's and St. Mary's.

The original dedication of the Mission was 'St. Augustine, Apostle of England'. The additional dedication of 'Our Lady' was made when the new church was opened 10 July 1938 on land belonging to the convent and school of the Rosminian Sisters from Loughborough. An appeal for funds for this new church was made in terms which one can only describe as lyrical. "Lincolnshire in the past was a great and intensive hive of Catholic life and monastic traditions, and was a rare jewel in the British Crown. Why should it not be so again? .. Help us to 'crown' Barton with a noble church, a worthy House of God, and a home for the priest."

The title of the parish was changed about 1984 to 'St. Augustine Webster', Prior of the Carthusian monastery of Melwood in the Isle of Axholme and one of the proto-martyrs of the English Reformation.

The second church proved difficult for the small community to maintain, one of the reasons being that repairs, particularly to the tower "which had been put up by builders who were more used to houses than churches" were going to be prohibitively expensive. So the decision was taken to demolish the church and replace it with a smaller church. This was dedicated 27 May 1988. The presbytery was retained as a parish centre as, from 2001, the parish could no longer have a resident priest.

As long ago as 1860 the Mission had its 'poor school', opened by Fr. Burge OSB in the saddle room of the Swan Inn, Fleet Gate. It was enlarged in 1878 and an independent school added two years later. This school was still in existence in 1901, but closed by 1905.

Tribute must be paid to the many Benedictine monks of Ampleforth, beginning with Fr. Lawrence Burge in 1848 and ending with Fathers James David Parker and John Edward Parker in 1949, who served Barton-upon-Humber until the parish was handed over to the diocesan clergy.

BARTON-UPON-HUMBER,
(Our Lady & St. Augustine) St. Augustine Webster - Convents

Sisters of Mercy
In 1887 the Sisters of Mercy established themselves in a house on Providence Terrace, Holydyke, and took over the work of teaching in the schools. They moved in the following year to a house in Castledyke, but left in 1889.

Sisters of St. Joseph of Peace in 1889 took over the work begun by the Sisters of Mercy, but they left a year later.

Rosminian Sisters of Providence in 1930 acquired a property known as Bardney Hall, on the southern outskirts of the town and opened a day and boarding school dedicated to 'Our Lady and St. Oswald'. Bardney Hall convent is first mentioned in the diocesan yearbook of 1931. The convent was in existence for some twenty years but was closed in 1950.

BELPER

Our Lady of Perpetual Succour

As early as 1853 the Nottingham Cathedral Chapter had "agreed that there was an immediate necessity of beginning a Mission at Belper as soon as means could be provided." But nothing happened until, in 1857, the Sisters of Mercy of Derby, who needed a country house to restore the health of the Sisters, since this was being affected by the sewage-farm adjacent to their convent on Nottingham Road, bought a 'fine residence' at the southern extremity of Belper on the road to Derby. Here they opened a school, and their chapel served a local congregation which then numbered nearly a hundred. They also provided quarters for a priest, but there is no evidence that a priest was ever there in permanent residence. Bishop Roskell is, however, said to have lived there for a time and to have served the convent as its chaplain.

After four years this first attempt at organised Catholic life at Belper had to be abandoned. Due to local prejudice, nearly all the Catholic workers in the town were discharged by their employers and forced to seek a livelihood elsewhere. There was also an outbreak of preternatural phenomena in the convent, which became eventually uninhabitable. In 1861 the Sisters returned to Derby

Over forty years were to pass before the Mission could be revived. In the meantime, there were two short-lived attempts to establish Mass-centres in Belper. In the years 1880-1883, Mass was said once a month on a weekday in the house of a Mr. Gallimore in Bridge Street; and from 1897 to 1900 Mass was said every Tuesday in the house occupied by Dr. McElligott.

The opportunity for a second foundation of this Mission was provided in 1904 by the War Office. At Easter in this year the Sherwood Foresters were under canvas on a site between Belper and Ambergate. Canon James W. Browne of St. Joseph's, Derby was asked (as Acting Chaplain to the Forces in the district) to say Mass for them. He rented for this purpose an auctioneer's sales room in King Street, opposite the main entrance to the railway station. The venture proved unexpectedly successful, and enough civilians attended Mass together with the troops to prove the need for a permanent Mission at Belper.

At the end of the three months' camp, Canon Browne accordingly obtained permission from Bishop Brindle to continue the Mass centre for the benefit of the civilian Catholics in Belper. At the same time, he moved it to a large room on the upper floor in the premises of Mr. Medley, a jeweller in King Street. This room later formed part of the Franciscan convent and for some years was used as a parish hall. For the next five years the Mass centre was in a somewhat anomalous position - due to its origin in a temporary army chaplaincy - for it was served from St. Joseph's, but situated in the Parish of St. Mary's, Derby.

The final step of erecting Belper as an independent Mission was taken in 1909. On 18 December in this year Fr. Joseph Stewart took up residence in a house on Spencer Road. On the first Sunday of 1910 he dedicated the Mission to 'Our Lady of Perpetual Succour' – in token of his particular devotion to Our Lady under that invocation. A full-sized, indulgenced picture of Our Lady under this title, erected by Fr. Stewart in the old King Street chapel in 1913, may still be seen in the new church in Gibfield Lane. Although Fr. Stewart, in his nine years as parish priest, found it impossible to erect a permanent church, he did valuable work in breaking down the Protestant bigotry with which Belper was peculiarly affected at that time. Year by year he preached a course of sermons to non-Catholics in November; and in the First World War years he aroused great sympathy for the Catholic Church by his work for the Belgian refugees and for the three military hospitals in the neighbourhood.

His successor, Fr. Louis Drury, moved the chapel to an empty shop at 70 King Street in October 1918. A flat over the shop served as a presbytery. A first attempt to buy a site for a permanent church was frustrated early in 1919 by a former owner who bought back the site rather than see it fall into Catholic hands. The present site in Gibfield Lane was bought. A church, designed by J. Sidney Brocklesby of Merton, Surrey, was built and opened by Bishop Dunn on 19 December 1919 The funds for this work came largely from an Ambergate convert, Humphrey Johnson, whose last contribution made the church free from debt in October 1923. Mr. Johnson was ordained priest in 1930 and, after a short period in the Diocese of Nottingham, transferred to Birmingham. He died in 1958.

Only seven years after its opening, the church was condemned as unsafe, and a new church had to be built.

In January 1937 Franciscan Minoresses opened what was initially a fee-paying school in King Street. The school began with thirteen pupils one of whom was non-Catholic. Three months later, there were thirty pupils. Both convent and school were moved to Quarrybank House in 1946, when the school was given the name St. Elizabeth's. Pupil numbers increased to such an extent that, in 1958, a new building had to be erected on land adjacent to the convent. Pupils have continued to be involved in the local community, and, for instance, in the 1990s, they took part in the Derbyshire custom of well-dressings.

In the 1980s the church was realigned and a new parish hall was built.

BELPER, *Our Lady of Perpetual Succour – Convents*

Sisters of Mercy came to Belper in 1857 and opened a school. Their chapel served the local congregation. The Sisters remained until 1861 when they returned to Derby.

Franciscan Minoresses opened a house, in 1936, in the old King Street property and the following year opened a school. In the 1990s the Sisters moved to a smaller house in Cherry Tree Avenue where, although no longer involved in the school, they continued to serve the parish in other capacities. The Sisters finally left Belper in 2007.

BIRSTALL

St. Theresa

On 15 October 1938 the Rosminian Fr. John Fevez, who at the time was priest-in-charge of the Mission of Barrow-cum-Sileby said the first Mass in Birstall, attended by fifty-one people, in Hillsborough School on Curzon Avenue. This was probably the first Mass in the district since the Reformation. The advantages of forming a self-contained missionary centre at Birstall had already been noted. The Soar Valley Missions had previously been served partly by Loughborough, and partly by a priest of Ratcliffe College. In neither community could a priest live and be completely free for the work of the villages. Birstall, however, could be the residence of a group of priests whose interests could lie wholly in that direction. Thus, it served as a convenient centre from which the Rosminians could care for their chain of village Missions in the valley of the Soar as well as providing for the new housing estates which developed to the north of Leicester between the two World Wars.

Soon after the first Mass had been said, Fr. Denis Horgan of Grace Dieu was appointed as priest-in-charge of Birstall to carry out this project. He was soon able to buy a site for a church in Wanlip Lane, and for a while the Birstall Social Club was used as a Mass centre. With the outbreak of the Second World War, severe restrictions were placed on the erection of a church. Per.ission was granted for a dual-purpose building, a church-hall. The foundation stone of this simple hall/chapel, built by Messrs. Harlow of Long Whatton, was laid on 25 May 1940.

A lot happened in 1941. Hitler's armies invaded Russia; London, Coventry and other English cities were blitzed; and America entered the War with a retaliatory attack on Japan. But in that same year of global conflict involving much destruction and loss of life, the Church of St. Theresa at Birstall in rural Leicestershire was opened by Bishop McNulty on 12 January. Fr. Horgan having secured a priests' house on Wanlip Lane, the bishop erected the Parish of Birstall, and Fr. Horgan went into residence as its first parish priest.

From the first, the new parish had charge of the village Mission at Rothley. In 1943 a more convenient presbytery was obtained at 53 Front Street. It was now possible to accommodate an assistant priest, and Syston was added to the parish. From 1947 Barrow-on-Soar was cut off from Sileby and entrusted to the growing community at Birstall, which for some years regularly had a complement of at least three Fathers of the Institute of Charity.

On 3 October 1986 a plaque to commemorate the 1941 church was unveiled in the presbytery grounds on Front Street. The congregation then made their way to Wanlip Lane for a concelebrated Mass after which they "promenaded leisurely" to the presbytery for a convivial evening with plenty of food and – one may imagine! – a modicum of drink also.

A new church, a substantial part of the funding for which came from the Murphy family, was opened on Front Street in 1988. A parish hall is situated between the church and the presbytery.

Towards the end of the twentieth century, due principally to shortage of Rosminians available for parish work, Barrow-on-Soar was cut off from Birstall, leaving only Rothley as a chapel-of-ease.

BOLSOVER

St. Bernadette – served from St. Philip Neri, Mansfield

Although an important nucleus of Catholics, perhaps dependent on the Jesuit Mission at Spinkhill, seems to have survived in Bolsover up until the end of the seventeenth century, it appears that the Catholic Faith was gradually extinguished during the next two hundred years. At a visitation of the Spinkhill Mission held in 1883, Bishop Bagshawe found there was not a single Catholic in Bolsover.

The transformation of Bolsover from a picturesque market-town, sheltering beneath an enormous castle, into an important mining centre brought some influx of Catholics by the end of the nineteenth century. (Markham Colliery, just outside the town, closed in 1993.) To provide for these, Fr. Charles Froes opened, in 1903, a Mass centre behind the house of Mr Street at 1 High Street. Mass was said in a wooden hut which bore the title 'St Joseph's.' At this time, Fr. Froes was Missionary Priest at Clowne. In the following year he moved to Shirebrook while continuing to serve Bolsover. This Mission came to an end in 1928 on the retirement of Fr. Froes, who died two years later and is buried in the cemetery attached to the church in Shirebrook.

In 1942 a new Mass centre was opened in an upper room behind the residence of Mr. Kennington in Market Place. In the following year a derelict property at 59 High Street was bought by the diocese, and a stone stable block was adapted by voluntary labour to form the new chapel. After a new church, designed by John Rochford, was built in 1967, the barn continued to be used as a parish social centre, until it was sold in 2005 to fund renovation in Bolsover and in Shirebrook. The new church was renovated in 2007. The church is situated on a confined site in the centre of the village adjacent to the old barn which previously served as the church. High Street lies close to the centre of Old Bolsover on its south side. There is space at the rear of the church originally earmarked for a presbytery, affording a panoramic view towards the Peak District. On its street frontage it is flanked by older stone-built properties, including the Blue Bell public house.

BOLSOVER, *St. Bernadette – Convent*

Presentation Sisters came to Bolsover from Shirebrook in 1981 and remained there until 1986 when they moved to Warsop.

BORROWASH

St. Hugh – served from Chaddesden

From December 1896 until April 1909 Mass was said at the 'Wilmot Arms Inn', Borrowash, in an upper room hired for the purpose. Throughout these years Borrowash was served from St. Mary's,

Derby, from where Canon Thomas Byrne used to travel by horse and cab. In 1909 the new chapel of Alvaston was opened in the same parish, and since it was no longer possible to spare a priest to serve Borrowash, the Mass centre was closed.

A new Catholic centre in Borrowash was established in 1945 when, on 8 May, the property known as 'Borrowash House' standing in twelve acres of ground on Derby Road to the west of the village was bought by the Diocesan Rescue Society. In the course of the year building operations were carried out to adapt it as a babies' home. The management was entrusted to the Sisters of St. Joseph of Peace and the formal opening of 'St Joseph's Nursery' took place on 28 May 1946. In 1951 the babies were transferred to Colston Bassett, but Borrowash House was retained by the Sisters as a maternity home until 1975.

On 30 June 1959 Bishop Ellis blessed and opened St. Hugh's chapel-of-ease on the Derby Road. Two things are worthy of note here. One: The bishop had stipulated that any Catholic church for Spondon must be built on a site facing the main road between Spondon and Borrowash. Two: all new parishes were to be named after English saints, and there was no church in the Derby area dedicated to St. Hugh of Lincoln. Thus, a church dedicated to St. Hugh (whom one might regard as an honorary Englishman!) was built on the Derby Road.

Borrowash became a separate parish in 1961; prior to this, it had been served from St. Alban's, Chaddesden. Borrowash had a resident priest until 2015 when it was returned to the pastoral care of the priest and people of St. Alban's.

BORROWASH, *St. Hugh – Convent*

In 1946 **Sisters of St. Joseph of Peace** opened a convent in Borrowash House where, under the auspices of the Diocesan Rescue Society, they looked after babies, then mothers and babies, and, finally, mothers. Borrowash House closed in 1976 and so did the convent, and the work was transferred to West Bridgford.

BOSTON

St. Mary (Our Lady of the Holy Rosary)

The Catholic Faith had disappeared completely from Boston before the end of Penal Times. A report of 1781 shows that at that date there was not a single Catholic in the town.

However, an influx of Irish construction workers following the passing of the 1809 and 1818 Fen Drainage Acts brought a large Irish Catholic population to Boston and almost certainly gave rise to the need for a Catholic church there. By the mid-1820s the district around Norfolk Street became known as 'Irishtown'.

In 1825 the Jesuit Fr. Bernard Addis came to reside in Boston. Fr. Addis had at his disposal the small private fortune which had been his until the time of his entry into the Society of Jesus. With this he built a presbytery. For two years he said Mass in one of the rooms of his house, and then, in 1827, built the present church seating about two hundred. The necessary funds came from the same source as the presbytery, and thus the new church was opened free of debt, which meant that – according to the practice at that time – it could have been consecrated when it was opened. However, the church was not consecrated until 1946. The Frenchman, Fr. Joseph Gattie, parish priest from 1913, had made plans to do so even to the extent of buying the consecration candlesticks and painting the consecration crosses on the walls of the church. But he died quite unexpectedly in January 1935 before the ceremony could be carried out. The intentions of his successor as parish priest were thwarted by the outbreak of the Second World War. When eventually the church was consecrated, someone had managed to find the consecration crosses purchased by Fr. Gattie.

In 1879 Bishop Bagshawe reported to Rome that Boston had a good-sized handsome church, served by Fathers Herman and Peter Sabela, brothers who had fled Germany during the time of the persecution of the Catholic Church under Otto von Bismarck. Both of them served the Diocese of Nottingham with great distinction for the remainder of their lives. In the same Report, Bishop Bagshawe noted that there were 309 Catholics in Boston, and that 47 children attended the school.

The date of the foundation of the school is not known but it was probably in the mid-1850s since the founder was Fr. Chépy, who came to Boston in 1854 when the Jesuits ceased to serve there. Additions were made to the school around 1898. In 1884 Bishop Bagshawe laid the foundation stone of St. Mary's School, which remained on the same site near to the church until 1983, when it transferred to a "more commodious location". In 1899 the school had 300 pupils who were taught by seven Sisters of Charity and two pupil teachers. A schools' inspector's report from the end of the nineteenth century contains these encouraging comments. "Discipline is maintained chiefly by kindliness and gentleness and not by that hateful instrument of child-torture – the rod. Corporal punishment, except in rare cases, is replaced by words of reproof, kindness and encouragement, which the Sisters of Charity [of St. Paul] know so well how to employ."

St. Bede's School opened in May 1967 and for several decades provided secondary education for the Catholic children of South Lincolnshire. It was clearly a very active place in which, in addition to their formal education, pupils became involved in the local community (for example, by revamping the garden at a local elderly persons' unit) and beyond (for example, by collecting items to help distressed people in Romania). In the early 1990s the school staff began to have some of their training days at The Briars Diocesan Youth Centre. In spite of the fact that "life was never dull" at St. Bede's, the school was forced to close in 2011.

One of the more noticeable features of the Boston area at the end of the twentieth century and beginning of the twenty-first was the influx of people from eastern Europe and, in particular, from Poland. This had a significant impact on the character of the Parish of St. Mary, and currently (2017) three weekend Masses are celebrated in Polish in addition to those in English. It is probably in this context that, to the original title of 'St. Mary' was added, in the early twenty-first century, 'Our Lady of the Holy Rosary.'

BOSTON, *St. Mary – Convents*

Servants of the Sacred Heart of Jesus opened a convent in 1875, and began teaching in the school. This venture did not prove successful, and the Sisters left Boston in 1877.

Sisters of Charity of St. Paul the Apostle came to Boston in 1886. Their coming was largely made possible by a Miss Frances Smith, who, with her relatives, paid for the convent and the adjoining ground and cottages. As well as teaching in the school, the Sisters exercised many other pastoral ministries in the parish. Their departure from Boston in 1978 was the occasion of great sadness but also of deep gratitude for their faithful service which had lasted for almost a century. Their work in the wider community was acknowledged by, among other things, the presentation made to them by the Mayor of Boston of a plaque bearing the Borough's coat of arms.

BOURNE

(Sacred Heart and) St. Gilbert

Woodlands stretch to the west of Bourne, and the flat, black-soil Fens to the east. The rich soil has long brought in an annual influx of harvest workers, many Irish and Catholics among them, from June to October. Six miles to the north lies Sempringham where, in the mid-twelfth century, Gilbert, a son of the local squire, founded the only medieval English religious order; it was named after him, the Gilbertines. One member of this Order, Robert Manning, saw the light of day (to avoid the pun 'born in Bourne') in Bourne about 1264. Manning wrote 'Handling Synne', a classic which was largely responsible for making the version of English used in the Midlands the recognised standard of literary English. In Penal Times, the recusant Thimelby family had their home at the Red Hall, near the former railway station. The Bull Inn is pointed out as the birthplace of that arch-enemy of the Catholic Faith, Queen Elizabeth I's Secretary, Cecil. If this place is the same as the 'Bull Hotel' where Fr. Cyril Horspool was living in the late 1940s, this is a remarkable irony.

The first mention of Catholics in Bourne in post-Penal Times is in 1883, when there were two of them, although the numbers increased in the summer when large numbers of Irishmen came for seasonal work. In 1911 there was one known Catholic in Bourne, a lady from Montrose. A first Mass centre was opened in 1924. From this year until 1927 the chaplain to the Xaverian Brothers at Deeping St. James came each Sunday to say Mass in the Angel Hotel. There was then a break of four years. Mass resumed in

1931, at first in the Corn Exchange, and then, before the end of that year, in the Co-operative Hall, North Street. Fr. Horspool bought a modernised army hut, capable of seating a congregation of 150. This was erected on Exeter Street (now known as St. Gilbert's Road) and dedicated to the Sacred Heart. It was opened on 11 January 1950.

But the need for a more permanent building was keenly felt by parishioners. Fr. Patrick Peppard SCJ, the parish priest, stated that he wanted the building to be designed as a church that could be used for social activities rather than, as was often done, a church hall that could be used as a church. It was not until 1976 that the permanent combined church and hall was built. The new church was dedicated to the local saint, Gilbert of Sempringham. But after a lot of reflection on the part of parishioners and priest, and out of consideration for the work of the Sacred Heart Fathers who had served Bourne and Deeping for some thirty years, the recommendation to rename the parish 'Sacred Heart and St. Gilbert' was made to Bishop Malcolm McMahon in 2012. He gladly gave his approval and this is the title the parish now bears.

BRIGG

St. Mary (The Immaculate Heart of Mary)

Brigg is the heir of the northernmost outlier of that chain of Catholic communities which in Penal Time stretched along the line of the Lincolnshire Wolds. In 1778 there was a chaplaincy, four miles to the north-east, at Worlaby Hall. Brigg was already a Mass station, served on one Sunday a month by the chaplain from Worlaby.

It is recorded that, from 1770 to the breaking out of the French Revolution in 1789, the Reverend Robert Newton (alias Fawcett) said Mass at Brigg on the fourth Sunday of each month at the house of a Mr. Bernard in Bigby Street. This has been identified with a Georgian house, still existing in 1922, which had a back entrance in Bigby Street, but whose front faced on to Wrawby Street. It contained a windowless top floor room, with altar rails and with a square confessional-hole cut in the door of one of the adjoining rooms.

It cannot be established with certainty that Mass was said at Brigg between the departure of Fr. Newton and the arrival from Louth, about 1794, of Fr. Jean Toussaint Froment, formerly confessor to King Louis XVI. Fr. Froment remained in Brigg until his death in 1810. The absence of any record of the registration of Brigg chapel among those of 1792 might suggest that the Mass station had been abandoned by this year. On the other hand, it seems certain that chaplains continued to reside at Worlaby Hall and it may be presumed that they would continue the work of Fr Newton at Brigg.

There existed at this time a little Catholic cemetery at Kettleby, two miles to the east, and the last burial can be dated to 1792. In 1848 this cemetery was obliterated to make way for the new railway.

After the death of Fr. Froment there is a gap of five years in the records. This ends with the arrival, in 1815, of another French émigré, Fr. Pierre Louis Moulin. With him came a Fr. Jacques Thomas Moulin, who is described as his brother, although he was younger by some thirty-eight years! A Mr. Musgrave gave them a plot of land, just outside the town on the Scawby Road and erected for them a cottage in which they lived. With their own hands they built a chapel of roughly cemented rubble as an annexe to the cottage. Fr. Pierre Moulin died here in 1822, and Fr. Jacques Moulin in 1836. For at least five years before 1823, they served the chapel at Worlaby Hall.

Except for short periods, when Brigg was amalgamated with Barton or Osgodby, a priest was in residence until 1860. At some date during this period the little chapel was extended by the addition of a stone built sanctuary.

It was always difficult to find priests for remote Missions, and this difficulty was met in 1848 by the transfer of Brigg to the Oblates of Mary Immaculate, one of whom served the Mission for the next seven years. In 1855 it reverted to the diocesan clergy, but five years later the shortage of clergy compelled the bishop to amalgamate Brigg with Gainsborough and from 1860 to 1875 the town had no priest of its own.

This period of decline came to an end in 1875, when the recently converted Sheriff of Lincolnshire, Mr. Valentine Cary-Elwes, of Brigg Manor House, promised to pay the stipend of a priest and at the same time adapted the coach-house of his residence to serve as a church which he dedicated to the 'Immaculate Heart of Mary'. This building remained the property of the Cary-Elwes family until about 1920, when they left the Manor House and conveyed the church to the diocese. (One of the sons of Valentine, Dudley Cary-Elwes, was Bishop of Northampton 1921-32).

The foundation stone of a new church on Barnard Avenue was laid in July 1964 and the church was blessed and opened in September of the following year. The report in the diocesan yearbook of the opening of the church notes that [although] "the plans for this church were completed before the details of the new liturgy were known, .. the requirements were largely anticipated." The old church was demolished in 1968. A parish hall adjacent to the church was opened in 1990.

The first school in the parish was opened in 1874. It consisted of one room in the Town Hall, rented by Mr. Cary-Elwes. Several years later, in the time of Fr. Patrick Conaty, a school building was erected. In 1885 it was noted that the school belonged to Mr. Cary-Elwes and had forty-five scholars. The school was housed in a number of places in the town and moved to its present site in 1966. However, in 1922, after the Cary-Elwes family had left the Manor House, Rosminian Sisters of Providence opened the 'Manor House Convent School', an independent fee-paying boarding and day establishment. This school existed alongside St. Mary's Primary School for some years and closed in 1971. Meanwhile St. Mary's School continued to grow. In 1972 it expanded beyond its four classes, and it continues to attract pupils from a very wide area of North Lincolnshire.

BRIGG, *St. Mary – Convents*

Rosminian Sisters of Providence took possession of the Manor House when the Carey-Elwes family vacated it in 1919, and they remained there until 1959 when they left Brigg. They handed over this school to the

Poor Clares of the Immaculate Conception (of Newry) who began to teach in the primary school in 1953. These left Brigg in 1989.

Sisters of Mercy In 1890 there was a convent of the Sisters of Mercy in Brigg. This cannot have lasted for a very long since it is not mentioned in Bishop Bagshawe's five-yearly reports to Rome in either 1885 or 1895.

Presentation Sisters were in Brigg from the mid-1990s until 2007.

BURTON-ON-TRENT

Stapenhill, Our Lady of the Most Holy Rosary

Stapenhill lies on the eastern bank of the River Trent opposite Burton. It is now within Staffordshire. In 1850, it formed part of the administrative County of Derby, and so continues to belong to the Diocese of Nottingham. In 1955, the district was cut off from the Parish of Swadlincote to form an independent Mission which, however, in a reversal of roles, it (2017) serves.

The church, a former Methodist chapel dating from 1907, was acquired by the Diocese of Nottingham in the early 1970s and, although it is not of special architectural or historic interest, by virtue of its elevated situation above street level it contributes to the historic character of Stapenhill, a suburb of Burton-on-Trent.

Blessed Robert Sutton Secondary School opened in 1964 and is now known as Blessed Robert Sutton Catholic Sports College.

BURTON-ON-TRENT

Winshill, St. Joseph

A chapel-of-ease to Stapenhill, Burton-on-Trent. The building now serving as St. Joseph's Church was formerly the Winshill Institute and dates from 1888. A building of some local historical interest, it was acquired by the Diocese of Nottingham in 1967, and has been modified somewhat to meet the requirements of its new usage. This was where the priest's residence was fixed, as were the parish primary school – opened in 1965, and the secondary school (the latter opened in 1964 and dedicated to the priest-martyr Blessed Robert Sutton, who was born in Burton-on-Trent).

BURTON-ON-TRENT – *Convent*

The **Presentation Sisters** opened a convent and private school here in 1954. The school catered for children aged 5-11. During the 1950s about 50 students, divided into three mixed age classes, were provided with a traditional, academic, Irish - Catholic education by, mostly Irish, Sisters. However, with the building of a parish primary school the Sisters realised that a private school would not be needed and because of failing finances and falling vocations, the school closed in the mid-1960s and the convent closed in 1966.

BUXTON

St. Anne

The return of the Catholic Faith to Buxton in the nineteenth century was due almost entirely to the tourist traffic of the town. From Roman times people were attracted to the area not only by the beautiful scenery but also by the warm springs which emerge near the River Wye with a constant temperature of 28 degrees Celsius.

In 1837, when there was probably not a single Catholic family resident in Buxton, the priest from Leek began to come occasionally to say Mass for the visitors from Ireland. From August 1845 Fr. James O'Farrell of Leek began to say Mass every Sunday during the season. It appears that he was able to secure the use of a small room which was reserved for Catholic purposes and which was spoken of as a 'chapel'.

The connection with Leek ceased in 1848. In this year the Mass centre was taken over by Fr. John Joseph Collins of New Mills. This arrangement lasted for the next four years. But then the situation changed dramatically. In 1850 Fr. Edward McGreavy, of the Diocese of Down and Connor, came to Buxton seeking a cure for his rheumatism which was so severe that, at first, he needed crutches and a bath-chair in order to move about. His health soon improved and, as it did, he began to say Mass for the Catholic visitors to Buxton initially at his house at 10 or 12 West Street; later, at the house of Mr. Robert Nall in High Street. At other times Mass was said in the house of Mr. Anzani - then the only Catholic resident in Buxton - in Spring Gardens. In the 'season' the greater numbers wishing to attend Mass made it necessary sometimes to move the Mass centre to Mr. Anzani's 'Bazaar' or to the Old Town Hall.

By 1852 the health of Fr. McGreavy was so improved that Bishop Hendren appointed him Missionary Priest of Buxton and separated the Mission from the parent church of New Mills. Some considerable progress had already been made. The Grimshawe family of Errwood Hall had given considerable assistance, and Dr. Darwin had adapted a large room in his house in Scarsdale Street to serve as a chapel with seating for a congregation of sixty.

In 1860 Bishop Roskell noted that there were eighty Catholics resident in Buxton but that many sufferers from rheumatism came to the town to receive the benefits of the waters and the baths, and that Fr. McGreavy had bought land on which to build a church, a presbytery and a school. That same year, on 26 July, the foundation stone of the present church of St. Anne was laid by Bishop Roskell. He returned to open the completed church on 16 July 1861 and the future Cardinal Manning preached on that occasion.

This original building of 1861, designed by the notable Catholic architect, J. J. Scoles, consisted of a simple nave in the Early English style. The plans provided for the subsequent erection of a tower and spire, but these have never been added to the building. The present sanctuary, together with the two side-chapels dedicated to the Sacred Heart and to Our Lady of Lourdes were added in the time of Fr. John Theodore Hoeben (1885-1900).

The church was consecrated on 26 July 1897. The sanctuary was reordered in the late twentieth century, retaining some good quality fittings from the late nineteenth century including the sanctuary reredos and pulpit. In 1980 the sacristy roof and organ loft were removed as part of a scheme to extend the presbytery.

In 1879 the Catholic population of Buxton was one hundred and twenty-five. In 2013 it was estimated at 5,000.

The land bought from the Duke of Devonshire by Fr. McGreavy for the church was of considerable size, and an area of some 1,545 square yards was earmarked for the erection of an elementary school. The project was, however, shelved until the arrival of Fr. Hoeben in 1885. He began by renting a very small room in the old town hall, where he organised a 'private' school with a Mr. & Mrs. Gorton as master and mistress. This seems to have been opened at about the same time as St. Anne's School, i.e. 1888. The latter began with one teacher and 36 'scholars.' By 1896 there were 78 children looked after by three teachers. Two years later, Presentation Sisters arrived in Buxton to begin a long and fruitful association with the parish and school. By 1958 there were 380 pupils on role from the ages of five to fifteen. When St. Thomas More Secondary School was opened in 1958, this relieved some of the pressure since the older boys and girls were transferred to there. In 2017 there were just over 400 pupils on roll. The school serves all areas of the High Peak. Children also travel from across the borders of Staffordshire and Cheshire to be part of the school community. Approximately sixty per cent of the pupils are Catholic, but whether of the Christian faith, other faiths or no faith, the children are very proud of their school. St. Anne's School moved to its present site in 1972, and its original premises now house St. Anne's Community Centre.

No account of the Parish of Buxton would be complete without mention of the shrine of Our Lady, Queen of the World, at Corbar on the Hayfield Road on the outskirts of the town. First established in 1955 on the initiative of the then parish priest, Fr. Alfred Baldwin, it was renovated and rededicated almost forty years later.

BUXTON, *St. Anne – Convent*

A convent of **Presentation Sisters**, founded from their Livesey Street, Manchester house, on 23 April 1898, was the first convent of this Congregation in the Diocese of Nottingham. From Buxton were founded, between 1904 and the late 1950s, almost all the convents of the Presentation Sisters in the Diocese. This fact alone gives some idea of the importance of the Buxton foundation. After exercising various ministries in the parish for more than a century, the last Presentation Sister left Buxton in 2004.

CAISTOR

St. Thomas More - served from Market Rasen

The market-town of Caistor is of Roman origin. It lies at the northern end of the Lincolnshire Wolds, where many Catholic families survived through the days of persecution. Some of these seem to have survived at Caistor well into the nineteenth century. A manuscript note of Fr. John Abbot, Missionary Priest of Osgodby (1836-1838) records that he handed over the care of Caistor on 31 January 1837 to Fr. McDermott of Brigg. A note such as this implies a least a recognisable Catholic congregation, and probably a Mass centre.

It was not, however, until 1876 that a regular Mass-centre appeared in the town. This was served by Fr. Amadeus Gavois of Osgodby. In his 1879 Report to Rome, Bishop Bagshawe refers to a domestic chapel of Mr. Smith at Caistor, where "Mass is sometimes said". There must have been a reasonable attendance since, at a visitation of September 1881, Bishop Bagshawe gave instructions that a school-chapel was to be erected in the town. The project did not materialise and, in fact, the Mass centre was closed in 1882.

In 1958 a nineteenth century former printing works in Bank Lane was acquired for Catholic worship; prior to that various premises around the town had been used, including the British Legion hall and the Red Lion public house. The church, dedicated to St. Thomas More, was opened by Bishop Ellis on 8 May 1960. It was significantly altered in the late 1980s and was consecrated in June 1991. Included in the revamped church are two nineteenth century stained-glass windows depicting St. John the Evangelist and St. Anne, brought here from E.W. Pugin's St. Gregory's Church at Longton, Stoke-on-Trent, as well as some fittings from the former convent of the Sisters of Nazareth in Birmingham. From 1950 Mass was said each Sunday by the Sacred Heart Fathers of Market Rasen until that parish was taken over by the secular clergy in 2008.

CALVERTON

St. Anthony – served from Southwell

Calverton lies three and a half miles to the north-east of Arnold, a suburb of Nottingham. The opening near the village in 1952 of a new colliery, described as one of the most up-to-date coalmines in the world, was one of the more ambitious projects of the National Coal Board after its formation, and brought a considerable number of Catholic workers into the district.

A Mass centre, served from Good Shepherd, Arnold, was opened in 1953. Two years later, an acre of land was acquired on Mansfield Lane, and a building intended to serve as a church on Sundays and as a hall during the week was opened in August 1957. The intention was to have, ultimately, a church, a hall and a presbytery on the site. This intention was never able to be fully realised, and the 1950s building long outlived its expected lifespan of some ten years. Soon after Easter 1993 the old building was demolished, and part of the land acquired in 1955 was sold off. The money raised from this helped towards the cost of a new church, designed to serve social as well as liturgical needs, on the same site. The church was opened on 15 December 1993. From the beginning, the Catholic community of Calverton has always maintained strong links with other Christians in the area.

The colliery closed in 1999 and, although Calverton boasts a small industrial estate providing some local employment, it has mainly the character of a large commuter village.

CASTLE DONINGTON

(St. John Fisher) Church of the Risen Lord – served from Melbourne

Although during the First World War, Mass was celebrated in Donington Hall for German officer prisoners interned there, it was only in 1928 that a Mass centre as such was established at Castle Donington. The congregation was small, and in the early years Mass was said only one Sunday in each month. Later, this was increased to two Sundays a month and the Moira Arms was used as the Mass centre. After seven years of unaided effort, the local Catholics were able to erect on Mount Pleasant as a chapel a wooden hut measuring thirty feet by twenty feet. This was opened on 29 September 1935 and was dedicated to St. John Fisher who had been canonised that same year. Owing to the natural increase in the congregation, and to an influx of workers at the power station opened in the late 1950s (and closed in the mid-1990s), this chapel was found to be inadequate in size. For some years from 1948, therefore, Mass was also said at the power station hostel and at Donington Hall during the time that this hosted a home for refugee children.

Castle Donington has always been served from Melbourne. In 1959 a redundant Church of England school on Castle Hill was purchased and was opened 13 May 1960 as a replacement for the chapel on Mount Pleasant. By the end of the 1970s, however, this building was showing such signs of deterioration which it would have been too costly to repair that, after much heart-searching on the part of priest and parishioners, the decision was taken in 1983 to demolish it and to accept the kind offer of hospitality from St. Edward's Anglican church.

For almost a decade Sunday Masses were celebrated in St. Edward's and weekday Masses (when not celebrated in Melbourne) were celebrated in the homes of parishioners. But there was a feeling among parishioners that they wanted their own church and, in April 1992, the first turf was cut for a new dual-purpose church, designed by Eberlin and Partners, to be built on the site of the old school which site had in the intervening years been rented to the local council as a car park. Six months after the first turf had been cut, the first Mass was celebrated in the new church now called 'The Catholic Church of the Risen Lord.'

Early in the twenty-first century, the Parish of Melbourne & Castle Donington was split, and for about a year, Melbourne was served from Swadlincote, and Castle Donington from East Leake. Since 2005, the two parts of the parish have been reunited.

CHAPEL-EN-LE-FRITH

St John Fisher and St Thomas More – served from Marple Bridge

For years after the Reformation the hamlets surrounding Chapel-en-le-Frith had been a stronghold of the Catholic Faith; but most of these gave up the unequal struggle soon after the death of Elizabeth I, and there is no certain evidence that the Faith survived continuously to modern times. There were, however, enough Catholics in the town to justify the opening of a Mass centre by Fr. John Joseph Collins of New Mills in 1848. This centre survived only two years.

The present Mission owes its origins to Fr. George Holland of Buxton. In 1928 he called a meeting of Catholics resident in the district and although he himself was to die before the end of the same year, the meeting bore fruit in the purchase of the site on Horderns Road where the presbytery and church now stand. It seems also that he began, at the same time, to say Mass occasionally in the chapel at the Constitutional Hall.

His work was continued by his successor at Buxton, Fr. Luke Prendergast who, in 1933, moved the Mass centre to the Picture Palace in Eccles Street and in the following year transferred the care of the Mission to Fr. John Joseph Cafferkey of Tideswell. He, in turn, moved the Mass centre to the Town Hall in 1935. On the death of Fr. Cafferkey in 1944, the Mission was reorganised in such a way that Chapel-en-le-Frith was given the status of the parish church and Tideswell became its chapel-of-ease.

The foundation stone of the new church, dedicated to Saints John Fisher and Thomas More, was laid by Monsignor Payne in 1936. The architect was Mr. Lowcock of Bakewell and Buxton. Local workmanship was used to a notable extent. The carved-oak altar was the product of two years' labour by Fr. Cafferkey himself one of whose hobbies was carpentry. The greater part of the money required for the building was provided by Mr. and Mrs. Carter of Hathersage. The church was opened by Bishop McNulty on 25 September 1937. In his address, the bishop pointed out that the patron of the medieval parish church of Chapel-en-le-Frith, St. Thomas Becket, had - like St. Thomas More, one of the co-patrons of the church being dedicated this day – died "for the freedom of the Church and for the freedom of the English people"; and he referred to the fact that he himself (the bishop) had been present in Rome in 1935 when Saints John Fisher and Thomas More were canonised. The presbytery, built ten years after the church, was first occupied at the end of 1947. The interior of the church, apparently stripped of original fittings in the 1970s, was some years later refitted with salvaged Gothic-style fittings and joinery. For example, the 1910 pulpit and Gothic wall panelling is from Angmering and the stone font and altar top from Belper. The painted decoration to the east wall has been restored and dado panelling installed in a Gothic design that echoes the salvaged joinery. The marble altar structure was made by the Gillick family in 2009. The open-backed pine pews are probably original. The sanctuary is lit by a small plain three-light window set high above the altar, probably an insertion, filled with 1950s stained-glass of the two martyrs to whom the church is dedicated. The nave windows are glazed with plain leaded glass.

The church was built on the western edge of the small town of Chapel, on a side road in a suburb of inter-war housing. It is not visible from the main road.

CHARLESWORTH

(Broadbottom) Immaculate Conception – served from Hadfield

This chapel-of-ease within the Parish of Hadfield is in the somewhat curious position of lying within the Diocese of Nottingham, but serving a congregation drawn almost exclusively from the Diocese of Shrewsbury. The Administrative Parish of Broadbottom is itself situated in the County of Cheshire; the Chapel of the Immaculate Conception is situated in the County of Derbyshire, with the River Etherow, marking the county boundary, flowing beneath its very walls. Except for a small number of Catholics who come down from the Derbyshire village of Charlesworth, most of the congregation comes from Broadbottom and Mottram in the Diocese of Shrewsbury.

Mass was said in Broadbottom during the late eighteenth century in property belonging to Charles Bostock, and from 1875 in the committee room of the village Co-operative Store. A Mass centre of some sort was first opened in Charlesworth by Monsignor Herman Sabela of Hadfield in 1894. Later in 1894, the site of the chapel was presented by Lord Howard of Glossop, and building began that summer. The church was opened by Bishop Bagshawe on 26 August 1896.

The church is in a rural setting on the banks of the River Etherow, below the village, now popular with commuters to Manchester. The attractive wooded grounds laid out by Monsignor Sabela in the 1890s include a statue of the Sacred Heart mounted on a rockery plinth facing the road and a stone-built grotto over a spring.

The church is a local landmark, notable for its little altered interior with a fine set of Gothic altars by Boulton of Cheltenham. The architect was Mr. Oswald Hill of Manchester, and the contractors Messrs. Storrs of Stalybridge. In accordance with the taste of the times, its altars are somewhat ornate, and this tendency has been maintained in the colourful murals executed by Mr. A. Jarvis of Stockport at the decoration of the church in 1937. The cost of the original fabric and fittings was all paid off before the chapel was opened in 1896. In 1936 the sanctuary was adorned with mural paintings of Saints Thomas More, John Fisher and local martyrs, and with Christ the King over the chancel arch; these have since been covered or removed.

It was at first intended to establish Broadbottom as an independent parish. A priest was sent to reside near the chapel in 1895, and a succession of missionary priests kept up until 1915. After that date the slump in the cotton industry made it impossible for the congregation to maintain its own priest, and the Mission reverted to the status of chapel-of-ease to Hadfield from that year until 1953. Some attempt was made in 1920 to raise funds for a presbytery and a part of the necessary money was collected, but the project of re-establishing Broadbottom as an independent Mission was not realised at that time. From 1953 to 1971 Broadbottom was served from Glossop, St. Mary Crowned. In the latter year Broadbottom became an independent parish, and a presbytery was built in 1980 in Gamesley, a nearby post-war estate. Since 1999 Broadbottom/Charlesworth has been served from Hadfield.

St. Margaret's Primary School was built at Gamesley. This is now federated with All Saints Primary School, Old Glossop.

CLAY CROSS

St. Patrick & St. Bridget – served from Alfreton

The very Irish dedication of this Mission is sufficient indication of the nationality of its original congregation. When the bituminous coal of Clay Cross was first worked in the 1840s, it seems that a considerable number of pit sinkers came from Ireland. Others came later when the ironworks were opened in 1847. These immigrants were able to hear Mass at Wingerworth Hall, three miles to the north. When this passed out of Catholic hands, the congregation was kept in being by a Mass centre at Birdholme. This closed in 1858 and the problem of providing for the congregation living in Clay Cross became acute.

Fr. Arthur McKenna, Missionary Priest of Ilkeston from 1860 to 1863, was alive to the spiritual indigence of the whole district. In his short period of office at Ilkeston, he opened Mass centres at Riddings, Mansfield, and, in 1861, at Clay Cross. In the following year Fr. McKenna obtained the tenancy of a chapel at Clay Cross, and the future of the Mission was assured.

The chapel appears to have been of curious origin. It was built by a non-Catholic butcher named Slack, and was nothing more than a private financial speculation. He was prepared to hire it out to any religious body that would pay. The Catholics were willing and able to do so, and it opened as a Catholic chapel on 1 June 1862, when Fr. Brindle SJ, uncle of the future Bishop Brindle, said Mass.

Throughout the episcopacy of Bishop Roskell, Clay Cross remained a chapel-of-ease, served sometimes from Ilkeston and sometimes from Chesterfield. From 1875 it became an independent Mission and was thus one of the first of many parishes founded by Bishop Bagshawe. During the long pastorate of Fr. Daniel Meenagh (1881-1915) the Mission attained some degree of prosperity. It acquired a presbytery, and a chapel-of-ease at Alfreton. It also attained some degree of notoriety when the parish priest made public his reasons for disagreeing with Bishop Brindle's policy regarding a private chapel in the home of a wealthy parishioner.

For some reason - possibly the migration of Irish labourers to new work - the parish fell suddenly in numbers from 365 in 1878 to no more than 100 in 1883. After this major disaster, the financial position of the parish became extremely precarious, and on the death of Fr. Meenagh in 1915, the bishop found it impossible to appoint a successor. There followed a depressing period of ten years, during which various expedients were adopted for keeping the Mission in existence. Twice a priest was sent to live at Clay Cross, but these attempts at revival were short-lived and more often than not Clay Cross was served by any church which could lend the services of a priest. A more hopeful period began in 1925, from which year Clay Cross has achieved stability as a chapel-of-ease to Alfreton.

Nothing is known of the first chapel of 1862 except that it had one hundred and twenty sittings and was described as 'Gothic'. The present church in Thanet Street was opened in 1882. It was much altered in the 1980s when the adjoining detached house was bought and the former presbytery was demolished. The nave was then extended and a new sanctuary was built on the site, between the house and the church. At the same time, the interior was reordered and the former sanctuary was adapted for use as a sacristy.

CLAY CROSS - *Convent*

Franciscan Minoresses

From 1903 the Novitiate of the Franciscan Minoresses was at the Mother House in Melton Mowbray until 1983 when it was moved to Clay Cross. But in 1964 St. Clare's Convent was opened. Within the grounds of Saint Clare's Convent there is a purpose-built Franciscan House of Prayer and Solitude, 'The Portiuncula', where laypeople, Catholic and non-Catholic, as well as clergy and Religious can come in search of peace and quiet.

CLEETHORPES

Corpus Christi

As it is the nearest seaside resort to South Yorkshire, Cleethorpes receives an annual influx of visitors in the summer. But it has also the character of a residential suburb of Grimsby, and its Catholic population has consequently some degree of stability. On 1 July 1914 Canon Patrick O'Donoghue, of St. Mary's, Grimsby, celebrated Mass in the Technical Institute (later, the Library) on Isaac's Hill. In the following years, Mass was offered in various places such as the Pier Pavilion, the Theatre Royal, the Scout Hut, and the Reynolds Street Schools. Until 1937, when Fr. Bernard Grimley was appointed the first parish priest, Cleethorpes was served from St. Mary's, Grimsby.

The first church, a construction of brick, with a small domed campanile and Romanesque affinities, was opened in 1930. It served well for some sixty years, but in the 1990s, when it was planned to extend the church, it was discovered that there were fundamental problems with the foundation. So the decision was taken to demolish the 1930 church and to build a new one on the same site while using some items from its predecessor. New fittings include two large stained-glass windows on either side of the sanctuary, (Annunciation and Christ the King) given by a family in the congregation, and windows designed by local schoolchildren under the direction of John Dean, stained-glass artist.

The foundation stone of the new church was laid in July 1995 and the first Mass was celebrated in the new church in December of that year.

St. Joseph's Catholic Primary School was opened in 1977. It became a Voluntary Academy in 2012, and a Nursery was opened in September 2015.

A secondary school, Holy Family Catholic Academy, opened in September 2013. This replaced St. Andrew's College, a joint Catholic and Church of England School, and, prior to that, St. Mary's Catholic High School. Holy Family Academy was rated 'Good' by OFSTED in all four inspection categories as a result of the inspection in June 2015.

However, in spite of the 'Good' OFSTED rating, the low number of students enrolled in the academy has meant that there were serious questions concerning Holy Family's viability, and the Department for Education, the Nottingham Roman Catholic Diocesan Education Service, North East Lincolnshire Council and Holy Family Catholic Academy Trust had been working to ensure the best future for staff and pupils of the academy. As a result of these discussions, the Nottingham Roman Catholic Diocesan Religious Education Service announced, in March 2017, that the Wellspring Academy Trust would assume the sponsorship of the academy from 1 September 2017.

CLEETHORPES – *Convent*

The **Sisters of St. Joseph of Peace** opened St. Hugh's Nursing Home in 1938. It was the first in England to be conducted by this Religious Congregation. Two houses in Princes Road were bought for the purpose. One served as a convent. The other, with additions which made it one of the most up-to-date establishments of its kind in the country, is a nursing home with 30 beds (including three children's cots) divided among 15 wards. A new chapel was opened at the convent by Bishop Ellis in 1950. In 1980 the nursing home and the maternity wing were upgraded. Although the Sisters of St. Joseph of Peace have not run the nursing home since 2001, their work in the parish continues where, living in the presbytery, they serve as Parish Sisters performing a valuable and much appreciated role in the community.

As part of the reorganisation of Catholic life in North-East Lincolnshire in January 2017, Cleethorpes now forms part of the Parish of the Most Holy and Undivided Trinity encompassing, Grimsby, Cleethorpes, and Immingham.

COALVILLE

(The Transfiguration)
St. Wilfrid of York

It seems that Mass was first said in Coalville by the Cistercians of Mount St. Bernard Abbey. In 1875 and the following year they said Mass each Sunday at Rock House. The venture was then discontinued.

An assistant priest was appointed to Whitwick in 1897, and Fr. Matthew Joseph O'Reilly of that Mission was therefore enabled to provide Sunday Mass at Coalville. A private house on the Ashby Road, nearly opposite the Post Office, was used as the Mass centre.

Although the attendance at Mass was originally no more than twenty, after nine months the congregation had grown too large to be accommodated in a private house. The centre was therefore moved to a dance hall; but the rent asked for was more than the congregation could pay. They used the dance hall for six months, and then were rescued from their financial straits by Mr. Charles Tyler, a local non-Catholic hotel proprietor. He offered, free of charge, the use of his 'theatre-hall'. (This still existed in 1915, and was then known as the 'Picture Palace'.) Even in those days of improvisation, a theatre-hall might have been considered of doubtful suitability, but Bishop Bagshawe made a personal inspection, and declared it fit for a Mass centre. This venue was in use for two an a half years. In 1900 a corrugated-iron chapel, dedicated to St. Saviour, was built at the expense of Mr. Edwin de Lisle of Garendon on a site previously secured by Canon O'Reilly of Whitwick, and opened by Bishop Bagshawe. The presbytery, adjoining the temporary chapel, was built sometime in the years 1910-1915.

From this time the congregation made repeated requests to the bishop for a priest of its own, but the financial resources of the Mission were hardly sufficient to support a priest. In 1910 the people were able to promise a very small amount - one third of which was to come from a single extra-parochial benefactor from Whitwick - and on this slenderest of security

Bishop Brindle sent Fr. Joseph Degen in 1910 to be the first parish priest of the Mission.

From these unstable beginnings, Fr. Degen, in spite of much – sometimes misguided - opposition created an enduring parish. For twenty-three years, he carried on a vigorous apostolate by means of verbal and printed propaganda, followed up by intensive instruction. The Mission flourished with various educational (including a parish library) and recreational activities. The result was an unusual number of conversions which gave a distinctive character to the parish.

A site for a permanent church was bought some time before 1915. Ambitious plans were then drawn up for a large church in the Pointed Style with transepts and steeple. Funds sufficient for the purpose were available in 1939, but the outbreak of the Second World War made it impossible to proceed with the project.

In 1955 a more central site on London Road was purchased. The foundation stone of a church dedicated to St. Wilfrid of York was laid in 1959. Canon Patrick Balfe, Parish Priest of Coalville 1957-1976, chose St. Wilfrid as the patron of the new church "because of his acknowledged loyalty to the See of Rome." The church was blessed and opened in June 1961 and consecrated on 21 September 1967. A presbytery adjoining the church was built around the same time. The site opposite was retained until the 1990s as a parish hall with social club, but was subsequently closed and demolished, retaining the land as a car park for the church. In the early 2000s the large presbytery was subdivided to create a flat for the parish priest upstairs and a weekday chapel, parish offices and a large meeting room at the rear.

St. Wilfrid's Church and its presbytery are set back from the frontage of the busy London Road a little to the east of the centre of Coalville. The area is mainly residential but the Anglican Christ Church is on the opposite side of the road. St. Wilfrid's makes a modest positive contribution to the streetscape.

In 1956 a Mass centre, dedicated to St. Thomas More, was opened in Ellistown, where Mass had been said at various places for several years previously. This closed in 1970.

A primary school, dedicated to St. Clare, was opened in 1976. Prior to this, there had been a day and boarding school successively conducted by three different Congregations of Religious sisters.

COALVILLE – *Convents*

Several religious communities of women have been established at Coalville at different times and have been involved in education.

The **Portuguese Sisters of St Dorothy** were here in 1915. They conducted a day and boarding school, which seems to have survived until the 1960s long after the Sisters of St. Dorothy had left.

The **Ladies of Mary** from Croydon and Sydenham occupied the convent on Forest Road from 1930 to 1945.

Poor Clares of the Immaculate Conception (of Newry) 1945-1990.
This was the first of six houses of this Congregation to be opened in the diocese.

In 1918 there was a convent of **Ursulines** (refugees from Belgium) in Coalville, but as they are not mentioned in the first edition of the diocesan yearbook (1921), it is presumed that they had returned to Belgium by this point in time.

COTGRAVE

Our Lady of Grace – served from West Bridgford

Cotgrave, although only a few miles south-east of Nottingham, retains something of a village character. Cotgrave colliery opened in 1964 and miners from all over the country moved to the area. To meet the needs of the Catholics among them, Fr. John Gilroy CSSp. was appointed to the new Parish of Keyworth and Cotgrave in 1973. Initially, Mass was celebrated at the Miners' Youth Centre. The priest lived at Candleby Lane in the village. In 1976 a hut (formerly part of a school) was acquired from Newark and brought to Cotgrave where the first Mass was celebrated on 5 December of that year. But the hut church on Candleby Lane, referred to from 1980 as "The Church of the Immaculate Heart of Mary", was "small, draughty and dingy". In 1989 Bishop McGuinness gave permission to build a new church; and September 1990 saw the opening of this new church with the dedication changed to Our Lady of Grace. Cotgrave colliery closed in the 1990s.

Around this time the designation of the two centres changed. Hitherto, Keyworth had been seen as the parish centre and Cotgrave a Mass centre or chapel-of-ease. Then Cotgrave was given the main listing in the diocesan yearbook and Keyworth was served from Cotgrave as a chapel-of-ease. Currently – 2017 – Keyworth is served from East Leake and Cotgrave from West Bridgford.

CROWLE

The Blessed Sacrament and St. Norbert - served from Gainsborough

The Isle of Axholme has been from time immemorial one of the most isolated districts of the diocese. It was, as its name implies, originally an island, formed by the Rivers Trent, Torn, Don and Idle. In 1626 the Dutch engineer Cornelius Vermuyden carried out adrainage scheme which changed its character. But its communications remained poor until the construction of the M180 motorway in the late 1970s. Crowle is the principal market-town in the north of the Isle of Axholme.

The mid-nineteenth century saw the industrial development of Crowle and its rural hinterland, and the influx of a large number of Irish labourers, whose nearest Mass centre was then at Howden. It was in this context that an Italian immigrant named Girolamo Vaccari, who anglicised his name as James Walker, took the initiative in founding a Mission. Prior to settling down as foreman of the gas-works in Crowle, he had toured the Midland and Eastern counties of England as an organ grinder and had also kept a second-hand furniture shop at Thorne in Yorkshire. In the course of his travels he married Miss Hannah Rogers of Bungay, who was to co-operate generously in his apostolic work.

A census taken by the Walkers showed that there were about 500

Irish labourers in the Isle. They sought the aid of Fr. William Harris of Gainsborough. On Easter Sunday 1862 the first Mass in Crowle was said at the Assembly Rooms, adjoining the Fishmongers' Arms. A year later, a regular Sunday Mass was instituted - apparently once a fortnight, for Fr. Harris was at that time saying Mass on alternate Sundays also at Gainsborough, Retford and Brigg. When visiting Crowle, Fr. Harris stayed at the home of the Walker family. It was the meeting-place for Catholics who wished to see the priest, and was also used by Mrs. Walker to teach the Catechism to the children. This was displeasing to some of the townsfolk as the Gas Company owned the house. Mr. Walker was given an ultimatum - either to give up his work for the Church or to leave the house. He chose to leave.

This incident underlined the need for a resident priest. Mrs. Walker wrote to solicit the aid of Mr. Young of Kingerby. He became interested, and in October 1868 bought a half-acre site on Field Side to the east of the village. To find a priest was another matter. A diocesan priest could not have existed on the meagre resources the Mission could provide. Mr. Young remembered that England's first Premonstratensian house, founded in 1143, was Newhouse near Brocklesby, not twenty miles from Crowle. So he wrote to Abbot Chrysostom de Swert of Tongerloo, near Antwerp, and offered to build a house and church if the Canons Regular of Premontré (also known as Premonstratensians or Norbertines – after their founder, St. Norbert of Xanten) would come over to England and make a foundation. The abbot visited Crowle in April 1871 and agreed. This was to become the first Premonstratensian house to be established in England since the Reformation. The Sub-Prior of Tongerloo, Fr. Martin Geudens, volunteered to go to England, and took temporary lodgings with the Walkers at Crowle in September 1872.

Building had already begun. The foundation stone of the church was laid on 7 July 1871. It was designed in the Early English style by Hadfield of Sheffield and constructed in brick. The first portion was opened by the Abbot of Mount St Bernard on 15 October 1872. A presbytery large enough to contain a whole community was built at the same time. Bishop Roskell came on 15 June 1874 to lay the foundation stone of a new chancel, which was opened on 21 April 1875. In his five-yearly Report to Rome of 1875, Bishop Bagshawe noted: "The new church, residence and schools belong to the Premonstratensian Canons of Tongerloo, who have two priests there; these take charge of the Catholics of the Isle of Axholme, about 378 in number, of whom 191 are at Crowle. They sometimes say Mass at a chapel at Epworth, belonging to Mr. Dawson of Hull." By 1885 the Premonstratensians had purchased for the diocese a piece of land, and built on it a school-chapel at Luddington, a place within the Mission, where about 100

Catholics resided. In 2016 Mass was still being said at Luddington on the first Friday of each month.

The fiftieth anniversary of St. Norbert's Church was celebrated with great pomp and circumstance in July 1922 when, among other things, stirring and enthusiastic sermons were preached by Fr. Alban King OP.

Apart from the erection in 1949 of an oak belfry, the church has remained almost unaltered since that date. The bell turret with its green copper spire forms a bold skyline feature and is an important local landmark. The modern parish hall and school buildings are located behind the church and house. The church contains a number of furnishings of note and with the house forms a good group in the conservation area, although the house has been marred by unsympathetic recent alterations.

The school dates from January 1873, when a lay school-mistress began to take classes in the reception-room of the Priory. A new school building was opened in March 1875. In 1879 the school had 70 pupils.

Another wing was added in 1926 "to house the growing numbers of Catholic children whose families were moving into the area." In 2016 there were about 120 pupils in the school which, in 2012, had become a Voluntary Academy.

In 1982 the Premonstratensians decided that they could no longer staff the Priory, and the parish was given over to the secular clergy. At the start of the twenty-first century, it was found impossible to have a resident priest for Crowle, and it has been served from Scunthorpe from 2000-2002 and from Gainsborough since 2003.

CROWLE, *The Blessed Sacrament and St. Norbert - Convent*

A community of **Presentation Sisters** was founded in Crowle from Buxton in 1935. As well as teaching in the private school – this had twelve pupils - the Sisters visited some of the outlying districts of the extensive parish in order to prepare children for the sacraments and engaged in other forms of parish ministry. They also began to teach in the parish school in the same year. They left the parish in 1961, but a Sister from Scunthorpe continued to travel to Crowle from Scunthorpe to teach in the school until 1983.

DEEPING ST JAMES

Our Lady of Lincoln and St. Guthlac – served from Bourne

The modern Catholic history of Deeping, seven miles north-east of Stamford, begins in 1880 and is tied up initially with the Waterton family. The antiquary Edmund Waterton (1830-87) purchased Deeping Manor in 1879. Like his father, the naturalist Charles Waterton, Edmund was a devout Catholic and had been educated at Stonyhurst College. Soon after his arrival in Deeping St. James, Edmund Waterton converted a stable for use as a Catholic church, and it remained in use until 1968. The Watertons left Deeping in 1891 and the Manor was purchased by the Marquis of Exeter. But links with the Waterton family were not severed for good. Edmund Waterton was a great collector of religious artefacts and three exceptional and precious objects remain in the church which was built in the late 1960s to replace the chapel which had served the Catholics of Deeping for the better part of a century.

After the Watertons left Deeping Manor, Mass continued to be celebrated each Sunday in the chapel until about 1914. Then it seems to have ceased until 1919, when the Xaverian Brothers established their novitiate in Deeping. The Brothers purchased the Manor in 1932 (it was demolished in the 1960s).

In 1942, owing to the war conditions, the Xaverian Brothers' Preparatory School of St. Edward the Confessor was moved to Deeping St. James and the novitiate was moved to Clapham. The school moved back to Sussex at the beginning of 1946 and the novices returned to Deeping where they remained until 1954 when they left the diocese for good.

In the 1960s new housing estates were built at Deeping St. James, providing the opportunity of a site for a new church. The new church, dedicated to Our Lady of Lincoln and the hermit of Crowland, Saint Guthlac (died 714), was blessed and opened by Bishop Ellis in May 1969 the first Mass having been celebrated there the previous Christmas.

The Sacred Heart Fathers served the Bourne and Deeping St. James area from 1957 until 1984.

DERBY

Christ the King (Mackworth)

The Parish of Christ the King on the Mackworth Estate, cut off from St. Mary's in 1960, was the third parish to be founded from the mother church within a quarter of a century. The most important thing, as always, was to find somewhere where Mass could be celebrated. In this case, a hut in the grounds of the local Army Drill Hall was made available by the Commanding Officer. This, of course, was only a beginning. The site for the church was purchased in 1962. On it was built a church which also served as a parish and community centre and, in addition, housed some classes from St. Mary's Primary School. This building was opened in 1963. The first Mass in the new building was celebrated by Bishop Ellis in the presence of a congregation of more than six hundred. Initially a small house on Lilac Avenue was purchased as a temporary presbytery to be replaced several years later by a presbytery adjacent to the church.

To meet the needs of the people of Mackworth and district, a new church, described as "a good example of a post-War church ..., with an inventive plan and dramatic internal spaces" was opened on the same site in June 1972.

The history of the parish is then relatively uneventful until the 1990s when the Catechetical Centre at Highfields had outgrown its available space. But there was space available in the parish centre at Mackworth and this was used, from 1993, to house the Diocesan Centre as a base for the work of catechesis and adult formation in the diocese. A number of other, smaller, bodies also took up residence. But when the Diocesan Schools Office outgrew the available space at Willson House in Nottingham, it was relocated to Mackworth, and the smaller bodies were squeezed into other areas, or found alternative accommodation.

When Fr. John Guest took on the Parish of Ashbourne in addition to Mackworth, the Mackworth presbytery became vacant and was used for several years as extra office space, but reverted to being a presbytery in 2013.

DERBY

English Martyrs (Alvaston)

This Mission is situated at Alvaston within the boundaries of the City of Derby. A brick chapel was opened here in April 1909 on a site given in 1906 by Mr. John Doherty, brother of a former Mayor of Derby. For the next eight years, Alvaston was served from St. Mary's, Derby, and for one year from St. Barnabas' Cathedral. From 1918 to 1921 and then for one further year there was a resident priest, but for the following fifteen years, Alvaston was once again served from St. Mary's. Since 1937, when it became an independent parish, Alvaston has always had a resident priest. At the time of its opening it was noted that, due to the great increase in the Catholic population of Alvaston and Allenton (which latter at that time formed part of St. Joseph's Parish), the original church of 1909 had become "woefully inadequate" for their accommodation, and the hope was expressed that, should a school be erected in Allenton, Mass could be offered there on Sundays and so make it possible for the church at Alvaston to cope for a few more years. The present church was designed in a style not unlike St. George's, Derby. The foundation stone was laid on 16 March 1952. The completed church was opened with great solemnity by Bishop Ellis on 10 May of the following year. The opening day began with Solemn High Mass at which the bishop preached. After lunch there was a procession of the Blessed Sacrament from the Convent of Mercy established the previous year at Greenhill House, Alvaston, to the newly-opened church. Some thousand people, led by the bishop and about thirty priests, took part in the procession. On arrival at the church, Solemn Benediction was given, preceded by a sermon and concluding with the 'Te Deum.' The church was packed to overflowing.

The presbytery, attached to the north-west end of the building, was added in 1971 and a new parish hall provided in 2004-5.

St. John Fisher School serving Alvaston and Chellaston, has seen many changes since it began as a private school in the Convent of Mercy in January 1953. It became a voluntary aided primary school in 1960. There were, in 2017, approximately 228 pupils in the school on its present site in Alvaston Street.

St. Thomas More Secondary Modern School, Allenton, was opened in 1957. In the 1970s it amalgamated with St. Ralph Sherwin to form St. Benedict's Comprehensive.

DERBY, *English Martyrs – Convent*

The **Sisters of Mercy** opened a convent in December 1952 and, early in the following year, an independent primary school. They continued to teach after it became a voluntary aided primary school. When the last teaching Sister retired in July 1996, marking the end of forty-four years of direct involvement of the Sisters in the primary school, the decision was taken to close the house. The remaining Sisters moved to the Bridge Gate community from where they are still able to keep contact with the sick and housebound in Alvaston.

DERBY

Holy Family (Allestree) – served from Derby, St. Mary's

The Parish of Holy Family was created in October 1970 when the Derby suburbs of Allestree and Quarndon were separated from St. Mary's Parish where many previous generations of parishioners from these areas had worshipped. A parish priest was appointed and land was purchased in Blenheim Drive, Allestree. On this land a church/hall was built; it was blessed by Bishop Ellis.

Loans from parishioners enabled the parish to pay a deposit on a nearby house as a presbytery. In the early days Mass was celebrated here during the week. The vicar and parishioners of the local Anglican Church of St. Nicholas kindly offered the use of their hall for the celebration of Mass on Sundays until the church/hall was completed.

In 1994, and again in 1999, the building was extended and reordered to provide additional facilities.

The founding parish priest was Father Brendan O'Callaghan. His inspiration in establishing the parish was the teaching of the Second Vatican Council with its emphasis on the active role of the laity in the life of the parish. That grounding has stood the parish in good stead over more than forty years, particularly over the difficult period in the early 1990s when it lost its resident priest and became, once again, the pastoral responsibility of the priests at St. Mary's.

Despite not having a resident priest since then, Holy Family has preserved its identity as a separate parish whilst sharing many activities and resources with St. Mary's. This is amply demonstrated from information on the parish website which shows how a parish without a resident priest can survive and prosper when it has involved lay people working closely with a supportive parish priest.

DERBY

Holy Spirit (Sinfin) - served from Derby, St. George's

In 1977, the Queen's Silver Jubilee year, Derby was granted its charter as a city; and the Parish of Sinfin and Chellaston was established from St. George's, Derby. Chellaston had had a church building since 1971, but it was not until 1981 that Sinfin got its own church. Prior to that, Sunday Mass was celebrated at the Moorfields Assessment Centre and at Sinfin Ecumenical Church while the Catholic community in Sinfin was gradually being built up. In 1980 a timber building which had previously served as a social club in Spondon was bought, dismantled, removed to Sinfin and re-erected on a large greenfield site on Redwood Road. The timber building was adapted for use as a church, complete with sacristy, meeting room and a Blessed Sacrament Chapel for weekday Mass. Bishop McGuinness opened the Church of the Holy Spirit during a Lenten Station Mass on 23 March 1981.

From its beginning, Holy Spirit was much involved with the local community. A good example of such involvement is the fact that the church, in the 1990s, was providing a base for an Asian Over-60s Drop-In Centre.

Eventually with the falling numbers of active clergy in the diocese available, the Parish of Sinfin and Chellaston was a prime candidate for being split up. Thus, in 2000, Chellaston was allocated to English Martyrs, Alvaston, and Sinfin returned to the care of St. George's.

DERBY

Our Lady of Lourdes (Mickleover)

In the seventeenth century, Mickleover was a rural community of four hundred individuals, but in the nineteenth century it grew significantly as it became the home of some of the owners of the industry that grew up in Derby. Growth was also affected by the coming of the railway in the 1870s and the building of the Pastures Hospital in 1850.

Major growth started in the 1950s with the building of the Brisbane Road Estate followed by the Silverhill Estate in the 1960/70s. Further developments to the south of Uttoxeter Road took place in the 1980s.

In the late 1950s Fr. Douglas Key of St. Joseph's, Derby, had foreseen the need for the establishment of a new parish in Mickleover. With this in mind, he arranged for a bus to collect people from Mickleover each Sunday and bring them to St. Joseph's for the 9.30 Mass.

The next stage was when, on 29 October 1961, Fr. Edward Byron, the first Parish Priest of Mickleover, celebrated Mass in the Memorial Hall on Station Road. Three years later, Mickleover Lodge on Uttoxeter Road was purchased. This became, and still remains, the presbytery. On Maundy Thursday, 7 April 1966, the first Mass was celebrated in the 'temporary' church. (This now, with extensions, serves as the Parish Centre.) Just over a year later there took place the first canonical visitation by Bishop Ellis.

It soon became obvious that the original church building was not capable of meeting the needs of a growing Catholic population - 837 (1967);

870 (1968); 936 (1976), and so on to 1350 in 2014. So the decision was taken to build a new church. After a lot of careful preparation over several years, work began on the new church in September 1981, and the first Mass was celebrated there ten months later. Bishop McGuinness, assisted by twenty-eight priests, dedicated the church on 7 October 1982.

The celebrations of the twenty-fifth anniversary of the parish in 1986 began with a barbeque on a wet and windy September evening and continued for some time afterwards in a somewhat calmer way! In 2004 the church entrance was extended to form a gathering area.

Over the years, a tremendous amount of work has been done both within and beyond the confines of the Catholic Church not least in reaching out to less able members of society. The booklet produced in 2011 to mark the Golden Jubilee of the parish bears the sub-title "Fifty years of walking together in faith" and gives many examples of such work. This "walking together" has been done whenever possible with fellow Christians of other traditions. Not all the activity has, however, been of equal importance. The parish records note, for instance, that in autumn 1985, a burglar alarm was fitted to the presbytery after the parish priest's dog slept soundly through a robbery!

DERBY

St. Alban
(Chaddesden)

The overspill of Derby's population beyond the River Derwent to the north had begun before the outbreak of the Second World War. From 1931 Mass was celebrated at the Crown Club in Spondon, and the growing number of Catholics there were hoping to get their own parish and priest. But, it seems, the large estates being built around the village of Chaddesden, included in the Borough of Derby from 1968, prompted a decision to build, eventually, a church there. Thus it was that Monsignor James Hargreaves, Parish Priest of St. Mary's, Derby, began, in 1943, to celebrate Sunday Mass in a health centre in Sussex Circus on the Roe Farm Estate. A site for a church was bought in 1946, and two years later, two War Department Nissen huts were bought and set up on the site. One of these formed the church, and the other the sacristy. The arrival and setting up of 'The Hut' has been compared to the arrival of the Ark of the Covenant among the Jewish people! The Catholic population continued to grow steadily and much work was put into raising money for a new and permanent church. This was designed by Reynolds and Scott of Manchester in Romanesque Style. The foundation stone was laid by Bishop Ellis on 3 October 1953, and the building was opened on 26 June 1955. A presbytery was built off the generous sacristies to the north of the church. To the south side of the church two low one-storey prefabs provided a parish hall and a social club.

It was time now for Chaddesden to branch out on its own, and so Fr. John McLean was appointed as the first parish priest. Since the new parish priest had also the heavy responsibility of Secretary to the Diocesan Schools Commission, he was immediately given a curate. During the next thirty years the parish continued to grow. In view of this, it was considered that the church was too small.

So, in the 1960s, the apse of the church was demolished and transepts were constructed on either side of a new, much larger sanctuary. The new extensions were blessed in September 1966, and the whole building was consecrated ten years later - almost twenty years after the first blessing. Unfortunately, the quality of the building this time was not the same as that of the original church and the flat roof leaked badly. By now numbers of those attending Mass had begun to decline and could no longer fill the extended church. Moreover, the leaks could not be fixed economically.

Fr. Gerald Murphy was appointed parish priest in October 2000 with the instruction by Bishop McGuinness, among other things, to demolish the extension! Over the next few years, this was done. Part of the land and the presbytery were sold off for development; and the money thus raised helped to fund the ambitious project of renewal. Although the original church was retained, significant alterations were made. These included the reorientation of the sanctuary to the centre of the south wall of the nave. While all this work was going on, Sunday Masses were celebrated in St. Alban's School. In September 2005 the now vastly altered church was reopened for worship. In 2003 a new parish centre was built off the south end of the old sanctuary area and a much smaller bungalow presbytery was built at the front of the site where the old prefabs had been.

It had long been a hope, consonant with Bishop Ellis' frequently expressed view that he would rather open a school than a church, to establish a Catholic school in Chaddesden. This hope came to fruition when a primary school was opened in January 1957. Numbers of pupils increased rapidly in the early years – with as many as forty-six children in each classroom! So it was decided to build a completely new infant school, which opened in 1969. The two schools amalgamated in 1984, and in 1993 a nursery unit was opened.

The Church on Oakwood, an ecumenical venture on a new housing estate, was dedicated 29 May 1993; it is served from Chaddesden. This is one of only three 'ecumenical' churches with Catholic involvement in England and Wales.

DERBY, *St. Alban (Chaddesden) - Convent*

Presentation Sisters

The convent was originally known as "The Grange" and was formerly owned by Mr. and Mrs. Carlin. Both were fervent Catholics and, in their ageing years, greatly desired that their home should be used for some religious purpose. With this in view, they offered "The Grange" to Bishop Ellis who, in turn, offered it to the Presentation Sisters as a more suitable location for the novitiate and the Mother House than was Cressbrook.

The Sisters moved to Chaddesden in 1957, and the novitiate remained there until the early 1970s. but the Chaddesden convent remained the central house of the Derby group until the Union of several Presentation Congregations took place. In February 1977 the Presentation Convent, Chaddesden, became the Provincialate House of the newly formed English Province of the Union of Presentation Sisters.

The Presentation Sisters left Chaddesden in 1988.

DERBY

St. George and All Soldier Saints

The erection of the fourth of Derby's churches was made possible largely through the generosity of Peter Bresser, a local farmer, who, as a thank-offering for the safe return of his son from the First World War and in memory of those who didn't, donated land for a church in Village Street. A certain Henry Pinchbeck offered to finance such a building. The latter had long been interested in providing the Parish of St. Joseph with a worthier church. For this purpose, about the year 1910 he contributed a sum of money towards the purchase of a site at the corner of Normanton Road and Hartington Street. At the same time, he expressed his intention of leaving in his will a considerable sum of money for the erection of a church thereon. He did, in fact, leave a significant legacy, but not sufficient to carry out an ambitious plan. As the town was spreading rapidly to the south in the years immediately after the First World War, Canon James William Browne of St. Joseph's Parish decided to abandon the project for replacing St. Joseph's and to use the funds available to build a new chapel-of-ease in the Normanton area.

He therefore bought a site in Village Street and the foundation stone of a new church designed by Mr. Sidney Brocklesby of Merton, Surrey, was laid on 23 April 1920.

Dedicated to St. George and All Soldier Saints in memory of the forty-eight parishioners and others who had died during the First World War, the church was opened on 18 December 1920. It was served as a chapel-of-ease from St. Joseph's until 1928 and was then closed owing to a curious legal tangle. On the death of Canon Browne in 1925, it was found that the church was legally his private property. The matter was settled amicably, and the diocese was able to purchase the church from the Canon's executors for a nominal sum. But pending a settlement, it had become impossible to effect repairs necessary for the safety of the church. It was not until June 1930 that the church was able to be reopened. Before this could be done, however, the foundations and pillars had to be strengthened and the whole roof taken off and reconstructed.

After this setback, the congregation attached to St. George's increased so rapidly that in 1945 it was considered advisable to separate it from St. Joseph's and to form it into an independent parish. The church was consecrated on 23 April 1948.

A reordering took place in the 1980s when the stone altar was removed. A parish hall was built on the adjacent site in the mid-1960s and a lightweight link provided between the buildings during the 1990s.

For many years, children from St. George's attended St. Joseph's School, and the senior children went on to St. Thomas More, Allenton, which was opened in 1957 and closed in 1986. St. George's Primary School was opened, with 167 pupils, in 1964. By 1995 the school had 310 pupils, and in 2016 347. Since the closure of St. Thomas More School and its amalgamation with St. Ralph Sherwin School to form St. Benedict's, most of the pupils from St. George's Primary School, which converted to an Academy in 2012, have received their secondary education there.

DERBY

St. Joseph

In the opinion of a former diocesan archivist, the late Canon G. D. Sweeney, whose father had been head-teacher of St. Joseph's School in the early part of the twentieth century, the history of this Mission has been singularly uneventful, and there is little to record beyond a series of dates which mark a steady development. The site of 1,488 square yards on Gordon Road was bought in 1876 by Monsignor Arthur McKenna of Derby, St. Mary's. At that time, it stood on the southern limit of the built-up area of the town. There were no formed streets between Mill Hill Lane and the new barracks, which since that same year had been in the course of erection in Normanton. It was, in fact, mainly with a view to serving the needs of the troops that this site was chosen. The first chapel was opened by Bishop

Bagshawe on 26 November 1878. In his quinquennial report to Rome of 1885, the bishop noted that "A large piece of ground has been purchased at the other end of the town of Derby, and a handsome school-chapel has been erected there. Mass is said there every Sunday, and the school is attended by 123 boys and girls."

Until 1891 St. Joseph's was served from St. Mary's. In that year a presbytery was built. The cost of this was met largely by a legacy from Monsignor Thomas Sing, formerly of St. Mary's, who also left a further sum to the infant Mission. When Fr. Isaac Hanks came, in 1891, to be the first missionary priest, he found himself in the happy position of being entirely free from debt.

Since the chapel was used during the week as a school, it soon became imperative to build a permanent church. The foundation stone of the new church was laid by Bishop Bagshawe on 29 April 1896. Cardinal Vaughan came to open the completed church on 25 February 1897. Architecturally the church had little to recommend it, and proposals were made to replace it by a worthier building in 1910. But the greater part of the legacy with which it had been hoped to build this church failed to materialise. And as much money as became available was utilised on the construction of St. George's.

In 1985 a new church was built on Burton Road, and the Gordon Road church was sold to the Polish community, who renamed it St. Maximilian Kolbe after the Polish priest who gave his life for a fellow-prisoner in the concentration camp of Dachau in 1941.

DERBY

St. Maksymilian, Kolbe, Polish Church. (Formerly St. Joseph's)

A parish centre replacing an earlier one on Mill Hill Lane and attached to the new church was opened in 2013.

The first school-chapel was used as a school from 1879 until 1908. In less than thirty years the school became inadequate for the number of children, and in 1907 it was condemned. Twelve further months of grace were given to it by an arrangement which provided for the transfer of the Infants' Department to the church. Meanwhile, on 18 March 1908, the foundation stone was laid of a new building in Cromwell Road, and in the summer of the same year St. Joseph's School was opened. The first phase of a primary school on Mill Hill Lane was opened in January 1971 and for some years it supplemented the earlier school on Cromwell Road. In 1973 the primary school was divided into separate Junior and Infant schools. These were reunited in 1983 to form the new St. Joseph's Primary School.

DERBY, *St. Joseph – Convent*

In the late 1890s, at the request of Canon Browne, several **Sisters of Mercy** began to teach in the parish school. Initially, they travelled from the Bridge Gate convent each day; but in 1899 they purchased a house in Mount Carmel Street. This enabled them, in addition to their work in the parish school and in the 'private school' which they opened, to be involved in other parish activities. They provided part of the teaching staff of the school and also, for a time, maintained a private school. The convent was closed in 1923, but Sisters continued working in the school until 2004 when they left the parish although they still (2017) have some involvement with the parish youth club.

DERBY

St. Mary

In spite of the strong Catholic survival in other parts of the county, the Church in Derby had a somewhat tardy development, although not too far from Derby – at Yeldersley near Ashbourne – there was a priest resident before the end of the seventeenth century.

Catholic worship in the town can be dated from 1766. But while Nottingham, Leicester and Lincoln had provided themselves with a public chapel before the close of the eighteenth century, the Catholics of Derby were still attending Mass in the club room of an inn. This was the 'Old Ship Inn', kept by a Mr. Smith in the Corn Market, and presumably in use as a Mass centre until the erection of the first public chapel.

The Catholic history of Derby seems to have differed in one other respect from that of the other county towns in this early period. Unlike Nottingham, Leicester and Lincoln, Derby owed little, if anything, to the clergy who had emigrated from France in the face of the French Revolution.

The first public chapel was opened about 1813. It was a diminutive building in the Pointed Style, and stood in Chapel Street, where also the priest had his residence.

Originally built to accommodate one hundred people, and subsequently enlarged to hold three hundred, the chapel soon proved to be too small. Whereas in 1829 there were twenty Catholic families living in Derby, by 1840 the numbers had risen to about three thousand individuals. This very substantial increase was due not only to the birth-rate but also to other factors such as a considerable number of conversions and a significant influx of immigrants from Ireland. John Talbot, who later became the sixteenth Earl of Shrewsbury, promised to assist in the erection of a new church when he came into the family estates. Encouraged by this, Fr. John Challoner bought the present site on Bridge Gate.

Fr. Challoner died in 1836, and it fell to his successor, Fr. Thomas

Sing, to erect the present Church of St. Mary. He chose Augustus Welby Northmore Pugin, a recent convert, as the architect. Pugin's designs for St. Mary's were ambitious, and the church is considered to be one of the most successful of his works. Moreover, it was the first of many buildings on which he and the builder George Myers collaborated.

The foundation stone was laid by Father Ignatius Spencer, and the completed church was dedicated by Bishop (later Cardinal) Wiseman on 9 October 1839. The occasion has achieved a certain fame in the pages of history. The Earl of Shrewsbury came with Pugin and de Lisle to the opening. They found that the music was to be provided by lady sopranos and a full string orchestra. In disgust at this outrage to their liturgical feelings, they gathered up the Gothic vestments they had lent for the occasion, and rode off without waiting for the ceremony! E.W. Pugin added a Lady Chapel in 1855.

In October 1921 a memorial brass to the forty parishioners of St. Mary's killed in the First World War was unveiled, and in their memory, too, the church was lighted throughout by electricity.

Early in the eighteen-year pastorate of Monsignor Payne, extensive restoration of the church was undertaken since it was discovered that much of the original stonework was faulty. Among other things, the tower was found to be unsafe. Once this had been attended to, an eight-foot statue of Our Lady was erected on the top of the tower and so arranged so that it could be illuminated at night. The church was reopened on Trinity Sunday, 3 June 1928. (However, in the course of further restoration to mark the one hundred and fiftieth anniversary of the opening of the church, the statue had to be removed before the roof of the tower collapsed.)

The centenary of the opening of St. Mary's was celebrated in October 1939 in a rather subdued fashion due to the outbreak of the Second World War the previous month, and the fear of possible air raids. One way in which this was reflected was that instead of a rather lavish luncheon planned for two hundred and fifty people, a more modest meal for fifty-three was cooked in the presbytery and served in the community room of the Convent of Mercy!

The sesquicentenary of St. Mary's Church in 1989 was marked by, among other things, the bringing forward of the chancel arch and the construction of a new altar. The Pugin high altar was left intact, while the removal of Pugin's ironwork screen allowed for large numbers of priests to concelebrate.

A parish centre was opened in May 1996.

At the time St. Mary's Church was built, the area served from St. Mary's was immense. Apart from temporary chapels at Ashbourne on the western border and Ilkeston on the eastern, it was the only church in the whole of the southern half of the county. In the fifty years during which Monsignor McKenna was parish priest (1866-1916), St. Mary's became the mother church of the Missions at Derby, St. Joseph; Derby, Christ the King; Matlock; Alfreton and Alvaston; and its territory was, accordingly, considerably reduced.

In the second decade of the nineteenth century, Fr. Challoner opened a school with a regular attendance of twenty-six boys and thirty girls. Little is known about the origins of the school in Edward Street, but it is said to have been built before 1859 when Canon Sing left Derby. Confusion about the early years of Catholic schooling in Derby increases when we learn that the Society of the Holy Child Jesus founded an elementary school in 1846 and by 1848, when these Sisters left Derby, there were a hundred and forty children on the books. In addition, more than a hundred factory girls attended night school every evening. In 1847 the Holy Child Sisters opened a boarding school for the daughters of the gentry; this closed when they left Derby.

When the Society of the Holy Child Jesus left, their work in education was taken over by the Sisters of Mercy who came to Derby in 1849. In 1874 the Sisters of Mercy reopened both a private day school and St. Philomena's Independent Secondary School for Girls in Bridge Gate. Shortly after the Second World War, the senior portion of St. Philomena's moved to Highfields. By the end of the 1920s, the old school on Edward Street could no longer accommodate the growing number of pupils, so a new school with capacity for six hundred pupils – seniors, juniors and infants - was opened in 1931. Six years later, four acres of land on the Nottingham Road with a house attached were secured for the purpose of a secondary school for boys, but this seems never to have materialised. In 1967 St. Mary's Secondary School was opened on Duffield Road. In 1971 St. Philomena's Convent High School and St. Mary's Secondary Modern School merged to form St. Ralph Sherwin Comprehensive School. Several years later, St. Ralph Sherwin and St. Thomas More Comprehensive School in Allenton amalgamated to form St. Benedict's. This merger enabled greater opportunities for the Sixth Forms of both schools. St. Philomena's Junior School closed in 1992, and St. Mary's Primary School moved to its present site on Broadway in 2002.

DERBY, *St. Mary - Convents*

Derby's first convent was the birth-place of the **Society of the Holy Child Jesus.** On 13 October 1846 Mother Cornelia Connelly arrived with three companions. This remarkable woman was American by birth. She married an Episcopalian minister and had already raised a family when both decided to enter the Catholic Church. They then agreed to separate - he to become a priest, and she to enter a convent. Pope Gregory XVI commissioned Cornelia to found a new Society for the education of Catholic children in England. Bishop Wiseman, then Coadjutor of the Midland District, persuaded her to make her first foundation in Derby.

This convent had a remarkable, but short-lived success. For some obscure reason a dispute arose between the Sisters and the clergy of St. Mary's, and the Sisters transferred to St. Leonard's, Sussex, in 1848.

Sisters of Mercy from Kinsale took possession of the Nottingham Road Convent, previously inhabited by the Holy Child Jesus Sisters, on 17 October 1849. They immediately started work in the day and night schools which were already set up. and to these they added an orphanage, a house of mercy, and a teachers' training college. Ten days after their arrival in Derby, the Sisters commenced the visitation of the poor and sick in their homes. On 30 May 1850, the first public ceremony of a nun entering the novitiate and receiving the religious habit took place in the convent chapel.

At the close of the Crimean War the prestige of the Sisters was immense. Mother Mary Francis Bridgman of Kinsale and three others had been nursing in the hospital at Balaclava. When, in 1856, they returned to the community at Derby, they were brought from the station in a carriage drawn by four greys, and found a military guard of honour waiting at the convent.

Meanwhile the Nottingham Road building had proved itself dangerously unhealthy. An alternative convent was provided in 1862 by the Honourable Mrs. Beaumont, who gave up her residence next to St. Mary's to the Sisters. She had already done much for them, and had settled on them a substantial endowment. Her house still remains in use as the nucleus of the present convent.

Currently (2017) Sisters of Mercy are at six places in Derby where they carry out a diversity of ministries in accordance with their particular charism.

Presentation Sisters opened a convent in 2008. Two years later this closed and was reopened in 2017.

DERBY

St. Ralph Sherwin (Chellaston) – served from Alvaston

In 1948 Fr. Simon Nolan of St. George's, Derby, began to say Mass in various places in Chellaston. An upper room behind the 'Rose & Crown' was used for Sunday Mass until 1951, in which year a room attached to the 'New Inn' was rented and reserved exclusively for Catholic purposes. From 1965 to 1971 the Catholics of Chellaston worshipped in the Old People's Hall on Maple Drive. In 1971 a new multi-purpose chapel-of-ease dedicated to St. Ralph Sherwin was opened on Swarkestone Road, and in 1977 Chellaston was linked with Sinfin to form a new parish.

In May 1996 St. Ralph Sherwin along with St. Peter's Anglican Church and Chellaston Methodist Church signed an Ecumenical Covenant. This was the fruit of more than twenty years of members of the three communities in the area coming to know, trust and love one another so that they bear joint, and therefore more effective witness to Christ.

In 2000, due to the shortage of available clergy, the Parish of Sinfin and Chellaston was split with Chellaston being given into the care of Alvaston, and Sinfin returning to the care of St. George's. For a number of years, a series of plans have been under consideration to replace the current structure with a proper church, while selling a portion of the land for development.

DUFFIELD

St. Margaret Clitherow - served from Belper

In the Middle Ages, Duffield, a village several miles north of Derby, was a settlement of considerable importance and even had its own castle built by Henri de Ferrers. By the nineteenth century, the major occupation in the village was framework knitting. In the middle years of the twentieth century, a large housing estate was built to the south of the village centre.

A Mass centre, served from Belper, was opened in 1954 at the British Legion Club, Tamworth Street.

In 1981 a chapel-of-ease was built in Hall Farm Road on land purchased some years previously by the diocesan trustees. It was noted at the time of the opening of the chapel that there was sufficient land left over on the site for "a larger church and a presbytery" if the need for these were ever to arise. The need didn't arise! However, in 2006, the chapel was extended to improve the facilities including a meeting area, and the spacious grounds offer opportunities for outdoor events. Duffield is but one of an increasing number of parish communities in the diocese surviving, and even thriving, without a resident priest.

EARL SHILTON

Saints Peter & Paul – forms part of South West Leicestershire Team Ministry

For many years before the erection of the Earl Shilton parish, the local Catholics had been able to attend Mass at the domestic chapel of the Worsley-Worswick family in Normanton Hall (1875-1917). This was served initially by the Dominicans of Leicester and Hinckley. But in 1907 a secular priest, Fr. Ernest Grimes, came to reside at the Hall, and in the following year he moved to Earl Shilton where he erected a temporary church in Mill Lane and became the first parish priest of an independent Mission. The Catholic school adjacent was erected in 1910 for the education of eighty children, a convent and priest's house being added later. Fr. Grimes left in 1912, and the parish had no resident priest until 1917. In 1921 the stone and marble altar, which formerly stood in the chapel at Normanton Hall, was presented to the church by the Worsley-Worswick family.

One or two snippets of parish life have been recorded in diocesan yearbooks. Thus, in June 1942, a garden party was held in the grounds of The Mansion in aid of the School Extension Fund. It was attended by between 400 and 500 people. The attractions included a baby show and a display of country dancing by the St. Peter's Girl Guide Company. The "outstanding attraction" of the day was a midsummer pantomime performed by the schoolchildren. The play, the incidental music and the songs were all written by the parish priest, Fr. Colin Mitchell. On 8 June 1958 Bishop Ellis presided at Solemn High Mass to celebrate the Golden Jubilee of the parish.

The new Church of St. Peter and St. Paul was designed in 1982 to replace an old Methodist chapel which formerly served the parish. The church and hall were located next to the existing presbytery and the development was undertaken in conjunction with the adjacent housing development called The Cloisters. The architect was D.J. Montague of Derby. The fittings include a stone altar carved with a sheaf of corn and a large figure of the Risen Christ on the east wall. Both of these are the work of the local sculptor Carmel Cauchi, who was also responsible for the glass doors under the gallery engraved with the figures of St. Peter and St. Paul. Cauchi also did some notable work in the late 1970s Church of St. Peter, Leicester.

A school called 'Earl Shilton R.C. School' was opened with 53 pupils in November 1910. There are some fascinating entries in the school log book. One of these, dated 12 April 1911, reads: "The Head Teacher, A. M. Clutterbuck, is leaving the school, as she is not allowed to manage the children as she thinks best, but has to cane them in accordance with the order of the managers, even after she has forgiven the children." The school was first called 'St. Peter's' in 1929. The school has several times been extended – in 1933, 1964, 1989, 2001 and 2013.

EARL SHILTON – *Convents/religious houses*

Dominican Sisters of the Congregation of King William's Town, South Africa. They opened a private boarding school in Mill Lane in 1936. This closed two years later. Intermittently during the 1930s and 1940s the convent was empty and was used for, among other things, a hosiery factory.

Sacred Heart Fathers took over the property vacated by the Dominican Sisters and used it as a preparatory seminary. This was transferred to Cheshire in 1949. The property was then taken over by the

Rosminian Sisters of Providence. From 1949 until 1955 they taught in the primary school.

EAST LEAKE

Our Lady of the Angels

Most of that part of Nottinghamshire which extends to the south of West Bridgford towards Loughborough was beyond the reach of the Mass until very recent times. The opening of a chapel at Ruddington in 1939 improved the situation in the northern part of this area. To the south, the gap was filled by the opening of a Mass centre at East Leake in 1952. Within three years the average attendance rose from an initial twenty-five to over sixty. The Rosminian Fathers of Loughborough, who during these years had said Mass each Sunday in the Village Hall, decided that a permanent church was an immediate necessity.

In the early summer of 1953 Captain and Mrs. Roulstone of East Leake - although not Catholics themselves - very generously presented the Rosminian Fr. Horgan of Loughborough with a building site. Architect's plans were prepared by Mr. Norris of Stafford. The work of building was entrusted to the Loughborough firm of Mr. H. Hammond and began in March 1954. Three months later the foundation stone was laid by Bishop Ellis. East Leake was served by the Rosminians from 1952 until 1969 when it was handed over to the diocesan clergy. The presbytery was built in the late 1970s, and more recently an attached parish hall has been built at the back of the church. The church has some interesting features, including an organ originally from Nazareth House, Hammersmith; a church bell – 'Little Freddie' – cast in 1842 for the old St. Winefride's Church, Shepshed, later removed to St. Aloysius', Hathern, and finally, in 2002, to East Leake. Since it was not possible, at the time of its construction, to gauge the future size of the congregation, the original building was small, but designed to allow of future expansion. The church has been significantly altered during the sixty years since it was built, and an outstanding feature, over the church door, is the Jubilee Mosaic portraying the Annunciation.

EASTWOOD

Our Lady of Good Counsel

Eastwood is a former coal mining town in the Broxtowe District, lying on the Nottinghamshire / Derbyshire border. Its most famous son was D.H. Lawrence, who perhaps over-romanticised the place when he wrote of his childhood home that 'Robin Hood and his merry men were never very far away.' The nineteenth century saw a great expansion of Eastwood, due to the growth of the coalmines, ironworks and the network of canals and railways across the Erewash Valley. It has been estimated that some ten per cent of those working in these expanding industries were Irish Catholics. The nearest Mass centre however was at Ilkeston.

The modern Catholic history of Eastwood has a not inappropriate connection with the Carthusian Priory of Beauvale founded in 1343, whose ruins lie to the north-east. St. Robert Lawrence, its last but one Prior, was one of the proto-martyrs of 1535 as was his immediate predecessor, St. John Houghton. All that remains intact today of the monastery is the Prior's Lodging. A post-Reformation house, known as Beauvale Mansion and situated on the monastic site, was used in the nineteenth century as a country seat by Earl Cowper. The Earl's sister was the Catholic writer, Lady Amabel Kerr, and she several times spent the summer vacation at Beauvale Mansion. The difficulty with which she herself found in getting to Mass was shared by a colony of Catholic labourers, mainly of Irish descent, who had settled at Eastwood to work on the canals and railways during the nineteenth century. Lady Amabel took steps to overcome the difficulty. She is said to have first attempted to establish a Mass centre at Beauvale Mansion. This attempt was apparently unsuccessful; and she then, with the aid of her husband, Admiral Lord Walter Kerr, leased a dwelling on Derby Road, Eastwood, known as Ellerslie House. This was turned into a chapel, with rooms reserved as a priest's lodging. The date of these operations remains uncertain. But Mass was certainly said once a month in Eastwood from 1880, and this is presumably the opening-date of the temporary chapel on Derby Road. From 1888 Mass was said each Sunday.

It appears that Eastwood was first formed into an independent Mission in 1889, and in this and the following year, the priest also served Long Eaton. In 1891 the Mission apparently lost its status as a parish, but regained it in 1895, when Fr. Arthur Howarth came to reside. He was a member of the Congregation of Our Lady of Good Counsel, then existing with its Mother House at Ilkeston, and this probably explains the dedication given to the church which was erected during his tenure of office. The site of the present church on Hill Top was acquired, again through the generosity of the Kerr family, erected entirely at their expense, and opened by Bishop Bagshawe in October 1898. It is a pleasing and convenient, if undistinguished, building in brick Gothic. Its most notable feature is the so-called Lawrence Chapel. This was erected in the 1930s as a thank-offering for a miraculous cure attributed to the intercession of St. Robert Lawrence, Prior of Beauvale. It was formed out of the original sacristy, and a new sacristy was built at the same time which links up the church with the presbytery. The altar stone in this chapel was found among the ruins of Beauvale Priory and was probably used by St. Robert Lawrence himself. It was brought to the church in 1942 by Fr. Martin Finneran. The crosses have been re-incised and in recent years Mass for the conversion of England has usually been said on it each Tuesday. The altar stone is of Bulwell limestone, is six feet long, three feet wide and six inches deep; and it weighs half a ton. The church was consecrated 24 April 1947. A pilgrimage to Beauvale in honour of Saints (since 1970) John Houghton and Robert Lawrence was organised for the first time in 1936. The Beauvale Society was founded in 1978 to promote devotion to these two local martyrs, and a diocesan pilgrimage takes place every year on the Sunday nearest to 4 May, on which day in 1535 Saints John Houghton and Robert Lawrence were martyred at Tyburn with fellow-Carthusian, Saint Augustine Webster, and two other priests. Mr. & Mrs. T. Whyte, the current owners of the land on which the visible part of the ruins is situated, have developed the site and generously opened it up to visitors.

The presbytery was built at the same time as the church by Lord Walter Kerr. There is also a parish hall, erected sometime after the First World War. The presbytery was extended in 1975 to designs by Reynolds and Scott, providing a meeting room, sacristy, small kitchen and garage. Seven years later, a new parish hall was built from designs by Montague Associates of Derby. In 2008 an extensive scheme of refurbishment and re-ordering of the whole complex, including the consecration of a new altar, was carried out under the direction of John Halton Design Ltd. of Lincoln. A porch/narthex at the west end and an extension to the parish hall were built at about the same time.

The parish had for many years a chapel-of-ease, situated over the

Derbyshire border at Heanor. Constructed of wood and asbestos, and no more than thirty feet in length, it was opened in 1929. At first it was dedicated to Our Lady of Good Counsel, but this was changed in 1938 when it was renamed the Sacred Heart. The chapel was closed in 2004 and the site sold off for development.

After much hard work by priest and people, and many setbacks, the Priory Primary School was opened in 1963 and was staffed by Sisters of Loreto and lay teachers. It became an Academy in 2012.

EASTWOOD – *Religious communities*

The **Brothers of Mercy** bought Stainsby Hall, Smalley, near Heanor, and transferred to it a school for boys evacuated from the south of England. In June 1948, a Novitiate of the Congregation was also opened in the Hall. The Brothers of Mercy left the diocese in the mid-1950s.

Although **Sisters of Loreto** had been on the staff of Priory Primary School since its beginning, they had to travel each day from their convent on Beechdale Road. It was only towards the end of 1969 that they were able to take up residence in Eastwood. Even after their involvement in the school ceased, the Sisters remained in Eastwood where they exercised a variety of ministries and finally left Eastwood and the Diocese of Nottingham in 2004.

EXTON

St. Thomas of Canterbury – served from Oakham

On the death of his father in 1856, Charles George Noel, Viscount Campden, succeeded to Exton Hall as the second Earl of Gainsborough. He was a convert, and at once opened a chapel in a room in the Hall. This was served from the first by a resident chaplain. Up to that time, Mass had not been said within the whole county of Rutland for approximately a century.

On 29 December 1857 the first stone of a permanent chapel was blessed by Bishop Roskell and laid by Viscount Campden. The chapel was officially opened on 7 July 1859, the Feast of the Translation of Saint Thomas of Canterbury. Archbishop (later Cardinal) Manning of Westminster preached the sermon on this occasion before a large gathering of prelates, clergy and friends. Thus, after three hundred years, Mass was publicly resumed in a Catholic church in Rutland. The red vestments worn on that occasion were made from robes worn by the first Earl of Gainsborough at the coronation of Queen Victoria. This chapel was built on the east of the Hall and was designed by Mr. C .A. Buckler in a thirteenth century style. Among the products of the Gothic Revival, it must be considered undoubtedly one of the more successful.

Lord Gainsborough also provided a house to serve as a presbytery, and erected a school, which was in existence by 1876, if not earlier. The school had 29 pupils in 1879; 41 six years later, and 52 in 1898. Sisters of Charity of St. Paul taught in the school from 1885 until 1918. When the school eventually closed, the building became St. Mary's Social Centre. This was sold in the 1980s by the Catholic Church and is now a private house.

Tudor Cottage was, until 1964, the picturesque residence of the priest. It is apparently a conversion of a pre-Reformation chapel, and was the most ancient priest's residence in the diocese. The priest now (2017) resides in Oakham.

Although Exton has always been a small parish - in 1960, for example, it was listed as having 188 parishioners - it has not been inactive. Over a period of twenty months at the beginning of the 1960s, 2847 copies of Catholic periodicals were distributed in the parish.

EXTON - *Convents*

Sisters of Charity of St Paul the Apostle had a small convent at Exton from 1884 to 1918, and taught in the school.

Sisters of the Assumption. The Sisters came to Exton Hall in 1946 where they ran a girls' boarding school, and the community became an independent house of the Congregation the following year. Their chaplain also looked after the Catholic residents of Exton. In 1952 the Sisters moved to Hengrave Hall, Bury St. Edmunds and the Noel family reoccupied Exton Hall.

GAINSBOROUGH

St. Thomas of Canterbury

In the early years of the nineteenth century, Gainsborough was the third largest town in Lincolnshire. The first attempt to establish a Mission here was made in 1823 when Bishop Milner sent Fr. T. McDonald to the town. The reasons which prompted the bishop to take this step are obscure. At this time, it was almost unknown to send a priest to a mission field where there were neither endowments nor a large number of Catholics to secure an income for the priest. As far as is known, there had been no tradition of Catholicism in Gainsborough during the previous century, and the congregation must, in 1823, have been made up of a few Irish of modest means. A quarter of a century later, their numbers had not risen above 130.

Possibly it was the difficulty of maintaining himself which caused Fr. McDonald to withdraw after a year. His successor lasted another two years before moving to Retford, where he had obtained a temporary church. After 1826 the town was no longer the residence of a priest. For another nine years Gainsborough had a Mass centre, but even this was abandoned in 1835 and the first Mission was at an end.

The second Mission began in a very small way in 1844. In this year, Fr. James Egan of Brigg is reported to have said Mass 'occasionally' in a club room at Gainsborough. Four years later, his successor, Fr. John B. Naughten OMI, rented a large room to serve as a chapel. Until 1852 Mass was said only on Monday mornings; but from this year the priest divided his Sundays alternately between Gainsborough and Brigg.

The year 1861 was the beginning of a period of expansion. Bishop Roskell sent Fr. William Harris to Gainsborough and made it the centre of a notable missionary effort in north-west Lincolnshire. He retained the care of Brigg, and opened Mass centres at Crowle and Epworth. The existing Mass centre at Retford was handed over to Fr. Harris in 1862. By saying two Masses in two different places each Sunday, it was possible to have Sunday Mass once a fortnight in Brigg, Gainsborough, Crowle and Retford.

One by one, these Missions were separated from the parent church: Crowle and Epworth in 1871; Brigg in 1875; Retford in 1877. This last, however, was restored to Gainsborough in the years 1878-1880. (However, in his Quinquennial Report to Rome of 1895, Bishop Bagshawe noted that Gainsborough had a chapel at Retford.)

The present church was begun in 1866 and opened by Bishop Roskell on 3 June 1868. Its architect, Mr. Hadfield, designed it on twelfth century Gothic lines. The material is brick, and it held, in its original form, 150 people. The cost of erection was met by Mr. Young of Middle Rasen. The presbytery was erected at the same time.

On 25 January 1920 Bishop Dunn reopened the church after substantial redecoration and thereby "inaugurated the new regime at St. Thomas'". "The whole church has been magnificently redecorated in thirteenth century style in keeping with the building ... Members of the Guild of the Blessed Sacrament in their scarlet robes were present. .. the re-decoration of the church is a direct result of the indefatigable efforts of the parish priest (F. Richmond) "backed by the willing cooperation of his flock." "From a cold and uninviting interior, the church has been transformed into a harmony of colour and light."

Ten years later, on the patronal feast (29 December), the first Solemn High Mass in the presence of the bishop since the Reformation was celebrated, and the relic of St. Thomas of Canterbury was exposed for veneration. On this occasion, Celebrant, Deacon and Subdeacon wore "exquisite new red and gold vestments", which had been made by the sister of the two drury priest brothers and by a Miss Naylor.

A school was opened in 1877 by Fr. Michael Gorman. It was staffed by Sisters of Mercy. To this primary school they subsequently added a secondary school for girls. In 1879 it was noted that 219 children, as yet mostly Protestant, attended the two schools (one for infants). Six years later we find that there are two large schools attached, one attended by 123 boys and girls, the other by 103 infants; also an upper class girls' school, with nineteen pupils, mostly boarders.

In 1883, contemporaneously with the establishment of the Nottingham seminary, Fr. Gorman established a 'St. Joseph's Collegiate Seminary for Young Gentlemen', also described as "an upper-class boys' boarding school" (it had fourteen pupils) Apparently Fr. Gorman was the headmaster and his curate, Fr. Henry Cafferata, and a lay-master formed the teaching staff. Unfortunately, the whole educational structure collapsed under the weight of debt and in 1887 convent and schools were all sold to meet liabilities. Hence there is no mention of schools in Bishop Bagshawe's Quinquennial Report to Rome of 1890, nor in the Reports for 1895 and 1898.

Another sixty years were to pass before the next attempt to provide a

Catholic school in the town. In 1948 the Poor Clares of Newry took a house known as 'The Cedars' in North Marsh Road and opened an independent school. By 1951 this had outgrown its premises and the convent and school moved to Lea Hall, two miles to the south of the town.

The story of the Catholic Church in Gainsborough has been most recently (2016) comprehensively told by Alison Richards and is a good illustration of how a community can grow and thrive in spite of – perhaps even because of – many changes, not least of having had almost forty priests in a century and a half.

GAINSBOROUGH - *Convents*

Sisters of Mercy These Sisters came from New Ross, County Wexford, and staffed the primary school which was opened in 1877. They subsequently added a secondary school for girls. The Sisters of Mercy left Gainsborough before 1890.

Poor Clares of the Immaculate Conception (of Newry)
In 1948 the Poor Clares of Newry came to Gainsborough where they opened an independent school. Three years later, convent and school moved to Lea Hall, the former home of Lincolnshire naturalist and antiquarian, Sir Charles Anderson. In 1963 the Parish Council bought the house and six and a half acres of land and demolished the house in 1972. The Poor Clares left Gainsborough in 1991.

GLOSSOP

All Saints

Glossop became the property, albeit not a very important part, of the Howard family in 1606. This changed around 1729 when Ralph S. Howard built Glossop Hall. Upon his death in 1737, the Hall was normally occupied by Howard family agents among whom were members of the Eyre family, a very influential Catholic family in north Derbyshire. The Eyres were among those responsible for bringing back Catholic priests to Glossop. Matthew Ellison, who towards the end of the eighteenth century succeeded the Eyres as agent to the Howard family, requested the Vicar-Apostolic to send a priest who would reside in Glossop rather than just visit there. Fr. Joseph Barbe, one of the many French priests who had fled to England to escape the horrors of the French Revolution, arrived in 1803. By 1810 a small chapel close to the Hall had been erected. Several years after Fr. Barbe left Glossop, he was succeeded, in 1831, by another Frenchman, Fr. Theodore Fauvel, who was to spend the whole of his priestly life (he died in 1865) at Glossop. In theory, Fr. (later Canon) Fauvel was chaplain to Glossop Hall, and his unfailing cheerfulness and inexhaustible store of anecdote enabled him to work in close co-operation with his patron. But at the same time he was a devoted missionary priest, and his thick-set figure became a well-known sight on the roads between Woodhead and the hills overlooking Buxton, for he almost always chose to make his visits on foot. In his lifetime he saw the gradual transformation of his chaplaincy to the form of a canonical parish. A new church at Glossop (1836) took the place of the chapel adjacent to the Hall; New Mills, Hadfield, and Marple Bridge were cut off from his enormous district, and even in Glossop he saw the foundations laid for a second parish by the erection of schools in Howardtown.

For more than a century the Howard family maintained the priest of the Mission as their chaplain. All the property of the Mission belonged to them until the sale of their Glossop estates upon the death of Francis Howard in 1924. The Mission property was then transferred to the diocese for a nominal sum.

The foundation stone of the present church was laid in February 1835 by Thomas Ellison Esq. on behalf of the Duke of Norfolk, and the church was opened on 19 July 1837. The architect, M. E. Hadfield, born in Glossop, was a nephew of Matthew Ellison, agent for the estate, and All Saints was an early fruit of Hadfield's partnership with John Gray Weightman. The cost of the church was defrayed by the Duke of Norfolk. The connection with the Howard family is marked by one of the stained-glass windows which depicts Saint Philip Howard, Earl of Arundel, who died in 1595 while under sentence of death for the Catholic Faith. Another window commemorates Blessed Nicholas Garlick, a native of the nearby village of Dinting. The church, which saw extensive improvements in the early part of the twentieth century, was eventually consecrated in 1936. Further changes took place in the early 1960s and in 1979.

The one hundred and fiftieth anniversary of the completion of the church was celebrated over several months in 1986. A Musical Evening was held in April. A garden fête on 14 June marked the beginning of four weeks of events concluding with a Parish Dance on 12 July. But the highlight of the celebrations was a concelebrated Mass of Thanksgiving on 8 July presided over by Bishop McGuinness at which a homily "both informative and amusing" was given by Monsignor Purdy, a former Parish Priest of All Saints; and the Duke of Norfolk planted a weeping beech tree in the church grounds.

The presbytery, Royle House, was erected about the time of Fr. Fauvel's arrival in 1831.

The parish has one of the oldest schools in the diocese. The first building was erected by contributions from the congregation, from Thomas Ellison Esq. and from all the Protestant gentry in Glossop! It was opened on 15 February 1835. Less than ten years later, this building was found to be inadequate, on account of the large Irish population which had flowed into the town after extensions to the mills. New schools were therefore built at the expense of Miss Kate Ellison on land leased from the Duke of Norfolk in November 1844. The Duke subsequently bought this school building and it has remained in use, with extensions completed about 1932, until the present day. In 1887 All Saints became an all-age school until 1949; and eleven years later, it became a primary school.

GLOSSOP, *All Saints - Convents*

Sisters of Mercy

A small group of Sisters of Mercy from Nottingham came to Glossop in 1849 and remained here for three years.

Sisters of Charity of St. Paul the Apostle

These Sisters arrived in 1853 and remained in All Saints' Parish for fifty years. During this time, they opened convents at St. Mary's, Glossop, and at Hadfield.

Presentation Sisters

In 1903 the Parish Priest of All Saints asked Reverend Mother Calasanctius of Buxton if she could spare some Sisters to teach in All Saints' School to take the place of the Sisters of Charity of St. Paul who were leaving the parish. Mother Calasanctius was able to meet this request with the support of Lord Howard of Glossop, who provided his coachman's cottage as a temporary residence for the Sisters until the convent could be opened. So began a century long involvement of the Presentation Sisters with All Saints. One of the founder members of the All Saints' community, Mother Angela Scallon, remained at All Saints for forty years and was involved in other parish activities in addition to teaching in the school. The Sisters left the parish in 2005.

GLOSSOP

St. Mary Crowned – served from All Saints, Glossop

The project of establishing a second Mission in Glossop was mooted as early as 1854. In that year Fr. (later, Canon) Theodore Fauvel of All Saints erected the first school, dedicated to St. Mary, in the Howardtown district and he intended to follow this with the erection of a church. The need for it had arisen with the influx of Catholic operatives in the previous decade, consequent on the enlarging of Wood's Mill, and on the building of Sumner's Mill in 1846-7. Their houses rose huddled on the hillside above the mills, while the Church of All Saints lay secluded in the quiet village atmosphere of Old Glossop.

When, in 1861, the American Civil War broke out and the mills had to close for lack of cotton, the project was shelved. Canon Fauvel died in 1865, and was replaced by Fr. Charles Tasker. In this same year he revived the project and opened a Mass centre, probably in St. Mary's Schools, which, in the archaic taste of the time, he dedicated to 'St. Marie'.

It appears that this centre was closed in 1877. There is some confusion in the records of the events of the next few years, but on 15 March 1882 the Parish of St. Mary's was erected by Bishop Bagshawe, and Fr. Tasker moved from All Saints to become its first Parish Priest. In the same year a school-chapel was erected as an addition to the schools in St. Mary's Road, the expense of which appears to have been borne, either wholly or to a considerable extent by F. J. Sumner Esq., JP DL of Park Hall, Glossop, and owner of the Wren Nest Mills, Glossop. This had been built by Matthew Ellison, agent of the Howards, in 1815.

The new parish had become a possibility mainly through the generosity of Mr. Sumner. But the erection of the school-chapel was not the end of his munificence towards the parish, He had often expressed his intention of building a large church in the district around his mills and although he died suddenly intestate at the Ascot race meeting in 1884, his heirs and executors respected his intentions, and the present fine church is the result.

The church is striking for its vast scale and internal height (70 feet/23 metres), making it the largest Catholic non-Cathedral church in the north of England. The style is Early English, and the church was designed by Mr. A. E. Dempster of Birmingham. In spite of changes over the years, the church retains some good quality late nineteenth century fittings such as a Caen stone Gothic high altar and reredos, along with panelled stone communion rails with iron gates in situ. The foundation stone was laid by Bishop Bagshawe on 3 July 1886 and the church was 'solemnly opened' on 18 August 1887. In this context, a whole week of celebrations took place. At the Pontifical High Mass on 18 August, the choir sang Haydn's Mass No. 1 accompanied by a "full band". The 'porch' and the 'vestibule' of the church were, for many years, known to the parishioners as, respectively, the 'summer' and 'winter' doors.

Sometime before the death of Canon William Hawkins in December 1919, St. Mary's received a large and important relic of St. Clement, Pope and Martyr. This was formerly kept at the Church of Our Lady of Mount Carmel, Corby Glen, Lincolnshire, and at the earnest petition of Canon Hawkins, made to and granted by Bishop Brindle, was translated to St. Mary's, Glossop. A beautiful reliquary was provided, and it was a condition of the translation that a suitable altar should be built; this was erected by the end of 1928. Both the altar and the floor of the chapel, dedicated to Pope Saint Clement, are of Carrara marble. The chapel is a memorial to Canon Hawkins, who had served at St. Mary's from 1906 until his death. The altar was consecrated by Bishop Dunn on 14 July 1930. When St. Mary's Church was redecorated in 1981, St. Clement's Chapel was renamed Our Lady's Chapel.

The Stations of the Cross, erected as a memorial to Canon Hawkins, are by Mayer of Munich.

Some external reconditioning was carried out in 1928 in the course of which the bell turret was reconstructed in hard white Hollington stone and a statue of Our Lady, carved from Portland stone by Boulton of Cheltenham was erected on the tower. In line with the changes consequent upon the Second Vatican Council, a new altar was erected in 1981.

The first schools in St Mary's Road were opened by Canon Fauvel in the mid-1850s. On 24 June 1882, Mr. Sumner laid the foundation stone of the main block of the new schools designed by F. C. J. Hadfield. Improvements were carried out in 1922. After the Second World War a further pre-fabricated classroom was erected on a site opposite the west end of the church. A new St. Mary's School on Gladstone Street was opened in 1969. Adjoining the church to the west is St. Philip Howard Catholic Academy. Officially opened in June 1962, it became a designated 'Sports College' in the early 2000s and was converted to an Academy in 2015.

Around 1930 Moorfield House, Glossop, for several years housed 'St Michael's College for Late Vocations.' The Principal of the College was Mr. Cecil Brereton. The College is not mentioned in diocesan yearbooks after 1933, so it is presumed that it closed around that time.

GLOSSOP, *St. Mary Crowned - Convent*

The Sisters of Charity of St. Paul the Apostle opened a convent in Shaw Street in 1876, to take up the work of teaching in the schools. The choice of this Congregation for this work was the natural consequence of their presence, since 1861, in the neighbouring Mission of Hadfield, and they had been in All Saints', Glossop, since 1853. They left in 2004.

GRANTHAM

St. Mary the Immaculate

Grantham is one of the two town Missions of Lincolnshire which date from before 1778. The priest at the end of the eighteenth century was Fr. John Busby, and, as he died 3 April 1794 at Barrowby two miles west of Grantham, and was buried in the village churchyard four days later, it is probable that his residence was fixed in that village. There can be no reasonable doubt that he said Mass in the town although the exact place cannot be ascertained. His immediate successor, Fr. Laurence Boyne (1795-1809) said Mass in Russell's Court, Westgate, and this centre may have been in use in the time of Fr. Busby.

Like almost all the Lincolnshire Missions in the early nineteenth century, Grantham was for a time kept in being through the services of a French émigré priest, in this case Fr. Jacques Gabriel Yver of the Diocese of Bayeux. He came to work in Grantham in 1810. In Fr. Yver's time, Grantham was the centre of a widespread Mission; for it is recorded that at least in his last eight years at this Mission he also spent one Sunday a month at Newark and another at Colston Basset. Grantham at this time had Sunday Mass only twice a month. In his later years, Fr. Yver resided permanently at Newark where he is regarded, by himself among others, as the founder of that Mission. However, there being no church in Newark at the time of his death in 1835, he was buried, in accordance with his own expressed wishes, in a vault beneath the floor of the church in Grantham. Fr. Yver's immediate successor as the priest at Grantham was Fr. William Wareing, who later became Vicar-Apostolic of the Eastern District and subsequently first Bishop of Northampton.

The circumstances which led up to the purchase of a presbytery in 1831 and the erection of a church are somewhat fortuitous. The Tempest family of Broughton Hall, Yorkshire, had relatives at Coleby Hall near Lincoln, and it appears that on one of their visits they went to Grantham. Among the party on this occasion was Thomas Peter Tempest, already a student for the priesthood. He noticed that at the junction of Barrowby Road and the Great North Road (later known as North Parade) there was for sale a large house and a site suitable for a church. He bought it with his own patrimony and, in February 1831, laid the foundation stone of the church. It was opened by Bishop Walsh on 1 May 1833. The architect was Mr Edward Willson of Lincoln, brother of Fr. Robert William Willson of Nottingham, later to be first Bishop of Hobart Town, Tasmania. Subsequently described as "an undistinguished classic-revival building, long, narrow and rather gloomy", the church measured 86 feet by 26 feet and originally seated 350. The greater part of the original cost was met personally by Fr. Tempest. In accordance with longstanding tradition, the altar was at the eastern end of the church. However, in 1884, shortly after the beginning of the twenty-nine year ministry of Fr. Peter Sabela, a refugee from the Bismarckian persecution of the Catholic Church in Germany, the church was extended by building a new sanctuary at its western end. On 7 September 1919 a beautiful stained-glass window, erected to the memory of members of the Machine Gun Corps who had passed through their training in Grantham, and had given their lives in the service of their country, was dedicated. It was the first World War One memorial in Grantham. Designed by Alexander Gascoyne of George F. Gascoyne & Son, it depicts the Annunciation. The lower part of the window (including the dedication panel) was removed in 1965 when the depth of the window was reduced to allow for the corridor behind. In the aftermath of the Second Vatican Council, the church was extended yet again, and the altar was moved to its present position on the north side of the church. Along the south wall in the main area of the church are to be found the moving and expressive painted Stations of the Cross (1976-77) by Vincent Wells, a parishioner.

It is said that a school was organised about the same time as the opening of the church; and that the church was used as a school room. Fr. Tempest, probably in his first years as Missionary at Grantham (1834-1839) built a separate school-room, himself acting as architect. The result was not satisfactory and the upper floor had to be supported on props! A new infant school was built in 1887 and further additions made in 1895. In 1928 a completely new primary school was built on Sandon Road. It was opened by Bishop Dunn on 8 November of that year.

Blessed Hugh More, a native of Grantham, was put to death in 1588 for his Catholic Faith. It was not inappropriate, therefore, that when, in September 1966, a secondary school was opened in Grantham, it should be dedicated to him. It began with sixty-three pupils – not a large number; but at that time, the problems which were later to beset small schools were still well on the horizon. When the school celebrated its twenty-first birthday, the hope was expressed that this celebration would launch the school into its next twenty-one years. Despite the fact that there was a question mark about the future of the school, the staff and pupils of the Blessed Hugh More School decided to commemorate the four hundredth anniversary of the execution in 1588 of their Patron, with a play 'They Climb Heaven' written by Fr. Jonathan Cotton. Regrettably, the school – built originally for 150 pupils – was closed in July 1989 since which time there has been no provision for Catholic secondary education in the Grantham area.

The nineteenth century Harlaxton Manor, near Grantham, currently owned by the University of Evansville, Indiana, served as a novitiate for the British Jesuit Province in the 1950s and 1960s.

GRANTHAM, *St. Mary the Immaculate – Convents*

In 1898, the **Sisters of St Joseph of Peace** had a convent here.

They handed it over in 1901 to the **Sisters of Mercy**, but the venture did not take root and the Sisters left the town in 1903.

GRIMSBY

St. John Fisher

St. John Fisher Hall, Scartho, was built in the 1960s and has always been served from St. Mary-on-the-Sea Church. It had the appearance of a hall intended to serve a church that was never built, although it was used for a Saturday evening Mass and other Masses.

However, St. John Fisher Hall was the main social centre of the Parish of St. Mary-on-the-Sea since it had facilities not available at St. Mary's, and it was therefore used for fund raising and social events. It has also been widely used by the local community for activities such as Line, Sequence and Ballroom Dancing as well as Weight Watchers, Slimming World, Keep Fit and Tai Chi.

As part of the reorganisation of Catholic life in North-East Lincolnshire, St. John Fisher Hall was closed in January 2017, and the area it previously served now forms part of the Parish of the Most Holy and Undivided Trinity encompassing Cleethorpes, Grimsby and Immingham.

GRIMSBY

St. Mary-on-the-Sea

Grimsby is one of the two Lincolnshire Missions founded in the decade (1840-50) during which the county formed part of the Eastern Vicariate. In 1846 the Manchester, Sheffield and Lincoln Railway Company began construction of the Royal Docks. Many Irish labourers were employed in this work. At this time, Grimsby came within the boundaries of the Mission of Louth. It is recorded that Fr. Henry Hall of Louth sometimes walked the fifteen miles through the night to say Mass in Grimsby at 4.0. am and then walked back to say a second Sunday Mass in his own church. Unfortunately, it seems impossible to establish the date when he first said Mass in the town.

In 1850 Bishop William Wareing, Vicar-Apostolic of the Eastern District, came to make a personal enquiry into the condition of Catholics in the town. The story of his visit throws considerable light on the difficult conditions that then prevailed in this part of Lincolnshire. He had booked rooms at the 'White Hart', but was put out with his luggage into the street when the landlord discovered that he was a Catholic bishop. He was rescued from this predicament by a Protestant lawyer, Mr. Brooks, who gave him hospitality in his own house.

The bishop's visit resulted in the appointment of Fr. Patrick Phelan to Grimsby. He arrived on 29 September 1850 - the same day as the restoration of the Hierarchy. The Mission was, therefore, born at the same moment as the Diocese of Nottingham.

Fr. Phelan took lodgings, and rented a room as a Mass centre in the old Baltic Warehouse, near Price and Potter's Sawmills. Later, he transferred the Mass centre to the ware-room at the river-head, belonging to the Earl of Yarborough. While the Irish were in the town, it seems that a sufficient income was available to maintain a priest. However, in 1852, the work on the Royal Docks was completed and many of the Irish left; those who remained were not enough to support a priest. By the end of the year, Fr.

Phelan found his position impossible and the Mission was closed.

Nearly three years were to pass before Mass was again said in Grimsby. The revival of the Mission followed a visit to the town made by Bishop Roskell in the autumn of 1855. He found it impossible to provide for a resident priest in the town, but arranged with Fr. Henry Swale of Brigg that he should come by rail every other Sunday to say Mass in Grimsby. He said Mass at first in a private house, but later rented a ware-room at the river-head that had formerly been used. The appointment of a resident priest to the Mission was due to Mr. John Bethell, the owner of two creosote factories in the town. Mr. Bethell was a convert, the brother of Lord Westbury, one-time Lord Chancellor of England, and was patentee of the method of preserving timber by means of creosote. He had one day been dining with Cardinal Wiseman, and had asked how best he might work for the good of the Church in this country. The Cardinal advised him to found a Mission in some town where none yet existed.

Mr. Bethell acted on this advice and made a promise to Bishop Roskell that for a period of five years he would pay for the maintenance of a priest and for that of a school-master. The bishop then sent Fr. George Bent to reside in Grimsby. He arrived at the beginning of April 1856.

For three months Mass was celebrated in a low room, reached by a dirty flight of stairs and a narrow passage. Few could stand upright. A heap of potatoes occupied one corner and a pile of onions another. Horses stamped in the stables below and poultry cackled in the room above. Fr. Bent then found premises which were at least slightly more suitable!

He had at first rented lodgings for himself in Cleethorpes Road, but in the summer of 1856 was able to rent a house at the back of the Oddfellows' Hall with a large yard and a room suitable for a school. He began to say Mass on Sundays in the Oddfellows' Hall - which at the time had an unsavoury reputation for its theatrical performances and political oratory - and opened a school in the largest room in the hired presbytery. The school was under the care of a certified headmistress.

Fr Bent in 1859 handed over the care of the Mission to the young Fr. George Johnson, who was to remain at Grimsby for twenty-five years. The Mission, as it survived for a century and a half, was largely his creation. The first step forward was made in June 1863 when he opened a temporary chapel built in the yard of the presbytery.

The five-year covenant for the priest's maintenance made by Mr. Bethell had meanwhile expired. He continued his grant, however, until his death on 22 February 1867. Fortunately for Grimsby, another benefactor was already waiting to take his place.

Sir John Sutton was a convert who, on the death of his father in 1855, had come into considerable property and a substantial annual income. He had residences at Norwood Park, Nottinghamshire; Lynford Hall, Norfolk; and Skeffington Hall, Leicestershire. But he preferred to reside in Bruges, where, in 1859, he had founded and endowed a college to educate priests for service in England, Scotland and Wales. (Some half dozen of the more than one hundred and twenty men trained in this seminary worked in the Diocese of Nottingham.) Sir John's wife, Emma, whom he married in 1844, died the following year; he remained a widower, devoting his great resources to the good of the Church. He had some interest in Grimsby, for he owned the whole village of Great Coates, three miles to the west of the town. As early as 1859, he had begun to contribute to the income of the Grimsby Mission. On the death of Mr. Bethell, he agreed to increase this significantly.

Attempts to buy a site for a permanent church began in 1860. The story behind these attempts is somewhat of a curiosity. Fr. Johnson appears to have been something of a politician, and after his first failure to obtain land from Mr. Heneage in 1860, he gave his assistance in the elections of the following year to Mr. Heneage's Tory opponent. His candidate was successful - by 12 votes: as Fr. Johnson had secured 22 votes for the Tory interest from Sir John Sutton's tenants at Great Coates, he took upon himself the credit of this success. When next, in June 1868, he tried to buy land from Mr. Heneage on the site of the old pre-Reformation church of St Mary in the High Street, this was remembered against him. The price was raised far beyond his means and he had to abandon his project.

Fr. Johnson made a quick recovery. Learning that Mr. Heneage's agent was the son-in-law of the prospective Liberal candidate for the 1868 election, he went to him and, in his own words, "offered him all the political aid I could in exchange for his services." His change of politics was made easier by Liberal support for the disestablishment of the Church of Ireland. In the event, his support proved ineffective, and the Liberal candidate was defeated. But the agent was not ungrateful, and was able, in 1869, to negotiate the conveyance of rather more than an acre of land on 'Heneage's Hill'. Sir John Sutton paid the money necessary for the purchase. He also engaged Mr. Buckler as the architect and intended to defray the costs of building. But Sir John died before he could carry out his intentions.

With his death, the financial resources of the Mission were considerably reduced. The ambitious plans of Sir John Sutton could not be carried out. In 1874 a school-chapel was built, together with a presbytery. Where the money came from is not clear. Part of it certainly was contributed by the Honourable Mrs. Fraser of Hainton, who also bought additional land to bring the site up to two acres.

Nine years later, one more benefactor came forward to make possible the erection of the present monumental church. This was Mr. Thomas Arthur

Young who had for some time laid aside a considerable sum of money for church purposes. He had at first planned a new church at Lincoln, and then had turned his thoughts to a seminary at Market Rasen. On neither of these projects did he come to an agreement with the bishop. He therefore devoted the money to the present large brick Gothic Church of St. Mary's, where his memory is perpetuated in the Young Chantry. This church was opened in 1883.

After its erection, the church was further enriched by its previous benefactors. In 1884 the Honourable Mrs. Fraser provided the altar and reredos for the Sacred Heart Chapel; three years later, she erected an altar in the Young Chantry in memory of her deceased husband, Colonel The Honourable Alexander Fraser. Mr. Young, in 1888, provided the carved oak stalls and sedilia in the sanctuary.

The pioneer work of Fr. Johnson (he became a Canon of the Cathedral Chapter in 1877) was now at an end. He left the Mission and the diocese in 1884.

By the beginning of the twentieth century, the Grimsby Mission had almost all the material equipment necessary for parish life. The need was now to be not for internal development, but for the erection of new parishes within its wide territory. The first of these was the Parish of St. Peter, erected in 1909 in the West Marsh area of Grimsby. (Cleethorpes followed in 1937.) The first priest of St. Peter's was Fr. Joseph Feskens, one of the more than a dozen priests from Belgium who, over a period of a hundred years, worked in the diocese. He served St. Peter's for thirty-three years until his death, after a long illness, on 9 October 1942. In the late 1950s St. Peter's became a chapel-of-ease to the Parish of St. Pius X where a new church was built in 1958. The Church of St. Peter was demolished in 1969.

Canon Johnson's successor at St. Mary's, Canon Joseph P. Hawkins (1884-1913), was also to leave an indelible mark on the parish, so much so that his funeral in July 1913 was attended not only by Catholics but by many other townsfolk. A year after his burial in Cleethorpes Cemetery, his body was exhumed and reburied in a vault beneath St. Mary's Church.

The fiftieth anniversary of the opening of the church was celebrated "with all the Church's stately ceremonial" on 17 August 1933 with a High Mass followed by a public luncheon in the Town Hall. Although the church had only one bell, a merry peal was sounded through loudspeakers from a gramophone record; and a detailed account of Bishop McNulty's sermon at the High Mass was given in the diocesan yearbook of the following year.

The church was redecorated in 1908 at the time of its Silver Jubilee celebrations, when the sanctuary was enriched with wall paintings. At some point (possibly in the 1960s) the sanctuary paintings were covered over, but early in the twenty-first century some of them were uncovered and restored. In 1979 the church was reordered, with a new altar and lectern. In 1983 a narthex was formed under the western gallery.

The first school – 1856 - was in a shed in the grounds of a rented house in Upper Burgess Street where Father Bent lived. He had the shed converted into a schoolroom and this continued to be used until better premises were acquired. In 1870 a piece of land was bought at Holme Hill and a new school was built on it several years later. The first properly designated St Mary's School opened in September 1874. In 1885 we learn that "360 children attend the school, of whom over 200 are Protestants". Once on the new site the school was able to expand and, since 2012 known as 'St Mary's Catholic Primary Academy', it still occupies the Wellington Street site.

In 1884, shortly after their arrival in Grimsby, the Sisters of St. Joseph of Peace became involved in the parish school, and the following year they opened 'St. Francis Xavier Academy' in the convent. In 1890 they built 'St. Francis Xavier Convent School'. This school remained an important part of the life of Grimsby for the next eighty years until it closed in 1970.

As part of the reorganisation of Catholic life in North-East Lincolnshire, St. John Fisher Hall, Scartho, previously served from St Mary-on-the-Sea, and St. Pius X Church were closed in January 2017, and the whole of North-East Lincolnshire now forms part of the Parish of the Most Holy and Undivided Trinity encompassing, Grimsby, Cleethorpes and Immingham.

GRIMSBY, *St. Mary-on-the-Sea - Convent*

The **Sisters of St. Joseph of Peace**, newly-founded by Bishop Bagshawe, chose Grimsby as the site of their very first convent in January 1884. It was dedicated to St. Francis Xavier.

The work of the Sisters did much to break down the anti-Catholic prejudice which lingered in Grimsby up to the Edwardian age. Their work changed its character. They gave up teaching in the elementary school, and, in addition to the work in the convent school, engaged in the care of deprived children. St. Anthony's Home in Victor Street was bought in 1899 and opened the following year as an orphanage. The orphanage closed in 1957. The Sisters, having – among other things – run a day-centre for homeless people - finally left Grimsby in 2006 after more than one hundred and twenty years of devoted service.

GRIMSBY

St. Pius X

The church was built to serve a new housing estate, on land given by Sir Alec Black, a Grimsby ship owner who died in 1942. Development did not start until May 1955 (the foundation stone was laid by Bishop Ellis in November of that year), and the first service to be held was Midnight Mass at Christmas 1957. The church, designed by Reynolds & Scott, and with provision for seating 380, was solemnly blessed by Bishop Ellis on 12 June 1958. Wilkinson & Houghton of Cleethorpes were the builders. The church was dedicated to Pope Pius X (canonised in 1954), and was the daughter church of St. Peter's, Grimsby, (demolished in 1969). A degree of amusement was caused by the fact that, for some time after the building of the Church of St. Pius X, the local Rating Department continued to address its communications to "St. Peter-on-the-Sea." The writer of an article in the diocesan yearbook for 1956 commented: "While Grimsby must perhaps strain its claims to beauty, it is surely appropriate that St. Pius X, Patriarch of Venice, should find a home in Grimsby, which, if not built on water, certainly draws its living from it." St. Pius' Church was significantly reordered in the early 1990s, but some artefacts from St. Peter's Church, were retained. These include a fine polychrome statue of St. Peter and a wooden baptismal font.

As part of the reorganisation of Catholic life in North-East Lincolnshire, St. Pius X Church was closed in January 2017, and the area previously served by the church now forms part of the Parish of the Most Holy and Undivided Trinity encompassing Grimsby, Cleethorpes and Immingham.

HADFIELD

St. Charles Borromeo

The story of the foundation of this parish is one of extreme simplicity. On the one hand there existed a considerable Catholic population, employed in the mills along the banks of the River Etherow; on the other and, coming to meet the needs of this population, was the apostolic munificence of the first Baron Howard of Glossop. From the fusion of these two factors emerged a parish furnished on an exceptional scale with the buildings necessary to its life. When Lord Howard had bought an extensive site, and had erected thereon a massive church, presbytery and schools, all the diocese had to do was to provide a priest. And this was done in 1858 when Fr. Bryan O'Donnell was sent from New Mills to minister to the Catholics of Hadfield and surrounding area. His stay was not long, since he died four years later, aged 38. In 1885 Bishop Bagshawe noted that: "Hadfield is a rapidly growing town, of 3000 inhabitants, mostly cotton-weavers, two miles to the north of Glossop. ..The Catholics of Hadfield number 630. They are nearly all poor and rough, but on the whole are attentive to their duties."

Three members of the Sabela family had come from their native Germany in the 1870s as refugees from the 'Kulturkampf.' One of them, Peter, served at Grantham for almost thirty years. When he died in 1911, his sister Anna, who had been his housekeeper, moved to Hadfield where their elder brother, Herman, had been parish priest since 1886 and where he died in 1914.

The Church of St. Charles Borromeo, opened on 18 February 1858, is one of the largest churches in the diocese. About 1884 Lord Francis Fitzalan Howard demolished the existing Lady Chapel on the north side of the sanctuary in order to build a Howard family vault. A new chapel, above this vault, was erected in 1940. The oak altar in the chapel to the south side of the sanctuary is another link with the Howards: it comes from the old domestic chapel at Glossop Hall. The high altar, erected by the congregation in 1882 as a memorial to their late pastor, Fr. Edward Hickey, was rebuilt in 1975. The church was consecrated on 26 May 1926.

About 1860 a small organ, built by Wheildon & Roberts, had been erected in the west gallery. With the passing of years, "it had deteriorated so that many of its pipes spoke with wheezy voice, or not at all. Its action required an elephantine touch, and its hand-bellows gave raise to those tragi-comedies of wailing exhaustion in the midst of a grand climax." Its replacement in 1937 was paid for from a legacy left by a parishioner, Mrs. Hannah Jackson. Many other changes in the church building and furnishings have taken place to meet the demands of new liturgical and pastoral insights.

The Howard family sold their Glossop estate in 1925. Most of the estate was bought up by sitting tenants, including the Diocese of Nottingham, which acquired the church, the presbytery, the school and their surrounding lands very cheaply! Enclosed within the same spacious site as the church are the presbytery, the primary school, a convent, and a parish hall. Both presbytery and schools date from 1858.

The first school appears to have been opened soon after the arrival of Fr. O'Donnell in 1858. Over subsequent years, many changes took place. Like most schools, St. Charles' was originally an all-age school. In 1961 St. Charles' became a junior and infant school. However, once the division into primary and secondary schools came into effect, means had to be found to provide secondary education for older pupils. The Blessed (now – since 1970 - Saint) Philip Howard (multi-parochial) School was opened in 1961 on a site adjacent to St. Mary's Church, Glossop. A new St. Charles' Primary School was solemnly blessed by Bishop McGuinness and opened by the Duke of Norfolk in July 1975.

HADFIELD, *St. Charles Borromeo – Convent*

Sisters of Charity of St Paul the Apostle came to Hadfield in 1861. Initially the Sisters were housed in a four-bedroomed cottage until they moved into St. Joseph's Convent, built at the expense of a Mr. Dalton, in 1887. The Sisters left Hadfield in 1977 after serving the Hadfield parish in many capacities for more than a hundred years.

HAINTON

St. Francis de Sales – served from Market Rasen

The earliest mention of Hainton after the end of Penal Times comes from the year 1792, when a Catholic school in the village (but not a chapel) was registered at the Lindsey Quarter Sessions. Nothing more is known of this school, and it is impossible to say at what date it was closed.

In any case, the Mission at Hainton is the lineal descendant of the Penal Times Mission at Sixhills. Both estates, in the early nineteenth century, were in the possession of the Heneage family. The head of the family, although no longer a Catholic at the turn of the century, continued to make provision for those of his relatives and dependants who kept to their ancient Faith.

The chapel and chaplaincy at Sixhills survived until 1836, when it was moved to Hainton to accommodate the ill-health of Frances Heneage, who was unable to attend Mass at Sixhills, which lies about two miles north-west of Hainton.

At the same time the present chapel was built at Hainton Hall, together with a priest's house. According to one account, the cost of erecting the chapel was borne by the Protestant head of the Heneage family; according to another, it was Mr. George Fieschi. His wife's Christian name, Frances, undoubtedly explains the rather unusual dedication of the chapel to St. Francis de Sales.

This Mission existed for a long time on the generosity of the Heneage family. Up to 1883, and possibly later, an annual stipend was paid by Mr. Heneage to the priest; but the chapel and presbytery remained his property. In 1856 Canon Francis Cheadle (1806-1886), described by his bishop as "very able and pious, and highly respected," moved to Hainton, where he spent the remaining thirty years of his scholarly priestly life. Prior to this, he had been the first Administrator of what, in 1850, became the Cathedral Church of the Diocese of Nottingham. A year before Canon Cheadle's death, Bishop Bagshawe, in his Quinquennial Report to Rome, noted that "Hainton is a small village of 100 inhabitants ... The Church, for 100 people, and the Presbytery, both belong to Mr. Heneage, a Protestant in whose grounds they stand. The Mission has no school, and only about 55 Catholics." Since the congregation was never large enough to justify the full-time services of a priest at a time when priests were urgently needed elsewhere, in 1916 Hainton was amalgamated with Market Rasen, reverting to the status of chapel-of-ease. It has remained such ever since.

HASSOP

All Saints

The main interest of Hassop lies in the chaplaincy which was maintained almost continuously during Penal Times at Hassop Hall. Since 1498 this had been in the possession of the ever-faithful Eyre family. When the First Catholic Relief Act was passed in 1778, the Hall already possessed an interior chapel. This was duly registered at the Bakewell Quarter Sessions under the Act of 1791. The chapel was served by a secular priest resident at the Hall.

The present Mission, situated opposite the Hall gates, was made possible through the generosity of Thomas Eyre of Hassop who died in 1792. In his will he left a considerable sum of money in trust to provide an income for a missionary priest. (It is recorded that this endowment, with a reduced principal, was extant as late as 1875). He also left a sum of money which was to be invested and accumulate interest with a view to buying land and building a church and presbytery.

The fortunes of the Eyre family underwent an apparent change in 1814. In this year the fourth Earl of Newburgh died without issue, and his title was assumed by Francis Eyre of Hassop Hall, his half-cousin. In doing so he proved mistaken; but the rise in Francis' fortunes undoubtedly prompted him to take steps to provide a church of greater dignity than the old chapel in the Hall. In 1816 he built the presbytery, and in the following year gave land for the church. Funds were available for building the church, since the original legacy of 1792 had now increased sufficiently to pay for this.

Thus the church erected in 1818 stands a worthy memorial to the loyalty of the Eyres to the ancient Faith. The family did not long survive their achievement. Both sons of Francis Eyre died without offspring, and the estate of Hassop passed to their sister Dorothy. On her death in 1853 the property passed to her husband, Colonel Leslie.

Now that the grandeur of the Eyres has departed, the church at Hassop stands remote and isolated in its tiny hamlet below the high bleak ridge of Longstone Edge. The main strength of the parish now lies in the daughter Mission of Bakewell, founded from Hassop in 1888.

The spirit of the times in which it was built dictated the use of a classical style for the church of 1818. The architect of the Hassop chapel (now All Saints Church) was Joseph Ireland. His pupil, J. J. Scoles, who went on to become a noted architect also specialising in Catholic churches, acted as clerk of works. The design of this building is based on St. Paul's Church, Covent Garden, by Inigo Jones. Possibly it is the best example of this style in the Diocese of Nottingham. The massive Doric columns of the portico, surmounted by a heavy pediment, and the situation of the building, elevated high above the road, certainly recapture the spirit of a Greek temple to an exceptional degree. The interior tends to the Baroque. Over the altar is a Crucifixion of some merit by Ludovico Caracci. The altar rails are of a much later date than the fabric of the church and are, like the Stations of the Cross, from the time of Fr. Arthur McKey (1886-89). Fr. McKey was a young priest when he came to Hassop, and after a few years felt the need for a bigger challenge than a small country parish. With the bishop's permission, he set out for the Antipodes, but shortly before reaching his destination he had a seizure resulting in his early death in his fortieth year. For the early history of the parish we are indebted to a handwritten account (1899) by Fr. (later Monsignor) William Baigent, Parish Priest of Hassop 1896-1902.

The presbytery did contain a Priests' Library established by Thomas Eyre who, at his death in 1792, left an endowment for its upkeep. In the 1950s this library was moved, for safekeeping, to St. Hugh's College, Tollerton, but was subsequently sold by the diocese and its contents dispersed.

The first school was at one time housed in the club room of the 'Devonshire Arms' at Calver. In 1859 Colonel Leslie, widower of Dorothy Eyre, Countess of Newburgh, built the existing school building on the Baslow Road. This was closed around 1872, but reopened by Fr. McKey in September 1887. At one time it had forty pupils on the register. By 1924 it had fallen to twelve, and government aid was withdrawn. It was accordingly closed. However, by 1898 there was a 'mixed' school at Hassop. This must have closed at some point soon afterwards, since it is not mentioned in 1904. In 1926 a private school was opened by the last headmistress, Miss Dykes, but this courageous venture lasted only until 1929.

In 1972 pastoral responsibility for the Parish of Hassop and Bakewell was entrusted to the care of the Holy Ghost Fathers, who have maintained their connection with the diocese ever since. The church is the only Grade I listed church building in the Diocese of Nottingham.

HINCKLEY

St. Peter - forms part of South West Leicestershire Team Ministry

The Parish and Priory of St. Peter trace their ancestry to the chaplaincy maintained in the eighteenth century by the Turville family at Aston Flamville Hall. In 1734 Fr. John Clarkson OP was sent to be chaplain at the Manor House and from there he seems to have ministered to Catholics in a wide surrounding area. In 1746 the Hall was sold by Mr. Carrington Francis Turville, who then went to live abroad. It seems probable that, until his death in 1749, he continued to maintain a Dominican priest in the district; for in his will he left a large sum of money to the Friars Preachers on condition that they assigned a certain amount each year for the upkeep of a priest on this Mission. Fr. Matthew Norton OP, who previously had been chaplain at the Hall, remained in the district with the new status of missionary priest. He "took over the Mission" on 29 June 1739 . But the work of the town was more important than that of the countryside, and he moved his residence to Hinckley in 1765. Through an intermediary, he bought a small house on the outskirts of Hinckley, and converted one of the rooms to serve as a chapel. He was twice called away from Hinckley on business connected with the Dominican Order but finally returned there in 1780 to spend the last years of his life. He died in 1800, and the tombstone of this founder-priest of this Mission may still be seen in the churchyard at Aston Flamville.

Meanwhile the French Revolution was bringing a new factor into the development of the Mission. From 1658 the English Dominican Province had been centred on Bornhem in the Low Countries. As the armies of the Revolution approached, the English Dominicans evacuated Bornhem and fled to England. Among these was Fr. Ambrose Woods OP, who before his profession had owned considerable property in the neighbourhood of Hinckley. He settled at Carshalton, Surrey, and opened a school known as 'Bornhem House'. This school seems to have existed in Surrey for approximately the period 1794-1813. It was then moved to Hinckley. Here it had a continuous existence until 1854. Advertisements of the time describe it as the 'Hinckley Catholic Academy' with accommodation 'for twelve young gentlemen' at fees of £50 per annum. Its closure was perhaps due to the necessity of transferring the staff to the new foundation at Woodchester.

Around the school a community of Dominican Friars began to form and was given the status of a Priory. The first part of the first church, together with the priory, was built and opened in 1824. From this year until the opening of Woodchester in 1854, Hinckley was the headquarters of the Dominicans in England and the residence of the Provincial. Even after the opening of Woodchester, the Provincials resided there at various periods, and from 1885 until 1898 a college and novitiate for the province was attached to the priory.

At the time of its erection, the church was considered as 'preposterously large'. In 1885 a tower, chancel and sacristies were added. The building consisted of little more than an oblong nave with round-headed windows, and was aptly described by Bishop Bagshawe in his visitation of July 1882 as being of "no style"; but, he added, it is "in good repair".

The building so dismissed by Bishop Bagshawe was replaced in 1960 by an equally large building typical of the time. Capable of seating 800, it was built with provision for future extension! But the new building was not well-maintained and eventually it had to be demolished. A new church of more modest proportions incorporating some of the items of its predecessor was built on the site and was dedicated on 12 December 1993. In 1989 the English Province of the Dominican Order found it necessary to withdraw from Hinckley where they had laboured for more than two hundred years. At the end of a concelebrated Mass on 14 September 1989, the Dominican Provincial "in a simple but moving ceremony" handed to the 'Dominican' Bishop of Nottingham, Malcolm McMahon, the keys of the priory to symbolise the transfer of control from the Order to the diocese. A large parish hall was built under the second diocesan parish priest, Fr. Frank Daly, who uses the parish as the centre for his valuable work with people in the diocese with special needs.

St. Peter's, founded more than two and a half centuries ago, continues, together with fellow Christians of other traditions, to witness to the Good

News of Jesus Christ in word and in action.

The first part of a parish school was built in 1842. Needless to say, many changes have taken place since then. Thus, in 1885, there were 175 pupils who were taught by Third Order Dominican Sisters. A new infants' school was opened in 1908, and many further developments have taken place since then. St. Martin's, Stoke Golding, which had begun as an independent day and boarding school in 1948, subsequently became St. Martin's Catholic High School and, later, St. Martin's Catholic Academy.

A second church in Hinckley, dedicated to the Sacred Heart, was opened in 1951. It closed in 1988.

With the departure of the Friars, there was a contraction of the outlying duties of the parish, and even the chapel-of-ease at Burbage (opened in 1956) was closed. The final connection with the Dominican Order was severed when the community of Sisters at Stoke Golding left the area and the chapel was no longer used as a Mass centre.

HINCKLEY, *St. Peter - Convents*

At the close of 1848 the **Dominican Canonesses of Brussels** had a house in Hinckley. They seem to have left within twelve months.

In March 1933, three **Dominican Sisters of the Congregation of King William's Town**, South Africa, established a convent, St. Albert's, and opened a private independent school there; this closed in 1987 and the remaining Sisters moved to Stoke Golding. St. Martin's Convent, Stoke Golding, opened in 1948, was closed in 2011.

HOLBEACH

(St. Joseph's Oratory), Holy Trinity

From 1955 Mass was said first in the Lower Games Room at the Chequers Hotel and subsequently in the Anglican church hall in Church Street. In 1957 the Premonstratensians of Spalding established an oratory, dedicated to St. Joseph, at The Tenters, Holbeach. Fr. Patrick Mulligan looked after the oratory. In 1965 he purchased an orchard at the junction of Foxes Lowe Road and Fleet Road from a Miss Doris Mawby, a non-Catholic. Miss Mawby was so impressed by Pope John XXIII that she was glad to sell the land so that a Catholic church could be built. On this site, the Church of the Holy Trinity was built and officially opened in October 1966. Fr. Mulligan continued to live at The Tenters until the erection of the presbytery in 1974. The district seems to have become a separate parish in 1966 with Fr. Mulligan as the first parish priest. After his death in 1993 Holbeach was served from Spalding by the Premonstratensians. Responsibility for both parishes passed from the Priory at Storrington to the Abbey of Kilnacrott in County Cavan, and back to Storrington.

Eventually, the Priory could not staff the parishes and gave both parishes into the care of the diocese. For some years, priests from Kilnacrott came to serve in Spalding and Holbeach while living in Spalding. But, with the passage of time, Kilnacrott could no longer find the priests to maintain their presence in the diocese and the last Premonstratensians left in 2008 handing over the care of both parishes to the diocesan clergy. In 2011 Fr. Paul Lloyd came to reside in the presbytery, and was appointed the first diocesan Parish Priest of Holbeach in 2013.

HOLBEACH – *Convent*

Sisters of Providence of the Immaculate Conception. From 1994 until 2011 two Sisters of Providence of the Immaculate Conception resided in the presbytery performing an invaluable role as Parish Sisters.

HORNCASTLE

Christ the King – served from Woodhall Spa.

The post-Reformation Catholic history of Horncastle begins with the foundation of a struggling Mass centre in 1905 - which has been struggling ever since. Its meagre fortunes may be described briefly as follows.

While Fr. Dumons was at Woodhall Spa (1905-1911) he said Mass each Sunday in a hall which is now the British Legion, Bank Street, Horncastle. In the interregnum (1911-1913) following the departure of Fr. Dumons, Mass was said only occasionally. His successor was appointed in 1913, and in the same year he gave Horncastle the dedication of Corpus Christi, but said Mass there only one Sunday in the month. This arrangement continued until 1920.

From 1920 to 1935 the Mass centre was abandoned. The Capuchins of Panton, who at that time were serving Woodhall Spa, then began a Mass each Sunday at the Lincolnshire Road Car 'bus station. They left Lincolnshire in the following year (1936) and a secular priest was sent to Woodhall Spa, with the additional duty of serving Horncastle. The priest lived for the first year at Woodhall Spa, but from 1937 to 1940 had a house in North Street, Horncastle. In 1937 the centre was given a new dedication - Christ the King. From 1940 the priest of the double Mission lived at Spilsby, and for some years from 1948 the centre for Mass was at the Bull Hotel, Horncastle.

Since 1982 a weekly Sunday Mass has been said in the Anglican parish church of St. Mary by the priest from Woodhall Spa.

HUCKNALL

Holy Cross

At the time of the Dissolution of the Monasteries, Hucknall was a village of twelve houses in a clearing in Sherwood Forest, six miles from Nottingham along the old road to Mansfield. It had close associations with Newstead Abbey the ruins of which can still be seen three miles to the north-east. The Augustinian Canons from the Abbey (or Priory, as it should more accurately be called), served the village church until their house was dissolved in 1539. The Industrial Revolution increased the population to some five thousand by the middle of the nineteenth century. The inhabitants were then engaged mainly on the manufacture of shawls and hose. In 1861 sinkers began work on the new pits; coal was first mined in 1864. The population rose sharply to twelve thousand within a decade, and among the new arrivals were many Catholic colliers from Whitwick, Bloxwich and other areas.

Bishop Bagshawe saw the urgent need for a Mission at Hucknall, and in November 1879 commissioned Fr. John Cantwell, a member of the cathedral staff, to do what he could towards a foundation. Fr. Cantwell began to say Mass the same month in a room in Whyburn Street. The room measured thirty feet by twenty-five feet, and was held from a Mr. Smith on a seven-year lease. It appears that this temporary chapel served the needs of the Mission for the next eight years. On 1 August 1880 the bishop sent a priest to reside at Hucknall, and the temporary chapel was dedicated to the Holy Cross. In its early years, the Mission extended also to Bulwell, where a Mass centre was opened in 1881. For twelve years the Bulwell Mass centre was served by the priest from Hucknall.

The erection of the church was due largely to the generosity of Mr. and Mrs. James Hanlon, who came to reside at Hucknall in 1885. Two fields - part of a legacy left to Mrs. Hanlon by her mother, Mrs. Mellors - were laid out as a housing estate. One of the streets was named Carlingford Road, and is itself a reminder of Mr. James Hanlon, who came originally from Carlingford. A site on this street, large enough for church, school and presbytery, was then donated by the Hanlons. The foundation stone for the new building was laid by Bishop Bagshawe on 14 September 1886 and the opening took place on the feast of the Finding of the True Cross, 3 May 1887. Two-thirds of the cost of the erection of the church came from the Hanlons, and the remaining third from Major Worsley-Worswick who had an interest in the neighbouring Annesley colliery. A presbytery was erected at the same time, the necessary money being loaned for the purpose by Mr. and Mrs. Hanlon.

The "beautiful new church, with school and presbytery" was a high, brick Gothic building in the early Decorated Style. The Stations of the Cross were of some merit, but there was little else of artistic value in the building. A new altar with altar rails was erected after the First World War as a memorial to those of the parish who had died for their country; it was blessed by Bishop Dunn on 31 December 1919. Later the same day, the bishop presented Patrick Griffin (9th Notts. and Derby Regiment) with the Military Medal, which he had won for "bravery in the field of battle." A mortuary chapel opening from the west wall of the sanctuary, contained the tombs of Mr. James Hanlon and of his wife. It was constructed in 1906. The church was consecrated by Bishop Dunn on 14 September 1926. "This was the year the miners went on strike, and all that was possible was done to relieve the distressed families, especially those where there were children." Bishop Dunn gave Canon Michael O'Reilly, (Parish Priest of Hucknall 1905-1936), a sum of money to start a soup kitchen.

The original church on Carlingford Road was replaced in February 1960 by a church on Watnall Road. Some of the items from the Carlingford Road church were transferred to the new church thus emphasising continuity. These included: marble altar in the Lady Chapel; Communion rails, and the Stations of the Cross. The new church has some fine modern stained-glass by Joseph Nuttgens and Patrick Reyntiens. A visitor from Denmark who had asked for Mass to be said in the church for Lord Byron (buried in the Anglican churchyard at Hucknall) paid for the mosaic over the front door, depicting the arms of the canons of Newstead Abbey.

The old church, having been used for some years as a social club and, later, for other purposes, was sold in 1994.

The old chapel in Whyburn Street was also used as a school from 1871. Perhaps it moved to another site in 1884, for there is mention in the records of the opening of a school on 21 April of that year, and Major Worsley-Worswick is said to have made himself responsible for its maintenance. The same benefactor was certainly responsible for erecting the first part of the primary school in Carlingford Road which was opened in 1886. When it opened, there were 80 boys and girls between the ages of 4 and 12 on roll. The only teacher was Miss L. Dixon and she was helped by the parish priest, Fr. John MacDonnell, and at times his housekeeper lent a hand! In 1905 the school was condemned as inadequate, but structural additions, carried out in the following year, enabled it to survive. A new site of two acres on Watnall Road was bought in 1952, with a view to erecting a new school, church and presbytery. The site proved inadequate and eventually land on Walk Mill Drive was obtained, thus separating school and church. The new school was opened in 1967. In 2012 Holy Cross School converted to an academy and became part of the Pax Christi Multi-Academy Trust.

HUSBANDS BOSWORTH

St. Mary – served from Market Harborough

This Mission lies on the extreme southern border of Leicestershire, on the watershed from which flows the River Welland to the east and the River Avon to the west. It was, therefore, remote enough from sheriffs and lords lieutenant to preserve the Catholic Faith through the days of persecution. In all probability, Husbands Bosworth Hall has never been without Mass. On the death of the last of the Fortescues of Husbands Bosworth in 1763, the Hall passed to the Turvilles, in the ownership of which family it still remains. They carried on the traditions of their relatives, and a succession of chaplains at the Hall can be traced, serving a domestic chapel, from the latter part of the eighteenth century down to the days of Catholic Emancipation.

The present church was built in 1875 by Sir Francis Fortescue Turville KCMG. It is a successful revival of the Pointed Style and constructed in stone. To the north of the chancel there is a chapel of St. Joseph, added after the founder's death, by Lady Lisgar in which may be seen relics of Blessed Adrian Fortescue (martyred 10 July 1539) and the tomb of the founder. The Baptismal Registers begin in 1794.

At one time, the Mission had its own school. It was in existence by

1879 when it had fourteen pupils. By 1885, it had been enlarged, but was attended by only fifteen children. It appears to have continued to at least 1907, and to have closed sometime between 1907 and 1921.

ILKESTON

Our Lady and St. Thomas of Hereford

The Parish of Ilkeston owes its importance to its geographical position. It is the natural metropolis of the fifteen-mile Erewash Valley, thickly populated and heavily industrialised, which runs almost due north and south from its source near Sutton-in-Ashfield to its confluence with the River Trent near Long Eaton. Ilkeston stands high upon the ridge that flanks the Derbyshire bank of the River Erewash. Situated almost exactly halfway along its course, it was the obvious choice for a Mission when, in the early days of the diocese, Bishop Roskell began the first attempt in post-Reformation times to evangelise the valley.

Early in 1858 the bishop decided to separate Ilkeston from the Mission of Derby from where, for at least a year beforehand, a priest had 'occasionally' come to say Mass. He sent Fr. Charles Tasker as the first resident priest. Soon after his arrival, Fr. Tasker gained possession of a building situated on the Nottingham Road and described as an 'empty lace-factory' and sometimes as a 'warehouse'. This was converted for use as a chapel and served the Mission for some four years. He was not, however, successful in establishing himself in residence at Ilkeston. Before the end of 1859 he was forced, possibly through lack of funds for his maintenance, to retire to Derby. It appears he continued to serve Ilkeston for another year, while living at St. Mary's.

His successor was Fr. Arthur McKenna, who came straight from the Venerable English College, Rome, newly-ordained, to be a true Apostle of the Erewash valley. His Mission extended over the whole length of the river, and the watershed to the north, to include the present Parishes of Alfreton, Mansfield and Kirkby-in-Ashfield. He established a Mass centre at Riddings (1860); began the Mission at Clay Cross the following year;

and established a Mass centre at Mansfield the year after that. In 1862 he opened a schoolroom-cum-chapel on Regent Street.

Fr. McKenna's work at Ilkeston came to an end in 1863, when he was appointed assistant priest and, later, Missionary Rector in Derby. After a short interregnum, a worthy successor was found in another newly-ordained priest, Fr. Hugh O'Neill. He spent eleven years at Ilkeston, and by the time he left, in 1878, the church had been enlarged by the addition of an apsidal sanctuary (1875) and the Mission had been provided with elementary schools (1876), housed initially in the church. There was also a presbytery and garden. With the arrival of Bishop Bagshawe in 1874, a great impetus was given to the erection of new parishes. Among them were Clay Cross and Mansfield, both of which had been started from Ilkeston. In the following decade the Mission was further truncated by the erection of the parishes at Long Eaton (1883) to the south and at Eastwood (1889) to the north. From this date its boundaries remained stable until the separation of Stapleford as a new parish in 1947. As a mother-church, Ilkeston can therefore count no less than five parishes among its immediate progeny.

The long pastorate of Canon Philip James McCarthy (1887-1908) brought the parish some degree of fame. He instituted, in 1891, an annual pilgrimage to the ruins at Dale Abbey which for a time attracted pilgrims from all over the country. In the following year, he erected in the church at Ilkeston a shrine of 'Our Lady of Dale' as the centre of an organisation known as the 'Roll Call Union of Honour of Our Blessed Lady of Dale.' This, together with another association 'to honour St. Philomena' (who also had a shrine in the Ilkeston church), attracted a clientele from all over the world, and numbered many thousands of members. His attempts to found an orphanage for boys in the town (1892) and a Diocesan Congregation for men, known as the 'Oblates of Our Lady of Good Counsel' (1892-1900) both proved abortive. A relic of the latter survived for many years in the periodical 'Dowry of Mary' which was first published at Ilkeston as the organ of the Oblates. Canon McCarthy died on 2 July 1908 - and the life of the parish has since continued in a more tranquil routine.

Attempts to provide Ilkeston with a church more in keeping with its importance as the centre of the Erewash district began after the First World War.

On 25 July 1921 Bishop Dunn laid the foundation stone for the present church. Under the foundation stone there was deposited a leaden casket containing: a copy of the previous week's "Ilkeston Advertiser" and "Ilkeston Pioneer"; a copy of "The Times" of 25 July; a parchment bearing the names of the bishop, the Vicar Forane, the parish priest, the architect, the builder and the Chairman and Secretary of the Building Committee together with a 1921 penny, and a one pound and a ten-shilling Treasury note.

The architect was Charles W. Hunt of Ilkeston; the builders were Messrs. Lehane & Co. of Darley Dale. Constructed of Darley Dale rock-faced stone, it has been described as "a striking and idiosyncratic Gothic design of the interwar period, old fashioned for its date, but nevertheless of some interest. Its tower with crown spire is a local landmark."

The complete plans provided for a nave of five bays with hammer beam roof, leading to an apsidal sanctuary; north and south aisles terminating in apsidal chapels dedicated respectively to the Sacred Heart and to Our Lady; a circular baptistery on the south-east side of the sanctuary, faced on the north side by the priest's and choir sacristies, with organ chamber above, At the western end, both aisles were provided with entrance doors, and provision was made for a tower.

The building work was carried out in stages. Three bays at the west end were completed by Easter 1922. By 1930 the building, with the exception of the tower, was complete. On 24 May of that year the church was consecrated by Bishop Dunn. It appears that the dedication to Our Lady and St. Thomas of Hereford was first given in 1875, when an apse was added to the original church. The reason for the latter part of the dedication is that St. Thomas, Bishop of Hereford (1275-82), was a member of the Cantilupe family, who were Lords of the Manor of Ilkeston.

The present church was furnished by degrees. The high altar was of Darley Dale stone and the rood figures were painted by Mr. Carlin of Chaddesden. The timber altars to the Sacred Heart and Our Lady were installed by 1930, as was the font. New benches, Stations of the Cross, organ frontal and a western porch were added later, in the 1950s. As part of the reordering in the early years of the twenty-first century, the original Darley Dale stone high altar was cut down and brought forward, and the altar rails were removed. However, the hanging rood painted by Mr. Carlin remains in situ, as do the timber altars in the side chapels. At the same time, an extension, with choir gallery, was added at the west end. The new altar was consecrated 23 October 2008. The parish hall dates from 1990.

The parish's first school dates from no later than 1876. In 1879 about 54 children attended the school. Six years later, there were 90. The school was extended sometime in the 1880s, and in 1898 it had 119 pupils.

The all-age school was eventually replaced by a secondary modern school, St. John Houghton, in 1965, and by a primary school, St. Thomas, in 1974.

Dale Abbey Pilgrimage

Within the boundaries of the parish lie the ruins of Dale Abbey. Little of this survives above ground except the arch of the east window. As the Abbey was dedicated to Our Lady, its ruins formed a convenient centre for pilgrimages the first of which was organised from Ilkeston in 1891. In the Lady Chapel of Ilkeston parish church is a shrine of Our Lady of Dale. The seated statue of Our Lady reproduces features found in what is said to have been the seal of Dale Abbey. The altar stone of the Lady Chapel is the one used by Bishop Bagshawe when he pontificated at an open-air Mass in the ruins of the abbey on 18 May 1891.

The custom of pilgrimages to Dale Abbey appears to have lapsed early in the twentieth century, but was revived about 1935, and then petered out towards the end of the twentieth century.

IMMINGHAM

Our Lady Star of the Sea

Immingham is of medieval origin. In the Middle Ages, it was the seventh largest port in England. In its more recent history, work on the new Immingham Docks of the Great Central Railway began in 1906. Three years later, the Belgian Fr. Joseph Feskens was sent to begin a Mission which was intended at first to comprise both Immingham and the West Marsh district of Grimsby. He founded the Parish of St. Peter, Grimsby, in 1909, and he opened a Mass centre at Immingham for the benefit of the labourers working on the new docks. For some years he cycled to Immingham to say an early Mass there before cycling back to say Mass in Grimsby. However, the new docks failed to attract a large housing settlement, and most of the permanent workers were able to live in Grimsby. Therefore, the Mass centre was gradually wound down, closing in 1920. It reopened on an occasional basis at the end of the decade. Nothing further seems to have happened until the mid-1950s when a Mass centre was reopened and served from St. Peter's, Grimsby, until the end of the 1960s when Fr. Frank Murray of the Sacred Heart Fathers was appointed Port Chaplain for the new container port. Immingham became an independent parish in 1965.

From January 2017, Immingham has formed part of the Parish of the Most Holy and Undivided Trinity encompassing, Grimsby, Cleethorpes and Immingham, while the Port Chaplaincy is served by Fr. Colum Kelly, a priest of the Diocese of Leeds.

KEYWORTH

St. Margaret Clitherow – served from East Leake.

In the late 1950s Canon John Buckley of West Bridgford began to look for a site for a church in Keyworth. His search was not successful during his lifetime (he died in 1965), and it was only in 1983 that the present site on Willow Brook was obtained. In the intervening years, Mass was celebrated in a variety of places – private homes; the British Legion building; the local Anglican and Methodist churches and, very significantly, Mary Ward Teacher Training College.

Mary Ward Teacher Training College opened in 1969 on a twenty-seven acre site on the outskirts of Keyworth. It had a capacity for five hundred and forty students. In addition to its primary purpose, it remained a focal point in the Catholic life of Keyworth for the next eight years. For the whole period of its existence it was staffed by Sisters of Loreto. When it became known that the College was to close, "all the ministers of the non-Catholic churches at once offered the use of their churches." Since the Methodist church building was the largest and the most suitable, this was the offer that was accepted, and the Catholic congregation used the Methodist church for Sunday Mass. The church hall on Willow Brook was then built: it was opened by Bishop McGuinness on 24 October 1984.

In the early years, Keyworth was part of the Parish of West Bridgford and, later, of Radcliffe-on-Trent. Subsequently, along with Cotgrave, it became an independent parish and remained thus until Cotgrave was allocated to West Bridgford and Keyworth to East Leake.

KEYWORTH, St. Margaret Clitherow - Convent

A community of **Loreto Sisters** was based in Keyworth where they staffed Mary Ward Teacher Training College from 1969 to 1977.

Sister Mary Beuno OP has been involved in Cotgrave and Keyworth from 1984 to the present.

KIRKBY-IN-ASHFIELD

All Souls (Our Lady, Help of Christians)

A Mass centre dedicated to St. Joseph was opened on Forest Street in 1923 by Fr Charles Payne of Mansfield. The foundation stone of the first church in Sherwood Street was laid by Bishop Dunn on 20 May 1925. It was opened by him on 4 November of the same year and the dedication at this time was changed to All Souls. In 1947 Kirkby was erected as a parish, but two years later the priest was withdrawn, and All Souls reverted to the status of a chapel-of-ease to Mansfield. But from 1972 it has, once again, had its own priest.

The congregation, however, outgrew the church on Sherwood Street, and a plan was devised to build a church, a church hall and presbytery on School Street. The hall would be built first and would serve as the church until the new church was built. But the plan as originally envisaged did not materialise, and the church hall, opened in 1970, has continued to serve as the church. A new hall and presbytery were built in the mid-1970s. The dedication of the parish changed once again, in 1975, this time to 'Our Lady, Help of Christians.'

LEICESTER

Holy Cross

The Catholic Mission in Leicester was revived in 1746 in the chapel of Belgrave Hall. In 1774 Fr. Peter Robson OP came to reside in St. John's Lane (later known as Causeway Lane) where, as well as in Belgrave, he said Mass. His Mission might well have been described as that of Leicestershire rather than of Leicester. The four other Missions of the county at this time hugged its southern and eastern extremities - Hinckley, Husbands Bosworth, Eastwell and Neville Holt. All the north and interior of the county fell to the care of Fr. Robson. This situation was to endure for another sixty years.

The early Dominicans and their Mission led a precarious existence. Twice, in 1779-1780 and 1783-1785, the priest was withdrawn to Hinckley. At these times Mass was said alternately in Leicester and Hinckley, the congregations taking it in turns to walk the twelve miles that separated these places. Their priest also covered the distance on foot - not with his flock, but alone, to avoid detection. In 1785 Fr. Matthew Norton OP was forced to leave the district altogether and retire into Yorkshire. A common informer had claimed the statutory reward for delating a priest who had said Mass, He did not get it. The magistrate was able to force the informer to drop the charge by a threat of prosecution for debt!

Leicester's first chapel was erected by Fr. Francis Xavier Chappell OP in 1798. It was built behind the houses down an entry off Causeway Lane. Its form reflected the peculiarly unfavourable circumstances of Leicester at this time. While the contemporary chapel at Eastwell (near Melton Mowbray) was built boldly at ground level, that at Causeway Lane was constructed after an older plan as an upper chamber reached by an outside flight of stairs. Both the door from the entry and the door into the chapel had peep-holes to scrutinise incomers; and a second escape led onto the road at the back of the chapel. The site was near that of the old medieval church of St. Michael; and this dedication was consequently adopted. Two round-headed windows over the altar were the only feature which marked this building as ecclesiastical. Later, it is believed that a circular stained-glass window, with a dove representing the Holy Spirit, was inserted; subsequently it was transferred to a position over the pulpit in the old Holy Cross. The chapel remained in use for occasional Mass until 1850, if not later. It was demolished in 1939 to make way for a new road leading from Belgrave Gate to High Street.

Fr. Chappell served Leicester for thirty years, and left in 1815. At the beginning of this period, the atmosphere had been so anti-Catholic that he was obliged to take on the guise of a gardener as he walked about the town. At the end, the small Catholic community was on the point of adventurously building the first Holy Cross.

Two names stand out among those who carried through this undertaking. Among the laity, there was Mr. Richard Raby from Garstang in Lancashire, a pioneer of wool manufacturing by machinery. He had erected a factory, and a house for himself, in the old Vauxhall Gardens. This stood at the corner of Friars Causeway and Sycamore Lane, and the site was cleared at the end of the nineteenth century to make room for the Great Central Station. Mr. Raby paid for the site of the future church in Wellington Street, and contributed towards the cost of the building almost all that he possessed.

The drive and inspiration behind the new venture came from Fr. Benedict Caestryck OP, who served Leicester from 1815 to 1834. He had come originally to this country under the pressure of the French Revolution, and, like so many foreign priests of that time, had none of the diffidence which prevented some of their English confrères from bringing the Catholic Faith before the hostile public. Soon after his arrival, the Leicester congregation seems to have become too large for St. Michael's. Sunday Mass was therefore said in an unidentified warehouse, the use of which was withdrawn by its owner at midsummer 1817. It is known that, at one time, Mr. Raby's factory was used for Sunday Mass. The most probable date for this would seem to be from the middle of 1817 to the opening of the church in 1819. The progress of the building can be followed in the pages of the 'Ordo and Laity's Directory' for these years. By 1816 the site had been bought, and Fr. Caestryck had begun to solicit financial help for his 'poor and numerous congregation'. By September 1818 the work had begun, and before the end of the following year the first Church of Holy Cross was opened.

The new dedication owed its origin to a relic of the True Cross which was entrusted to the church. It had belonged to the Dominican Cardinal Howard, who had been Lord Almoner to Charles II's Queen, Catherine of Braganza. The relic passed from Cardinal Howard to Bornhem Priory in the Netherlands, and thence to England again with the Dominicans. About

1877 it was removed from Leicester to Haverstock Hill, but was returned in 1931 when the new church was opened.

The church of 1819 was little more than an oblong box of brick, with stone facings and pointed windows which entitled it to be described as Early English in style. A substantial donation from the Earl of Shrewsbury made possible the addition of a groined and painted ceiling to the original plans. There is some reason to believe that these plans were drawn up by Bishop Milner himself.

In the course of time the church was enlarged and altered beyond recognition. A chancel, separated from the nave by a rood-screen of carved wood, was added in 1848. A Lady Chapel was built in the same year. The windows of the new additions - three lancets behind the high altar, and four in the Lady Chapel - were filled with stained-glass. In 1887 the Lady Chapel was given an apse.

Shortly after 1877 a new aisle was added to the church. When Cardinal Manning arrived to bless and open the new aisle, he was escorted from the station, riding on a white horse! The two who had done so much to build Holy Cross, Fr. Benedict Caestryk and Mr. Richard Raby, were buried within its walls.

The earliest known residence for the priest in Leicester was a small house in Wellington Street near the corner of Dover Street, used in the twentieth century as a repository. Fr. Caestryk went to live there in 1817 and, while the church was being completed, adapted the front room on the first floor as a chapel for daily Mass, and the corresponding room on the ground floor as a confessional. In 1824 he was able to build a priest's house on a site of 409 square yards which he had bought to the south-east of the church. Additions to it were made in 1843 and in 1861 and the quadrangular layout of house and church was then complete. Except for the years 1834-1835, when a secular priest served the Mission as delegate of the Dominicans, Holy Cross has always been served by the Friars Preachers. The community was given the status of a Priory in 1882.

As early as 1911 it became apparent that the church of 1819 was hardly adequate in size and far from suitable in view of the importance which the Priory had by then attained. Fr. Vincent McNabb OP, the Prior at that time, began the work of gathering funds. A site for the new building was acquired in various stages. A house and factory on a site of 475 square yards in Wellington Street were bought in 1914. The house adjoining was bought in 1919; and a third house, previously in the possession of the Dominican Province and known as 'Corpus Christi House' was transferred to the Priory in 1924, thus completing the area required. About this time the advisability of moving the whole project to a site further from the centre of the town was debated. But land proved impossible to obtain, and the historic position of Holy Cross was retained.

The first sod for the foundations was cut on 25 April 1928, and the foundation stone laid by Bishop Dunn on 14 September of the same year. Funds permitted the erection of no more than half of the priory church provided for in the plans. The completed portion was blessed on 30 April 1931, its high altar was consecrated on the following 2 May, and the new Holy Cross officially opened on the feast of The Finding of the True Cross, Sunday 3 May 1931. The church was finally completed and consecrated on 14 May 1958. The priory church was subsequently completed following the plans from 1928, but in a simpler and more economic style.

The primary school can claim to be one of the oldest in the diocese. Two schools were opened in 1824: one, in Belgrave Gate, was set aside for infants and later developed into the Mission of St. Patrick's; the other was built in Wellington Street and is now known as St. Clement's Hall. The site for the primary school in New Walk was bought in 1884, the foundation stone was laid by the Earl of Denbigh on 31 July 1886, and the completed building opened on 6 June 1887. Holy Cross Primary School transferred to Stonesby Avenue in the Parish of St. John Bosco in 1966.

As an aside: Bishop Dunn visited the Holy Cross Branch of the Catholic Women's League in February 1920 and, among other things, "gave a stimulating address, in which he warned the branch of the dangers of 'Apathy'".

The Dominicans, along with the Rosminians, were responsible for much of the post-Reformation pioneering missionary work in Leicestershire. Not to be overlooked either is the spiritual and pastoral impact of the Cistercian monks of Mount Saint Bernard Abbey (founded in 1835.) Holy Cross itself deserves preeminently to be styled the mother and head of most of the churches of Leicester and Leicestershire. Dominicans were at work in Loughborough before the establishment of that Mission in 1833 and in Market Harborough before the coming of the secular clergy in 1872. The revival of the Catholic Church in the Loughborough area from the 1840s, owes much to the activity of the Rosminian Fr. Luigi Gentili and his confrères. These two Missions covered an enormous area, but the whole of the Borough of Leicester and its environs remained under Holy Cross. Since that time, the city parishes of Sacred Heart (1883), St. Patrick (1894) and St. Peter (1897) were carved out of its home territory, and the Friars Preachers pioneered the Missions of South Wigston, Aylestone, Oadby, and Knighton before handing them over to the diocesan clergy. The erection of the Parish of St. Thomas More, Knighton, in 1947, left Holy Cross with no more than a much reduced area of the City of Leicester, in no way commensurate with its widespread spiritual influence. In addition to the Parish of Holy Cross, the Dominican Friars serve a Mass station at the village of Woodhouse in a fourteenth-century chapel. They are also responsible for the chaplaincies to two universities, Leicester and De Montfort, and to the Leicester Royal Infirmary.

LEICESTER, *Holy Cross – Convents*

Some **Third Order Dominican Sisters** came to Leicester towards the end of 1859 but remained there for only a matter of months.

Dominican Sisters from Haverstock Hill arrived in 1875. Their first convent was in Abbey Lane, from where they moved in 1879 to Millstone Lane, and later to London Road, at the corner of University Road. The Sisters at first taught in the schools both of Holy Cross and St Patrick's. After the opening of the Sacred Heart schools in 1884, they went there to teach, and gave up their other commitments. They also opened a private school of their own at the London Road convent. From 1906 their work changed in character. In that year they moved to Dane Hills, in St. Peter's Parish, and devoted themselves to the nursing of incurables.

A house in West Walk was taken in 1908 by a group of women who, from 1923, have been known as the **Corpus Christi Carmelites**. They engaged in the instruction of converts, the visitation of the sick and those in prison, and other works of mercy. The community became affiliated to the Carmelites, and opened houses in North America and the British West Indies. The Leicester house was closed in 1927. In 1952 they returned to the diocese where, under the auspices of the Nottingham Diocesan Catholic Children's Society, they opened 'Carmel', a home for children aged five to sixteen, at Kirby Muxloe near Leicester. This closed in 1993. The community moved to the Parish of St. Thomas More, Knighton, for some years before closing in 2011.

The **Sisters of St Dorothy** conducted a private secondary school for girls on London Road from 1916 to 1940. In this latter year they returned to Portugal and their convent was then taken over by the

Franciscan Minoresses who converted it into a private nursing home for medical, surgical and maternity cases. Changing needs of apostolates and lack of personnel led to the decision by the Sisters to close the hospital which they did in 1976. When the convent closed, the Sisters dispersed to their other houses within the diocese and beyond.

LEICESTER

Blessed Sacrament

The development of housing estates to the south of Leicester after the First World War made it necessary to establish a Mission in the Braunstone district. By 1929 Canon Francis Caus of St. Peter's hoped to build a church dedicated to St. Joseph. The project was shelved when a more suitable site on Gooding Avenue became available and it was found that the Dutch Province of the Blessed Sacrament Fathers was willing to take charge of the new Mission.

On 17 September 1938 Bishop McNulty laid the foundation stone of the Priory, known as 'Eymard House'. It was opened on 3 October 1939. Twelve novices came into residence, and it was hoped that this would lead eventually to the formation of an English Province of the Congregation. The Priory was named after Saint Peter Julian Eymard, Founder of the Congregation of the Blessed Sacrament. In 1951 the House was transferred to the American Province of the Congregation.

Two priests of this Congregation took up residence at Braunstone in 1935. They said Mass each Sunday at the Working Men's Club and set about the erection of a temporary wooden church. This was opened by Bishop McNulty on Holy Saturday 1938. The temporary wooden church lasted for almost twenty years and was closed on 18 May 1957.

In 1944 the population of the parish was temporarily swollen by the arrival from Italy of the American 82nd Airborne Division which took over Braunstone Park for its camp to prepare for the invasion of Normandy in June that year. The Americans had their own Mass in the wooden church, celebrated by their own chaplain.

On 5 July 1956 Bishop Ellis laid the foundation stone of a new church; and less than a year later, on 25 June 1957, he solemnly blessed and opened it. A main focus of the new building was a throne on which the Blessed Sacrament could be perpetually exposed for adoration, this being a focal point of the spirituality of the Blessed Sacrament Fathers. The interior of the church was remodelled in the late 1970s and following years to meet the changing needs of the congregation and liturgical requirements. The church is a good example of a familiar Roman Catholic type, the mid-twentieth century Italianate brick basilica, of which there are several in the Leicester suburbs.

In 1990 the Blessed Sacrament Fathers, who had meanwhile established other houses in Britain, withdrew from Braunstone and the parish was entrusted to the care of diocesan clergy. Eymard House was sold as it was too large for parish use, and a small presbytery was built to one side of the site which also has a parish hall at the far end of the oval site in Gooding Avenue.

LEICESTER, *Blessed Sacrament – Convent*

Corpus Christi Carmelites. This Religious Congregation was founded in 1908 in Leicester, but the Sisters left there in 1927, returning in 1952 to open a convent and children's home in the village of Kirby Muxloe. Both the convent and the children's home closed in 1993.

LEICESTER

Mother of God (New Parks Estate)

From the end of the Second World War, the western fringes of Leicester were rapidly covered by new housing estates. From 1952 Catholics were able to attend Mass on Sunday at the White House Schools, New Parks Estate. This Mass centre was initially served from St. Peter's. In 1957 a church designed to seat four hundred people was built at the junction of Glenfield Road with New Parks Boulevard. The 'Taking Stock' Survey of 2011 noted that "While the exterior [of the church] is unassuming, the interior is of considerable architectural quality, with a series of tall parabolic arches defining the bays of the nave", commenting favourably on the fact that "the interior is relatively little altered and contains a number of original furnishings of note."

Mother of God was established as a parish in 1960. A church hall was opened in September 1967. Mother of God has the distinction of being the only parish in the diocese to have had a bishop as parish priest. Bishop James McGuinness lived there until he succeeded Bishop Edward Ellis on the latter's retirement in 1974, and he came back to consecrate Mother of God Church on 21 November 1975.

The Silver Jubilee year of the parish was marked initially by a severe setback when, in March, the parish hall was broken into and set on fire. The damage done to the hall was repaired in time for the Silver Jubilee Thanksgiving Mass on 11 October 1982.

For a short period from 2003, Mother of God was once again served from its parent parish, but since 2008 it has once again had its own resident priest.

Reflecting the changing demographics of the area in recent years, Mass is celebrated once each month in the Syro-Malabar Rite as well as in the Latin Rite.

LEICESTER

Our Lady of Good Counsel

After the First World War, slum clearance began in the crowded district around St. Patrick's, and there was a corresponding expansion of the city to the Belgrave area of Leicester. Hence the erection of a new church which in time was to supplant the old St. Patrick's. Some 1,722 square yards of land with a frontage on Canon Street were bought in July 1920. The church, a brick building "simple but eminently serviceable" with a main entrance opening onto Moira Street, was erected on this site and blessed by Bishop Dunn on 22 August 1922. It was the work of the Leicester builder, Mr. F. J. Bradford. The church was intended to serve eventually as a parish hall, and to be superseded in time by a worthier structure. Fr. George Holland of St. Patrick's bought a house suitable for a presbytery in 1920. He came to live in this house, and the new church of Our Lady of Good Counsel became the parish church, while St. Patrick's, until its closure in 1940, served as a chapel-of-ease.

There was a similar transfer of the old St. Patrick's Schools to Harrison Road. The foundation stone was laid by Bishop McNulty in May 1936, and the complete schools - retaining the title of St. Patrick - were opened the following year.

The name of St. Patrick for a church was not lost either, and a new building on the Beaumont Leys Estate was put up in the late 1950s under Fr. Lawrence Hill. A new presbytery and parish hall incorporating a social club were also built on the site.

In the early 1960s it was proposed to build a new Church of Our Lady and adapt the old church as a hall. This did not come to fruition, however, and the church on Moira Street was eventually superseded, but not by a building on the same site. Canon Leo McReavy bought a site in the Rushey Mead area and a new church, presbytery, and combined parish hall and social club were erected at the corner of Gleneagles Avenue and Peebles Way and opened in March 1975. The church has been described as "a striking small modern church on a radial plan, designed by a well-established firm of church architects and reflecting several of the 1970s currents in church design."

In recent years, the Church of Our Lady of Good Counsel has become the focal point in Leicester for the Divine Mercy devotion.

LEICESTER

Sacred Heart

Until 1882 no priests other than the Dominicans had served in the city of Leicester. In that year Bishop Bagshawe sent the fifty-four year old Frenchman Fr. John Salius-Grin, whom he described as a "gentle, pious and useful priest", to live at 33 Mere Road and establish a new Mission in a large and growing suburb in the south-east of the town. He at first used a room in this house as a Mass centre. Subsequently, he adapted a hired room in Farnham Street as a temporary chapel.

A corrugated-iron chapel, known as the 'Tin Tabernacle', was built in 1890. Temporary in intention, it served the parish for thirty-four years. The present church may be described as an adaptation to an English environment of the Romanesque Style. Below the church, which is located on a slope, is a parish hall, capable of seating 300 people. The foundation stone of the church was laid on 21 May 1923, and the completed building was opened the following year.

The construction of Sacred Heart Church was almost the life-work of the Dutchman Canon Henry Lindeboom who came to the parish in 1905. On his arrival, he found a tin chapel, a most inadequate school, and a rented presbytery. When he left, thirty-three years later, Sacred Heart was a confident and flourishing parish with a fine church and schools which were "at least adequate for their times". In 1954 he came back to preach at Sacred Heart on the patronal feast. At the end of his sermon, he collapsed and died.

In the late 1970s a new presbytery was built between the church and the school. The church was reordered in the early 1990s.

In 1945 a chapel-of-ease, dedicated to St. Margaret Mary, was erected on the eastern edge of the parish and served this purpose until 2003, when it was handed over to the Polish community since their previous church, St. Paul's in the Highfields area of Sacred Heart Parish, was becoming too expensive to maintain.

According to the practice of the time, the school came before the church. This first portion of the school which lasted until the 1970s opened in 1886. For six years it was used also as a chapel. In 1895 an infant school was added, and the greater part of the building was erected sometime in the years 1897-1905 by Fr. Arthur Lepère. With the growth of the community it became clear that a new school was needed, and this was finally achieved in the late 1970s.

LEICESTER, *Sacred Heart – Convents*

Dominican Sisters taught for a number of years in the school. Their departure must probably be dated to 1906.

Sisters of St Joseph of Peace in 1934 opened a small convent on Mere Road, from which the school was partly staffed. The Sisters left the parish at the end of the 1950s.

LEICESTER

St. Patrick

As its name implies, the Mission of St. Patrick was founded in a district largely populated by a faithful but poverty-stricken, Irish congregation. The work of the Dominicans from Holy Cross had begun in this district as early as 1824. In that year, they founded an infant school in Belgrave Gate. This, together with the nearby chapel of St. Michael in Causeway Lane, was to form the nucleus of the Mission.

Fr. Thomas Nickolds OP is credited with the founding of the Mission in 1854, in which year a school-chapel, dedicated to St. Patrick, was opened in Royal East Street. This first chapel of St. Patrick may claim continuity with the older St. Michael's Chapel of 1798. Fr. Nickolds had used this old chapel for lectures on Christian doctrine on Tuesday evenings, and for Mass on Wednesday mornings until at least 1850. It seems probable that the Causeway Lane chapel was closed to public use only when St Patrick's had been erected to take its place.

In 1873 Fr. Cyril Bunce OP was sent from Holy Cross to reside in Archdeacon Lane and St. Patrick's became a Mission independent of the mother-church. The priests' house was as poor as those of their congregation - a double cottage opposite the chapel, which in 1946 formed part of a button factory. Fr. Bunce collected money both from his own congregation and from Ireland, and in 1876 was able to erect a new church of St. Patrick attached to but distinct from the parish school.

Until 1894 the Mission was in the hands of the Dominicans. Bishop Bagshawe then sent one of this own clergy, Fr. William A. Hawkins, who – by reason of his forceful character and physical powers – was well suited for such a parish. For twelve years he kept the peace as few others could have done. The church was hemmed in by public-houses. At one side of it stood 'The Woolcomber'; at the rear was 'The Horn of Plenty'; in Royal East Street, within a stone's throw of the church, was 'The Shamrock', a favourite haunt of the Irish population. Fr. Hawkins increased his financial resources by shrewd negotiations. In 1894 he bought 'The Woolcomber' and 351 square yards of land adjoining the church and sold it four years later. After it had lost its licence, it was bought back in 1911! In the latter part of the nineteenth century at least, the numbers of Catholics in St. Patrick's Mission exceeded those in Holy Cross.

After the First World War, as a result of town clearance, many people moved to the outskirts of Leicester. Naturally, this had an impact on the congregation of St. Patrick's. The Irish dwellings disappeared, and factories, a car park and a bus station took their place. In consequence Fr. George Holland moved his residence to the Melton Road district in 1921 and in the following year opened the Church of Our Lady of Good Counsel. St. Patrick's was then served from the new church as a chapel-of-ease. It was finally closed on Whit Sunday 1940. The schools were similarly transferred, in 1937, to new buildings on Harrison Road – in Our Lady's Parish. English Martyrs Comprehensive School on Anstey Lane was opened in 1964.

From 1950 until the opening of the 'new' St. Patrick's Church on the Beaumont Leys Estate on 17 March 1959, Mass was celebrated each Sunday for the Catholics of this area in the Leicester Stadium by one of the priests from Our Lady's. It is perhaps out of a sense of loyalty to the original St. Patrick's that until the mid-1950s, the second parish in Leicester (after Holy Cross) is listed in diocesan yearbooks as "St. Patrick and Our Lady of Good Counsel." Only from 1956 is the order changed to "Our Lady of Good Counsel and St. Patrick."

St. Patrick's became independent from Our Lady's Parish in 1961. The parish hall was built in 1964, the presbytery in 1972. The church was re-ordered in the early 1980s.

LEICESTER

St. Peter

The early history of this parish follows a pattern common at the end of the nineteenth century. A priest was sent to the district with the bishop's blessing and very little else. The early period was one of uncertainty, as priest after priest failed to cope with the difficulties of the situation, and ended only with the advent of one who made the development of the parish the work of his whole life.

In February 1896 Bishop Bagshawe sent Fr. John R. Kane to reside at Ferndene Villa, Streeton Road. The district had previously been within the jurisdiction of Holy Cross. He lasted three months during which time he said Mass in his own house. Fr. Kane had five successors within the next seven years! Mass was said at first in the King Richard's Road Board Schools. By 1900 a warehouse in Noble Street was hired to serve as a temporary chapel, together with a priest's house adjoining it. In 1898 Bishop Bagshawe noted that a new Mission of St. Peter had been established in Leicester and a large piece of land had been bought on which to build a school-chapel. For the time being, a good presbytery and two large rooms had been hired and one of these rooms had been set out to serve as a church.

Stability came in 1903 when a young Belgian, Fr. Francis Caus, was appointed to the Mission. The twenty-eight years of life that remained to him were devoted to St. Peter's. St. Peter's Church, the first of many in the diocese to be built by Mr. F. J. Bradford, a parishioner, was opened in 1905. (The north aisle, memorial chapel and sacristies were added in 1919.) The church was a simple brick structure with no architectural pretensions, but it was warmly devotional. St. Peter's Guild Hall on King Richard's Road, which served the parish for social purposes, was opened on 14 October 1937. The site for this was given by Mr. Bradford.

The church on King Richard's Road served for some seventy years until, in the 1970s, Leicester City Council's plans for a new road scheme included the compulsory purchase and demolition of the buildings of St.

Peter's. A new site on Hinckley Road was bought with the compensation award. Work began on the new site in January 1977, and by the end of the year the new presbytery was completed. Work continued on the new church and hall. The last Mass in the old church on King Richard's Road was said at lunchtime on the feast of Saints Peter and Paul, 1978, and the first Mass in the new church was said the same day in the evening after a Procession of the Blessed Sacrament from the old to the new church. The new church was consecrated on 5 October 1978. Among the distinguishing features of the church are the cut-brick bas-reliefs of Christ with Peter and the Apostles, and the Stations of the Cross by the Maltese sculptor Carmel Cauchi, a local resident, who also did work at the 1982 Church of Saints Peter and Paul, Earl Shilton.

Many years passed before satisfactory provision was made within the parish for the education of children. The problem was met partially by the Sisters of the Nativity, who, in 1918, opened both a secondary school for girls and a private elementary school on Glenfield Road. These were closed in 1939 when the Sisters moved to Evington Hall in what was then Sacred Heart Parish.

The primary school of Christ the King in the Parish of St. Peter was the first to be built under the Diocesan Development Plan which followed the 1944 Education Act. A magnificent site opposite Dane Hills Convent was bought in 1945. Plans were drawn up by the architect, Mr. Harding, and the contract for building was awarded to Messrs. Calverley. The foundation stone was laid by Bishop Ellis on 17 December 1950. A previously existing mid-Victorian building on the site, known as 'Ashleigh House' was demolished to the ground floor, and the remainder used as administration block, dining room and kitchens. From this, two wings fan out, one for infants and the other for juniors. The new school was opened for use in 1951, followed by a formal inauguration early in 1952. In September 2015 the school expanded onto a second site near to the original one.

LEICESTER, *St. Peter - Convents*

Dominican Sisters of the English Congregation of St. Catherine of Siena (Stone) bought a site on Dane Hills in 1904 prior to which time they had been resident within the Parish of Holy Cross. It was their intention to establish a home for incurables. The foundation stone of the first portion was laid on 24 August 1905 and the building was opened on 29 September 1906. This provided accommodation for thirty patients. A new chapel, built by Mr. F. J. Bradford to the plans of Messrs. K. Bedingfield and P. H. Grundy, was opened in 1928. This enabled the old chapel to be converted into a ward for ten patients, and a further twelve beds were made available in 1930. The accommodation provided for the Sisters up to this time was far from satisfactory. A new convent was therefore built; it was opened by Bishop McNulty on 30th April 1937.

Sisters of the Nativity of the Blessed Virgin came in 1918 and remained there until 1939 when they moved to Evington Hall, now in St. Joseph's Parish.

Daughters of Divine Charity in 1949 bought a house on Fosse Road North, close to the former Convent of the Nativity. On 11 February of that year they opened it as St. Teresa's Hostel for Business Girls. The venture proved to be an outstanding success in providing a home both for girls working in Leicester and for students. The hostel and the convent appeared to have closed in 1962.

LEICESTER

St. Joseph

The story of this parish began when, in 1938, Mr. F. J. Bradford presented to the Parish of the Sacred Heart a site of two acres on Uppingham Road, on which stood some farm buildings. Work began later that year to convert the stable and cowshed into a church, parish hall, and a priest's house. The first Mass was celebrated on Christmas Eve of that same year.

St. Joseph's was separated from the Sacred Heart to form a new parish in 1942. Fr. James Leahy was the first parish priest, serving here for thirty-four years in the course of which time he oversaw – among other things – the building of the second and third churches.

The urban territory of the parish is residential in character; but it also covers a large rural area to the east of Leicester up to the Rutland boundary. A Mass centre at Billesdon, the geographical centre of this district, served the scattered Catholics of the countryside from 1945-1954.

The second church was built in the early 1950s with the intention of its becoming a parish hall. The third and present church was opened on 24 September 1968. Considered by the 'Taking Stock' Survey of 2011 to be the most striking post-War church in Leicester, it is an early and original design by Thomas E. Wilson, who designed several other churches in the Diocese of Nottingham. The interior has been altered significantly since it was built. The high altar has been remodelled on an enlarged dais opposite the gallery; and the dramatic impact of the interior has been further increased by the stained-glass by Harry Cardross of Goddard & Gibbs, installed in the windows of the narthex under the gallery in 2002.

St. Joseph's Primary School was opened in 1962 adjacent to the chapel-of-ease, Our Lady of the Rosary.

St. Paul's Secondary School was formed in 1977 from Evington Hall Convent School and Corpus Christi Secondary Modern School on Gwendolen Road. The Gwendolen Road site was sold and new buildings were erected on the Evington site and opened by Bishop McGuinness in 1985. A three-storey new building was blessed by Cardinal Vincent Nichols in March 2015 while he was in Leicester for the re-burial of King Richard III.

The Watermead Apostolate came to St. Joseph's in February 2001, having begun its music and publishing apostolate in 1994 in the Parish of St. Theresa, Birstall.

LEICESTER, *St. Joseph – Convents*

The **Sisters of the Nativity of the Blessed Virgin** purchased Evington Hall in 1939. This Congregation, founded in France in 1818, made its first settlement in the Nottingham Diocese in Market Harborough in 1904. From that time until 1918 the Sisters conducted a boarding and day school in that town, after which they transferred their convent and school to St. Peter's Parish, Leicester, where they also kept a private elementary school. The venture at Evington was eminently successful, and by 1946 their independent grammar school for girls had 210 pupils. In 1955 the Sisters of the Nativity were amalgamated with the

Sisters of Charity of St. Paul the Apostle who then took over Evington Hall Girls' Grammar School and continued to be involved in education in the parish after the grammar school was amalgamated with Corpus Christi Secondary Modern School. The Sisters of Charity left Leicester in 1992.

The **Sisters of St. Joseph of Peace** came to the parish in 1961 at the invitation of the then parish priest, Father James Leahy, to open a new Mission in the Goodwood / Scraptoft area of Leicester. The Sisters' apostolate in the parish has included instruction of converts, parish visiting, hospital chaplaincy and education in St. Joseph's Primary School.

LEICESTER, *Holy Rosary Church – has always been served from St. Joseph's*

A chapel-of-ease dedicated to Our Lady of the Rosary was built, in 1958, on a site on the Netherhall Estate large enough for a permanent church and presbytery, although these were never built.

LEICESTER

St. Edward the Confessor (Aylestone)

A Mass centre in the Aylestone district of Leicester was first opened by the Dominicans of Holy Cross on Christmas Day 1915, when the first Mass, attended by forty-one people, was celebrated in a room above a bake-house in Knighton Lane. As a result of growing numbers, just over a year later the local Catholics gathered in larger premises, this time over a stable also in Knighton Lane. The present church, with a seating capacity of 250, was opened by Bishop Dunn on 3 May 1922. It was designed, by Mr. Clement Streeton, a Leicester architect, and built by Mr. F. J. Bradford, the builder of many other churches in the diocese. The church had a vestibule made intentionally large enough to accommodate bath-chairs, bicycles, etc.! In 1937 the district was cut off from Holy Cross and formed into a parish, with St. John Bosco on Saffron Lane as a chapel-of-ease. Fr. John Dewar, the third parish priest, served St. Edward's for forty-three years. A bungalow presbytery and a parish hall, blessed and opened in 1998, complete the site on Aylestone Road.

LEICESTER, St. Edward the Confessor – Convent

Corpus Christi Carmelites were responsible for a great degree of pioneering work in the parish in its early years and, from 1993 to 1996, were resident in the presbytery as Parish Sisters.

LEICESTER

St. John Bosco – served from St. Mary's, South Wigston

The club-chapel of St. John Bosco owed its erection to an unusual degree of lay initiative. Two young men of the Morrisey family in Sacred Heart Parish, together with their sister, decided that a club was needed for the young Catholics in the new housing estate around Saffron Lane. A plot of land on Stonesby Avenue had been offered in 1933 by a Mr. & Mrs. Burns. Permission to build a temporary structure was given with the proviso that the building could be moved should an interested buyer wish to purchase the plot.

With the aid of Mr. F. J. Bradford, the Leicester builder, the Morriseys erected a brick club-house. It was opened on 1 November 1936. The Dominicans of Holy Cross gave it every assistance and, from Christmas 1936, began a Sunday Mass for the people of the district. The building was constructed in such a way that a 'sanctuary' area could be screened off from the remainder when social activities took place. The altar came from the Dominican Convent at Dane Hills; the tabernacle was a gift of Mr. Burns' sister; the ciborium and chalice were given by the Morrisey family, and a set of vestments by the monks of Mount Saint Bernard Abbey. St. John Bosco was initially attached to the Parish of St. Edward the Confessor, Aylestone, which, in 1937, had been detached from Holy Cross to become a parish in its own right.

St. John Bosco, covering the Saffron Lane and Eyres Monsell Estates, was cut off from Aylestone in 1958 to become a separate parish. In the mid-1960s a piece of land on the Eyres Monsell Estate was purchased from the City Council, and here was built a hall which was also used as a church at weekends. A presbytery was built adjacent to the hall. The original chapel on Saffron Lane continued to serve in addition to the hall-cum-church on Pasley Road on the Eyres Monsell Estate until a new church was opened in September 1984.

Holy Cross School in Holy Cross Parish was relocated to Stonesby Avenue in 1966.

Within the parish lies Glen Parva Young Offenders Centre. For seventeen years, Sister Teresa Joseph, a member of the Corpus Christi Carmelites, was an Assistant Chaplain there, for which service she was awarded the MBE.

LEICESTER, *St. John Bosco – Convent*

Presentation Sisters, resident in the presbytery, have served as Parish Sisters since 2002.

LEICESTER

St. Mary (South Wigston)

As so often in the Leicester area, the pioneer work at South Wigston was carried out by the Dominicans of Holy Cross. The occasion for the work at South Wigston was, in the first place, the erection in 1880 of the Glen Parva Barracks, home of the Leicestershire Regiment. The first Mass was said in the barracks on 29 August of that year, and continued until 1896 for the benefit of the troops and other Catholics of the neighbourhood. (The question has been raised as to whether the parish would have been started at all had it not been for the presence of the barracks.)

It seems that, for reasons no longer known, this first Mass centre ceased to exist in 1896. Four years later, the Dominicans called a meeting at Holy Cross to consider the provision of a permanent chapel. This resulted in the purchase of a site on Countesthorpe Road, South Wigston, in 1901. The first plans drawn up provided for a structure in corrugated-iron. This did not meet with the approval of the people, who wanted a more substantial and permanent building, and the present brick structure was opened by Bishop Brindle in July 1905. It is one of the earliest of the series of churches built by the Leicester builder Mr. F. J. Bradford. A porch and a choir gallery were added in 1913. The period of the First World War saw a number of refugees from Belgium in the area and during the same period and, indeed, at least as late as 1925, as many as a hundred soldiers from Glen Parva Barracks would march to St. Mary's for Sunday Mass. In 1937 the district was separated from Holy Cross and erected as a parish under the care of diocesan clergy. In 1980 a large new addition was made on the south side of the old church and the building was reorientated. More recently, the front porch has been altered and extended.

The presbytery was built in 1953. Significant alterations to the church building were made in the late 1970s. Until a presbytery was built next door to the church in 1953, the priest lived at Glen Parva Manor, the home of the Bailey family.

In the mid-1980s St. Mary's Parish hosted, the first parish in the diocese to do so, a parish-based programme of preparation for Confirmation designed by Fr. Ken O'Riordan and Sr. Ellen McGrath of the Diocesan Catechetical Centre.

St. John Fisher Primary School, on the borders of Wigston and Oadby, was opened in 1966. It converted to an Academy in 2012.

LEICESTER

St. Thomas More (Knighton)

About 1940 the Dominicans of Holy Cross began to say Mass each Sunday at the Craddock Arms, Knighton. In 1945 Mass was moved to the Royal Army Ordnance Corps Hut in Ratcliffe Road, and the following year to a disused Methodist chapel in Chapel Lane, used during the rest of the week as a Girl Guide Headquarters. In 1941 a plot of land at the junction of Knighton Road and Southernhay Road was bought with a view to building a chapel-of-ease to Holy Cross. Numbers of people attending Mass increased to such a degree that, in August 1947, Bishop Ellis erected the Parish of St. Thomas More, Knighton, the first parish in the diocese to be dedicated to that saint alone. For the next few years, Sunday Masses were celebrated in the disused Methodist chapel and in the convent chapel of the Franciscan Minoresses on London Road.

In 1947 the house adjacent to the original site was purchased as the priest's house.

The foundation stone of the church was laid by Bishop Ellis on 28 October 1950; but it was not until 6 July 1952 that the completed building could be opened. Built to the designs of Messrs. Reynolds and Scott, the Manchester architects, it was soon recognised as "a fine example of modern architecture and building." The church was consecrated in 1972 and, several years later, a statue of St. Thomas More was installed over the main entrance. The interior of the church has been reordered several times, initially in the early 1970s prior to the consecration of the church. In preparation for the Golden Jubilee of the parish in 1997, the church was reordered in a more radical fashion. The parish room and sacristies were substantially rebuilt and enlarged and the opportunity taken to make some improvements to the accommodation in the presbytery.

An independent junior school for boys and girls, dedicated to Our Lady of the Angels, was opened in September 1954 by Poor Clares of Newry. This was replaced, in 1965, by a purpose-built primary school on Newstead Road. It was given the title 'St. Thomas More', and for some years was staffed by Poor Clare Sisters of Newry and lay people.

LEICESTER, *St. Thomas More – Convents*

Franciscan Minoresses

After the Sisters of St. Dorothy returned to Portugal in 1940, the premises they had occupied (at that time still in Holy Cross Parish) were converted by the Franciscan Minoresses into a private nursing home for medical, surgical and maternity cases. This opened on 1 May 1941. Its success was immense. Besides the original convent (No. 362 London Road) the two adjoining houses were bought to extend the nursing home. One of these, purchased in 1951, provided living quarters for the Sisters; and two rooms on the first floor were converted into a new chapel, opened by Bishop Ellis on 8 December 1951. The Sisters closed St. Francis' Hospital in 1976.

Poor Clares of the Immaculate Conception (of Newry) in 1954 bought a large house in Ratcliffe Road, opposite the church, and opened it as a convent in June of the same year. The Sisters taught initially in an independent junior school, 'Our Lady of the Angels' and, subsequently, in its replacement, 'St. Thomas More Primary school.' In later years, the Convent on Ratcliffe Road eventually proved too large for the dwindling numbers of Sisters and was sold, and a smaller house on Southernhay Road on the far side of the church was purchased. Eventually in 1995 the Sisters left the parish and sold the property.

Corpus Christi Carmelites opened a convent close to the church and worked in the parish for some years, before they too left in the late 1900s.

LEICESTER

Immaculate Conception (Oadby) - served from St. Thomas More, Knighton

The Mass centre at Oadby, on the south-eastern outskirts of Leicester, was founded by the Dominicans of Holy Cross in 1940. It was called into being by the necessities of wartime, but its usefulness preserved it in being after the emergency ceased. The centre has been described successively as the Working Men's Institute (1940-1941), The Institute, Main Street (1941-1948) and The Institute, New Street (from 1948).

When, in 1947, the new Parish of St Thomas More was formed out of the district between Holy Cross and Oadby, the care of the Mass centre was transferred from the Dominicans to the Parish of South Wigston. Various factors including a degree of anti-Catholic sentiment even as late as the 1950s hindered the acquisition of land on which to build a church. The present site was not finally acquired until 1960 and there was then a further delay while funds were raised for the new building. But these hindrances were eventually overcome and Oadby became a separate parish in 1961. From that year, Sunday Masses were celebrated in Launde School by kind permission of the Leicestershire Education Authority. Three years later Fr. John Feeley, the first parish priest, cut the first sod for the new church. The church was opened on 8 December 1965, the day on which the Second Vatican Council closed, and was consecrated in July 1976. The original form of the church was a simple rectangular building with a short projecting addition at the front and a porch to the left made from two glazed wooden screens and a blind brick wall. Both church and presbytery were designed and built with flat roofs. The church in particular leaked constantly. Eventually both buildings had pitched roofs added with red clay tiles on the church and brown concrete tiles on the presbytery.

A parish is more than bricks and mortar; and it is more than a closed community. So it is that, like most other parishes, Oadby has always looked beyond its own denominational and geographical boundaries. To give one example: as its Millennium Project, Oadby established a link with the village of Stauceni in Moldova, a former 'state' of the Soviet Union. One purpose of this link, which became known as the 'Moldova Project', was to provide food for children and elderly people.

OADBY, *Immaculate Conception – Convent*

Sisters of St. Joseph of Peace took up residence in the presbytery in 2016.

LINCOLN

St. Hugh

At the end of the Penal Times, the city of Lincoln had probably the strongest Catholic community of any town in the present diocese. By 1778 the Jesuit Fr. Richard Knight had already spent fourteen years as its missionary priest. He is said to have occupied a house in Bank Street, near to its junction with Silver Street, and owned by Mrs. Winifred Heneage. This house was stone-built and dated from the seventeenth century. Previously it had served as the parsonage of St. Swithin's; later, at the end of the nineteenth century, it was occupied by Mr. Danby, a solicitor.

A room in the upper floor of this house was used as a chapel. The ceiling was extremely low. Those who were present when the Vicar-Apostolic came to administer Confirmation noted that his mitre touched the roof. And the people who went to Mass in those days had memories of Fr. Knight laying his brown wig upon the altar until he had finished vesting.

As the Society of Jesus was suppressed in 1773, it was not possible to find a Jesuit to succeed Fr. Knight when he died in 1793. He was therefore succeeded by a French émigré priest, Fr. Guillaume Bertrand. Fr. Bertrand, like many other émigré clergy, initially acted as a tutor to a local family; in his case, it was the Sibthorps of Canwick Hall, one of whose members, Richard Waldo Sibthorp, became, in 1842, a priest of the present Diocese of Nottingham, and died in Nottingham in 1879. He was buried in the Sibthorp family plot in Canwick Cemetery. In 1799 Fr. Bertrand built the first diminutive chapel in Silver Street. It measured forty feet by twenty feet, and - in addition - had a sanctuary some twelve or thirteen feet square. The Catholics at this time felt at any rate confident enough to ignore an order from the Mayor of Lincoln that they should obliterate a brick cross on the facade.

The Jesuits once more took charge of the Mission in 1823. Fr. Bertrand (also known as Beaumont) had returned to France five years previously, and what happened in the interim is not known. The Mission remained in the care of the Society of Jesus until 1869 and was then transferred to the diocesan clergy.

In 1853 the chapel was lengthened and raised, and completed by the addition of transepts and an apse. It was dedicated to Saints John the Baptist and John the Evangelist, and has been described as a 'plain, Romanesque building.'

Soon after the departure of the Jesuits, there began the long and involved negotiations which ended with the erection of the present church in 1893. The arrival in 1875 of Canon William Croft, who served the parish for more than fifty years, ushered in an era of fund-raising and growth which resulted in the erection of the present Church of St. Hugh, opened by Cardinal Vaughan in December 1893. Mr. T. G. Young of Middle Rasen, in 1870, intervened and offered to defray the whole cost of a new church and a seminary in exchange for the Silver Street site. The site was sold to Mr. Young and architect's plans were drawn up by Mr. Hadfield; but these failed to meet the approval of the new Bishop (Bagshawe) in 1874, and Mr. Young withdrew his offer. Whatever happened is perhaps reflected in the bishop's Quinquennial Report to Rome of 1875, in which he noted that he had "visited Lincoln and had seen some of the principal Catholics." He went on to say that: "The state of the congregation appears to be fairly satisfactory." But then he crossed out this sentence and replaced it with: "The state of the congregation would probably admit of improvement."

Ten years later Bishop Bagshawe noted that: "There are about 848 Catholics in the Mission, of whom some are persons of wealth, the great majority being poor. [Furthermore,] the church is small, holding only 250 persons. [But] there are good hopes of a suitable church being built before long by one of the congregation." He noted also that the presbytery was small and poor.

It was not until 1889 that the project was resumed. Widespread appeals throughout the diocese brought in the necessary funds. By 1890 and presbytery in the heart of the city had been purchased, and a large part of the cost of it had been collected. The new church retained the old dedication until 1898, and was then rededicated to St. Hugh of Lincoln. A porch was added in 1909. Bishop Dunn consecrated the church on 27 January 1927. Several months later he returned to Lincoln to consecrate the two side altars. Over subsequent years a significant number of alterations have taken place, most recently in the first decade of the twenty-first century. The interior of the church was refurbished in 2008-10.

The origins of the first primary school are uncertain. In 1875 there is mention of a 'disused' schoolroom, and as it adjoined one of the side walls of the chapel, it may be conjectured that the first elementary school dates from the same time as the reconstruction of the chapel carried out in 1853. The school was revived by Fr. Austin Rowley, and given new premises in 1882. A short-lived attempt to found an independent grammar school, dedicated to 'Little' St. Hugh, was made in 1927 by a Captain Malden.

St. Hugh's Primary School transferred from the centre of Lincoln in 1993 and is now located in Saints Peter and Paul Parish.

The mid 1980s witnessed an almost unique event in the history of the diocese. Mgr. Hugh Atkinson, who had been Parish Priest of St. Hugh's for more than thirty years, changed roles with his curate, Fr. Thomas McGovern who became parish priest while Mgr. Atkinson became the curate. This arrangement lasted for several years until Mgr. Atkinson's age and health required him to retire altogether, although he continued to live in the presbytery until several months before his death.

LINCOLN, *St. Hugh – Convent*

A small group of **Sisters of Providence of Ruillé-sur-Loir** (founded in France in 1806) arrived in Lincoln from Woodhall Spa in 1902 and established a community on Greestone Stairs (not far from St. Hugh's Church). They started a boarding and day school for girls, St. Joseph's Convent, which was successful and soon outgrew these premises. In 1911 they moved into the recently vacated boys' grammar school property in Upper Lindum Street and continued to expand (until numbers grew to more than 400 among whom at least 80 were boarders). In 1983 due in part to a lack of vocations and the increasing age of the community, the school was sold to and administered by the Parents' Association under the name of St. Joseph's School, with some involvement and help from the Sisters for a while. (In 1993/4 it amalgamated with the Cathedral School and Stonefield School to become The Minster School.) The other Sisters became involved in the parish schools or in parish work and continued to serve the community in a different way, and they still do. The Sisters moved to a smaller house in Our Lady's Parish in February 2014.

LINCOLN

Our Lady of Lincoln

In spite of the strength of the Catholic community in Lincoln in the days of persecution, its recent development has been slow. Until 1933 the whole city was served from St. Hugh's. Canon Hunt then opened a Mass centre at a shop in the St. Giles district. Before the end of 1933 the centre for Mass had been moved to the Co-operative Hall, and then to a temporary wooden church at The Oval. To emphasise the importance of Our Lady in the history of Lincoln, a local craftsman made for Our Lady's Church a stone statue of Our Lady of Lincoln which is a copy of a statue in Lincoln Cathedral.

On 1 February 1943 the district was erected as an independent parish. The present church was opened in 1964 and consecrated in September 1975. In 1998 the sanctuary of the church was richly redecorated. A parish centre connected to the church dates from 1981, and further alterations were made in 2001.

But the Church is more than just buildings as a delightful article in the diocesan yearbook for 1989 boldly informs us. "Christmas in the historic City of Lincoln would not be the same without the singing of Our Lady's Carollers." For almost twenty years they had sung in hostelries and restaurants around the city collecting money for various local charities.

More important than collecting money, their aim was to draw people's attention to the real meaning of Christmas. The Carollers and church choir have also appeared on television and radio and had made tapes of carols which they sold to raise money for the repair of the church roof!

In order to relieve the chronic overcrowding of the old primary school of St. Hugh and to meet the needs of the many children in the new estates to the north and east of the city, a new primary school was built in the early 1960s. Providing places for 280 children in eight classrooms with a spacious hall and kitchen, it came into use in September 1962. The 'official' opening did not take place until the following May since in the autumn of 1962, the bishop "was too deeply engaged in the preliminaries of the Second Vatican Council to be able to come to Lincoln at that time" – a useful reminder that the Church is universal as well as parochial or diocesan!

LINCOLN, *Our Lady – Convent*

Sisters of Providence of Reuillé-sur-Loir

These Sisters, who had been in Lincoln since 1902, moved to Our Lady's Parish in February 2014, where they continue to serve the community in a variety of ways.

LINCOLN

Saints Peter & Paul

A site for a new church in the Boultham district of Lincoln was bought by Monsignor William Croft in 1916. But it was not until 1944 that a regular Mass centre was opened, served from St. Hugh's. The centre was at first established at Boultham Hall where Mass was said in an upstairs room. In 1948 a storage hut was bought and was erected on the site to serve as a temporary chapel, and was dedicated to St. Peter. This was subsequently enlarged and, in 1958, Mass was said in the hall of St. Peter and St. Paul School which had been opened in 1955. On 2 May 1966 Bishop Ellis laid the foundation stone of the new Church of St Peter and St Paul, which opened the following year. (It was noted that Saints Peter and Paul Church cost almost twice as much as Our Lady of Lincoln Church, completed three years earlier!) Preaching at the consecration of the church on 12 September 1968, the Apostolic Delegate, Archbishop Igino Cardinale, speaking of the Catholic community, reminded the congregation that their sense of community should not be "restricted to these holy precincts. When you leave the walls that now surround you, they must stretch out with you into the troubled world. For although God dwells in this house, he craves much more – to dwell in the temple of your body. The true Catholic must carry the Church with him wherever he goes."

After the closure of St. Hugh's College, Tollerton, in 1986, the statue of Our Lady, the "Faithful Virgin", which had stood in the entrance hall of the college since its earliest years, was brought to Saints Peter and Paul Church. The narthex of the church was remodelled in 2001 by John Halton Design Ltd., who also modified the sanctuary floor and canopy over the tabernacle in 2008.

The parish centre was opened in 1995.

In 2014 a new statue of Our Lady was dedicated in Lincoln Cathedral. This statue was and is a reminder of the city and Cathedral of Lincoln's pre-Reformation dedication to the Mother of God. A number of Catholic parishes and individuals were among those who contributed to the cost of the new statue; this in itself was a gesture of reconciliation between Anglicans and Catholics. As an expression of gratitude, the maquette (preliminary model) of the statue was presented to Mgr. Thomas McGovern by the Dean of Lincoln Cathedral and now occupies a place of honour in St. Peter and St. Paul Church.

Saint Peter and Saint Paul Catholic High School was founded in 1955. It is a mixed Catholic Academy, with Specialist Science College status, serving Lincoln and the wider community. In 2016 there were six hundred pupils on roll including Sixth Formers.

St. Hugh's Primary School transferred here from the centre of Lincoln in 1993.

LONG EATON

St. Francis of Assisi

Long Eaton, the southernmost of the chain of Missions lying along the River Erewash, probably owes its origin to the initiative of Bishop Bagshawe. It dates from a time when the bishop was engaged in bringing the Mass to the outer fringe of population around Nottingham.

In his Quinquennial Report to the Holy See in 1885, Bishop Bagshawe wrote: "A piece of land has been bought at Long Eaton, a place of 6000 inhabitants 8 miles from Nottingham, and an iron church has been built on it lately capable of holding 120 people. There are about 50 Catholics there, who have been much neglected." A church of corrugated-iron had been opened on 4 November 1883. Two years later an attempt was made to establish a resident priest, but the small congregation proved insufficient, and within a year the priest had to leave. Apart from anything else, there had been a lot of opposition to the prospect of having a Catholic church in the town. A series of articles and letters in the 'Long Eaton Advertiser' included a comment to the effect that the priest of Long Eaton had made a mistake in coming to the town. For, one gentleman wrote to the editor: "He may collect a few Irish labourers, a few women and girls, but the Pope's influence will not be very great for some time in Long Eaton because the people have too much good sense."

A second, this time successful, attempt was made in 1895 and since then Long Eaton has always had a resident priest, and it has been a parish in its own right. The presbytery was built in 1923. The lace trade, Long Eaton's staple industry, was in depression, but in spite of this, the building fund for a new church steadily increased "thanks to the energetic efforts of the Men's Committee, well supported by the congregation". The corrugated-iron church which had been supposed to stand for five years had, by 1929, reached the stage where "the rain came in through the roof in places and it was .. so cold that on occasions the holy water and the oil in the sanctuary lamp froze solid!" The foundation stone of the present church was laid on 13 June 1929 and the completed building was opened the following year. The next major development of the church occurred in 1995 in an attempt the better to reflect changes in the Church's thinking and worship in the aftermath of the Second Vatican Council. The result was a dramatic reordering of a modest red brick church of 1930, a reordering which included a curved sanctuary dais, axially placed font with sunken pool and artworks of a high order. In the 1970s a parish hall was built behind the church.

1965 saw the opening of English Martyrs' Primary School with 206 children from the Parishes of Long Eaton and Stapleford. Since the early 1980s pupils have come also from Beeston. In 2013 English Martyrs Catholic Primary School became English Martyrs' Catholic Voluntary Academy.

LONG EATON, *St. Francis of Assisi – Convent*

In 1939 the **Daughters of Divine Charity**, a Religious Congregation of Austrian origin, opened a convent on Acton Road. There they established an independent school; it was known as "St. Marie's". The school closed when the Sisters left the parish in 1964.

Bishop Bagshawe noted, in 1885, that a large piece of land had been given at Long Eaton by Sister Mary Teresa of Jesus (Miss Everitt) a professed Discalced Carmelite, for a house of her Order which she hoped to found on it. It seems that her hopes were not fulfilled!

LOUGHBOROUGH

St. Mary of the Annunciation

There is some evidence that the Leicester Dominicans were active in Loughborough for at least four years before the advent of a resident priest. An extant baptismal certificate shows that there were, and a note added to the certificate states that 'The first meeting place of this body of Christians was in a room over the ironmonger's shop in Mill Street.' If the few local Catholics possessed a meeting-place, it seems probable that this was used, at least occasionally, for Mass. Even before 1829 there were certain private houses which were recognised as Catholic centres. Thus the home of an Irishwoman in the town was used by Fr. Thomas McDonnell of Birmingham when he came, in 1824, to give instructions to Ambrose De Lisle. A year later, on 21 December 1825, he came again to receive the new convert in the home of an Irish paviour outside Loughborough.

In 1833 a convert priest of the Midland District, Fr. Benjamin Hulme, became interested in the spiritual needs of the town. While he was staying with the Dominican Fr. Benedict Caestryck in Leicester, an Irish mother had brought her child in from Loughborough to be baptised. Fr. Hulme learned from her that there were a few Irish Catholics in the town, and he determined to do what he could for them. The tradition in the parish is that, in 1833, Fr. Hulme came to reside at Loughborough; that he lodged first in the public house on the Ashby Road, kept by Mr. McElroy, and said Mass therein. Later he bought a house, and used one room as a chapel until the erection of the church in 1834.

Anti-Catholic feeling seems to have been exceptionally furious in Loughborough. When, in 1834, Fr. Hulme built the first portion of the present church, a certain 'Aristogeiton' published 'An Address to the inhabitants of Loughborough and the vicinity on the erection of a Roman Catholic chapel in the town', and an angry protest appeared also in 'The Times'. In those days, challenges of this sort were not allowed to pass unanswered. Fr. Hulme replied with a 'Counter Address.' Moreover, the abilities of Fr. Hulme as a preacher seem to have won him some sympathy among the members of the Established Church. They formed the greater part of his congregation. Their sympathies, however, were quickly to evaporate when the priest sided with the Dissenters in their opposition to church rates. When his erstwhile supporters withdrew, the congregation was reduced to about a dozen and Fr. Hulme asked the Vicar-Apostolic to replace him by a priest more acceptable to the townsfolk. His work had not, however been in vain, for the registers show sixty-three baptisms performed in his five years as missionary priest.

For the next few years the Mission was in the care of Fr. Norbert Woolfrey of Mount St. Bernard Abbey. His work was fruitful, and the chapel-of-ease at Barrow-on-Soar dates from his time. There was a short interregnum, and then, in 1841, Bishop Walsh handed over the Mission to the Fathers of the Institute of Charity (Rosminians), who have served it ever since.

The Mission benefited enormously by the coming of the Rosminians. Its church was served by a community, and for some years was the most important centre of the Institute of Charity (Rosminians) in England. Four cottages in Hastings Street were bought, and these served as a novitiate from 1841 until it was transferred to Ratcliffe. The first 'Mission' ever given in England was preached at Loughborough in 1843 by Fr. Gentili and Fr. Rinolfi; and in the following year May Devotions were similarly introduced to English Catholics. Conversions followed in unusual numbers. Sixty-three were made after the first 'Mission' of 1843. Nearly a thousand were received into the Church during the long pastorate of Fr. Andrew Egan (1850-1889). Prior to this, during the brief pastorate of Fr. Luigi Gentili, the first priest in England to wear the cassock in the public streets, many of the principal figures of the Second Spring came to Loughborough. Among these were William George Ward, and William Lockhart (the latter was received into the Church at Loughborough in August 1843). Bishop Walsh brought Bishops Briggs and Brown to consult with Gentili in 1844, and the future Cardinal (since 2010, Blessed) John Henry Newman came in 1846.

Anti-Catholic feeling in the town, however, died hard. Fr. Fortunatus Signini had done much by joining forces with an Anglican lawyer to raise relief funds in Loughborough during the severe winter of 1841-1842. But the restoration of the Hierarchy led to a new outbreak in the November of 1850. Effigies of the pope and Cardinal Wiseman were burnt in the market-place. It was some small consolation that the demonstrators came afterwards to the priests and offered to burn the effigies of anybody else whom they might wish!

When Fr. Hulme first mooted the project of building a church, Ambrose de Lisle had pressed for the adoption of the Gothic style. Fr. Hulme, however, insisted on Renaissance architecture, and the first church proved to be inspired by a Leicester concert hall known as the 'Green Room'. The total cost of the church, house and site was met by a loan from Bishop Walsh.

By 1918 this church of 1834 had become inadequate for the congregation, and a building fund was opened. Bishop Dunn insisted that the work should not be begun until half the necessary money had been collected. Five years passed before this condition could be satisfied. The completed church was opened on 26 August 1925. The new portico consisted of a nave, built at right-angles to the old church, which became the sanctuary and transepts. Throughout, the Renaissance characteristics of the old portion were preserved, and a classical portico of monumental proportions makes an imposing frontage on Ashby Road. A new high altar was consecrated in 1933. The altar of Our Lady, Queen of Peace (donated by the Loughborough Sodality of the Children of Mary) and marble altar rails given by parishioners in memory of a former parish priest, were the work of Dinelli Figli of Pietrasanta, Italy. It was, no doubt, to everyone's great relief that the numerous parts of the altar and altar rails having been shipped from Livorno (Leghorn) to Liverpool and then by road to Loughborough were found to be quite intact: it took nine days, under the supervision of a member of the Dinelli family to assemble the various parts.

A Catholic primary school has existed in the parish since the 1840s. The current building on Hastings Street, like its predecessors, was erected in 1987 and is a purpose-built establishment for children aged between 4 and 11 years of age. Our Lady's Convent School, opened in 1844, closed in 2015.

De Lisle Secondary School was opened in 1959 to serve the Catholic community in a wide catchment area covering the whole of North Leicestershire. From its very beginning it has taken pupils from 11 to 18. In 2003, it received 'special science' status and was renamed De Lisle Catholic Science College, and from 2012 has been known as De Lisle College, a Catholic Voluntary Academy.

LOUGHBOROUGH, *St. Mary – Convent*

Rosminian Sisters of Providence

This convent owed its origin to Lady Mary Arundell, widow of Everard, 10th Baron Arundell of Wardour. She had visited Prior Park in 1839, and while there had met the Rosminian Fr. Pagani. Under his direction, she then devoted herself to a life of prayer and works of mercy. Her intention was at first to establish a convent for the Rosminian Sisters at Prior Park. But in the spring of 1843 she bought the property known as Paget House, Woodgate, Loughborough, and went to reside there. A domestic chapel was established in the house. Mass was said for the first time on the Feast of the Seven Dolours, 7 April 1843. This was the title subsequently given to the convent. At Lady Arundell's request, two Sisters were sent from the Mother House at Domodossola, and they arrived at Paget House in October 1843. These Italian Sisters learned enough English to take charge on 25 March 1844 of a school for girls which Lady Arundell had already opened at Paget House. It was the first day-school in England to be taught by nuns.

Lady Arundell died, after a short illness, on 2 June 1845 and was buried at Ratcliffe College of which she had been a notable benefactress. The convent she had founded was already flourishing, and was attracting English novices. Larger premises became necessary, and in 1848 a plot of land not far from the town was bought. The foundation stone of the new convent was laid on 30 May 1848 and the Sisters moved into their new home in what came to be known as Park Road in April 1850. Almost one hundred and sixty years later, they moved to smaller premises in Garton Road in Sacred Heart Parish.

LOUGHBOROUGH

Sacred Heart of Jesus

In the early 1950s land was acquired for a chapel-of-ease in the Shelthorpe district of Loughborough. Prior to the building of the Church of the Sacred Heart, Catholics from this area had been attending Mass in Our Lady's Convent School chapel. The foundation stone of the new building was laid by Bishop Ellis on 18 December 1954, on which occasion the bishop observed that this was the twenty-second time he had carried out such a ceremony in the last seven years. In little more than a year the church was ready for use, and the first Mass was celebrated in it on 19 February 1956, the First Sunday of Lent. The solemn blessing and official opening followed three months later, in May 1956. A history of the parish published to mark its fiftieth anniversary describes in detail some of the efforts that were made to raise funds and to build up the Catholic community in this part of Loughborough. Until Sacred Heart became a separate parish in 1963 and was handed over to diocesan clergy, Rosminians from St. Mary's cared for it. One of the Rosminians, Fr. John Barry, used to cycle over every Sunday morning to say Mass at Sacred Heart. Although the parish was handed over to the care of the diocesan clergy in 1963, the debt owed to the Rosminians who brought it into being should not be forgotten.

A great landmark in the history of this parish was the Ordination to the priesthood of one of its members, Frank Daly, on 18 July 1975. The occasion was made even more memorable by the presence and involvement of a number of children and adults with special needs, ministry to whom has always been a fundamental part of Fr Daly's life.

Sacred Heart Primary School, opened in September 1987, serves the Parishes of Sacred Heart, Loughborough, St Gregory's, Sileby, and The Divine Infant of Prague, Syston. Initially it was on Gray Street but it transferred to its present site on Beacon Road in 1995.

LOUGHBOROUGH, *Sacred Heart of Jesus – Convent*

Rosminian Sisters of Providence moved, in 2009, to Sacred Heart Parish from St. Mary's Parish, where they had been since 1843.

LOUTH

St. Mary

This charming town in North Lincolnshire was not only the starting point of the Lincolnshire Rising in 1536; it was also the birthplace in 1559 of St. Eustace White. Born into a Protestant family, he converted to Catholicism, whereupon he was disowned by his father. Eustace subsequently travelled to Rome to study for the priesthood and was ordained in 1588. Returning to England later that year, the year of the Spanish Armada, he began his ministry just as anti-Catholic feeling was reaching fever pitch. Like many of the priests who came back to England at this period, his ministry did not last long. After a mere three years he was arrested in Dorset. He was brought to London where, after a mock trial, he was sentenced to death and was hanged, drawn and quartered at Tyburn on 10 December 1591. He was one of the 40 Martyrs canonised by Pope Paul VI in 1970.

Almost two centuries later, it is highly probable that Louth had, in 1778, a resident priest. Records show that Fr Lawrence Hall, a Franciscan, died in the town on 12 March 1783. It is not known when he came to Louth, but as no priest is known to have resided at the ancient Heneage chaplaincy at Cadeby (six miles north-north-west of Louth) after 1767, it may be conjectured that the Cadeby chaplain transferred his residence to the town sometime between 1767 and 1783. Half a century before, Louth had five Catholic families to its credit, and there is reason to believe that at the time of the passing of the First Catholic Relief Act (1778) their numbers were still sufficient to explain the presence of a priest in the town.

A chapel of some sort was in existence by 1792, in which year it was registered at the Lindsey Quarter Sessions. It was situated in Eastgate, and was possibly established by Fr. Hall before 1783. There was a local tradition that Mass was said by Fr. Hall in Eastgate in premises which in the 1930s were occupied by the offices of the 'Louth Advertiser.' The tradition may, of course, refer to the later Fr. Henry Hall, who came to Louth in 1832 and remained there for more than thirty years.

There is no record of the residence of the priest between 1783 and 1790. In this latter year a former confessor of King Louis XVI, Fr. Jean Toussaint Alphonse Froment, escaped from the revolutionary tribunals of France and took refuge in Louth at the house of a Dr. Clarke whose daughters had been sent for their education to a French convent. Fr. Froment's exact movements are uncertain. It seems that he said Mass at a house in Westgate not far from the Anglican parish church. This was presumably after 1792, when the chapel in Eastgate was registered. It seems also that he moved to Brigg about the year 1794. But the Mission was never again to be left without a priest. Another émigré priest, Fr. Guy Bertrand, was at Louth from 1807 until his death in 1829. With him the supply of French refugee clergy came to an end. By now the Mission was so firmly established that the Vicar-Apostolic of the Midland District was willing to provide it with a priest.

There is a local tradition that at some time in this period Mass was said 'in the first building on the left through the arch in Ramsgate'. Nothing more than this is known of the existence of a chapel in these years. The main body of the present church was built in 1833 from designs by E. J. Willson, whose brother was Fr. Robert William Willson, priest in Nottingham 1825 to 1844 and subsequently first Bishop of Hobart Town, Tasmania. (Among other Catholic churches designed by E. J. Willson was St. Mary's, Grantham.) The sanctuary of the Louth church was added in 1845 or possibly later. The sacristy was extended in the 1870s. The church has been described as "pretty" (1875) and "handsome" six years later! The presbytery dates from 1835.

In 1860 a stained-glass window designed by a Mr. G.B. Musson was fitted at the west end of the church. It depicted Christ watching the widow casting her mite into the temple treasury, with the figures of St. Patrick and St. Bridget to complete the four lights. Underneath the window was the inscription 'Given to this chapel by the Poor Irish, A.D. MDCCCLX'. The window was a reflection of Catholic life in Louth in the middle part of the nineteenth century, when a large part of the congregation was made up of Irish who had come to work in Louth in the carpet factory which was then in existence. This window no longer survives.

Towards the end of the nineteenth century, Fr. Austin Rowley set up in front of the church a Calvary, but this was stoned to pieces by the anti-Catholic youth of the town.

A school was erected in 1877. In 1879 it had eighty-six pupils and in 1898 forty-one pupils. By 1909 it had ceased to exist, but the exact date of closure cannot be ascertained. In the late 1950s it was hoped to be able to get a community of Religious Sisters to open a convent school in Louth, but this did not materialise.

On 29 May 1920 the town of Louth was severely flooded, and twenty-three people lost their lives. St. Mary's Church, standing halfway up a fairly steep hill, was not directly affected. But the parishioners under the leadership of their parish priest, Fr. Scully, became actively associated with the relief work.

The sanctuary of the church was reordered in 1997, and more recently the church has been fitted out with a good collection of stained-glass partly in memory of Fr. Raymond Mendel, Parish Priest of St. Mary's from 1977 to his death in 2007. There is a modern parish hall behind the presbytery.

LUDDINGTON

St. Dympna

The Premonstratensian Fr. Geudens of Crowle began to say Mass in this village on the Yorkshire border in 1876. The small church was opened on 4 November 1877. Described as "a charming, modest Gothic chapel," it was built to serve the population of poor and mainly Irish agricultural workers who arrived in the Isle of Axholme in the wake of the potato famine in the 1840s. It was dedicated to St. Joseph and St. Dympna (or Dymphna,) an Irish martyr of the seventh century, by the Norbertines (also called Premonstratensians), who had established themselves at nearby Crowle in 1872. As at Crowle, the architects appear to have been Hadfield & Son of Sheffield. It has not been definitively established whether Thomas Young of Kingerby Hall helped finance the project, but this seems likely. However, it was clearly a church built on a low budget.

The bell in the little bell tower on the west gable was cast in 1880 by John Taylor of Loughborough.

From the very beginning it had the status of chapel-of-ease within the Parish of Crowle.

LUTTERWORTH

Our Lady & St. Alphonsus - served from Narborough

Lutterworth is remembered by most people in connection with the fourteenth century reformer, John Wycliffe, who has been described as the 'Day Star of the Reformation.' For Catholics however, in particular those belonging to the Diocese of Nottingham, this small market-town in south-west Leicestershire is significant as the place where Robert Sutton, a native of Burton-on-Trent, served as Anglican rector for several years in the 1570s. One Sunday in 1576 he begged pardon of his startled parishioners for having led them in error, told them there was no hope of eternal salvation outside the Church of Rome, got down from the pulpit, removed his clerical gown, jumped on a horse which had been prepared for him and headed for the continent. After a brief period of study at the English College, Douai, he was ordained priest and almost immediately returned to his native land. Here he laboured for some years until he was arrested in Stafford, where he was tried, condemned to death and hung, drawn and quartered on 27 July 1588. A shrine in his honour was erected in the church in 1949. Robert Sutton was one of the eighty-five martyrs beatified by Pope John Paul II in 1987. Among Blessed Robert's remains was a thumb. This had been in the possession of the Jesuits for some centuries since one of Robert's brothers was a Jesuit. In 1987 this relic was given to the Parish of Lutterworth where it is now venerated.

In post-Reformation times, it was only from 1873 that an occasional weekday Mass was said in Lutterworth by Fr. Martin, chaplain to the Earl of Denbigh at Newnham Paddox, over the Warwickshire border. This meagre arrangement continued for seven years. But the Earl of Denbigh was taking an interest in the infant Mission, and it was reported to the Nottingham Cathedral Chapter on 12 October 1875, that he had offered a house in Lutterworth with the object of establishing there the Oblates of Mary Immaculate. The project, however, did not mature.

A second Catholic peer then became interested in Lutterworth. Lord Braye succeeded to the title and to the family seat of Stanford Hall, four miles to the south-east of Lutterworth, in 1879 and immediately began the erection of a domestic chapel. In 1880 he brought Fr. Alfred Hazeland to serve the market-town and at the same time to be domestic chaplain at Stanford Hall. The dual arrangement was not entirely a success. But the stipend paid by Lord Braye undoubtedly enabled a priest to be kept in what otherwise would have been a financially impossible position.

Fr. Hazeland reported to the bishop in April 1880 that he had no practising Catholics, and no property, moveable or immovable. His Mass centre was at first 'a wretched loft over the stables in one of the inns of the town, lighted by sky lights and protected only by a roof, which was not proof against the inclemency of the weather.' The inn referred to appears to have been the Denbigh Arms.

Early in 1881 the Earl of Denbigh presented the Mission with the present site of three and a quarter acres on Bitteswell Road. On this site, a modest church, one of a number of dual purpose school-chapels said to have been designed by Christopher Wray, a brother-in-law of Bishop Bagshawe, was opened on 11 August 1881. (Another source says that the church was designed by Fr. Hazeland who, prior to his ordination, had been articled to an architect.) Although the church has been largely submerged by modern additions, something of the character of the original building survives inside. The Earl of Denbigh was one of the contributors to the cost of the presbytery and the church, but most of the money came from Fr. Hazeland's own patrimony.

By 1883 (and possibly from 1881) the chapel was also used as a day-school. This was run at an annual loss, borne by the priest himself, and in 1895 had no more than six pupils, of whom three were non-Catholic. It was therefore closed in 1895 or shortly afterwards.

A sacristy was added to the church in 1949. This was felt to be an improvement since "from time immemorial the priest had to vest in the presbytery."

In 1898 Fr. Hazeland was described as being "very infirm". In spite of this he survived for another forty-two years, dying in March 1940 at the age of ninety-two, having spent sixty years at Lutterworth! Fr. Hazeland (he became an honorary canon in 1930) used to delight in telling the story of how, when he was a young man, no insurance company would give him a policy because, they said, there was something wrong with his heart. In fact, until he was in his seventies, he used to cycle, averaging about a thousand miles a year.

During the Second World War, the number of Catholics in the Lutterworth area increased considerably since children had been evacuated from Sacred Heart Elementary School, Hammersmith, and Irishmen were working in the construction industry. For the latter group, a week-long 'Mission' was preached in September 1942 in the nearby village of Bruntingthorpe where most of them were housed. Mass was celebrated each morning at 6.30, and in the evening there were Devotions. It was noted that the contractors, Messrs. Wimpey and Co., did much to help in the success of the week.

LUTTERWORTH, - *Convent*

A community of **Poor Clare Colettines**, exiled from France because of the anti-religious laws, opened a convent in Bank Street in September 1911. The French Sisters returned to the Diocese of La Rochelle in 1922. Hope was expressed that the Poor Clares would be able to continue in Lutterworth since "a sufficient number of English ladies had joined the community". This hope was not to be realised, and the community was dispersed in 1925 or 1926. Before the 1920s were over, a group of Poor Clares came from Levenshulme, Manchester, to Nottingham and settled in Bulwell where they remain to this day.

MABLETHORPE

St. Joseph

The first Mission at Mablethorpe seems to have been a private enterprise on the part of Monsignor Gilbert Vincent Bull. In 1906 while Missionary Priest of Louth, he opened a Mass centre, where

Mass was said on Sundays during the holiday season. In the following year he built a small church, apparently at his own expense. He resigned the Mission of Louth in 1909 and for the next four years lived in Mablethorpe in a residence styled 'The Hermitage'. In 1913 he went to live abroad. Monsignor Bull rented 'The Hermitage' to a Mr. and Mrs. Webb with the request that they would do whatever they could to provide spiritual and material support for the troops stationed along the Lincolnshire coast. For several years the Webbs worked unceasingly for the soldiers, obtaining priests from various sources to minister to their needs; furthermore, the Webbs provided hospitality both by way of refreshments after Sunday Mass and by various social events. In 1918 Monsignor Bull sold 'The Hermitage' to a Church of England clergyman, Mr. Larkin, who eventually sold it to the Nottingham Holiday Home for Cripples. But Mass continued to be said at this seaside resort during the season until 1920.

For the next four years there is no record of any Mass centre in Mablethorpe. However, in 1924 the Capuchin Fathers of Panton reopened it on the same seasonal basis. A temporary chapel in Seaholme Road, commonly known as "the Catholic Hut", was opened in 1931. It was dedicated to Our Lady of Victories and was henceforth served from Louth. Monsignor Bull died in October 1937. In his will he left a substantial sum for the erection of a new church in Mablethorpe. With the help of this and other funds which had been collected, the foundation stone of the present church, a simple, well-proportioned brick structure dedicated to St. Joseph, was able to be laid by Bishop McNulty on 11 August 1938, and the church was opened the following year. The opening ceremony, carried out by Fr. Louis Drury of Louth, was described in eloquent terms. "The church .. stands within hearing distance of the constant roar of the sea, and it is here that Catholics not only from Mablethorpe and Louth but those from the large towns holidaying at this resort will kneel together in prayer." The original entrance to the church is flanked by holy water stoups said to be of twelfth century date and to come from Louth Abbey. If they are medieval, they have been heavily restored.

Mablethorpe has the distinction of having the first shrine to Our Lady of Fatima to be erected in England; it dates from 1937 during a period when Mablethorpe was being served by the Parish Priest of Louth.

At the beginning of the twenty-first century, the parish community, having for some time felt the need for a small meeting area, decided to build a large narthex which, while enhancing the external appearance of the church, could fulfil this and related purposes.

Mablethorpe was erected as an independent parish in 1956 and has had a resident priest since that time.

MANSFIELD

St. Philip Neri

The dedication of this parish is a reminder that it was the first to be founded by Bishop Bagshawe after he had come from the Oratory of St. Philip Neri to be Nottingham's third Bishop. He was enabled to do this through the generosity of a Mrs. Susanna White, who bought and placed at his disposal in 1876, a property known as The Manor House, situated in Ratcliffe Gate. The house was immediately adapted for use as a chapel, and opened for Sunday Mass in 1876. The property was conveyed to the bishop in June 1877, and by him to the diocesan trustees twelve years later.

Prior to that date, the Catholic life of the district had been desperately neglected. Some few baptisms from Mansfield are recorded in the Spinkhill registers up to 1862. From time to time the town seems to have come under the responsibility of the priest at Ilkeston. When Fr. Arthur McKenna was appointed to that Mission in 1860, he opened various Mass centres, one of which was at a house in Chandler's Court in Mansfield. But there is nothing to show that Mass was ever possible on a Sunday, or that it continued after Fr. McKenna's departure in 1863.

A priest was first appointed to reside in Mansfield in 1877. On 10 July of that year, a community of Sisters of Mercy from Nottingham took possession of the Manor House and opened a school. The Manor House, serving as a chapel, convent and school all-in-one, became somewhat overcrowded. In 1878 a chapel was built in the grounds. It was designed by Christopher Wray of London (Bishop Bagshawe's brother-in-law), and was in the form of a school-chapel - a standard type of building in the diocese for many years to come. In 1879 it was noted that "the school is managed by the Sisters of Mercy and is attended by 120 children, most of them being still Protestants." Was there an unspoken hope that the Protestant children wouldn't still be Protestants by the time they left the school? Six years later we read that "the Mission has a large school-chapel .... It is situated on the bishop's personal property, but the chapel, with a right of way to it, has been given to the Mission. A large house adjoining the chapel has been divided into two houses, and a half of it forms the presbytery." By this stage the school had 208 pupils. The Sisters of Mercy, who taught in the school, lived in one of the divisions of the house adjoining the chapel. They had a small chapel of their own, in which Mass was said, and the Blessed Sacrament was reserved during the week. In 1927 new schools were built to replace the original one of 1877.

Collections for a site on Chesterfield Road for a church and ancillary buildings were begun in 1907, and the land was finally purchased – through a third party – two years later. The economic conditions and the First World War prevented Fr. Joseph Prince from building the new church. During this time Fr. Prince and the laity of Mansfield were heavily involved in work with the soldiers at Clipstone Military Camp. Nothing further was done until Fr. Charles Payne arrived in April 1921 to take charge of the parish. The financial effort that followed was extraordinary. Bishop Dunn laid the foundation stone of the new church on 6 June 1923. The completed building – described as "Mansfield's answer to the London Oratory" and as "a bold and triumphant exercise in Italian Baroque" - was consecrated, debt-free, on 24 March 1925. It was on this occasion that Fr. Payne was appointed Vicar General of the diocese. He was to serve in this role under three bishops until his death in December 1944.

A prominent feature of the church's interior decoration, completed in 1934, is the use of copies of paintings of the Italian School for the walls and half-dome of the sanctuary. While this work was being done, the church was closed for a while and was reopened in December 1934. The work must have been very impressive since it was suggested that "After, perhaps the wonderful Blessed Sacrament Chapel in St. Barnabas' Cathedral, the roof of St. Philip Neri's Church is by far the richest piece of decoration in the Midlands." In the 1990s an extensive programme of restoration was undertaken which necessitated the church being closed for almost a year.

Even at the time of its opening this church was far from adequate for the needs of a vast parish, which, besides the Borough of Mansfield, included the Urban Districts of Mansfield Woodhouse, Sutton-in-Ashfield and Kirkby-in-Ashfield as well as a number of colliery villages. St. Philip's was then the only Catholic church for a civil population of well over a hundred thousand. Before long, St. Philip's had a chapel-of-ease at Kirkby-in-Ashfield (1923) – this became an independent parish in 1947. Two years later the priest was withdrawn from Kirkby, and it reverted to the status of a chapel-of-ease to Mansfield. But from 1972 it has, once again, had its own priest. Sutton-in-Ashfield was also established as a Mass centre from St. Philip Neri's (1931). It became an independent parish in 1956 but from 2012 has been served from Kirkby-in-Ashfield. From 1955 to 1971 Mansfield Woodhouse served as a chapel-of-ease to St. Philip Neri's. In 1963 the Parish of St. George, Rainworth, was erected from part of St. Philip Neri's, and shortly afterwards Forest Town was further detached from the same parish.

St. Philip Neri with St. Bede Catholic Voluntary Academy was formed by the amalgamation of St. Philip Neri First School with St. Bede's Middle School in 1984. The school is housed in the former St. Bede's building and was completely refurbished in 1986. In 2016 it was one of the largest schools in the Diocese of Nottingham with 420 on roll including a 78 place nursery.

All Saints Secondary School was opened in 1974 and became part of the Aquinas Catholic Academy Trust in 2014.

MANSFIELD, *St. Philip Neri – Convents*

Sisters of Mercy opened a branch house from Nottingham in 1877 and took up residence in the Manor House. An account of their work in the school is given above. Part of the agreement between the diocesan trustees and the Sisters in 1904 was that the Sisters should have "spiritual advantages – daily Mass etc. in return for their providing oil, wine, candles, linen, etc. for the use of the altar and chapel - also cleaning and keeping in repair". In 1926 the Sisters moved from Ratcliffe Gate to Norfolk Drive where they remained until 1974 when, due to, among other things, shortage of personnel, they returned to their Nottingham house.

A **Carmelite** Convent was opened at Crow Hill Drive in 1926, but moved to Offcote Hurst, near Ashbourne, in 1948.

Daughters of Our Lady of Good Counsel (Vocation Sisters) came to Mansfield in 1975 to the premises vacated by the Sisters of Mercy. The Sisters left Mansfield in 1987.

MANSFIELD

St. Patrick
(Forest Town)

St. Patrick, Forest Town, began as a chapel-of-ease from St Philip Neri in Mansfield. In 1956 a former Methodist chapel in Clipstone Road was acquired for Catholic use, with a view to redeveloping the site with a purpose-built church and presbytery. St. Patrick was made a separate parish in 1958. When the parish was erected, the Mass centre of St. George, Blidworth (established in the 1940s), was attached to it. The presbytery was completed in August 1964. The original church was converted into a parish hall - cum - social club, and a presbytery was built to one side of the site. The foundation stone of the present church, which has been described as "an economical design which is given some interest by its hexagonal plan form and varied roof profiles," was laid by Bishop McGuinness in February 1989 and was opened by him a mere four months later. The church occupies a large corner site on the main road through Forest Town, on the edge of the shopping area. There is a Methodist church and an old farmhouse opposite, the latter a reminder of the agricultural past of what is now a suburban area.

The parish also has a primary school which opened on 6 September 1966 with one hundred and thirty-four children. In time the parish began its own chapel-of-ease at Rainworth (1960) which, along with New Ollerton, it still serves.

MARKET BOSWORTH

Our Lady & St. Gregory
– forms part of South West Leicestershire Team Ministry

South-westwards from Charnwood Forest and Coalville to the Warwickshire border, Leicestershire tails off in an untidy tangle of small villages with poor communications. The largest of these is Market Bosworth. The Battle of Bosworth took place to the south of the town in 1485 as the final battle in the Wars of the Roses between the House of Lancaster and the House of York. Following the discovery of the remains of King Richard III in Leicester in 2012, the king's funeral cortège passed through the town on its way to Leicester Cathedral for his reburial on 22 March 2015.

A small Catholic congregation was formed in Market Bosworth - by the chances of time rather than by any explicit apostolic effort. Fr. Leonard Middleton of Earl Shilton said Mass once a month at the Red Lion in 1923-1924. The parish website noted in 2014, that "Catholics still meet at the Red Lion but now it is to sample its wares rather than for religious purposes." After Fr. Middleton's departure, the centre was apparently continued by the priests who served Earl Shilton, though for the next seven years this parish was itself often without a resident priest. From 1929 to 1931 the Mass centre was at the house of Mrs. Trivett, and was served (as also was Earl Shilton) from Coalville.

It seems that the initiative in building the present church, opened in 1931, came from Fr. Joseph Degen of Coalville. The land for the church was given by Sir Arthur Wheeler - a non-Catholic himself - but his sister, Mrs. Sutton, was a convert and it was she who donated the statue of the Madonna and Child which she brought back from Lourdes. The statue remains above the front door of the church for all to see. At the time of its opening, the church had capacity for 65 people, but this increased to some 200 following extensions given planning permission in 1975. In February 1933 an agricultural training centre for Catholic unemployed young men was opened nearby at Westfields Farm by the Midland Catholic Land Association. The farm comprised 188 acres, with a house for warden, chaplain and trainees. It closed before 1939.

For several years from 1964, the Holy Ghost Fathers had their house of studies at Wellsborough several miles west of Market Bosworth. Prior to this, their house of studies had been at Upton near Newark. Upton then became the novitiate.

MARKET HARBOROUGH

Our Lady of Victories

The Parish of Market Harborough has some claim to be considered the lineal descendant of the Penal Times chaplaincy, six miles to the north-east, at Neville Holt. A priest had resided with the Nevilles until 1848. From this year his place was taken by a visiting priest. The Dominicans from Leicester were serving the domestic chapel once a month in 1858, and in this year they opened a Mass centre at Market Harborough. The new centre seems to have been considered sufficient provision for the district, and the following year regular services at Neville Holt stopped. There is also a financial connection. Of the money spent eventually on the church at Market Harborough, slightly more than half was left for the purpose by the Frenchman, Fr. Nicholas Malvoisin, the last chaplain of Neville Holt, and the remainder was provided by a legacy of Miss Christina Neville.

The first Mass centre was in a small cottage, lent by Mr James Flint and adapted for use as a temporary chapel. Records show that in 1872-1873 the chapel (perhaps the same as that of 1858) was 'on the upper floor of a small cottage'; and from 1873 to 1877 they describe it as situated in a house on Western Terrace. A further note in the records shows that there was a small orphanage for girls attached to the Mission in 1869-1972, but no further information is available.

Fr. Richard Vandepitte came to reside in the town in 1872. Mr. Flint, trustee of the Mission funds left by Fr. Malvoisin and Miss Neville, presented him with a building site, and work on the church and schools began in 1876. Christopher Wray, a brother-in-law of Bishop Bagshawe, was the architect of the church the foundation stone of which was laid on 21 September 1876. On 16 August of the following year the new church and schools were opened with some considerable ceremony. The Bishop of Northampton celebrated the Mass; the Bishop of Nottingham was also present and Cardinal Manning performed the opening, preaching also in the evening. Originally the church was called 'St. Mary's'. This was because it was intended to house a seventeenth century statue from Flanders, and to become a place of pilgrimage. But this idea was abandoned since Market Harborough was felt to be geographically too remote for general easy access. The dedication was then changed to 'Our Lady of Victories', and opinions differ as to why this title was given. One suggestion is that it was the choice of Cardinal Manning, whose own Pro-Cathedral in Kensington had this title. In 1894 Peter Paul Pugin was employed to oversee a redecoration of the church and some additions to the buildings including the link between the church and presbytery. The work was completed in 1898 and partly paid for by Sir Humphrey de Trafford. The church was consecrated by Bishop Ellis on 5 May 1949. The church (and the presbytery, with the linking cloister) were listed Grade II in 1977. In 1979 an octagonal community centre, in the same style as St. Barnabas' Cathedral Hall, was built at the north end of the site to the designs of Eberlin & Partners, Nottingham. In 2001 the firm of John Halton Design was appointed to oversee a substantial enlargement of the church. The work was completed in 2005. It now represents a very interesting fusion of Victorian and twenty-first century Gothic architecture.

The primary school dates from the same time as the church. Additions were made to the school in 1910 and again in 1948. When the Presentation Sisters took over the running of the school in 1954, it was an all-age school ranging from 4 to 15 years with 230 on roll. There were seven classrooms, two of them in the dilapidated building attached to the presbytery, and the other five in huts in a nearby youth centre. Later the seniors were housed in a hall on Northampton Road, about twenty minutes' walk from the main school. In 1970 a new St. Joseph's Primary School was built on a separate site and the old school buildings were taken over for community use. The first phase of the present St. Joseph's Primary School was occupied in 1970. St. Joseph's converted to academy status in 2012 and now forms part of the Corpus Christi Catholic Academy Trust. In 2016 there were 195 pupils on roll at St. Joseph's with a maximum capacity of 210.

MARKET HARBOROUGH - *Convents*

Sisters of the Nativity opened a boarding school for girls in 1906, and remained there until 1918 when the Sisters moved to Leicester.

Presentation Sisters arrived in Market Harborough in May 1954 to provide teaching staff for St. Joseph's School. For the first few months they lodged with the Vocation Sisters at Hallaton Hall some eight miles away, from where they travelled by train each day to Market Harborough until they were able to move into their convent on Coventry Road in December of the same year. In addition to their work in the school, the Sisters gave religious instruction to the children at the American Air Base at Husbands Bosworth. Fr. Douglas Key, Parish Priest of Market Harborough in the 1950s, frequently took them to other villages in the parish so that the people could get a glimpse of 'his' nuns! Although no longer involved in the school, Presentation Sisters still perform apostolic work in the parish from the convent on Coventry Road.

Daughters of Our Lady of Good Counsel (often known as the Vocation Sisters) were founded, in 1945, by Edna John (Mother Mary Joseph). Their purpose was the discernment, fostering, and nurturing of religious and priestly vocations through giving talks, showing films, mounting exhibitions, advising religious orders, and so on. In the 1960/70s they began their ministry of counselling religious and clergy.

In 1951 needing larger premises, the Vocation Sisters bought Hallaton Hall, near Market Harborough, Leicestershire, where they were able to provide accommodation for twelve people considering their vocation in an atmosphere of prayer. They were also able to expand their other ministries, particularly in encouraging and advising Religious in their own search for vocations. On 25 September 1962 the Daughters of Our Lady of Good Counsel were canonically erected by Bishop Ellis as a Congregation. The Sisters left Hallaton in 1976.

MARKET RASEN

Holy Rood

In all but name Market Rasen can be considered as a foundation of Penal Times. The town had never been without its congregation of Catholics, who had heard Mass in the chapels maintained on the Constable estate at West Rasen or at Kingerby Hall, which had come into possession of the Knight family in 1702. One member of this family was Fr. Richard Knight SJ (1720-1793), who was Rector of the Jesuits' Lincolnshire District. It was he who, in 1782, established the Mission at Market Rasen, replacing that at Kingerby. In the same year Fr. Knight built at Market Rasen a presbytery with a chapel on the upper floor; and Fr. James Leslie SJ, previously at West Rasen, moved to Market Rasen as the first resident priest. His Mission and congregation remained the same; it was only the seat of administration which had changed.

In 1824 during the long and heroic pastorate of the Carmelite Fr. Francis Willoughby Brewster (born in 1770, he died in 1849), a new chapel, separate from the presbytery, was built on a more convenient site and still remains the nucleus of the present church of Holy Rood. It was opened on 14 September 1824.

The church was significantly altered when Fr. Algernon Moore (at Market Rasen 1867-1875) added north and side aisles and a tower from designs by Hadfield & Son of Sheffield. In spite of the piecemeal construction, the resultant church was architecturally successful. The interior has a Byzantine aspect and the capitals of the columns which separate the nave from the aisles are carved with a care unusual in the late nineteenth century. The exterior is of brick Gothic, apparently by Hadfield & Son of Sheffield, the architects who designed the church at Gainsborough in the 1860s. The cost of the enlargement was borne mainly by Mr. T. G. Young of Middle Rasen, a major benefactor of church building projects including the chapel at Osgodby.

The presbytery is unusually large. One tradition says that the Jesuits (who served the Mission until 1859) added the extra rooms in 1850 in order to accommodate some of their students. Another account attributes the extensions to Monsignor Thomas Sing (1859-1864), possibly with a view to establishing a diocesan seminary at Market Rasen, although this never materialised. In his Report to Rome in 1860, Bishop Roskell noted that Market Rasen possessed "an adequate church and school."

In 1975 the sanctuary was reordered to bring it into line with post-Vatican II liturgical requirements. Problems with internal valley gutters and subsequent timber decay led to a decision in about 1980 to remove the nave and aisle roofs and replace them with a large new roof of single span.

The Mission once had what was probably the oldest post-Reformation school in the diocese. Records show that this existed in 1780 - two years before the first chapel was erected. The school was closed sometime between 1893 and 1896.

After the departure of the Jesuits in 1859, the Mission was served by diocesan priests until 1949. In this year it was handed over to the Sacred Heart Fathers as a missionary centre from which they served Mass centres and where also was the headquarters of the Diocesan Motor (Travelling) Mission. The last Sacred Heart Father, Fr. Philip Bailey, a renowned historian, retired to Crowle after thirty-one years as Parish Priest of Market Rasen. The parish was then handed back to the care of the diocesan clergy.

Within the Parish of Market Rasen resides a **Diocesan Hermit**, Rachel Denton, who after a period of formation, made her Solemn Profession to Bishop Malcolm McMahon in November 2006.

MARKET WARSOP

St. Theresa – served from St. Philip Neri, Mansfield

This urban district of over ten thousand people lies at the crossing of the River Meden, five miles north of Mansfield on the Worksop road. From 1942 Mass was celebrated each Sunday by the priest of

Shirebrook, which lies three and a half miles to the west. The Hetts Lane Infant School was used as a Mass centre until 1947, and from that date until 1956 Mass was said in the Club Room of the Plough Inn.

In December 1956 Monsignor William Eric Grasar, then Vicar General of the Diocese of Nottingham and subsequently Bishop of Shrewsbury, blessed and opened a dual-purpose prefabricated timber building on High Street. At the time this was sufficient for the needs of the Catholic congregation there, and it was served by the priest from Shirebrook.

A new church was built and opened in time for Easter 1973. Consecrated on 20 February 1974, it was one of a series of churches in the diocese designed by John Rochford, who experimented with a variety of interesting roof forms. Taking full advantage of the steeply sloping site on Main Street, a hall was built underneath the church with access by external steps from the main door of the church. In October 1974 Market Warsop ceased to be served from Shirebrook and, along with Mansfield Woodhouse (taken from St. Philip Neri, Mansfield), became an independent parish. It continued as such until 1992 when, due to a shortage of priests, Market Warsop ceased to be an independent parish and was attached initially to St. Philip Neri, Mansfield and, from 2011, once again to Shirebrook.

MARKET WARSOP - *Convent*

Presentation Sisters established a convent in Market Warsop in 1986. In the 1990s they moved into the presbytery on Clumber Street from where they continue to play an active role in the life of the parish and community.

MARPLE BRIDGE

St. Mary

Situated at the point where the River Goyt takes up the waters of the Etherow before passing into Cheshire, Marple Bridge is by nature of some geographical importance among the western valleys of the Peak

District. It came within the sphere of activity of Fr. John Joseph Collins of New Mills (1839-1853) who was a notable apostle of the Vale of the Goyt. The present congregation may trace its continuous history back to 1848, in which year he established a Mass centre on the northern fringe of Marple Bridge at Compstall Road.

Although this venture was abandoned in 1850, Mass was said occasionally in private houses of the district until the arrival of Fr. Luke Livermore in New Mills in 1858. He was a Cistercian who, having worked in Hobart, Tasmania, with Bishop Willson, on his return to England took up pastoral work in the Diocese of Nottingham; and he made the foundation of the Mission at Marple the work of the last years of his life. In 1858 he established a Mass centre and before the close of 1859 was successful in building the present church, to which he was immediately transferred as its first missionary priest.

Financially, the enterprise was made possible only through the generosity of Lord Edward Fitzalan Howard, later 1st Baron Howard of Glossop. Besides bearing the main expenses of erecting the church, he for more than twenty years provided an annual stipend for the priest. When Fr. Livermore died in 1875, he left behind a parish of unusual solidity and stability - evidenced by the long years spent by successive priests in this Mission, where they have not infrequently remained until death.

If undistinguished in style, the somewhat squat Church of St. Mary is solidly built in Derbyshire stone and is devotional in appearance. The church was opened on 21 December 1859, but not consecrated until 17 May 1945. The delay in consecration is possibly to be explained by the fact that the church was leased from Lord Howard to the diocese in 1876 for 999 years. The church was defined as a private chapel until Lord Howard conveyed it to the diocese in 1921. In 1938 the interior of the church was redecorated by Hardman & Co. and oak panelling installed in the sanctuary, carved by Douglas Renwick of Hyde. The parish hall was built in 1935 in the pastorate of Fr. Louis du Boulaye.

In 1967 'Top' Marple, on the other side of the River Goyt, was cut off from Marple Bridge to form a new parish in the Shrewsbury Diocese.

The extensive grounds include a lawned garden and trees on the west side of the church and a burial ground, in use and extended in 2005, along the north side of the site adjoining a stream. A private path over the stream connects the church with the primary school to the north. A large tarmac car park laid out for ball games fills part of the slope between church and parish hall.

St. Mary's School was established before 1860 when a single stone-built classroom, for children aged 5-14, was added to the existing church building. This was a decade before the 1870 Education Act which proposed elementary education for all children. It was prophetic in meeting the needs of the time. The school then provided for the influx of Irish Catholics, who settled in large numbers and were instrumental in building our canals and railways. A similar classroom added in 1881 enabled the infant children to have a room of their own. For years this accommodation sufficed, and was thought to be luxurious in comparison to educational standards of the time.

During the Second World War, when the Channel Islands were under German occupation, the school was shared with a group of children who came to the district accompanied by two teaching Sisters from St. Peter Port, Guernsey.

After many years of hard campaigning, by the parish and school, the present St. Mary's School was built in three separate phases. Three classrooms were opened in 1970, followed by the hall, kitchen and administration wing in 1972. The building was completed in 1974 with the addition of an "Open-Plan" department. Most of the pupils of St. Mary's go on to Harrytown High School in the Diocese of Shrewsbury for their secondary education.

MARPLE BRIDGE, *St. Mary - Convent*

For over thirty years the parish had a convent of the **Faithful Companions of Jesus** - their only foundation in the diocese. It was opened in 1901 in Hollins Lane, moved in 1929 to nearby Mill Brow, and closed in 1932. A day and boarding school for girls was attached to the convent.

MATLOCK

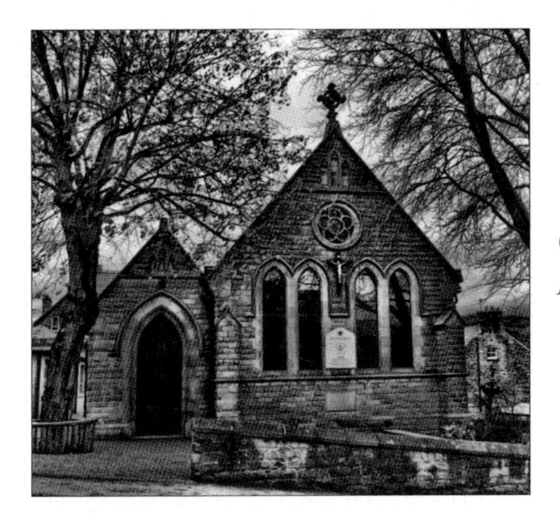

Our Lady and St. Joseph

This Mission is one of several founded by Monsignor Arthur McKenna of St. Mary's, Derby. On 23 April 1880 he said the first (as far as is known) post-Reformation Mass in an upper room of a house in Holt

Terrace, Dale Road, and Mass was celebrated on Sundays from that time. The same year, the site on which the church now stands was purchased. The church was built three years later and opened, on 16 July 1883, by Bishop Bagshawe with a Mass at which the choir from St. Mary's, Derby, sang Mozart's Mass No, 1. The church is a well-proportioned stone building in the Pointed Style. Monsignor McKenna had a devotion to St. Dismas, the Good Thief, and from the earliest years of the new Mission gathered funds to erect an oratory in his honour. He persevered in his project and in 1885 the Matlock church was enlarged by the addition of its unusual chapel of St Dismas. (The stained-glass window in this chapel is inscribed 'St. Dimas'.) The sanctuary was added in 1903 and the apse in 1934. The church was consecrated by Bishop McNulty in June 1935.

In 1884 a further piece of land was bought for a presbytery which was completed in 1896.

A parish hall was built in 1967, and the church liturgically reordered in 1969. Recent work has included the rebuilding of the parish hall in 2001.

Presentation Sisters opened a boarding school in 1927. This closed in 1989 and St. Joseph's Primary School, housed in the 'day' part of the former convent school, was opened in September 1990. At the time of the opening, thanks were expressed to the Presentation Sisters for their "love, support and generosity" in making these premises available.

MATLOCK - *Convent*

The P**resentation Sisters** came to Matlock in 1927. They bought Chesterfield House, a large property high above the town, overlooking the Derwent valley from the east. The house was renamed 'Mount St Joseph' and became an independent secondary school for day-girls and boarders. This was to be the first boarding school in England run by the Presentation Sisters. The school made great progress, and by the end of the first term (1927) it had 165 boarders. In July 1961 Cardinal Godfrey, Archbishop of Westminster, came to Matlock to be installed as Cardinal Protector of the Presentation Sisters The school continued to expand, and in 1962 a further building, Lilybank Hydro, was purchased; this provided, among other things, accommodation for the Nagle Preparatory School. In 1989 the convent school was closed. The 'boarding' part of the premises was turned into a nursing home – now known as the Presentation Care Home, and the 'day' part houses St. Joseph's Primary School. In addition to the Presentation Care Home, which also has provision for elderly priests, the Sisters have an archive and heritage centre housed in the laundry of the former girls' school.

MEASHAM

St. Charles Borromeo - served from Ashby-de-la-Zouch.

The sinking of coal-pits near this small village on the south-western borders of Leicestershire brought a number of Catholic miners to Measham. The Countess of Loudoun, living a few miles away at Willesley Hall, built a small church for their use. This church, first proposed in May 1881, was opened in December 1881. Designed by Christopher Wray, a brother-in-law of Bishop Bagshawe, it was a fine example of the school-chapel type of building characteristic of the latter part of the nineteenth century. It was served for two years from Lutterworth. From 1883 a priest resided in Measham in a house adjacent to the church purchased by Lady Loudoun for this purpose and was maintained by the Countess as her private chaplain. Until the death of the Countess of Loudoun in 1915, the church remained her personal property, but then was conveyed to the diocese.

On weekdays the church was used as a school. School logbooks survive from 1905 when the first pupil was admitted, and they tell a fascinating story of life in a village school in the early part of the twentieth century. The church building continued to serve this dual-purpose until the early 1960s when the present school was built on land behind the church and officially opened in July 1963.

The parish was not regarded as being too stressful a place for a priest to live and work. This is illustrated by the fact that Fr. Leo Moens, a Belgian priest, came to Measham in July 1916, initially for three months' rest. He remained for thirty-nine years and lived for another five years after his retirement! However, it cannot have been too easy for him in the early years since the diocesan yearbook for 1923 observed that: "Measham was nearly a dead parish until, at a special congregational meeting in 1922, the people promised their parish priest to put their shoulders to the wheel. The result up to the present time [1923] has been splendid in the increased attendance at Mass, generosity and good will." In 1941 there was a double celebration:

sixty years since the church was built, and twenty-five years since the arrival of Fr. Moens to whom a presentation was made. In reply, Fr. Moens said that "nothing spectacular had been accomplished during his twenty-five years [in Measham], but he thanked Almighty God that he had been able to minister to his people during that period, in a small and poor mining town." Fr. Moens was appointed an honorary canon of the diocese in 1957.

Understandably, after more than a century the original church building was showing signs of wear and tear. After much consultation and a certain amount of heartbreak on the part of those who had worshipped there for many years as had – in some cases – several generations of their families, the decision was taken to demolish the church and presbytery and replace the church with a church-cum-hall. As a reminder of the past, many of the artefacts from the original church were transferred to the new building which was opened on 17 April 2008.

MELBOURNE

Our Lady of Mercy and St. Philip Neri

The Mission at Melbourne owes its origin to the generosity of Lord Walter and Lady Amabel Kerr. Lord Walter and Lady Amabel had come into possession of Melbourne Hall on the death of Earl Cowper, Lady Amabel's brother. Within a few days of their arrival in Melbourne (May 1906) they converted the loft of a disused laundry building to serve as a temporary chapel. The first Mass was said on 6 May 1906 in this building, subsequently known as the Tea Rooms. Benediction of the Blessed Sacrament was given for the first time on 1 July 1906.

Lady Amabel Kerr had intended from the first to provide a permanent church, but she died within six months of the first Mass. The foundation stone of the present church was laid by Bishop Brindle on 19 July 1907 and the completed building opened on 10 May 1908. The following year the Lady Chapel was lined with oak panelling made in Belgium: this was given in memory of Lady Amabel by members of her family. In November 1929 oak panelling was erected in the sanctuary as a memorial to Lord Walter Kerr who had died in May 1927.

The Log Book of the Catholic Church, Melbourne, begins in 1906 and continues, with a number of gaps, until 1956. It contains various pieces of information, including ministry to the German prisoners held at Donington Hall during the First World War (they left finally in October 1919) and details of when successive parish priests took their holidays and who replaced them. We learn also that the first 'sewing meeting' was held at Rose Cottage, Penn Lane, on 27 September 1923: that on 31 January 1924, Miss G. Earp, Warden of the Guild of the Blessed Sacrament, was presented with an umbrella on her leaving Melbourne. Regarding an altar boys' outing to Matlock in October 1924, we learn, among other things, that the boys went to the pictures in the Hydro at Matlock where they saw "How to educate a wife." Comings and goings of various members of the Kerr family are noted also. And so on.

A priest has been resident in Melbourne since 1907. The addition of a presbytery was completed in December 1909. This, together with the church and all their furnishings, were provided at the expense of Lord Walter Kerr, GCB. Lord Walter and his wife, whose direct descendants are still living in Melbourne Hall, had been previously responsible for the establishment of the Parish of Eastwood. The church and presbytery remained in the ownership of the Kerr family until 1982 when they were handed over to the diocese. The priest of Melbourne has always been responsible for the Catholic community in Castle Donington.

MELTON MOWBRAY

St. John

Early editions of the 'Catholic Directory' give some racy notices concerning the foundation of this Mission. That of 1838 expresses the hope that in the following spring the building of a church will begin on a site at the Nottingham Road end of Melton. It continues: 'An orator, at a Reformation meeting which was [recently] held here, told the saints of Melton that there should not be a Catholic chapel in their town; but the Catholics of the town and neighbourhood appear determined to make him turn out a false prophet.' The 'saints of Melton' apparently gained some temporary success, for the edition of the 'Catholic Directory' of the following year states that the church could not be built because of 'religious prejudice interfering to prevent the land being sold for that purpose.' The same edition of the Catholic Directory added that "another site, equally eligible, had been purchased" and that "the funds for the erection are small, and will scarcely justify [the Catholics of Melton] in commencing, unless assisted by the charity of their friends"; and it goes on to give the names of those to whom donations could be sent.

Most probably the original congregation was largely comprised of Irish immigrants. But possibly there were some few whose families had kept the Faith from earlier Catholic centres in the neighbourhood. Of these centres, the most important was Eastwell, five miles north of Melton. But there were also Ashby Folville and Old Dalby, a few miles to the west, where Lady Bowater maintained a chaplain up to 1829. However this may be, the initiative in making the new foundation came principally from Fr. Thomas Peter Tempest, who had opened the neighbouring church of Grantham only a few years previously in 1833. He gathered subscriptions, and contributed generously from his own patrimony. In this he was aided by Mr. John Exton of Eastwell. This benefactor, besides a generous donation to the building fund, left a legacy which enabled the bishop, up to at least 1880, to allot a sum of money for the maintenance of the priest in the Mission.

The church, dedicated to St. John the Baptist, begun in 1839 and completed three years later, is "said to have been designed" by A. W. N. Pugin. An alternative explanation is that it was designed by Edward J. Willson, a friend of Pugin, who may have advised on such matters as the stone detailing, which is of high quality, and the stained-glass. In the 1980s, the sanctuary was reordered and the sacristies were rebuilt. When the church was opened by Bishop Walsh in 1842, there was much opposition from Dr. Cumming, then a well-known No-Popery lecturer. Fr. Anthony McDermott, the first missionary priest, had to live some miles out of town for the first six months. He then obtained the use of a derelict house, and was able to build a presbytery in 1844. In July 1921 "a new electric lighting system was installed."

For several years towards the end of the nineteenth century, there was no resident priest in Melton Mowbray, and the parish was served at one stage from the cathedral and at another from the seminary adjacent to the cathedral.

In the 1960s, at the time St. Peter's was being built, parts of the town centre where St. John's was situated were undergoing redevelopment. Part of this redevelopment involved the demolition of the priest's house and the reduction of the area around the church. The parish hall, which had been built at the same time as the church, was demolished in the 1980s. In the small graveyard attached to the church lies buried, among others, Mother Francis Murphy (1843-1927), Foundress of the Franciscan Minoresses.

Although the records speak of 'a humble beginning of a school' in 1843, the venture seems to have been short-lived. Another school was erected by Fr. Austin Rowley in 1864, but fell on evil days before the end of the century. There is mention of a schoolroom in 1875. Ten years later, the school had forty-six pupils and a certificated mistress. The school returns of 1895 suggest that there was a virtual boycott on the part of the Catholics. Twelve of their children at this time were at Protestant schools, while the only children attending St. John the Baptist's were four non-Catholics. The school was closed in the late 1890s.

This hiatus in Catholic education in Melton Mowbray did not last long, for it was in 1900 that the Franciscan Minoresses came to the town and almost at once opened a private convent school, initially with four pupils. In 1902 an advert appeared headed "St. Joseph's Franciscan Convent and High-Class Boarding School for Young Ladies, conducted by the Missionary Franciscan Sisters."

In the following decades many changes were made. The foundation stone of the present St. Francis Primary School was laid by Bishop Ellis in February 1957. A year later, the junior pupils transferred from their classrooms in the convent to brand new classrooms in the present school. The senior school closed in 1968.

During the 1960s funds were raised for a new church intended to serve the area north of the town centre where many new houses had recently been built. This church, dedicated to St. Peter, was blessed by Bishop Ellis on 13 July 1964. In 2008 the confessionals and Lady Chapel on the south side of the building were combined to create a large multi-purpose area with ancillary facilities and a new main entrance.

MELTON MOWBRAY - *Convents*

The **Little Company of Mary** which had been founded in Nottingham in 1877 had a convent in Melton Mowbray from 1881 to 1884. During their time in Melton, the Sisters taught in the school.

The **Franciscan Minoresses**. Their Foundress, Mother Francis Murphy, and several of her Sisters, arrived in Melton Mowbray in December 1900.

At that time they were known as the 'Missionary Sisters of St. Francis' but in 1910 they were given their present name 'Franciscan Sisters Minoress.' The Tower House on Dalby Road, which the Sisters acquired in 1903, became and remains the Mother House of the Congregation. Mother Francis Murphy died on Christmas Eve 1927 and is buried in the small cemetery beside St. John's Church in Melton. Among the many ministries of the Sisters is the leadership of a group of Franciscan Companions who meet regularly at the Convent and are also active in the parish.

NARBOROUGH

St. Pius X

This Mass centre, opened by the Blessed Sacrament Fathers of Braunstone in April 1939, lies five and a half miles south-west of Leicester. For about four years Mass was celebrated each Sunday in a doctor's surgery in Church Lane. Then the congregation moved to a room in the Narborough Arms Hotel. Meanwhile the congregation was raising funds to purchase a site for a church. On this site on Narborough Road, a small church was built. The first Mass there was celebrated there at Christmas 1957, and the official blessing and opening by Bishop Ellis took place on 25 April 1958. The building, which seats approximately one hundred and twenty, was designed as a church and a hall.

In 1965 Narborough, which had hitherto been served by the Blessed Sacrament Fathers of Braunstone, became a parish in its own right and has remained so until the present day. A presbytery was built the following year, and the church building was later provided with a sacristy and a separate parish hall. The hall was enlarged and refitted in 2004.

NEW MILLS

The Annunciation – served from Marple Bridge

The greater part of the population of north-west Derbyshire has always been concentrated in the two valleys that carry the waters from the Kinder massif towards the Irish Sea. To the north of Kinder, the deep valley of the Etherow contains a group of parishes which all derive from a single source, the Parish of All Saints, Glossop. Glossop had the services of a priest from at least 1803. The Goyt valley runs due north for some twelve miles from Axe Edge before taking up the waters of the Etherow at Marple and carrying them on to the Tame at Stockport. A well-defined chain of parishes lies along the banks of the Goyt, and New Mills is the mother-church of them all.

In November 1839 Bishop Thomas Walsh, Vicar-Apostolic of the Midland District, sent Fr. John Joseph Collins to take up residence at New Mills. But it is also probable that Mass had been said in the village as early as 1832. If so, one may conjecture that the foundation of this first Mass centre was the work of the apostolic Frenchman Fr. Theodore Fauvel, who had come to Glossop the previous year.

From the correspondence of Bishop Walsh, it is clear that New Mills was chosen as a residence for a priest because it was a convenient centre for the many mill-villages along the Goyt. From the first, then, New Mills had the character of a centre of missionary activity, and the four parishes which derive from it are the fulfilment of its early destiny.

Things were not easy for Fr. Collins. Monsignor William Croft, in the information he collected, at the beginning of the twentieth century, for a history of the diocese (never published), noted that: "It was in the year 1844 that the first stone of the church was laid to the great annoyance and disgust of some people of the district, who at that time were greatly biased against the Catholic Faith. This enmity persisted to such lengths that they determined that when it should be erected, to level the church to the ground and --- some fifty or sixty of these evilly disposed individuals on one occasion marched up to the church determined to carry out this design. This bitterness of feeling, however, gradually abated and Father Collins had the happiness and consolation of witnessing the accomplishment of his desire."

It was in accordance with the spirit of the times that the church erected at New Mills in 1845 by Fr. Collins should be monumental in size. Nottingham St. Barnabas had been completed the previous year; Derby, St. Mary's was six years old; and an age which believed in quality rather than quantity was responsible for the splendid venture at New Mills. St. Mary's Church was consecrated on 17 May 1895.

Soon after the erection of the church, Fr. Collins turned his attention to the establishment of Mass centres in the valley. In 1848 he began to say Mass at Chapel-en-le-Frith and at Compstall - the forerunner of the Mission of Marple Bridge. In the same year he took over the existing Mass centre at Buxton, which, though geographically separated from the Goyt valley by the high ridge of Edge Moor, was linked by its communications more closely to New Mills than to Leek, on which it had previously been dependent. The work was more than one man could do. An assistant priest was for a short time (1848-1849) obtained for New Mills, and afterwards the burdened lightened by the residence at Buxton by the crippled Fr. Edward McGreavy.

On the death of Fr. Collins in 1853 the division of the parish began. His successor inherited New Mills and the northern villages, while Buxton became an independent Mission. When Fr. Luke Livermore, a Cistercian of Mount Saint Bernard Abbey, came to New Mills in 1858, his main effort was directed to the erection of a new parish at Marple Bridge, at the confluence of the Goyt and the Etherow. Within two years he had succeeded, and Marple Bridge was cut off from New Mills in 1860.

In 1879 Bishop Bagshawe noted that New Mills had a handsome church served temporarily by the Rev. Patrick Tobin. The Blessed Sacrament was reserved there. The Catholics numbered 466, and 87 children attended the school. The congregation was poor, and many were very indifferent. Six years later, he repeated his opinion about the congregation and observed that most of the population of New Mills, a town of 7000 inhabitants about sixty-four miles from Nottingham, were engaged in cotton-weaving. The bishop added that, as well as the church with a capacity for 300 persons, there was a fair presbytery, a large garden, and a good school. The Catholics numbered 380.

Between New Mills and Buxton, the largest centre of population is Whaley Bridge. The left bank of the River Goyt is in Cheshire and consequently in Shrewsbury Diocese; and it is there that the greater part of the population is housed. But the beginnings of the present Mission were made on the right bank of the river by Fr. William McKenna of New Mills in

1897. He had some sort of chapel, dedicated to St. Joseph, at Elnor Lane. In the following year, however, a Mission was begun on the opposite bank by the chaplain of Errwood Hall, higher up the Goyt valley and in the Diocese of Shrewsbury. It seems that for some years the two Missions faced each other across the river. But in 1907 the Shrewsbury Diocese made certain the survival of its own Mission by providing it with a resident priest. The Elnor Lane Mission was closed in 1918, and its congregation absorbed by the church on the other bank.

Thus, by the close of the century, New Mills had become the spiritual progenitor of three parishes in the basin of the Goyt. The Mission at Chapel-en-le-Frith might also claim New Mills as its founder-parish by virtue of the Mass centre in 1848. But this had lapsed in 1850, and when it was revived in 1928, the revival came from Buxton. With the foundation at Chapel-en-le-Frith, its district was cut off from New Mills, and thus the parish received its final form.

A school was built in 1860, on land previously acquired for the purpose; this building and a plot of land were sold for residential conversion and development in about 2005. The present St. Mary's Primary School is on Longlands Road.

NEW OLLERTON

St. Joseph – served from Mansfield St. Patrick (Forest Town)

Ollerton had its own Catholic history in Penal Times. The Markham family, together with the Molyneux family at Wellow, kept the Catholic Faith alive until the latter part of the eighteenth century. In 1774 six members of this community were confirmed at Worksop. Fr. Thomas Pickering of Aspley Hall near Nottingham is described in the Confirmation register as their 'Pastor'. This implies, according to the practice common at the time, that Fr. Pickering visited Ollerton at regular intervals to say Mass. But this little group of

Catholics had died out entirely by the end of the nineteenth century. In the twentieth century the congregation derived mainly from the influx of Catholics who came to find work when the pits were opened at New Ollerton after the First World War. St. Joseph's owes its financial origins to the Wright family, who were local coal-owners. The village was at that time part of the Parish of Mansfield, and Fr. Charles Payne, the parish priest, bought a site on Sherwood Drive in 1924. This site was subsequently enlarged twice by purchases of adjoining land in 1926 and sometime before 1940. In the mid-1920s, there were only three Catholic families in the Ollerton area. The first Mass was said on 27 May 1925, and the Plough Inn was used as the Mass centre for two years or more before the opening of the church. In 1927 Ollerton was cut off from Mansfield, and Fr. George Hickey became the first Parish Priest.

A presbytery was completed before the end of 1928. The foundation stone of the church had been laid by Bishop Dunn on 29 August 1928, and the completed building, a pleasing example of Romanesque construction in brick which harmonised successfully with the environment of the modern colliery village, was opened on 10 March 1929. (The colliery closed in 1994.)

Due to the proximity of the mine-workings, the church was found to be showing signs of subsidence. It was judged unsuitable for remedial work to shore up the building, and the decision was taken to demolish the building and replace it with a modern building. The new church, described as having a bright and welcoming internal character, was dedicated 20 October 1995.

Boughton Manor House was opened in 1960 as a junior independent school staffed by the Religious Sisters of Charity; it was to be the forerunner of St. Joseph's Primary School the first phase of which opened in 1962 and the second in 1970. Although 'officially' known as 'St. Joseph's Catholic Primary and Nursery School, a Voluntary Academy', it is usually referred to locally simply as 'St. Joseph's.'

NEW OLLERTON - *Convent*

The **Religious Sisters of Charity** (often referred to as the 'Irish' Sisters of Charity) opened a convent at Boughton in 1960. After a quarter of a century's ministry, they left the parish in 1986.

NEWARK

The Holy Trinity

The last pre-Reformation Catholic priest to serve in Newark, Fr. Henry Lytherland, was arraigned on a charge of treason for not supporting Henry VIII's claim to be the only Supreme Head of the Church in England and was executed in August 1538.

The traditional date for the foundation of the post-Reformation Mission (later known as 'Parish') of Newark is given as 1802 - the date of the first entry in the Baptismal Register. The earliest records of any detail show that in 1823 Mass was being said in Newark once a month by Fr. Jacques Gabriel Yver of Grantham. It appears probable, however, that from 1807 there was a regular monthly Mass at Newark and that before this date there was no regularity of service.

In those days it was still unusual to provide a Mission with a resident priest until an endowment had been provided. In the years 1824-1827 therefore, Fr. Yver bought various properties in Dovecote Close, Turnstile Close and Mill Gate. The rents from these properties were sufficient to maintain a priest. With the approval of the Vicar-Apostolic, Bishop Thomas Walsh, Fr. Yver moved from Grantham in 1831 to become the first Missionary Priest of Newark. A priest of the Diocese of Bayeux, Fr. Yver refers to himself as "the founder of the Mission of Newark." He died on 29 April 1835 and is buried in a vault below the floor of the Church of St. Mary the Immaculate, Grantham.

Although he began to collect funds for the purpose, Fr. Yver did not survive to see the erection of the first church. He apparently bought the site, and the adjoining house known as Newark Old Hall. This dated from 1603, and was the oldest building in the diocese to serve as a presbytery. The foundation stone of the church on Parliament Street was laid on 27 June 1836 by Fr. James Waterworth, who was to serve the parish for almost forty years, and the first Mass was celebrated by him on 2 July 1837. There was a "very numerous congregation" at this Mass - and there was no collection!

(This practice of 'no collection' was, one may surmise, soon abandoned!) The dedication of the church may possibly have been chosen in the light of the pre-Reformation history of the town since the Guild of the Most Holy Trinity of Newark had been of considerable importance in the later Middle Ages. It perished in the Suppression of 1546. But the last Alderman of the Guild became the first Alderman of the new Borough of Newark; and its last account-book became the first minute-book of the Corporation.

The Church of the Holy Trinity on Parliament Street served the Catholics of Newark for more than a hundred and forty years. In the 1970s it was realised that a new and larger building was needed. After a lot of hard work and some frustration due, in part, to basic faults in the structure, the present church on Boundary Road was opened in 1979. Together with Holy Trinity Primary School and Holy Trinity Community and Partnership Centre (the latter opened in October 2005), the church and presbytery make a great contribution to the life not only of the Catholics but of the wider community in Newark.

As elsewhere, the Catholic Faith in Newark has been lived and handed on by generations of laity, religious and clergy. When people enter the Church of the Holy Trinity, they may not notice the gravestone marking the spot where Provost James Waterworth, builder of the first Holy Trinity Church, was reburied when the old church was demolished. Awareness of this may remind them of the debt they owe to those who have gone before them in faith.

In the process of demolition of the old church in 1985, a curious thing happened. Below the spot where Provost Waterworth had been buried, a hitherto unknown body was discovered. Circumstances did not permit further investigation, but the body was exhumed and reburied in Newark Cemetery on 20 September 1986.

A Catholic day-school was in existence in Newark by 1841. With various enlargements and improvements, e.g. in 1879 it had 73 pupils; in 1885, 92; in 1912, 98; in the 1950s, 161, the school remained in existence until the building of the new school on Boundary Road which opened in 1969.

Cardinal Hinsley Middle School was opened in May 1965 and closed in 1984.

NEWARK – *Religious Communities*

Sisters of Mercy 1881-1882 provided teaching staff for the school.

Poor Clares of the Immaculate Conception (of Newry) opened a convent at Park House in 1953 and almost immediately began teaching in the parish school where one of them was headmistress from 1957 to 1967. The Sisters opened a convent school in 1954; this closed fourteen years later. But they remained in the parish exercising various ministries until 1995.

Benedictine Hermits of the Diocese of Nottingham

On 13 September 2013, after many years of discussion with Bishop Malcolm McMahon, the Elston Hermits, who had lived in the Newark Parish since 2009, were received by him into Full Communion with the Holy See having for many years previously served in another Orthodox Communion. On December 11 2013, the brethren renewed their vows of religious profession to Bishop Malcolm, vows which they had made initially some thirty years earlier.

On 11 July 2015, after they had served a short period as deacons, Bishop Patrick McKinney ordained the brethren to the presbyterate to serve as priests in the Diocese of Nottingham.

NORTH-EAST LINCOLNSHIRE

The Parish of the Most Holy and Undivided Trinity encompassing Grimsby, Cleethorpes and Immingham

For many years, North-East Lincolnshire had four parishes, viz., Grimsby, St. Mary-on-the Sea; Grimsby, St Pius X; Cleethorpes, Corpus Christi; Immingham, Our Lady Star of the Sea. In addition, St. Mary -on-the-Sea Parish had a chapel-of-ease, St. John Fisher Hall, at Scartho.

In 2016 Bishop Patrick McKinney, at the request of the two priests then working in these four parishes, comMissioned an independent review into all aspects of Catholic life in North-East Lincolnshire, including the number of places of worship, so that ways in which the Church could best grow and serve the wider community could be identified.

On the basis of this review, and after consultation with clergy and parishioners, the bishop, on 17 December 2016, announced his decision to close St. Pius X Church and St. John Fisher Hall with effect from 15 January 2017. The bishop said that, by concentrating resources on three churches rather than five places of worship, he would like the Catholic community to come together as one united parish to provide a powerful and effective witness to Christ in service to the wider community of North-East Lincolnshire. He saw this as a time of real opportunity and mission for the Catholic community in the area, and it was his prayer that the Holy Spirit would continue to help all Catholics – and every other Christian in this area – to deepen their faith and proclaim God's love in the wider community.

The new parish was given the name 'The Most Holy and Undivided Trinity.'

NOTTINGHAM

St. Augustine of England

The establishment of a Mission in the eastern part of Nottingham was among the first cares of Bishop Bagshawe. He separated the whole area from the cathedral parish in 1876, appointing Fr. Patrick Conaty to do what he could with it. No dedication was given to this Mission. Its centre, called St. Joseph's, was at the Kent Street Schools, where Mass was said on Sundays. On 22 November of the same year the site on Woodborough Road where St. Augustine's now stands was bought. It was a gift to the diocese from the ever-generous Mr. W. Dobson, of The Park, Nottingham.

In 1877 the eastern district of Nottingham was again subdivided, and the form of the present parish began to emerge. The Woodborough Road and Blue Bell Hill areas together formed a Mission which (for the first two years) was placed under the patronage of Our Lady of Dolours. Nottingham's first Nazareth House, known at the time as the Convent of St. Ann, had been established in this same year in three houses in Cranmer Street, The Sisters contributed a sum each year to the upkeep of the priest during the three years of their residence, and it seems probable that without this contribution the maintenance of a priest would have been impossible. In any case, Fr. Garvey, the first priest appointed to the Mission, had to share lodgings at 39 Heskey Street, with the priest of St. John's.

Between 1878 and 1880 the Mission was united with St. John's and placed under the care of Canon Christopher Monahan. A "handsome iron school-chapel, capable of accommodating three hundred people" was erected on the Woodborough Road on a site of 2070 square yards donated by Mr. W. Dobson. It was opened on 12 October 1879 with the new dedication of St. Augustine replacing the earlier title of Our Lady of Dolours. At this time, the new Mission of St. Augustine was separated from that of St. Joseph. It is possible that the money contributed by the Duke of Norfolk represented the whole cost of the building. Several years later, it was noted that a large part of the congregation of the new Mission consisted of English people in fairly easy circumstances and that they were, on the whole, good and devout Catholics. In 1880 a residence for a priest was found at 177 Woodborough Road. The combined Mission was then once more divided. Fr. Joseph Gernon became the first priest of St. Augustine's, while Canon Monahan returned to the Mission in Kent Street which now became known as St. Joseph's. About 1883 the Blue Bell Hill district was cut off from St. Augustine's and placed under the care of Canon Monahan as a preliminary to the establishment of St. Edward's. In addition to his parish activities, Canon Monahan organised the first of many pilgrimages outside the diocese, in this case to Holywell in North Wales.

The temporary chapel was to serve its purpose for over forty years. Its unprepossessing appearance was accentuated by its situation next door to the Emmanuel Parish Room - a building of similar construction. It became progressively more dilapidated and lost the battle with the weather even before its successor could be completed. For a short time before 1922 it was abandoned, and the congregation heard Sunday Mass in the largest schoolroom of the Sacred Heart Convent.

After the First World War a new church, "to take the place of the old corrugated iron structure ... which was razed to the ground in 1920", was planned on an ambitious scale by Mr. Brocklesby, the architect of the 1920 Church of St. George, Derby. The foundation stone was laid on 3 February 1921. Financial difficulties dogged it from the first, and building operations were suspended in the early months of 1921 due to lack of the necessary funds. The urgent need for a new building had prompted a beginning with very little money in hand.

In the end, the cost was almost twice the original estimate, and it took seventeen years to clear the debt. While the new church was being built, the congregation worshipped in St. Augustine's School in conjunction with Sacred Heart Convent. When the Lady Chapel of the new church was opened by Bishop Dunn in May 1922, there was a procession from the convent to what had so far been constructed of the new church. But since the new chapel would seat only about fifty, an open-air service was held, and Bishop Dunn preached to a congregation of more than a thousand. The remainder of the church was completed and opened early in 1923. But according to the practice of the time, the church could not be consecrated until the debt was cleared. When Father Maurice Parmentier was appointed to St. Augustine's in 1927, it was reckoned that the debt would not be paid off until 1959. However, as a result of an outstanding financial effort on the part of people and priest, not forgetting the contributions made in so many ways by the Sisters of St. Joseph of Peace, the debt was cleared in thirteen years and the church was consecrated by Bishop McNulty on 21 September 1940.

The tin chapel was certainly in use as a school in 1880, and had possibly been used for this purpose from the time of its opening in the previous year. Although, in 1885, Bishop Bagshawe was of the opinion that the Mission had a very good mixed school, attended by 110 boys, girls, and infants, only a few years later the government grant was nearly lost through inefficiency. In this crisis, the Sisters of St Joseph of Peace, then at Blue Bell Hill, were asked to take over the school. They taught continuously at St. Augustine's from 1889 until 1992. Although they quickly raised the standard of the school and earned the extra grant awarded for excellence, the school was threatened by a second crisis in 1892. The tin building was condemned as insufficient and insanitary. Funds for a new school were raised entirely through the initiative of the Sisters. By circulating the nobility, and by means of a Fair in the Albert Hall, they were able to build the schools in Northville Street, which were opened in 1896. In 1964 what had now become St. Augustine's Junior and Infant School moved to new premises on Park Avenue. The Sisters of St. Joseph of Peace opened Sacred Heart Secondary School for Girls at their Mapperley Road Convent in 1912. This was sold to the diocese in the mid-1960s.

By no later than the mid-1920s, the presbytery was located at 240 Woodborough Road, a short walk up from the church. In the 1970s the entire area of St. Ann's was redeveloped. There was widespread demolition, but St. Augustine's Church was spared. A new presbytery and parish hall were built on the site of the old school in 1974.

Since September 2000 St. Augustine's has been served from the cathedral.

NOTTINGHAM, *St. Augustine of England - Convents*

Sisters of Nazareth from 1877 until 1880, when they moved to Old Lenton.

The Mission remained without a convent for some years.

The Sisters of St. Joseph of Peace, who from their house on Blue Bell Hill, had been teaching in the schools from 1889, in 1892 established the Sacred Heart Convent at 30 Mapperley Road. These Sisters, besides conducting their own independent secondary school which opened in 1912 and closed in the mid-1960s, for many years supplied teaching staff for the primary schools at St. Augustine's, St. Mary's (Hyson Green) and Arnold as well as for Sunday schools in several other local parishes. In 1975 the Convent was relocated to Lucknow Avenue and closed in the 1990s with the remaining Sisters being rehoused in other convents of the Congregation.

Presentation Sisters in 2002 moved into the now vacant presbytery from where they exercise various ministries in the parish and beyond.

NOTTINGHAM

Our Lady of Perpetual Succour (Bulwell)

The foundation of a Mission in the Bulwell district of Nottingham was due primarily to the initiative of working-class laity. It has retained this characteristic ever since. There are no names of wealthy benefactors to record in the history of the parish.

The first move appears to have been made by some laymen, who asked Bishop Bagshawe to provide Mass in the area. He gave his approval. At that time, Bulwell was a village outside the city boundaries, and was attached to the newly formed Mission of Hucknall. A first Mass centre was opened in 1881 at a private house in Gedling Street, tenanted by a Mr. M. McDermott. The records of this Mass centre are obscure, but it seems improbable that Mass was said regularly every Sunday for the first four years.

In May 1885 Fr. John MacDonnell of Hucknall took a seven-year lease of a disused building in Downing Street, in that part of Bulwell then known as the Kiln Yards. This was opened in June 1885 as a chapel dedicated to Our Lady of Perpetual Succour. About the same time, the adjoining house was also rented, and at Easter 1890 the bishop sent a priest into residence. After two years of dire poverty, the priest was withdrawn. But Bulwell did not revert to the status of a chapel-of-ease to Hucknall. It appears to have retained its dignity as an independent Mission, and was served from various city parishes until, in 1898, another attempt was made to establish a priest in residence. The Mission led a struggling existence until 1911. A sudden and unexplained disaster then overtook it. Bishop Brindle closed the chapel, removed the priest, and not even a Mass centre was left in Bulwell for the next two years.

During these two years the hopes of the destitute congregation were kept alive largely through the efforts of the Sisters of St. Joseph of Peace from their Mapperley convent. They gathered the children for instructions, and were mainly instrumental in securing the use of a little hall in Hazel Street, for a Mass centre in 1913. This centre had an existence of seven years. But it is completely ignored in the official records of the diocese and it seems improbable that Mass was celebrated there regularly on Sundays.

A definitive revival began in 1920. Bishop Dunn assigned Fr. Austin Williamson to the work and loaned a sum of money with which the present site on Brooklyn Road was bought. Bishop Dunn notified the Duke of Newcastle's estate agent that "rather a curious situation has arisen. A committee of Catholics of Bulwell, very keen to make a start, have purchased an army hut recently at Newark. …They are anxious to start erecting it as soon as possible on the land at Bulwell," and he (the bishop) wondered how the Duke from whom he hoped to purchase the land would react to this initiative. The Duke's reaction was favourable and so the army hut was purchased and erected to serve as a chapel. When this had been done, largely through the voluntary work of the men of the congregation, the first Mass was said on 7 November 1920 and Fr. Williamson handed over to a Rosminian Father who took up residence at Bulwell. This new attempt at establishing a resident priest lasted only ten months, and the Mission reverted to the care of the Bishop's Secretary, Fr. Edwin Henson. The principal need of the parish was now a presbytery. For this purpose, Fr. Henson erected a bungalow in 1924. As soon as this was complete, the Mission was once more given a resident priest, Fr. Vincent Denny.

August 1926 marked the beginning of the thirty-four year ministry of Fr. (later, Canon) Bowman Augustus Short. It was under his leadership that the present church was built, paid for and consecrated. Soon after he came to Bulwell, a community of Poor Clares was established in the parish from Manchester via Hyson Green.

The present church, for which the foundation stone was laid on 27 July 1934, was designed by Mr. E. Bower Norris and Mr. F. M. Reynolds in an adaptation of Lombardic Romanesque. It was opened by Bishop McNulty on 8 May 1935. The final decoration was deferred, owing to financial stringency, war conditions, and colliery subsidence, until 1949. The principal feature of the decoration was a twenty-five feet mosaic, behind the High Altar, of the Last Supper. Mosaics were also provided for the rear walls of the chapels of the Sacred Heart and Our Lady. Once the debt had been cleared, the church was consecrated by Bishop Ellis on 8 May 1951. The church was significantly reordered in the 1970s, a reordering which included the removal of the baldacchino over the high altar; this opened up the mosaic of the Last Supper to full view.

The parish hall, built in 1932, served a number of purposes until it was demolished and replaced by a community centre in 2016.

A new presbytery, to accommodate two priests, was erected in 1939.

Shortly after the outbreak of the Second World War, the children from St. Mary's School next to the cathedral were dispersed (it was hoped at the time on a short-term basis) to various sites around the city. One of these sites was Bulwell. The then parish priest, Fr. Short, managed to convince the education authority of the need of schooling for Catholic children in the Bulwell area. Thus it was that the parish hall served as the primary school from 1939 until 1957 when the present school on Piccadilly was opened. Initially there were two classrooms divided by a folding partition. As pupil numbers increased, the wooden hut (the original church) adjacent to the parish hall was pressed into service as a third classroom. Until the new school was opened, Our Lady's was classed as 'St. Mary's (Derby Road) Annexe.' After the move to the new premises on Piccadilly, the wooden hut served for some years as a parish club until it was demolished.

NOTTINGHAM, Our Lady of Perpetual Succour, Bulwell - Convents

A community of **Poor Clares (Colettines)** came from Levenshulme, Manchester, to Nottingham in 1927 and moved to Bulwell about a year later into a building behind the new church. Subsequent enlargements provided further accommodation for the nuns including a novitiate. A convent chapel accessible to the public was opened 28 October 1958. The debt owed to the Poor Clares has not always been appreciated. In addition to their hidden life of prayer, among many other things, the extern sisters, having been away from home from Monday to Friday collecting alms, for many years often spent most of Saturday afternoon on their hands and knees polishing the church floor!

Little Company of Mary. A small community of 'Blue Nuns' were resident in the bungalow, the original presbytery, from 1981 to 1988. When these Sisters left, the bungalow was returned to residential use for retired clergy of the diocese.

After the departure of the Blue Nuns, Bishop McGuinness offered the property to the **Sisters of St Francis** who opened a counselling centre. As this work developed, a large hall (the McGuinness Centre) was constructed on land adjoining the bungalow, and opened in May 1988, but after the Diocesan Assembly of 2003, the McGuinness Centre was closed, and for some years served as the parish hall. In 2016, after the new parish centre was built, the McGuinness Centre was rented to Cafod.

NOTTINGHAM

Divine Infant of Prague, (Bestwood) – served from Bulwell

Whereas the Bestwood Estate was developed during the 1930s, Bestwood Park Estate was not built until the late 1950s and early 1960s. From 1956 Fr. Bernard Allen of Hucknall said Mass in the Bestwood Hotel. In the early 1960s Father Francis Lang, one of the priests of Bulwell, began to visit the houses on this new estate to ascertain how many Catholics there were and how their needs might be met. In December 1963 three thousand square yards of land were purchased from Nottingham City Council with the intention of eventually building a church, parish hall, presbytery and school. Two years later, a church-hall on Cherry Orchard Mount was opened in which Mass was said on Sundays by one of the priests from Bulwell, and every Sunday afternoon there was a Novena and Holy Hour. By 1967 there were two Sunday Masses; and in 1968 the chapel-of-ease was given the name Infant of Prague. In 1971 Father Michael Eastwood became the first Parish Priest of the new Parish of Infant of Prague, Bestwood Park – and his address (since the presbytery adjacent to the church dates only from the early 1980s) was Mosswood Crescent! Although a 'church' as such was never built, the church-hall was extended in 1978 to form a sanctuary, day chapel, sacristies and confessional. Thus, as has so often happened, the original dream of church, presbytery, parish hall and school has not been able to be realised in its entirety – but the Faith lives on even in small congregations.

The first phase of St. Margaret Clitherow Primary School with accommodation for one hundred and sixty pupils was built in the space of eight months, and opened in November 1970. The official opening by Bishop Ellis took place in July 1971. Over the years, there were further developments, and in October 2012 St Margaret Clitherow School became an academy and part of the Pax Christi Multi-Academy Trust.

For some years it has not been possible to find a resident priest for the parish, and the parish, since 2005, has been once again under the pastoral care of the priest at Bulwell. The presbytery is now let to tenants.

NOTTINGHAM

Sacred Heart, Carlton

The first move in the foundation of this Mission appears to have come from the laity. A Miss Pollard began by collecting local Catholic children for religious instruction in her house at Carlton. Subsequently, a deputation of local residents came to see Bishop Bagshawe, and asked him for a Mass centre. The bishop promised to send a priest monthly if suitable premises could be provided. Mr. W. Kirk then came forward and - as far as can be gathered from the rather confused records of the period - erected the building which formed the nucleus of the original school of St. Augustine (renamed Sacred Heart in 1990.) This remained for some time his own property, and was rented to the diocese. The bishop came personally to say Mass for the first time in the temporary chapel on 24 June 1877. Bishop Bagshawe appointed the Dutchman Fr. John Theodore Hoeben to be the first resident priest of Carlton.

The task of the new priest was to build a permanent church. He begged vigorously from as far away as Cardiff, Halifax, Scotland and South Africa! Mr. Kirk presented him with the site on Main Street, in front of the temporary chapel, on which stood four cottages. Two of these were demolished to make way for the church. The foundation stone was laid on 6 September 1883, and the completed church was opened by Bishop Bagshawe on 23 March 1884. At the same time, the two remaining cottages were converted to form a presbytery. Fr. Hoeben had previously lodged with Mr. Kirk. These buildings all survive, the presbytery still in use, the old church now used by a playgroup and the former school largely rebuilt as a community centre in 1992.

The first temporary chapel had been dedicated to St. Augustine. But in 1879, a school-chapel with the same dedication had been erected on Woodborough Road, Nottingham. The dedication of Carlton was therefore changed, in 1883, to the Sacred Heart. It was possibly the first church in the diocese to bear this title.

Shortly after the First World War, Carlton had grown to a district of some 18,000 inhabitants. The church was quite inadequate for its congregation. A site for a new church, adjoining the old, was bought in 1921. On 12 March 1930, after a considerable sum of money had been collected, the foundation stone was laid by Bishop Dunn, who also opened the new building on 27 January of the following year. It is a good example of the revived Catholic architecture of the inter-war years; of considerable size, well-lighted, and with all the dignified simplicity of the Romanesque style, to the traditions to which it clings rather more closely than later examples in the diocese. The debt on the church was paid off by persistent financial effort, including adverts in the diocesan yearbook, and it was consecrated by Bishop Ellis on 21 May 1945.

From its first erection, the temporary chapel of 1877 was used as a school. It retained this character, and also the dedication of St. Augustine, after the opening of the first church six years later. A new school on Southcliffe Road was officially opened in 1969. In 1990 the school's name was changed to Sacred Heart.

St. Bernadette's School on Sneinton Dale was built to serve the growing population in the Sneinton area of Nottingham. The foundation stone was laid on 9 December 1933, and Bishop McNulty opened the completed school on 6 September of the following year. The situation of the school made it a convenient centre for Catholics living on the awkwardly-placed new housing estate beyond the Nottingham suburban line towards Colwick. The school became a secondary modern school and subsequently a comprehensive school in the mid-1970s, but was closed in 1985 when it was found that there were "insufficient pupils to maintain the courses which every pupil has the right to experience. "

Almost since its erection, St. Bernadette's School was used as a Sunday Mass centre. For many years it was served from Our Lady & St. Patrick on London Road; but following the closure and relocation of the Church of St. Patrick in 1979, responsibility for St. Bernadette's was transferred to the care of the Carlton Parish. Even with the closure of the school, the Mass centre continued for many years to be used for the celebration of Sunday Mass.

From March 2017 Sunday Mass in Sneinton has been celebrated at the Anglican Church of St. Christopher. This arrangement has also led to common witness and Christian presence in the Sneinton area.

NOTTINGHAM, *Sacred Heart, Carlton – Convents*

Sisters of Mercy

The Sisters of Mercy from St. Mary's, Derby, opened a small convent at Carlton in August 1882 and continued teaching in the school until 1889, when they were obliged to leave through lack of financial support.

Sisters of St. Dorotea

These Sisters came to Nottingham in 1972 to work with the Italian community and initially had a nursery in the Arboretum area of the city. This nursery closed in 1984 and the Sisters moved to Carlton to continue their work with the Italian Mission until 2003 when they left the diocese.

NOTTINGHAM

Our Lady & St. Edward

After five years of confused experiments to provide for the Catholics in the eastern part of Nottingham, two Missions finally emerged in 1880. St. Augustine's formed one of these - and its territory at this time included the district around Blue Bell Hill. The other was under the patronage of St. Joseph. It had a school-chapel in Kent Street, and was under the care of Canon Christopher Monahan, who lived at 9 Northumberland Street. It was this Mission which ultimately developed into St. Edward's.

In 1883 Blue Bell Hill was still outside the boundaries of Canon Monahan's Mission. But before the end of the year he had obtained from the Nottingham Corporation a ninety-nine year lease on a plot of land at the corner of Hunt Street and Blue Bell Hill Road. It must be presumed that there was an adjustment of boundaries at this time, and that this district was detached from St. Augustine's and added to St. Joseph's. Mass was said on Blue Bell Hill for the first time in 1884. The Sisters of St. Joseph of Peace opened their first Nottingham convent in that year and their convent chapel - at the corner of Simkin Street and Blue Bell Hill Road - was made available to the public for Sunday Mass.

Canon Monahan had meanwhile run into some financial difficulty, for he found himself obliged to give up part of the site he had secured in 1883. Nevertheless, the foundation stone of the church on Hunt Street was laid in September 1885. On its completion, it was opened with some ceremony by Cardinal Manning on 21 July 1886. Although without architectural pretensions, the building was of some historic interest. It was the largest and most complete example in the diocese of the school-chapel type of building which became standard in the Age of Manning. The dedication to St. Edward the Confessor was probably prompted by the Christian name shared by both the Cardinal and Bishop Bagshawe.

For another year after the opening, the whole Mission retained its dedication to St. Joseph. From 1887 it was known as St. Edward's, and the district around Kent Street was handed back, together with the school-chapel of St. Joseph, to the cathedral parish. Canon Monahan lived in the old priest's house in Northumberland Street until his death in 1894. The presbytery in Blue Bell Hill Road was built by his successor shortly after 1895.

Fr. Herbert Ignatius Beale attempted, in 1896, to establish a Diocesan Congregation of men under the name of the Missionary Brotherhood of Franciscan Tertiaries. The attempt met with little success, and was abandoned in 1900. But an Association of St. Anthony of Padua, which Fr. Beale founded in 1898 and a shrine to the same saint which he erected in St. Edward's, were more successful and became known far beyond the boundaries of the parish.

An improvised school was organised in the Mission as early as 1884. The schoolrooms were a stable and a hayloft at the rear of Simkin Street. It appears to have been opened on 22 September 1884, and the teachers were Sisters of St. Joseph of Peace. Curiously enough, in view of later Franciscan developments, the school was dedicated to St. Francis. At the same time, a house in Long Hedge Lane was secured as a home for girls, but this was soon discontinued. Two years later, St. Edward's School, Gordon Road, replaced that on Simkin Street.

The Sisters of St. Joseph of Peace continued to teach, after its erection, at the St. Edward's school-chapel: possibly they continued to do so until the Franciscan Minoresses took over the work in 1899. These in turn handed over to a staff of lay teachers in 1903. The current school, called Our Lady & St Edward Primary and Nursery Catholic Voluntary Academy, was founded in 1960. It became an academy in September 2011 and, along with four other schools, formed the South Nottingham Catholic Academy Trust.

In the subsequent history of the parish, the most important event was undoubtedly the coming of the Friars Minor in 1930. Exactly seven hundred years had passed since the first coming of the Franciscans to Nottingham. Their pre-Reformation friary was established on the banks of the River Leen in 1230. Its site appears to have been bounded by Greyfriar Gate, Canal Street and Broad Marsh. The only recognisable relics are said to be some fragments of stonework alongside a watercourse which flows below Carrington Street. The friary came to an end on 5 February 1539, when it was surrendered to the king. However, a Franciscan connection in the diocese was reestablished before the Friars Minor came to the Parish of St. Edward on 15 May 1930, since the first Bishop of Nottingham, Joseph William Hendren, was also a Franciscan. The community was canonically erected as a Friary in September 1930.

Within six months of their arrival, the Franciscans began to negotiate for a plot of land at Gordon Road, higher up Blue Bell Hill, on which to build a new church. They were successful, and this site was further enlarged in August 1937 by the purchase of land sufficient for a new Friary and school. Shortly before the outbreak of the Second World War, permission had been obtained from the Board of Education for the erection of a new school and hall on this site. The war, however, prevented the execution of this project, and, when it was over, it was found necessary to shelve the erection of the school. In 1952 Bishop Ellis gave his consent to proposals for building a new church. The foundation stone - which contains an inserted fragment of stone from the pre-Reformation Nottingham friary - was laid by Bishop Ellis on October 13 1954, the feast of St. Edward. As this was the Marian Year, the title of the parish was changed to Our Lady and St. Edward. The new church was opened on 8 April 1956 although the sanctuary was not completed until 1966, the same year in which the friary was built.

In 2014 the Franciscan Friars left Nottingham once again not, this time, because of persecution, but because they could no longer provide the numbers of men sufficient to sustain a community. Saint Edward's was returned to the care of diocesan clergy, but the service rendered by these sons of St. Francis, especially to the poor and otherwise disadvantaged, will long remain in the minds and hearts of the people of Blue Bell Hill and beyond.

NOTTINGHAM, *(Our Lady &) St. Edward – Convents*

The **Sisters of St. Joseph of Peace** opened their first Nottingham convent in the summer of 1884. This also served as their Mother House and novitiate. Soon afterwards they opened a school. The Sisters moved to St. Augustine's Parish in 1887.

Franciscan Minoresses

In 1899 a community of religious women who had previously lived and worked in the Westminster Archdiocese without attaining canonical status moved to the Nottingham Diocese. Fr. Beale found a home for them at Beacon House and under his care they were organized into a Diocesan Congregation, called Franciscan Minoresses. They left the parish in 1903 and moved to Melton Mowbray where, since that date, they have had their Mother House.

NOTTINGHAM

(St. Peter) The Assumption (Beeston)

The first foundation at Beeston seems to have been an act of hope on the part of Bishop Bagshawe. In 1884 he appointed Fr. Peter Elkins as Missionary Priest of Beeston-cum-Long Eaton. A temporary chapel had been built at Long Eaton in the previous year. Beeston, where the priest resided, was the weaker centre. Mass was said in the billiards room of The Rising Sun public house in Middle Street, and the attendance was at first no more than ten. In his 1885 Report to the Holy See, Bishop Bagshawe noted that "A house has been taken at Beeston, an outlying, but wealthy and important suburb of Nottingham, where there are about 70 Catholics.

Two rooms thrown into one form a good chapel, which will hold nearly 100 people." In 1887 a further attempt was made to establish Beeston as an independent Mission. Fr. Gilbert V. Bull, newly ordained, was appointed as the first missionary priest. There were, however, no resources to maintain a priest, and after a short time, probably a matter of a few months, Fr. Bull was withdrawn. For one year more, Beeston was served as a Mass centre from the cathedral. It would seem that there was some sort of temporary chapel in existence at this time, for there is a tradition that the priest had once to fight off a gang of youths who demanded to know what was in the tabernacle. This incident, and the legal proceedings which followed, is said to have led to the closure of the Mass centre.

For the next eight years Beeston was left without Mass, and for five years after that it was cared for by Canon Edward Douglass, Administrator of the Cathedral and Secretary to Bishop Bagshawe. During that time, two young women, a Mrs Bagdurn (or Blagburn) and a Miss Robinson, took the initiative in keeping the fFaith alive. From about 1888 they collected the children and gave them religious instruction in the front room of a private house. In the early 1890s they were able to interest Canon Douglass in the needs of the dormant Mission. Two rooms in a small factory near Styring Street were rented and Mass was once more said in 1895. Beeston was apparently erected at this time as an independent Mission, for the Canon is found signing the Lenten Returns of 1895 as Rector of the Mission. Only seven adults had at first attended Mass, but when the Mass centre was removed shortly afterwards to an upper room at the old Humber Works, the congregation began to overflow and the permanence of the Mission was assured.

A site in Styring Street for a church was bought in 1897. Plans were drawn up by Mr. G. Hart; the building contract was awarded to Mr. Turner of Styring Street; and the completed church was opened by Bishop Bagshawe on Whit Sunday 1898. It served its purpose until it was replaced by the present Church of the Assumption. Once this had been opened, the old church was used by Age Concern and was eventually demolished in 2005. A year or two before the First World War, the congregation was significantly decreased when the Humber Works moved to Coventry. However, numbers rose again quickly with the opening of Chilwell Ordnance Depot after the outbreak of war in 1914. A war memorial at the rear of St. Peter's Church in the form of a massive replica of the Iona Cross was unveiled by Col. Sir Lancelot Rolleston DSO.

Efforts to raise funds for a worthier church were made sporadically from the first years of the twentieth century. Fr. Francis Hays was able to buy the present site in Foster Avenue, and laid the foundations of a church in 1939. The outbreak of the Second World War halted further progress.

After the war, Mr. Reynolds was engaged as architect to draw up new plans. Three sets of plans were turned down by the local authority as too elaborate and costly; the fourth and final set were approved in November 1951. As a preliminary, the foundations of 1939 - which had perished during twelve years of exposure to the elements - were removed. The work of building, entrusted to the Nottingham builders, Messrs. Sweeney and Palmer, began on 1 March 1952, and four weeks later Bishop Ellis came to lay the foundation stone.

The new church - a portion only of the building contemplated in the architect's plans - was opened by the bishop on 21 March 1954. At the same time the original dedication to St. Peter was replaced by that of Our Lady of the Assumption. This change may have been due to personal favours granted to the parish priest, Fr. Timothy Shanahan, on the Feast of the Assumption, or perhaps it was to commemorate the fact that Pope Pius XII had promulgated the dogma of the Assumption four years earlier. A side-altar is dedicated to Our Lady, and has a statue, carved in Italy, representing the Assumption. The same Mystery of the Rosary appears in a stained-glass window over the door. A new priest's house in Foster Avenue was opened in the same year as the new church. The sanctuary of the church was renovated in 1971, and five years later the building was extended. In 1984, the centenary year of the parish, a parish hall was built and was opened on 8 December of that year.

Since 1992 Beeston has been the principal centre in the diocese for Perpetual Exposition of the Blessed Sacrament.

NOTTINGHAM

St. Thomas More, Wollaton

The first move towards solving the problems of Catholics living in Nottingham's western housing estates was made in 1937. In that year the Bulwell parish founded a Mass centre in Aspley. The next move came four years later, when Fr. Francis McNicholas of St. Paul's, Radford, began to say Mass on one Sunday a month at Wollaton. Mass was provided fortnightly from 1943 and, since 1944, Mass has been said every Sunday.

A large site was purchased on the corner of Glenwood Avenue and Bramcote Lane on which, in the mid-1950s, a presbytery and a church-hall with accommodation for about 200 people were built. The intention was, as in so many cases, eventually to build a church, but this has not happened, partly because the congregation is relatively small and funding is an issue. Most plans have involved the sale of much of the site for housing development with the profit from the sale funding the difference between the parish money and the total cost of the project. The plans were further dogged by the presence on the site of badgers, a protected species. However, is spite of these setbacks, it is hoped that a new church will be built at Wollaton.

St. Thomas More became an independent parish in 1971 and had a resident priest until 2003 after which time it was served, once again, from St. Paul's until 2014, and from 2014 to 2015 from Borrowash. In 2015 it was once again given its own priest.

From 2017 Wollaton has been part of a team ministry with Aspley and Bilborough.

The parish was, for some years, the base for two successive chaplains to the University of Nottingham. In addition to the accommodation at Newman House in Beeston, the presbytery in Wollaton was used by the chaplains.

NOTTINGHAM, *St Thomas More, Wollaton - Convent*

The **Sisters of St Joseph of Peace** moved to Wollaton from St. Augustine's Parish, Nottingham, in 2000.

NOTTINGHAM

St. Paul (Radford/ Lenton)

The first steps towards the foundation of a Mission in the Radford district of Nottingham appear to have been taken in 1882. In this year a site was bought in Salisbury Street - close to the important road junction of Lenton Boulevard with Ilkeston Road. Prior to this, a chapel known as the "Brotherhood" was acquired or leased by the Catholics for use as a Mass centre.

A new school-chapel was opened in September 1897 in Salisbury Street. It is described in 1899 as a 'new school'. But the erection of a completely new building is hard to reconcile with its abandonment after only nine years. Possibly this school-chapel was, like so many others of the period, an adaptation of an existing building. When it opened, the Mission was provided with a staff of two resident priests, though the reason for this is not clear. Perhaps the Mission was intended to be of greater importance than its subsequent history suggests. Radford was the birthplace, in 1899, of the future Bishop Ellis, the first, and - so far - only native of the diocese to become its bishop.

For the first three years, the Mission appears to have flourished, but in 1900 there was a sudden and unexplained collapse. The resident priests were withdrawn, and St. Paul's became a chapel-of-ease to the cathedral.

An obscure attempt at reorganisation was made in 1904. The building in Salisbury Street was no longer used for Mass; in its place was what has been described as a 'chapel' in Redoubt Street - on the far side of Ilkeston Road. A resident priest was again assigned to the Mission. What happened to the Salisbury Street building is not clear. Probably it was sold, together with the site, in 1904. There seems to be no other reason for the move to Redoubt Street. If the series of school reports is to be trusted, the school continued to exist until 1905. But it may possibly have been housed in a building different from the first school-chapel. In any case, this re-organisation soon failed in its purpose. The school was closed in 1905, and in 1906 the Redoubt Street 'chapel' was abandoned, the priest withdrawn, and for the next ten years there is no record of Mass being said in Radford.

In its final form, the parish was the first-fruits of the episcopate of Bishop Dunn. A Mass centre, served initially from the cathedral and then from St. Edward's, Blue Bell Hill, was reopened in 1916. In 1918 Fr. Bernard George was sent to reside in the parish, and it was he who bought the present site on Lenton Boulevard. But it was not until 1929 that work on the church was begun. The foundation stone was laid on 30 July of that year, and the church, one of a series, including Good Shepherd (Arnold), and Holy Spirit (West Bridgford), built at the time by Mr. F. J. Bradford, the Leicester builder, was opened on 25 January 1930. The baptismal font is believed to be that from Lenten Cluniac Priory. The presbytery, popularly known as the 'Bird cage' since it was the home of Fr. (later Monsignor) Arthur Bird, was added in the early 1930s.

Over the years it became clear that the church and the presbytery needed to be extended, and that there was need of a parish hall. Plans for these were submitted in the early 1960s, but the work was not begun for several years. The first priority was to build a parish hall, which was then used for the celebration of Mass and other services while the church was extended. The church was extended by demolishing the sanctuary and lengthening the nave and constructing a new sanctuary. At the same time a belfry was added. The extensions and improvements were blessed by Bishop Ellis in November 1967.

In the early years of the twenty-first century, St. Paul's and St. Mary's, Hyson Green, were formally united to form a single parish.

NOTTINGHAM, *St. Paul – Convents*

In 1898 a convent of **Franciscan Minoresses** was established at Radford, and it seems probable that these Sisters provided the teaching staff for the school. The Sisters withdrew two years later.

Sisters of Nazareth

Within the limits of the modern parish lay the long-established convent of the Sisters of Nazareth. The first Nottingham house of this Congregation was opened in 1876 on Woodborough Road. In 1880 the Sisters moved to Priory Street, Lenton, (occupying part of the site of the old Lenton Priory). A new chapel, of Romanesque inspiration, was opened in the grounds in 1952, and the buildings were remodelled many times over the years.

In the early 1980s, as social circumstances changed, Nazareth House ceased to provide services for children. In the ensuing years, successive regulation and the demands for increasing standards of care for the elderly meant that the buildings could not be adequately modernised in an economic fashion. These factors, coupled with a declining number of vocations to the religious life, led to the decision by the Sisters of Nazareth to close many of their houses. Nottingham was one of these.

After more than one hundred and twenty-five years of service to the people of Nottingham during which one hundred and fifty-eight Sisters of Nazareth had cared for 2,225 children and 1,472 elderly people, the Sisters of Nazareth left Nottingham. Nazareth House very often hosted clergy meetings of various kinds, and many priests and Religious, including Bishop Ellis, who – after his retirement - served as their chaplain until shortly before his death in 1979, and Bishop McGuinness, were cared for by the Sisters of Nazareth.

Missionary Sisters of the Holy Rosary

The Sisters came to the diocese in 1976 and were based in St. Paul's Parish, where they were engaged in pastoral and social work. They also carried out mission appeals and vocations promotion. The Sisters withdrew from the diocese in August 1990.

NOTTINGHAM

St. Mary, (Hyson Green)

In its origins, this Mission is bound up closely with the Little Company of Mary. On behalf of this new Diocesan Congregation, Bishop Bagshawe signed, on 7 February 1877, the lease of a property in Lenton Street consisting of two small cottages and a dilapidated workshop. For this he agreed to pay the proprietor, Mr. Mellors, an annual rent. The first Sisters took possession on 19 March of the same year. They formed a chapel out of the largest of the rooms, and adapted two more rooms for use as an elementary school. These were blessed and opened by the bishop on 2 April 1877, and dedicated to the Maternal Heart of Mary.

This convent was to be, from the first, the nucleus of the new Mission. It was situated in the midst of newly-built streets at Hyson Green in which three hundred Catholics were known to be resident. Moreover, there was no place at that time, from the cathedral to as far north as Mansfield, where Mass could be said. Hucknall did not have the Mass until 1879, Bulwell not until 1881: their small congregations could meanwhile - and they did - trudge their way on Sundays to the convent chapel at Hyson Green. Lodgings were found for a priest at the house of a Mr. Tracy in Lenton Street, and Fr. John Burns - ordained two weeks previously - was sent to be the first Missionary Priest of what has since been known as St. Mary's.

For three years the crowded upper room at the convent was the Mission's only chapel. The congregation grew - largely through the heroism with which the Venerable Mother Mary Potter, Foundress of the Little Company of Mary, and her Sisters devoted themselves to the spiritual and material necessities of the poverty-stricken district. Forty-one converts were received into the Church during the first six months!

A site, in Beaconsfield Street, for a more permanent chapel was given to the diocese in 1878 by Mr. Samuel Limpenny, who was also a benefactor of St.Patrick's. A school-chapel was built to the designs of Mr. Christopher Wray, a brother-in-law of Bishop Bagshawe. The bishop's diary notes that, on 26 June 1880, the Hyson Green chapel was 'finished' and the date of opening must lie close to that time.

This building was to serve the needs of the parish for more than thirty years. But the era of school-chapels passed away, and on 1 July 1909, Bishop Brindle laid the foundations of the present church in Goodliffe Street. It was opened on 2 February 1910. A new presbytery in Belton Street was built at the same time. The debt on the church was paid off by 1911, but the church was not consecrated until 2 February 1931. The Lady Chapel, opened on 14 June 1939, was built as a memorial to Provost John McIlroy, who had served the parish for the entire forty-three years of his priestly ministry.

At the urgent request of Bishop Bagshawe, and despite her own misgivings, Mother Mary Potter agreed to provide, in 1877, schooling for the children of the area. Teaching was not, however, the calling of the Little Company of Mary, and this venture lasted no more than a couple of years. But a school was opened in 1882 in the new church building. The foundation stone of the school was laid on 6 April 1911; and the opening took place on 14 September of the same year. However, according to another source, the pupils moved to the new school in 1913. The old school-chapel was retained as St. Mary's Parish Hall. Some of the teaching staff for the schools were, for many years, provided by the Sisters of St. Joseph of Peace from their Mapperley Road convent. In September 1976 the school moved into new premises on Beaconsfield Street.

As in so many places, the demography of the parish has evolved over the decades. In the latter part of the twentieth century, there were very many new arrivals in the area of Hyson Green, Forest Fields and New Basford. Most of these people (at least by the end of the 1980s) were from the new Commonwealth. This has presented, and continues to present, significant challenges and opportunities such as integration.

NOTTINGHAM, *St. Mary – Convents*

The **Little Company of Mary** was founded at Hyson Green in 1877. Bishop Bagshawe noted, in his 1879 Report to Rome, that these Sisters "began the Mission and have largely contributed to the formation of it and of its school." The Congregation, devoted mainly to the work of nursing the sick in properly-equipped hospitals and nursing homes, soon grew. By 1893 the Little Company of Mary numbered eight houses: two in Italy, and one each in England, Australia, Ireland and the United States, Malta and South Africa. The improvised convent in Lenton Street became consequently an anomaly, and was demolished in 1922. Of some interest is the following.

A member of the Little Company of Mary, Sister Martina, was awarded the 'Medaille de la Societé Française de secour aux blessés militaires' for her service with the French Red Cross Society. She went to the military hospital at St. Germaine-sur-Laye early in 1917 and was there during some of the worst fighting. The men were brought in straight from the trenches, and there were generally between 200 and 300 men in the hospital. In the formal letter from the French Red Cross, tribute was paid to "the brave little Sister who has given so generously to our poor wounded the great solace of her care and prayers."

The Sisters moved, in 1922, firstly to West Bridgford, and, in 1929, to Woodthorpe.

In 1988 the Foundress of the Little Company of Mary, Mother Mary Potter, was declared Venerable, and in 1997 her mortal remains were reinterred in the north ambulatory of St. Barnabas' Cathedral. One of the Nottingham Express Transit trams was named after her in 2004.

In the spirit of the Venerable Mary Potter, the Mary Magdalen Foundation was set up by Sister Elizabeth Malone LCM, and under its auspices 'The Sanctuary' was opened in Hyson Green in 1990 to help alcoholics and their families.

The Mary Potter Health Centre was officially opened in September 2008.

The **Poor Clare Colettines** came to Nottingham from Manchester in 1927, and spent some months in a house in Beaconsfield Street before moving to Bulwell in 1928.

Sisters of St. Francis established a house in Forest Fields in 1979.

NOTTINGHAM

St. Teresa of Lisieux (Aspley)

Between the two World Wars, some eight thousand houses were built by the Corporation of Nottingham on the Aspley, Broxtowe, Bells Lane and Bilborough Estates. At the time, the whole district fell within the boundaries of the Bulwell Parish. Fr. Bowman Short, the Parish Priest, began to make efforts to find some centre for the Catholics on the new estate. His first attempt - an offer to purchase Broxtowe Hall - came to nothing! But he was successful, in August 1935, in buying the first portion of the present site. This was situated on Glencairn Drive, and had once formed part of the estate of Aspley Hall, where the Willoughbys had maintained a chaplain, Fr. Thomas Pickering (born 1703), for roughly forty years. Fr. Pickering died in March 1789 and was buried in St. Peter's Churchyard, Old Radford. The site bought in 1935 was subsequently twice enlarged; in 1946 the half acre on which the temporary church was situated was bought; and, in 1948, an acre was added - sufficient for primary and secondary schools.

The first Mass was said on 7 November 1937 in a classroom of the William Crane School. Before the end of the year, the size of the congregation had made necessary a move to the South Hall in the same school. In January 1947 a temporary church was brought into use. This was formed from a large, dilapidated wooden hut which was situated on the additional half-acre of land bought in 1946 and a considerable amount of voluntary labour went into the work of conversion. The church was fitted up over time, with altar rails from the cathedral and a reredos painted by a Bavarian ex-prisoner of war. The Mission had been transferred, in 1941, to the Hyson

Green Parish. It was cut off from there in October 1947, and became an independent parish with Fr. Emil Puttman as the first parish priest. For the next four years the priest lived in lodgings at 21 Aspley Park Drive until the presbytery in Kingsbury Drive was built in 1951. The parish also had a hall for social purposes, formed in 1949 from a Nissen hut.

In 1958 Fr. Puttman was succeeded by Fr. P. J. Neary, one of those priests who have "a genius for raising money without seeming to ask for it." Towards the end of the 1950s, it had become clear that the wooden church needed to be replaced, and a new church of unusual design was blessed and opened by Bishop Ellis on 4 May 1966, the first Mass having been celebrated at Christmas 1965. St. Teresa's was one of the first churches in the diocese to be built after the Second Vatican Council, and its design reflects some of the insights of the Council.

From 2017 Aspley has been part of a team ministry with Bilborough and Wollaton.

The foundation stone of St. Teresa's Primary School was laid in October 1952, and, in May 1954, it opened with two hundred and twenty-one pupils. By October of the following year the numbers had reached three hundred and twenty.

Bishop Dunn Secondary Modern School was built in 1965, and the Loreto Girls' Grammar School, which replaced St. Catherine's Grammar School for Girls in the cathedral parish, was opened in 1962. These two schools were amalgamated, in 1975, to form the Trinity Comprehensive. Trinity School became an Academy in July 2012. Along with Our Lady's (Bulwell), St. Mary's (Hyson Green) and St. Teresa's (Aspley) it forms the St. Barnabas Catholic Multi Academy Trust.

NOTTINGHAM, *St. Teresa of Lisieux (Aspley) – Convent*

In 1962, the **Loreto Sisters** opened a convent on Beechdale Road where they were responsible for the girls' grammar school which was transferred from the cathedral parish where it had been founded and run by the Sisters of Mercy. True to the spirit of their Foundress, the Venerable Mary Ward, spiritual formation was an important part of their work and, in 1975, the community house in Aspley became the centre of formation for those interested in religious life. The Loreto Sisters were also much involved with people having special needs; among other things, they made they made their house in Llandudno available to them for annual holidays. The convent closed in 1987.

NOTTINGHAM

St. Hugh of Lincoln (Bilborough)

Bilborough was one of many housing estates on the outskirts of Nottingham developed after the Second World War. In November 1949 an army hut in Leicestershire was purchased, dismantled and stored at St. Teresa's. Less than a year later, the hut was erected on an acre of land acquired from the Nottingham Corporation in June 1950. Seating 150, it was blessed and opened on 31 December 1950 by Bishop Ellis, the first Mass having been celebrated there on Christmas Day. Sometime before this, a parishioner overheard someone pose the question "I wonder who will have the first church [on this estate]; I bet it will be the Catholics." When the little church was opened, the hope was expressed that soon there would be a beautiful church, a hall and a presbytery on the site. It was not long before this hope was fulfilled. The new church was opened in 1964, a year before the new church in the parent parish of St. Teresa; a presbytery was built in the late 1970s.

Bilborough became a separate parish in 1968 with Fr. Brendan O'Sullivan ('Big Brendan') as its first parish priest. The fifth parish priest, Mgr. Edward Walker (died 2016), will be remembered not only for his work in the parish but also for his outstanding service over several decades in the diocesan marriage tribunal and with Marriage Encounter.

From 2017 Bilborough has been part of a team ministry with Aspley and Wollaton.

NOTTINGHAM

Corpus Christi
(Clifton)

As in the case of St. Teresa's, Aspley, the opening of a Mass centre on the Clifton Estate brought back the Mass to a chaplaincy of Penal Times. Little is known of the Catholicity of the Cliftons of Clifton Hall, but they certainly maintained a priest in the early part of the eighteenth century. The new venture was due to the spread of Nottingham to the south of the River Trent after the Second World War. A site for a church, school and presbytery was earmarked on the development plan of the Clifton Estate, and in 1953 a Mass centre, served on Sundays from West Bridgford, was opened in a builders' hut. When this hut was burned down by vandals, the congregation moved to a building owned by the Nottingham Cooperative Society where they used a billiard table as an altar.

The first parish priest, Fr. James McGuinness, was appointed in 1956. After building a primary school, dedicated to the local martyr, Blessed Robert Widmerpool, opened in 1957, and a secondary modern school, Corpus Christi, opened in 1958, his next task was to build a church. (From about 1956, Mass had been celebrated in Wimpey's Canteen.) Work on the new church began in November 1963. Bishop Ellis laid the foundation stone on 24 June 1964, and the first Mass was celebrated at Christmas 1965. Three months later, on 29 March 1966, Bishop Ellis blessed and officially opened the large new church, capable of accommodating 596 worshippers. Along with Good Shepherd, (Woodthorpe), and St. Teresa's (Aspley), Corpus Christi was among the first in the diocese to be conceived and designed in the light of the Second Vatican Council. The church is notable for its large and complete sanctuary; and its towering concrete campanile is a local landmark. As well as looking after the Clifton Estate, Fr. McGuinness was also saying Sunday Mass in Corpus Christi School, Wilford, and in Ruddington. In 1983, as Bishop McGuinness, the first parish priest returned to consecrate the church on the parish's patronal feast day.

In 1975, following the policy of turning all local authority-run secondary schools into comprehensives, Corpus Christi was amalgamated with The Becket School, a boys' grammar school on Wilford Lane, West Bridgford, run hitherto by the Augustinians of the Assumption.

Since September 2011, both The Becket School and Blessed Robert Widmerpool School have been part of the South Nottingham Catholic Academy Trust.

NOTTINGHAM

(Our Lady &) St. Patrick

The first steps towards the foundation of this Mission were taken no later than 1863 by Canon John J. Mulligan, at that time Administrator of the Cathedral. He took up the lease of a disused factory on Leenside and turned it into a school. From the first it had been his intention to establish a Mission in this district. The cathedral, Nottingham's only Catholic church up to 1867 - was too far away and perhaps too respectable for the many Irish immigrants who in dire poverty crowded the new streets below the old Lace Market. The former Jesuit Fr. Joseph Bond, one of Canon Mulligan's curates, was entrusted with the task of preparing for the new Mission. By the time he departed for the West Indian Missions, Fr. Bond had managed to collect a considerable sum of money for a church. Mr. W. E. Dobson, of The Park, Nottingham, was especially generous: he paid for the maintenance of the school, and contributed notably to the new church of 1883.

The little school adjoining The Turk's Head public house on Leenside was then reconstructed to serve as a church and presbytery as well as a school. Bishop Roskell, in 1867, sent the young Fr. John Harnett to be the first Missionary Priest of Our Lady & St. Patrick's. The remaining forty-two years of the later Provost Harnett's life were to be devoted to this one Mission! Bishop Roskell gave Fr. Harnett a chalice that had been given him when he left St. Patrick's, Manchester, to become Bishop of Nottingham.

(This chalice was used once again at the Mass marking the centenary of the parish.)

On 18 March 1872 Fr. Harnett purchased from the Nottingham Corporation three-quarters of an acre of land bounded by London Road, Narrow Marsh, Leenside and the Plumtre Hospitals Estate. Besides four cottages, the site contained the Red Lion Inn, and this added further to the cost as compensation had to be paid to the tenant when the public-house was demolished.

The first building erected on the site was a school. Its architects, Messrs. Evans and Jolly, planned it on lines which for those days were magnificent. Rising three storeys high, it was intended originally to house boys, girls and infants in three separate departments. The foundation stone was laid on Easter Monday, 6 April 1874, by Bishop Roskell; and it was opened by his successor, Bishop Bagshawe, on 18 January 1875. The boys' department on the top floor was condemned in 1911. A new school for senior boys was then built on Sneinton Dale and opened in 1933. This was dedicated to St. Bernadette, who had been canonised that year. The site on Sneinton Dale was bought by a legacy left by Miss Elizabeth Atkin, a cleaner at Boots' Chemists, who had devoted her whole life to the parish. The remainder of St. Patrick's School continued in use, but its days were numbered. The Sisters of Mercy from the College Street convent staffed the school from 1867 to 1875; the girls' and infants' departments from 1875 to 1892; and from that year until their withdrawal in 1912 the boys' and girls' departments. In 1963 the primary school was relocated to its present site in Wilford.

After the school came the presbytery. It was designed to hold four priests, and was completed in 1879. It is recorded that at one time the Sisters of Mercy used the basement of this presbytery to provide penny dinners for the children. It appears that the old temporary chapel on Leenside was closed in 1875. For the next few years, the school-hall of the girls' department was used for Sunday Mass.

The erection of the new church was considered a matter of some importance. Cardinal Manning came to lay the foundation stone on 21 August 1880. But the builders ran into considerable difficulty. The site lay on what had once been the bed of the River Leen, and was still marshy. They attempted to lay the foundations on the stone piles of what had once been a medieval bridge, carrying the road from London to Nottingham. These began to sink as soon as the superstructure was raised. The walls cracked. Eventually a sufficient foundation was provided by constructing large brick pillars in the crypt - which in the original plan was intended for use as a parish hall: the cracks in the walls were patched up, and the completed church was opened on 24 September 1883. A new community centre with a meeting room for The Grail Movement and a flat for the Grail Leader was constructed behind the church in 1968.

In 1979 Bishop McGuinness, on the advice of Canon Philip Soar and parishioners, decided to demolish the old church, where the final Mass was celebrated on 3 June, and to relocate it in a brown-field site in the Meadows area. The bishop laid the foundation stone of the new church on 14 February 1981 with the trowel used at the laying of the foundation stone of the original church in 1880. This was a gift from an American who had discovered it in a junk shop in Tokyo! The new church was consecrated on 22 October 1981.

The following year, Canon Soar together with his Anglican and Free Church colleagues performed a Service of Dedication of the "Meadows for Christ".

Because the new Church of St. Patrick was so far from its historic site, the decision was taken to change the parish boundaries, and the Sneinton area, with the care of the Mass centre at St. Bernadette's, was entrusted to the Parish of The Sacred Heart of Jesus on Carlton Hill. Canon Soar did not need to build a presbytery as he qualified for a council housing flat; this was situated in the block overlooking the church car-park. Upon his death in 1993, this economy had to be remedied and two houses in Mickledon Close were purchased and used as a presbytery during the time Father George Woodall was parish priest. When Father Woodall was appointed to the neighbouring Parish of Corpus Christi, Clifton, pastoral care of the Parish of Our Lady & St. Patrick was given to the cathedral from 2003-2014. In the September of this latter year, following the plans laid down by the consultation 'You are Living Stones' established by Bishop McMahon, pastoral care was given to the Parish Priest of Corpus Christi, Clifton.

NOTTINGHAM

Good Shepherd (Arnold/Woodthorpe)

The Parish of Arnold / Woodthorpe includes a considerable area of the city; but its church is situated outside the city boundary, in the Borough of Gedling. Its foundation was an unusual example of long-term planning. Immediately after the First World War, it became evident that Nottingham would spread towards the north-east, to link up with the old forest-village of Arnold. Fr. Edwin Henson, at that time Secretary to Bishop Dunn, set to work to provide for the future. In 1922 he began to say Mass in a room over the Co-operative Store, Front Street, and about the same time bought a site for the future church. This site was well chosen. Even six years later, when the church was built, it stood in open country, and the road that ran past it was little more than a cart track. Today it is the centre of a built-up area, and the fifty people who attended Mass in the early years had swelled to more than nine hundred by 2015.

In 1928 the Mass centre was transferred to a room in a disused factory at Daybrook, and the work on the church began almost immediately. Initially dedicated to the Sacred Heart, it was opened on 29 October 1929. A presbytery adjacent to the church was built in 1937. The church was almost identical in design with those built around the same time at Radford (Lenton) and West Bridgford. All three as well as several others in the diocese were erected by the Catholic builder, Mr. F. J. Bradford of Leicester. Described as "small and unpretentious [but] .. much loved by all who use it habitually", the Church of the Good Shepherd was consecrated on 22 June 1950. It was so small that an extension, forty feet by twenty, was added in 1952 to provide extra accommodation; and even this was not sufficient. So, in the early 1960s, plans were made to build a new church. Designed by the architect Gerard Goalen to seat six hundred, it was opened on 23 July 1964, the twenty-fifth anniversary of Ordination of the then parish priest, Fr. Bernard Mooney. It was consecrated on 27 October 1983.

Due to quite unforeseen (and perhaps unforeseeable) circumstances, substantial remedial work on the 'new' church had to be carried out from the late 1980s. In spite of these problems, the church was awarded, in 1998, a Grade II* listing by English Heritage.

Meanwhile, the first church and the buildings behind it which had housed the school in the early 1950s were then used as a parish hall until a purpose-built parish centre was built and opened in 2007.

In 1966 a chapel-of-ease dedicated to St. Gilbert was built in the Arnold area of the parish, but could not be sustained and was closed in 2001.

A site for a primary school was bought in the late 1940s, but the Local Education Authority considered that the Catholic child-population did not justify aided status. A two-form non-fee-paying independent primary school was therefore opened in September 1951. This was housed in a "temporary though commodious and useful parish hall" - formerly a R.A.F. hut measuring sixty feet by twenty - which had been erected beside the church in 1946. The 1952 extension to the church was also used, during weekdays, for the school. In 1961 the first phase of a new primary school was opened on Somersby Road. The children were taught by the Sisters of St. Joseph of Peace as well as by lay staff.

The first phase of Christ the King Comprehensive School was opened in 1971 to be followed by a second phase three years later. In October 2012 Christ the King School became part of the Pax Christi Multi Academy Trust which includes the four partner primary schools, Good Shepherd Primary, Holy Cross Primary, Sacred Heart Primary and St Margaret Clitherow.

NOTTINGHAM, *Good Shepherd, Arnold (Woodthorpe) - Convent*

Little Company of Mary

The Blue Nuns (Little Company of Mary) moved from Wilford Lane to establish their Convent Nursing Home at Woodthorpe in 1929. In addition to their work in nursing care, they exercised a number of other ministries in Good Shepherd Parish and further afield. Due to a significant change of circumstances, the Sisters relinquished their care of the nursing home in 1998 and eventually moved from the parish in 2001.

NOTTINGHAM

Polish Church Our Lady of Czestochowa

The Polish community in Nottingham is served from this church on Sherwood Rise.

NOTTINGHAM

Holy Spirit (West Bridgford)

In the middle of the nineteenth century, West Bridgford was a village of about twenty-four houses. By 1955 it was an Urban District with a population in excess of 24,000. The traditions of the parish relate that Mass was said for the first time in 1897 at Trent Lodge, subsequently part of the Becket School on Wilford Lane. At the same time, Fr. Francis Hays was appointed Missionary Priest. He did not, however, reside in his Mission, but lived at St. Patrick's Presbytery on London Road. The centre for Mass was very soon moved to an upper room in the pavilion of the Y.M.C.A. cricket ground, where the County Hall now stands. The exact date at which this first Mass centre ceased to function seems impossible to recover. One account states that it was abandoned in 1901 on account of the disastrous floods of that year. But the Catholic Directories continued to list it until the issue of 1906. The Mission certainly ceased to have any independent existence after 1902, when it was merged into that of St. Patrick. In its early days it was dedicated to the Sacred Heart. One permanent result of this first venture was the acquisition of a building site in Victoria Road. This was bought by Bishop Brindle in January 1904. West Bridgford was cut off from St. Patrick's to form a new parish in 1929.

Seven years after its purchase, building operations began on the Victoria Road site and, on 15 August 1929, Bishop Dunn laid the foundation stone of the Church of the Holy Spirit. The work was carried out by Mr. F. J. Bradford, the Leicester builder, and the design falls under no single architectural classification. It was not dissimilar to several other churches in the diocese of the same era, e.g. St. Paul's, Lenton. The completed church was opened on 8 June 1930. In 1937 the fortieth anniversary of the celebration of the first post-Reformation Mass in West Bridgford was celebrated with a Mass of Thanksgiving and an Evening Service at which the sermon was given by Fr. Francis Hays, who had celebrated the first Mass in 1897. In 1945 it was noted that the church, the presbytery and "other parochial property" were entirely free of external debt.

In the 1930s and 1940s floods were a major issue. In May 1932 the ground floor of the priest's house in Victoria Road was inundated by the waters of the River Trent. This house was sold shortly after 1937, and the present house in Charnwood Grove was purchased in its place. But in 1946 and 1947 the Trent again overflowed, and reached to within a few inches of the altar in the church.

The wooden parish hall next to the church erected by Fr. Robert Woodbridge (1937-47) served for various social functions until the late 1960s when it was replaced, in 1967, by a purpose-built social centre, with upstairs committee room and a downstairs bar.

The original church proved to be too small to cope with the number of worshippers. It was, therefore, demolished early in 1973, and until the new church, with seating accommodation for approximately 360, was opened in May 1974, the social centre was used for Mass and other services such as baptisms, weddings and funerals. Since the building of the new church, various experiments, some more successful than others, have been tried out in the decoration of the interior.

A primary school dedicated to St. Edmund Campion was opened in the parish in 1974.

In 1929 the Augustinians of the Assumption opened the Becket Grammar School for boys at Trent Lodge, on the site of the former convent of the Little Company of Mary. The school began with twenty-six boys but grew rapidly. Further accommodation was provided by the acquisition of an adjoining house, and playing fields were bought on the opposite side of Wilford Lane. New buildings were opened by Bishop McNulty on 8 July 1940. Two wings were erected, forming with Trent Lodge three sides of an open quadrangle facing Wilford Lane. The new wings increased the capacity of the school to two hundred places, and included classrooms, gymnasium, assembly hall, chapel, and - a sign of the times - a steel-lined air-raid shelter. A sixth-form science laboratory was added in 1954.

In 1975 the Becket Grammar School was amalgamated with Corpus Christi Secondary Modern two miles away. In the early years of the present century, a new school was built at the far end of Wilford Lane, almost at the boundaries with Corpus Christi and Our Lady & St. Patrick's Parishes. The new school took the name 'The Becket School' in deference to the older school, and the dedication 'Corpus Christi' vanished from use.

When the Assumptionists ceased to be involved in the Becket School, some of them took up various ministries in and around Nottingham. Worthy of particular mention is the work of a former headmaster, Fr. Roger Killeen who, in 1976, founded Emmanuel House in the Hockley district of Nottingham to support in a variety of ways homeless, vulnerable or isolated adults in and around the city.

In recent years, the parish has taken on pastoral responsibility, first for the parish of Keyworth and Cotgrave, and latterly, when the parish was divided, Cotgrave alone, while Keyworth was handed over to the care of the East Leake parish.

WEST BRIDGFORD – *Convents*

The coming of the **Little Company of Mary** (or Blue Nuns as they are usually known) to open a nursing home at Trent Lodge in June 1922, marked the beginnings of revival. Their chapel was open to the public, and at times they had a priest resident as chaplain. The Sisters left West Bridgford for Woodthorpe in 1931.

Sisters of St. Joseph of Peace transferred a mother and babies Home from Borrowash in 1976. This closed in about 1994 but the Sisters remained there, carrying out various ministries including counselling and involvement in the work of the Catholic Children's Society until 2015 when they left the parish.

OAKHAM

St. Joseph (and St. Edith)

Oakham shares with Derby and Lincoln the honour of witnessing an Elizabethan martyrdom, in Oakham's case that of the Venerable John Lion, a layman. Although no contemporary accounts of his martyrdom have been found, it is reasonable to speculate – on the basis of what is known about Oakham in the late sixteenth century and the general format of trials of Catholics at that time - that he was confined in the prison which once stood in Gaol Street, was condemned to death in the hall of the old Norman Castle - now the County Hall - and executed on the Uppingham Road. His execution took place on 16 July 1599.

For nearly three centuries after this, the post-Reformation Catholic history of Oakham appears to be blank. Then, in 1881, Fr. Emilius Van Dale of Exton Hall opened a Mass centre where he said Mass on alternate Sundays.

Charles George Noel, second Earl of Gainsborough, and founder of the Exton Mission, died in that same year (1881). His son and heir, the third Earl, determined to build a church at Oakham as a memorial to his father. The foundation stone was laid on 7 July 1883, and Bishop Bagshawe opened the completed church on 16 October of the same year. The church, on Mill Street, was dedicated to St. Joseph and St. Edith. Presumably the second part of the dedication was to commemorate Lady Edith Noel and her family. It had sittings for about one hundred and twenty persons. The new church was provided with a weekly Mass on Sundays (except from 1885 to 1895, when there was a reversion to the fortnightly arrangement) from Exton Hall until 1918. In that year Oakham was given its own priest. When Bishop Dunn erected the Stations of the Cross in the church in 1920, he also blessed statues of the patron saints, St. Joseph and St. Edith.

Over the years, the general growth in population including the Catholic population meant that the old church was too small for its purposes, so a new church, dedicated to St. Joseph, was opened 5 April 1975. This church was designed by Thomas Wilson, a local architect who built widely in the diocese in the 1960s, and it is very similar to his earlier church at Deeping St. James.

The old church on Mill Street served as a parish social centre for a while. It is still owned by the diocese but is currently (2017) leased to a hairdresser.

English Martyrs Primary School was blessed and opened in May 1965. In 2011 it was federated with St. Augustine's School, Stamford. Two years later, it joined the St. Gilbert of Sempringham Catholic Academy Trust.

In recent years, some of the parishioners have attempted to draw attention to the Venerable John Lion and to resurrect devotion to him. Such devotion was not lacking in the 1920s, since the 1921 issue of the Nottingham Diocesan Yearbook describes in some detail the inauguration of an annual pilgrimage in honour of the local martyr, calling it "the great event of the year, at least from a spectacular point of view." The day began with Solemn High Mass, and, in the afternoon, there was a procession in the form of a pageant through the streets of Oakham with halts at the jail in which John Lion is believed to have been imprisoned, the castle where his mock trial is said to have taken place, and the spot on the Uppingham Road where the gallows formerly stood. The event concluded with Benediction given from an altar erected for this purpose outside St. Joseph's Church. It is not known when or why the earlier devotion to the Venerable John Lion lapsed.

OAKHAM, *St. Joseph (and St. Edith) Convent*

A convent of **Franciscan Minoresses** (now of Melton Mowbray) was opened in 1899, but closed in 1901. During these years, the Sisters had a resident chaplain.

OSGODBY

The Blessed Virgin (Our Lady) and St Joseph – served from Market Rasen

The presence of a chapel in so small a hamlet as Osgodby needs some explanation. In 1785, the Young family of West Rasen bought Kingerby Hall, less than a mile west of Osgodby. For their own needs, they might well have reopened the chapel which had existed inside the Hall earlier in the century. Instead, they preferred to establish a public chapel where it might be of use both to themselves and to the scattered Catholics of the countryside. In 1792 they accordingly built the existing chapel, most of the money being provided by Mrs. Tunstall, a member of the family.

The chapel stands today as a perfect example of the type erected in this country as soon as the legislation of 1791 made it legal to erect Catholic chapels. On the ground floor is the residence for the priest; above it is the chapel proper. The type had been evolved during the thirteen years that had elapsed since the First Catholic Relief Act of 1778. This Act tolerated Catholics, but not Catholic chapels, and the buildings put up at this time were designed to have the appearance of dwelling houses. The type persisted, owing to the diffidence of the Catholic body, even after 1791.

In spite of the diminutive congregation, it was possible to provide for the maintenance of a priest by means of endowments. These yielded, as late as 1880, a yearly income of over £163 (about £13,700 in 2017.) It was certainly the intention of the founders to establish a priest at Osgodby from the beginning, but certain evidence which would prove the residence of a priest from 1792 is lacking. The series of known priests begins in 1793.

It must soon have become evident that the Mission was not large enough to justify the full-time services of a priest. About 1880 Bishop Bagshawe attempted to place it on a more rational foundation combining it with a Mass centre at Caistor, eight miles to the north-east. This was opened in 1876, and about four years later the bishop gave orders for the erection of a school-chapel at Caistor. For some reason not known, it was found impossible to carry out these instructions and in 1882 the Caistor centre was closed. Around this time, we read the following: "The Mission has a small chapel for 80 persons, & a presbytery, but no school. It has some lands and endowments for the priest, being an ancient Mission. It is served by the Rev. Amadeus Gavois. There are 44 Catholics." In 1895 there were about 30, and the number was roughly the same in 1904.

In 1949 a small community of Sacred Heart Fathers was established at Market Rasen, four miles away. It then became possible to withdraw the priest from Osgodby and to attach it to the Market Rasen Mission.

In 1976 the chapel was listed. Since it was used only once a month for Mass, the diocese was considering closure, but the listing ruled out demolition as an option. Instead, in 1982, a charitable trust, the Friends of Osgodby Chapel, was established to restore and maintain the building. Internal redecoration was carried out by students from Lincoln College of Art. The chapel, reopened on 7 May 1989, is served from Market Rasen and Mass is celebrated there once a month.

RADCLIFFE-ON-TRENT

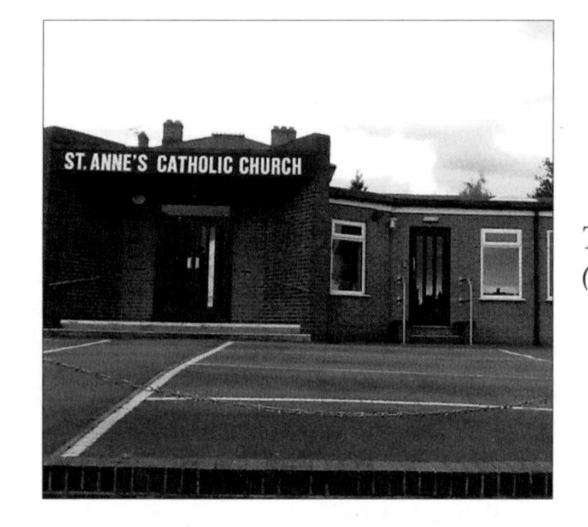

The English Martyrs (St. Anne)

This Trent-side village, lying rather more than five miles east of Nottingham along the old Grantham Road, took on the character of a dormitory for Nottingham in the years that followed the First World War. The new settlers contained an average proportion of Catholics for whom, in 1938, Fr. Robert Woodbridge of West Bridgford opened a Mass centre in 'The Lodge' at Wharfe End. In 1940 a corrugated-iron building in Shelford Road was bought and dedicated to The English Martyrs. Sunday Mass was said once a month until 1948 after which date it was said every week in a chapel which soon proved to be inadequate for the numbers of its congregation. The current church was "opened, blessed and dedicated to St. Anne" on 26 July 1962. The original intention was this should become the parish hall once a church had been built. This intention was never fulfilled and the hall has remained the church. In 1963 Radcliffe-on-Trent became a parish. However, the church/hall has been altered and extended over the years and now has catering facilities, a meeting room and extra seating all of which were provided in 1982. In the 1990s, the presbytery was extended, adding an office and a small reception room. A new sacristy was also built on to the hall. Finally, on 26 July 2002, the fortieth anniversary of its opening, St. Anne's Church was consecrated by Bishop McMahon.

RAINWORTH

St. George – served from Mansfield St. Patrick

The background to the erection of this church is rather unusual. For some years prior to 1942, Fr. John Cuddon (ordained 1909, died 1946) of the Southwark Diocese used to come and stay from time to time with his brother-in-law, Dr. Matthews, a general practitioner in Blidworth, some two miles from Rainworth. Because Fr. Cuddon was a sick man, he obtained permission to celebrate Mass in his brother-in-law's house. From the beginning of Advent 1942, Mass was said regularly in Blidworth by a priest from Mansfield. After the death of Dr. Matthews in 1946, his successor, a non-Catholic, allowed Mass to continue to be celebrated weekly in his surgery. At times during the Second World War, because of the demands for work in the pits, Mass attendance was very variable. Sometimes there were as few as eight people at Mass, and the future looked less than hopeful. But then the numbers increased to such an extent that the surgery was not big enough to contain them. So the Mass centre was moved to the Boys' Club in Belle Vue Lane, Blidworth, and it was given the name St. George.

In 1958 Bishop Ellis erected the Parish of St. Patrick, Forest Town, Mansfield, and assigned to the new parish the villages of Blidworth and Rainworth. Over the years, the people of St. George's had raised money and had bought a site in Rainworth on which the Church of St. George was built. It was opened on 12 July 1960.

A parish social club was opened in the former Palace Cinema twelve years to the day after the opening of the church.

RIPLEY

St. Joseph

Ripley is an ancient settlement which expanded rapidly from the late eighteenth century as coal, brickmaking and ironworking industries developed.

In the latter part of the nineteenth century, among the owners of the collieries and ironworks in the Ripley area were the Wright family who founded the Butterley Company. The family had a domestic chapel in their home, Butterley Grange, and Mass was celebrated there, at least on Sundays, for a number of years. When this chapel was closed, a new venue was found - the clubroom at the back of 'The Rose and Crown'. This soon proved inadequate to the needs of a growing congregation: in 1927 there were about a hundred Catholics living in Ripley. But hope was at hand. Mrs. Wright persuaded her husband to donate a piece of land on Butterley Hill as a site for a church, and on 28 May 1928 the foundation stone of the present church was laid by Bishop Dunn. Beneath the foundation stone was laid an oak casket containing: a list of parishioners, Catholic and daily newspapers, and current coins of the realm. The completed church, able to accommodate two hundred people, was opened on 10 December of the same year!

In the late 1930s parishioners of Belper and Ripley instituted the practice of going around the villages which constituted the parish and saying the Rosary in the homes of Catholics and – perhaps surprisingly for that time – of some non-Catholics too.

In 1953 Ripley was separated from Belper to form an independent parish.

For many years a wooden hut served as a parish hall in a carpark below the church. This was demolished and replaced in 2000 by a more substantial building with many facilities which are used not only by Catholics but also by other local people.

ROTHLEY

The Sacred Heart – served from Birstall

A first decade of apostolic work by the Rosminian Fathers came to a close about 1850. In the next seventy years, their only missionary foundation was that of Sileby. The foundation of Rothley in 1921 marked the beginning of a second phase of activity which has spread a network of village chapels all along the valley of the Soar.

The background to this and similar developments is given in the Nottingham Diocesan Yearbook for 1928. "The development of suburbs around all our larger towns, and the consequent migration of people to live 'in the country,' outside the busy centres of commercial life, makes it incumbent on ecclesiastical authorities to follow the population and provide suitable buildings for divine worship within easy reach of the new dwellings. Leicester is no exception to this general movement..."

The first Mass in Rothley was said by the Rosminian Fr. Keating in June 1921. Enderby House, in Howe Lane, was used as the Mass centre for the first three years. In 1924, some Dominican Tertiaries opened, at Corpus Christi House, what was described as a "Secondary School" for young boys and girls. This was used for Mass until the erection of a church in 1927. The convent was closed soon afterwards. The church is one of many designed and built by Mr. F. J. Bradford of Leicester. It was described as "eminently well-suited to its purpose, ... [and able to] meet the needs of the Catholics of the neighbourhood for many years to come"; and the hope was expressed that "buildings of this type could be multiplied in the diocese." The church was opened by Bishop Dunn on 19 July 1927. Served first from Ratcliffe College by the priest-in-charge of Sileby, since 1941 it has been attached to Birstall.

ROTHLEY - *Convent*

Dominican Tertiaries. From 1927, when they left Rothley, they came to be known as Corpus Christi Carmelites.

SCUNTHORPE

Holy Souls

In little more than half a century, Scunthorpe developed from a group of five villages in north Lincolnshire into an industrial borough with a population of more than 50,000. On All Souls Day, 2 November 1892, Fr. Michael Kirby of Brigg celebrated at a house on Mary Street what was probably the first Catholic Mass in Scunthorpe since the Reformation. This marked the beginning of post-Reformation Catholicism in the town. Five years later, Bishop Bagshawe sent Fr. Rupert McCauley to be the first resident priest. One year later he was replaced by Fr. John J. Hooker.

Sunday Mass was said at first in the drill Hall, but the thought of having this public building used in the long term as a place of Catholic worship caused a certain amount of disquiet among the townsfolk. This was perhaps one reason why the Belgian Fr. Leo Mouthuy (1907-1910) purchased, with the support of funds from the estate of Thomas Arthur Young of Kingerby Hall, land on Frodingham Road on which he built a wood and corrugated-iron structure affectionately known, like many similar buildings, as the 'Tin Tabernacle.'

With the arrival as parish priest of a former architect, Fr. Frederick

Askew, in 1910, things began to move quickly. Work started on a permanent church. The architects were Edmund Kirby & Sons of Liverpool, making this their only church in the Diocese of Nottingham. The church was opened in 1911, and the presbytery was completed in the mid-1920s, its building having been delayed due to a builders' strike.

The parish continued to grow in the following years, not least due to the influx of several hundred Irish workmen among others, and it became necessary in the 1930s to have an assistant priest for whose accommodation the presbytery had to be extended. In the 1930s Holy Souls' Parish was the third largest parish in Lincolnshire.

In 1954 part of the Parish of Holy Souls was cut off to form the new Parish of St. Bernadette in the Ashby area of Scunthorpe.

In the list of martyrs canonised by Pope Paul VI on 25 October 1970 there occurs the name of Augustine Webster. A graduate of Cambridge, he became a member of the Carthusian monastery at Sheen in Surrey and was then appointed Prior of Axholme (or Melwood) near Epworth. Along with two other Carthusians, John Houghton and Robert Lawrence and two other priests, he was hung, drawn and quartered at Tyburn on 4 May 1535. They were the first martyrs of the Reformation. Father John (Jack) Newsham, who came to Holy Souls in 1977, had earlier been Parish Priest of Eastwood in which parish lies the Carthusian monastery of Beauvale, home to Saints John Houghton and Robert Lawrence. On discovering that Melwood was not far from Scunthorpe, with the assistance of the Knights of St Columba, he instigated in 1981 an annual pilgrimage to Melwood in honour of St. Augustine Webster. This pilgrimage normally takes place in the first week of May.

The parish hall originally housed a printing business belonging to the Grasar family. This family was also responsible for publishing the 'Dowry of Mary' magazine from 1908 until 1958. One member of the family, William Eric, became a priest of the Nottingham Diocese in 1937 and then, in 1982, Bishop of Shrewsbury.

The hall was donated to the parish by the Grasars. It was burnt down in 2007, and a new hall with much better facilities was blessed and opened by Bishop McMahon in November 2011, the centenary year of the opening of the church.

As in every parish, the provision of Catholic education has always been a priority in Scunthorpe, but it was only in 1966 that Holy Souls got its own primary school dedicated to St. Augustine Webster.

SCUNTHORPE

St. Bernadette

1954, celebrated in the Catholic world as a 'Marian Year' since it marked the centenary of the definition of the dogma of the Immaculate Conception of the Blessed Virgin Mary, marked also the establishment of Scunthorpe's second parish, dedicated to St. Bernadette, the visionary of Lourdes. Fr. Albert Lakin of Holy Souls (1929-1949) bought, in 1940 a site in Ashby sufficient for a new church and priest's house. In 1939 he opened a Mass centre, which was housed in hired rooms (an Anglican church hall served the purpose at one time) until 1950. A temporary chapel was then built with voluntary labour, and opened on 26 October 1950.

The present church was consecrated in December 1980, and a parish centre, originally built as St. Bernadette's Catholic Social Club in 1965, was rebuilt and enlarged in 1999.

From April 1951 the temporary chapel served also as a school. It began with forty-eight pupils. Numbers increased rapidly. In 1954, three infant classrooms were added, built by voluntary labour including that of the first parish priest, Fr. Jeremiah McGillicuddy, in the space of five weeks! In July of the same year, the foundation stone for the present St. Bernadette's School was laid and the school opened its doors to more than three hundred pupils in September 1955.

Prior to the opening of St. Bede's Secondary School in September 1961 with 191 pupils and thirteen teaching staff, (including three Presentation Sisters) Catholic children of secondary age had to go to the all-age school in Crowle, twelve miles from Scunthorpe.

SCUNTHORPE, *St Bernadette – Convent*

Presentation Sisters opened a convent on Ashby High Street in 1951. During the half-century they spent here, the Sisters were involved, initially, primarily in formal education in three parishes and in four schools, but with the passage of time their apostolate expanded from being school-based to parish- based. They remained in the parish until 2002.

SHEPSHED

St. Winefride

The small market-town of Shepshed was the scene of the most fruitful of the apostolic labours of Fr. Luigi Gentili, a member of the Institute of Charity (usually known as Rosminians after their founder, Blessed Antonio Rosmini.) Gentili's success was extraordinary. His first lecture in the town was given on 7 August 1840 and twenty-five persons came to listen to him. By the end of the year he had received 67 converts, and this number rose to 200 adults and 100 children before the close of 1842. Some of these came from Belton, Osgathorpe and Grace Dieu, but by far the greater number were provided by Shepshed. Fr J. B. Pagani's 'Life of Gentili' gives an interesting insight into the religious life of the time, very different from the twenty-first century: "Not satisfied with previously calumniating the Catholic Church from the pulpits of error, they (the Anglican ministers) also sought out those who had received from Gentili any Catholic books, and took them away. They promised employment, with land to grow potatoes, and held out other advantages to induce them to renounce Catholicity and adhere to Protestantism. The parson at Shepshed, in particular, distinguished himself by his maniacal zeal, and did whatever he could to prevent parents from permitting their children to attend that Catholic chapel. He sent emissaries to distribute tracts calculated to excite ridicule against Catholic belief concerning images, indulgences, prayers for the dead, the Real Presence, etc. He engaged a curate to assist in opening a school for children, to whom lessons were given to learn at the precise time Fr. Gentili gave his instructions, and thus they were prevented from hearing him. At the same time also appointed by Gentili for adults, the parson began to give a No-Popery lecture." This, however, only stimulated the people's curiosity to hear Gentili, and the first No-Popery lecture was also the last. Fr. Gentili moved from Grace Dieu to Loughborough in 1842 and finally left the area three years later. He died in Dublin in 1848.

In January 1841 a site for the church, at the corner of Belton Street and Pick Street, was bought by Ambrose de Lisle. Since, however, funds for the building were not yet available, Fr. Gentili bought a disused Methodist chapel in Church Street, and converted it into a temporary chapel and schools. In the event, the costs of the church, designed by Augustus Welby Pugin, were kept low with the aid of the Grace Dieu tenantry, who provided and transported the stone without charge, and of the architect who refused to accept a fee for his work. Such money as was necessary came not only from the Shepshed congregation, but from Gentili's friends both in England and Italy. The foundation stone was laid on 28 March 1842 by Ambrose's son Everard, and the new church was opened on 18 November of the same year by Bishop Walsh, who at the same time consecrated the high altar. Pugin's plans provided for a nave with two aisles, a sanctuary, two side-chapels, and a crypt which was never used.

When Fr. Gentili left the district, Shepshed was established as an independent Mission. A small Rosminian community - two priests and two laybrothers - took up residence on 23 December 1845, at a house in The Flats, Pick Street, opposite the old church. For a short time (1849-1850) the novitiate of the Rosminians was also established here.

In 1852 the Rosminians withdrew from Shepshed and for the next year the Mission was served by Fr. John Wyse, a secular priest who – among other things - wrote the words of the hymn 'I'll sing a hymn to Mary'. In the following years, had it not been for the support given by the monks of Mount Saint Bernard Abbey, there would probably have been no Mass in Shepshed. In fact, there was no Sunday Mass from 1858 until 1862, when Fr. Angelus Van Paemel, one of a number of Belgian priests who served in Leicestershire in the latter part of the nineteenth century, came to Shepshed for one year before moving to Whitwick where he died in 1885. In Whitwick, he had as his curate, a fellow-countryman, Fr. John Aloysius Martens. In 1870 Fr. Martens moved to Shepshed, and then the almost dormant Mission got a burst of new life.

Fr. Martens (he was made Canon in 1891) spent the remaining forty-six years of his life in Shepshed where he "laboured with shrewd foresight and unflagging diligence for the flock entrusted to his care." He soon began a somewhat remarkable collection of property. In 1879 he acquired the cottages in Pick Street with a view to using the site for a new presbytery. A Belgian lady, Vicomtesse Marie Vilain XIII, gave him enough money to buy 2,200 square yards of land in Britannia Street on 8 March 1889 for the school. In the following year he bought, with the aid of a benefactor, a house in Pick Street. The same benefactor enabled him, on 28 September 1892, to buy the house in Charnwood Road known as 'The Elms'. Since 1895, when Canon Martens moved from Pick Street, this house has served as the presbytery, and the church is built on the adjoining site. In 1908 he purchased a disused United Methodist chapel in Hathern and dedicated it to his patron, Saint Aloysius. The chapel had closed by 2003. Canon Martens rounded off his collection of property in 1914, when he bought the 'White House' in Shepshed to serve as a home for aged and sick priests. This latter project never materialised, and the 'White House' served, in the early years of the First World War, to provide temporary accommodation for Belgian refugees.

Canon Bernard Hobson, who succeeded Canon Martens on the latter's death in 1916, "fulfilled a life-long ambition by erecting a new Gothic church of proportions which recalled the parish churches of the Middle Ages." It was to be his last work since he died in 1930, and he is buried near the side entrance to the church the foundation stone of which was laid on 4 June 1927 by Bishop Dunn. Some of the artefacts from the old church were transferred to the new church in time for its opening by Bishop Dunn on 10 April 1928. When the capital debt on the church had been paid off, it was consecrated by Bishop Ellis on 4 May 1945, the first church he consecrated after becoming bishop the previous year.

On Christmas Eve 1949, while the church bell was being rung for Midnight Mass, the rope broke and the bell was silent. Subsequent inspection revealed that the bell and its mounting were in a dangerous condition. The bell, which had come from the old Anglican church at Dishley near Loughborough, was recast and then consecrated by Bishop Ellis in April 1950. The seventy-fifth anniversary of the opening of St. Winefride's was celebrated with great enthusiasm in July 2003. One of those who took part in the celebrations observed that "It was like having a long weekend break without having to pack a suitcase!"

Shepshed's first Catholic school was opened by Fr. Gentili in a disused Methodist chapel which he had purchased in 1841 to serve also as a church. Separate day schools for boys and for girls were established in 1846, and the two schools were amalgamated in 1861. A new infant school was opened in 1896, and the remainder of the present school buildings dates from 1904. In 1959, the year in which De Lisle School in Loughborough opened, St. Winefride's was reorganised as a primary school.

SHIREBROOK (LANGWITH JUNCTION)

St. Joseph – served from St. Philip Neri, Mansfield

In the early years of the twentieth century, Shirebrook consisted of a mushroom growth of miners' cottages which had sprung up around the new pit. Among the sinkers were many Irish families. Some of these formed a committee which, in 1904, petitioned Bishop Brindle for a priest. They also adapted Cox's Barn, at the corner of Main Street and Central Drive, to serve as a chapel. Fr. Charles Froes, chaplain at Southgate House near Clowne, home of the Butler-Bowdon family, had opened a chapel at Bolsover in 1903. At the bishop's request, he transferred to Shirebrook. There he bought a corrugated-iron building on the recreation ground which had been erected to serve as an isolation hospital, but was never used for its original purpose. One part of this building served as a chapel, the other as the presbytery.

The foundation stone of the present church, erected on land bought from the Duke of Devonshire, was laid on 5 October 1907, and the church - a brick Gothic structure typical of its age - was opened on 29 August 1908. The building work was done by Irish labourers, and the early congregation was drawn from the local colliery. In 1964 a flat-roofed narthex was added at the west end of the church, as well as a sacristy off the north side of the chancel. At the time of the church's centenary in 2007, this narthex was replaced with a new and wider narthex and the church interior was redecorated at the same time.

Two chapels-of-ease were opened from Shirebrook, in Bolsover (1942) and in Market Warsop (1956).

After the First World War, Fr. Froes bought and erected an army hut in which he intended to open a school. The education authority refused to approve this project and the hut served as a meeting-room until 1947, when it was superseded by the present parish hall. Eventually, after a lot of hard work and some disappointments, St. Joseph's non-fee-paying Private School opened in April 1958 with forty children. By the autumn of that year the number had risen to 114. A new St. Joseph's Primary School for 150 pupils, solemnly blessed and opened by Bishop Ellis on 1 May 1963, was lyrically described in the following terms. "With its clean, graceful lines and airy lightness, [this school] brings a touch of much-needed beauty into the rather drab environment of a mining village. Its opening is the crowning of years of self-sacrifice on the part of priests, nuns and people." Over the years the school has been involved in many activities in the parish and beyond.

One of the many casualties of the decline of the mining industry in the late twentieth century was Shirebrook whose colliery closed in 1993.

SHIREBROOK (LANGWITH JUNCTION), *St. Joseph – Convent*

Presentation Sisters came to Shirebrook in 1958 in response to a request from Bishop Ellis to teach in the independent non-fee-paying school. Initially housed in the presbytery (the priest having moved out), the Sisters remained in Shirebrook until 1981 when they moved to Bolsover.

SILEBY

St. Gregory - served from Syston

Sileby is an old village which expanded in the mid-nineteenth century with the coming of the Midland Railway line. In the 1840s, soon after their arrival in the area, the Fathers of Charity (Rosminians) established, from Ratcliffe College, a Mass centre at Sileby. The present church, a modest Victorian brick Gothic chapel, of some architectural interest for the vigorous brickwork of the exterior, was opened in 1877, and was the first of the Rosminian Missions in the Soar valley. The first priest was Fr. William Lewthwaite, an Anglican convert ordained in 1854.

Initially the Rosminians found nothing but hostility in Sileby until some twenty years after their arrival in the area. The famine conditions of

1865 brought a change of mind. Many of the villagers came to the college for their daily food, and this contact with the Rosminian Fathers led some of them to attend instructions in the college chapel. No less than seventy children were brought by their parents to be instructed, and a school at Sileby became essential. Three thatched cottages were bought in the village and opened as a school in 1874. A school-chapel replaced these on the same site in 1876, but the first Mass was not said therein until 15th April 1877. The school is last heard of in 1885, and was then, apparently, closed.

In 1885 the Mission was united with Barrow-on-Soar to form an independent Mission of Barrow-cum-Sileby. Its history since that time has been somewhat confused. The priests of the Mission have been supplied at different times by the diocesan clergy and the Rosminians, and have resided for varying periods in the villages of Barrow (1885-1887, 1900-1902 and 1910-1920) and in Sileby (1903-1908) and also at Ratcliffe College. From 1947 one of the Rosminians from Birstall served Sileby until 1972, since which time the parish has been served by diocesan clergy.

SKEGNESS

Sacred Heart

Skegness was the first of a series of five Missions (the others were Sleaford, 1879; Woodhall Spa, 1895; Westborough, 1887, Welbourne, 1900) founded in Lincolnshire by Fr. Peter Sabela. While Missionary Priest at Boston, he began, in 1877, to say Mass at Skegness on one weekday each month. His brother, Fr. Herman Sabela, took his place in Boston in 1879, and obtained from the proprietor of the Seaview Hotel, Skegness, the use of a barn. This was fitted up as a chapel and opened on 18 July 1880. An assistant priest had been assigned to Boston, and this enabled Mass to be said in Skegness every Sunday. Fr. Herman Sabela continued to serve the Mission even after his removal to Sleaford in 1882. By 1885 Fr. H. Sabela had purchased a large site for a future Mission at Skegness of which he had the spiritual charge. It reverted to Boston after his departure from Lincolnshire in 1886. But it seems to have been peculiarly dependent on the personal interest taken in it by Fr. Sabela and in 1889 the temporary chapel was closed.

A refoundation was made in 1896 by the same Fr. Peter Sabela who had said the first Mass at Skegness in 1877. He was now Missionary Priest of Grantham, but seems to have exercised a roving apostolate in the county, and Fr. Philip Capron, the priest who resided at Skegness from 1896 to 1897, is described as assistant priest. From the latter date until 1908, Fr. James V. Davis was there, so it is legitimate to infer that, from about September 1898, when a small brick church was opened in Grosvenor Road, the Skegness district seems to have been an independent Mission. This first church bore the lengthy dedication of the Sacred Heart and Our Lady of the Holy Souls.

Between the two World Wars, the need for a much larger church became urgent. Sufficient money was raised by 1939, but the outbreak of war held up the project and halved the value of the funds in hand. New efforts were made, and at last, on 15 December 1949, the foundation stone was laid by Bishop Ellis. The architects, Messrs. Reynolds & Scott of Manchester, designed the new building with a view to accommodating a large seasonal congregation. The baptismal font, in Yorkshire stone, was subscribed for as a memorial to Fr. Charles Croucher, who died in 1947 after thirty years in the parish. When the new church was opened on 30 July 1950, the former lengthy dedication was shortened to the Sacred Heart.

Around 1999 the rather ramshackle presbytery was found to be uninhabitable, and a pair of semi-detached houses were built along Grosvenor Road next to the church. The first of the pair, next to the church, was designed as the presbytery, while the second was built for rental to bring in an income.

SKEGNESS *Sacred Heart – Convents*

The **Franciscan Minoresses** were here briefly (1900-1901).

Franciscan Sisters of the Holy Ghost conducted St. Peter's College, a day-school for junior boys from 1911 to 1918.

SLEAFORD

Our Lady of Good Counsel

The first missionary activity in Sleaford seems to date from August 1879, when one of the two Fathers Sabela began to give outdoor sermons for Irish harvesters, using a wagon (located on Sleaford cricket field, according to one source) as a pulpit. It does not seem, however, that Mass was said in Sleaford until 1881. In the December of the previous year, Fr. Sabela bought from J. T. Marston Esq. a building site in Jermyn Street. Work was begun in 1881 on the erection of a school-chapel. The foundation stone was laid by Bishop Bagshawe on 24 November of that year and it was opened 1 June 1882. At the time it was dedicated to 'Our Lady of the Immaculate Conception'.

When this new school-chapel was opened, Sleaford became an independent Mission with Fr. Herman Sabela as its first priest. A presbytery was built at this time - a large three-storey building whose size suggests that it might have been intended for a community of priests serving the surrounding district. As things turned out, it proved useful when the Conventual Franciscan Friars took over the parish in 1964.

Although the permanent Catholic population of Sleaford hardly rose above a hundred until the turn of the nineteenth century, it was considerably augmented in the harvest season by Irish labourers. The small school-chapel was at such times too small. On 14 September 1888 the foundation stone of the present church was laid, and it was opened in June the following year. It is not clear whether this building was a completely new one or simply a rebuilding of the school-chapel constructed a mere seven years earlier. Whatever the case, the present church is an ornate specimen of brick Gothic. The dedication was changed to 'Our Lady of Good Counsel' at the time of the opening. An oil painting of Our Lady under this invocation, believed to have been the work of Fr. Herman Sabela, who had some considerable artistic gifts as, indeed, did his brother Peter, was originally over the high altar, but was relocated to the south wall of the nave in the reordering of 2015. A new porch was added to the church in 1989. In the second decade of the present century, an ambitious and highly successful project was undertaken involving the restoration of some of the features of the 1889 church which had been altered in the aftermath of the Second Vatican Council. The sanctuary is outstanding.

After the building of the church in 1889, the old school-chapel of 1882 continued in use, with some additions. The school was founded in 1882 in what is now the church hall. It moved to the current site on The Drove in 1974 and was converted to become an academy in 2013.

SLEAFORD, *Our Lady of Good Counsel – Religious Communities*

Sisters of St Joseph of Peace staffed the school from 1897 to 1901.

Conventual Franciscan Friars served the parish from 1964 to 1993.

SOUTHWELL

Our Lady of Victories

In 1884 a Miss Sophia Sherlock gave an "excellent" site for a church, a house and schools as well as a donation towards a building fund. On the basis of this, Bishop Bagshawe hoped to be able "in time" to open a Mission there. This hope was not able to be realised for more than fifty years, and then only gradually. From 1945 Mass was celebrated at Southwell "by arrangement." It is only from 1949 that it is stated that this is explicitly "on Sundays", which leads one to believe that, prior to this, it may have been a weekday Mass. The initiative for the Mass at Southwell came from Canon Bernard Farmer of Newark. From 1950, Sunday Mass was celebrated at the WVS Hall., and, by 1956, in addition to Sunday Mass, there was an evening Mass on Holydays of Obligation.

Southwell was served from Newark until 1963 when it was given its own priest who, however, lived in Calverton while Calverton was being served from Good Shepherd, Arnold! The following year Southwell and Calverton became an independent parish with the parish priest living in Calverton until the early 1970s.

The foundation stone of the Church of Our Lady of Victories was laid on 7 October 1961, and the church was officially opened by Bishop Ellis on 12 September of the following year. Canon Farmer of Newark, whom one may regard as the founder of the Parish of Southwell and Calverton, died before the end of that month.

Among those present at the official opening of the church was the Provost of the Anglican Diocese of Southwell. Bishop Ellis, in his sermon, "spoke movingly" on devotion to Our Lady as a common bond between Catholics and [what were then called] our Separated Brethren. In the years since then, this bond has grown ever stronger, and it has become the normal practice for the Catholics and the Anglicans of Southwell to celebrate part of Holy Week together.

A bungalow presbytery was built next to the church in 1970. In the late 1990s an internal narthex with choir loft and organ was added to the church. This has proved to be a great blessing in providing more space and helping to keep the church warmer by eliminating some of the sources of draughts. In October 1999 a new parish centre adjacent to the church was blessed and opened by Bishop McGuinness. The church and parish centre together make a positive contribution to the local scene.

The Spiritans, or Holy Ghost Fathers, as they are usually known, opened their House of Studies at Upton Hall near Newark in 1945. This closed in 1972. During their time at Upton, the priests performed a valuable role in the pastoral care of the neighbourhood, and the students forged links with the (Anglican) Society of the Sacred Mission at nearby Kelham Hall.

SPALDING

Immaculate Conception and St. Norbert

Spalding in South Lincolnshire was famous for its Flower Festival in the latter part of the twentieth century, and it was on 7 October 1979, that in Spalding the first barcode was used in the United Kingdom.

Much more importantly, the first Mass in post-Reformation times was said at Spalding in 1872 by the Dutchman Fr. John Theodore Hoeben of Boston. For the next three years, Mass was said infrequently on a weekday. In this period there were not more than two Catholic families, and a few individuals, in the town. With the support of Mr. Thomas Arthur Young of Kingerby, the Premonstratensians of Tongerloo undertook to found a Mission on this almost virgin soil. A house was bought for them, 28 St Thomas' Street. The Premonstratensian Fr. Thomas Van Biesen arrived to take charge in December 1875. Spalding thus became the second Premonstratensian house in England, the first having been founded at Crowle in 1872. In 1879 Bishop Bagshawe noted that there were seventy Catholics in Spalding (although there were hardly any when the Premonstratensians arrived), and ten children attended the school.

Until the erection of the church, Mass was said in a chapel improvised from a room in the priest's house. The first portion of the church, designed by M. E. Hadfield & Son of Sheffield, was begun almost immediately. It was opened by Bishop Bagshawe on 13 November 1876. A new presbytery was built around the same time. The remainder of the church was erected in 1879 and seated about two hundred. It was consecrated in 1904. The whole expense of the building was borne by Mr. Young, and both church and presbytery belonged to the Premonstratensian Order. In addition to the church at Spalding, the Premonstratensians served the chapel in the home of S. Waterton Esq. at Deeping Waterton, some nine miles south of Spalding.

The Lourdes Grotto at Spalding was built and solemnly blessed on 17 September 1908, in the fiftieth anniversary year of the apparition of Our

Lady to St. Bernadette. From about 1910, an outdoor procession was held as part of an annual pilgrimage in honour of Our Lady of Lourdes. In the 1921 procession, about fifty banners were carried and eighteen bannerets representing the apparitions at Lourdes. In the 1922 procession, the choir was led by boys from the college at Deeping St. James.

A school was in existence by 1877 and new school buildings were erected in 1879. The cost of erection was again borne by Mr. Young. In 1885 the school had fifty-five pupils most of whom were Protestants. St. Norbert's School, which now (2017) has seven classes for pupils aged four to eleven, moved to its present site on Tollgate, the better part of a mile from the church, in 1964.

By the mid-1990s the church, priory buildings and old school buildings, by this time used as a parish hall, were all in need of refurbishment. Various plans were advanced trying to keep elements of the buildings partly for the sake of the sensitivities of the local people, but in the end the entire site was cleared in 2003 and new buildings consisting of church, hall, parish rooms and presbytery, were opened the following year. To emphasise the continuity, some of the furnishings from the old church - in particular, the crucifix, Stations of the Cross, tabernacle and marble font, were transferred to the new one. There is some fine modern stained glass to be found in the church. The church was consecrated on 8 December 2004, the Solemnity of the Immaculate Conception, by Bishop McMahon, who told the congregation that some of his fellow-bishops would not believe him when he told them he was going to consecrate a new church – in 2004!

Not long afterwards, it was announced that the Premonstratensians, who had served Spalding so faithfully for more a hundred and thirty years, would no longer be able to do so, and so Spalding and the neighbouring parish of Holbeach were handed over to the diocesan clergy in 2008.

SPALDING, *Immaculate Conception and St. Norbert - Convent*

Norbertine Sisters (Third Order) had a convent in Spalding from 1877 to 1882 and taught in the school during this time.

SPILSBY

Our Lady and the English Martyrs - served from Skegness

Described as "An Outpost of the Diocese", the foundation of a Mission at Spilsby in 1897 was almost accidental. Fr. Gilbert V. Bull had come to reside at nearby Halton Holgate in the previous year. His purpose had been to revive the Order of Sempringham, the only monastic Order of English origin, which had disappeared altogether at the time of the Reformation. The Order, however, refused to come to life again, and this left Fr. Bull free for missionary activity in the neighbourhood. He said the first Mass at Spilsby on 24 October 1897. For this purpose, he hired a room, apparently attached to a public house, and continued to say Mass there each Sunday until he left the area in 1900.

The original dedication of the Mission was to Our Lady of Good Counsel and St. Gilbert of Sempringham. This was changed to the present dedication when the church was opened for use in 1902.

The Mission might well have perished on the departure of Fr. Bull but for the interest taken in it by Mr. W. D. Gainsford of Skendleby Hall. About March 1899 he had bought a site for a church in Spilsby and had begun building operations at his own expense. The first portion of the church was completed and in use by the summer of 1902. Subsequent difficulties - including a lawsuit between Mr. Gainsford and the builder prevented the erection of the remainder until after the First World War. It was finally opened and consecrated in 1925. Mr. Gainsford lived long enough to witness the consecration. He died on 4 October 1926 and lies buried under the shadow of the church that he had built and endowed at his own expense.

The problem of finding - or rather sparing - a priest to serve so small a Mission has always been acute. Fr. Bull's successor continued to live at Sempringham House, Halton Holgate, for one year. This house was then given up. The Mission was then handed over to the Benedictines (1904-1906) and then to the Rosminians, who departed in 1907. During these years

(1904-1908) some stability was given to the parish by the establishment of an Ursuline Convent at Welham House, Spilsby. For nearly thirty years after the departure of the Rosminians there was no resident priest in the town. For the last nine years of this period, the Mission was served by the Capuchins of Panton. Their departure in 1936 precipitated a crisis in the Lincolnshire Missions, and in the reorganisation that followed, a priest was once more sent to reside at Spilsby. A year later the Horncastle Mass centre was transferred to the care of this priest. But the problem of finding a suitable priest's house had still to be solved. For one year (1937-1938) the priest resided at Woodhall Spa; then (1938-1940) at 21 North Street, Horncastle. There were two years (1940-1942) of lodging at Silverdale, Boston Road, Spilsby, followed by five more in a caravan on the plot of land adjoining the church.

The existing presbytery was built in 1947. In reply to a question as to why, after five years of living in a caravan, Fr. Waldo Judd (1942-1948) had finally decided to build a presbytery, he is said to have replied that it was to help the Dean carry out his responsibility of inspecting all parts of the parish property. The Dean in question at that time was a man of such ample proportions that he was unable to squeeze through the narrow doorway of the caravan, so he had ordered Fr. Judd to build a presbytery which would have a wider door than a caravan!

At the end of the nineteenth century Spilsby was also serving Skendleby and Halton Holegate. For many years in the twentieth century Spilsby was served from Woodhall Spa, but since 2008 has been attached to the Parish of Skegness. Spilsby is a good example – there are others – of a Catholic community flourishing without a resident priest.

SPILSBY, *Our Lady and the English Martyrs – Convent*

Ursuline Sisters had a convent at Welham House, Spilsby, from 1904 to 1908. In his 1904 Quinquennial Report to the Holy See, Bishop Brindle mentioned that three communities of Religious very recently expelled from France had come to his diocese. One of these was the Ursulines. It is reasonable to presume that these were the Sisters who came to Spilsby.

These Sisters came from Rouen and had a convent and high school. An advertisement for the school includes the following. "The course of studies includes the … usual branches of an efficient and refined English education, together with French, Latin, and the German languages" and adds that "It is worthy of note that English girls attending the School can follow the French curriculum without the expense of travelling abroad."

STAMFORD

Our Lady and St. Augustine

It cannot be ascertained with certainty when the Mass returned to Stamford after the Reformation. According to one source, there was a Mass centre at Stamford from 1784 to 1790; according to another, Mass was celebrated in the town earlier in the eighteenth century. It appears that a priest from the so-called 'Riding Mission' (referred to as such because of the large distances that had to be covered on horseback) said Mass regularly, albeit infrequently, over some decades and, from 1823, monthly.

Accounts differ as to where in the town Mass was said. It is known, however, that, in 1825, work began on a chapel in the yard behind 19 All Saints Street. When this chapel was opened in the following year, the 'Stamford Mercury' commented that "The building is of considerable size, though there are at present in Stamford few people of the Roman Catholic persuasion." In 1833 19 All Saints Street was demolished and the chapel was considerably enlarged. Two years later, Number 20 was purchased and became the home of the – since 1834 – resident priest, Fr. William Wareing, who, in 1840, became Vicar-Apostolic of the Eastern District and, ten years later, first Bishop of Northampton.

Wareing's successor but one, the Irishman Fr. Thomas J. O'Connor, spent almost the whole of his short priestly life in Stamford dying in 1861 at the age of fifty-five. His congregation consisted almost entirely of seasonal Irish labourers. It is recorded that, in the summer of 1845, over a thousand Irish harvesters were attending Mass, and that sermons were preached for them in Gaelic. Fr. O'Connor had influence over his flock in many ways, and he provided assistance to the poor from his own slender resources. Additionally, he was successful, where the police had failed, in imposing peace upon their frequent quarrels.

A larger church became a necessity. The Dolphin Inn on Broad Street was purchased for the parish by the convert Charles Ormston Eaton of

Tolethorpe Hall. Eaton also contributed towards the cost of building the present church for which plans were drawn up in 1862 by George Goldie. In 1863 the pub was demolished and the foundation stone of the church laid. The work was begun by Fr. James Daly, but he died in June 1864 at the age of twenty-nine. On the night before his funeral, his body lay in the uncompleted church, which was opened by Bishop Wareing on 6 June 1865. The new church was described at the time as "the prettiest modern Gothic erection in the town." It appears that the presbytery and schools, which flank the church in Broad Street, were erected at the same time. The belfry was added to the church in 1871.

Bishop Bagshawe, in his Quinquennial Report to the Holy See of 1885, referred to Stamford as "a very bigoted place." Six years after this Report was written there arrived in Stamford as parish priest, the thirty-five-year-old, newly ordained Fr. Joseph West. He was to spend the whole of his priestly ministry – fifty-one years – in Stamford where he died shortly before his eighty-sixth birthday. He was, by all accounts, quite a character. On the occasion of the Golden Jubilee, in 1941, of his Ordination, a local newspaper described him as "a loved and revered figure not only among adherents of his own faith", listing among his characteristics his ability as an after-dinner speaker, and a love of horse-riding, a pursuit in which he had engaged until quite recently. He had a great love for the Old Testament and this was reflected in his sermons and in his conversation. Clearly attitudes in the local community to Catholics had changed helped, no doubt, by the long ministry and the personality of Canon (since 1924) West.

As part of the redecoration of the church in the 1940s, new Stations of the Cross, were erected in memory of those who fell during the two World Wars, a gift of the departing American armed forces and "around the walls of the church beautiful English oak panelling was placed, giving a rich but dignified effect."

It was only in July 1952 that the church was consecrated in a "long and tiring service." Post-consecration celebrations lasted for a whole week and included a grand tea-party for the children and a dinner party for eighty-three members of the congregation at the Stamford Hotel. The parish priest observed that if the present (1952) generation were to emulate the example of zeal and courage of those great priests and laity of the past, they would leave, as their forebears had done, their mark upon this lovely old Lincolnshire town.

Much has been done since 1952 by way of reordering. Most recently the sanctuary ceiling has been cleaned and restored and the entire church redecorated. In 2016 the confessional was returned to its original location in the aisle beside the sanctuary, and the altar of St. Joseph's Chapel was brought forward to facilitate the celebration of weekday Mass there facing the people. The linenfold panelling was completed along the back wall of the chapel where the altar had been fixed to the wall.

At various times the priest of Stamford has served in other places, such as the domestic chapels at Tolethorpe Hall, the home of the great benefactor of Stamford, Charles Eaton, and that at Deeping Waterton, home of the Waterton family. For a while in the 1880s, but no longer by 1890, Oakham was served from Stamford.

St. Augustine's School was formed in 1852. Classes were initially held in a tenement behind the 'Olive Branch' in Saint Leonard's Street. The first purpose-built school opened in 1870 in what is now the parish hall.

In 1957 the junior school transferred to its present site in Kesteven Road, while the infants initially remained in the Broad Street building until additional classes were added to the Kesteven Road site.

STAPLEFORD

St. John the Evangelist – served from Ilkeston

In the early part of the twentieth century, Catholics in the Stapleford and Sandiacre area wishing to attend Sunday Mass had to make their way, usually on foot since few people had cars in those days, to either Long Eaton or Ilkeston, in either case a considerable distance.

A group of local Catholics approached Bishop McNulty in 1933 with a request for a Mass centre at Stapleford. An enquiry requested by the bishop as to how many Catholics there were in the area gave the result: roughly sixty-two including practising and non-practising. After some searching, a rather dilapidated loft over a disused stable was rented and converted for use as a chapel. This involved a lot of hard work including repairs to the floor and the construction of an outside staircase. One hundred folding chairs were bought, and a parishioner, a retired postman, made all the kneelers. The first Mass was celebrated in this chapel on 22 October 1933. Not long afterwards, Bishop McNulty himself came to celebrate Mass, and his request that the chapel should be dedicated to St. John the Evangelist in honour of his own patron saint was gladly accepted by the parishioners.

Eighteen months later, a site on Midland Avenue was bought where, on 6 October 1951, Bishop Ellis laid the foundation stone of the present church and on 2 November of the following year he solemnly blessed and opened it. It had been intended that the church should have a tower forty feet high but, for various reasons, this was never built. Between 1933 and 1947, Stapleford was served firstly from the cathedral, then from Long Eaton and, finally, from Ilkeston.

After the Second World War, an influx of Catholics made it desirable to form Stapleford into an independent parish, and Fr. Paul Klee was sent to be its first Parish Priest in 1947. A house in Lime Grove was bought to serve as a presbytery. This was given up in 1951 to economise funds for the church building. For the next three years, the priest lived at Borrowash House where the Sisters of St. Joseph of Peace had opened a mother and baby home. A presbytery at 11 Bessell Lane was completed in 1954 and a parish hall was built around the same time. Some years later, the presbytery was sold and a house behind the church was bought to serve in its place. When the parish ceased to have a resident priest in 2003, this house along with a sizeable garden was sold for development. Since 2005 Stapleford has been served from Ilkeston.

In October 1962 a dual-purpose chapel-of-ease was opened just off the main Nottingham-Derby road at Bramcote. The vision was to build a church and presbytery and, when this was done, the original building would serve as a parish hall. Unfortunately, this vision could not be realised, and the chapel, dedicated to St. Gregory the Great, closed in 1994.

SUTTON-IN-ASHFIELD

St Joseph the Worker – served from Kirkby-in-Ashfield

From the 1920s Mass was said in various private houses until, in January 1931, Fr. John Keogh, Parish Priest of St. Philip Neri, Mansfield, formed a chapel-of-ease by converting a room over a garage in North Street. This chapel was furnished from various sources. The altar came from the convent of the Sisters of St. Joseph of Peace in Mapperley; the benches from Long Eaton; the branch candlesticks came from the Great War Camp at Clipstone; the chalice was the gift of Mgr. Charles Payne, Fr. Keogh's predecessor in Mansfield.

When Fr. Keogh, "an admirable example of a priest who knew how to combine an active life with a life of prayer," died in 1940, he left a considerable sum of money for the building of a new church. Nonetheless, it took several years before the present site in Forest Street was acquired. Meanwhile the congregation continued to grow. Concerns about mining subsidence led to the architects, Reynolds and Scott, adopting a raft and beam reinforced concrete foundation for the new church. The difference in levels meant that it was possible to accommodate a large parish hall beneath the church. Work began on the new church in 1959; it was opened and blessed by Bishop Ellis two years later. A distinguishing feature of the church is its seventy-foot high bell tower, which can be seen for miles around. The presbytery, situated high above the road and accessible by a series of steps, is contemporaneous with the church. St. Joseph's Church was consecrated by Bishop McGuinness in 1986, at the time of its Silver Jubilee.

Sutton-in-Ashfield continued to be served from Mansfield until 1956 when it became an independent parish with its own parish priest. This arrangement lasted until September 2003, after which time and until 2012, it was – once again – served from St. Philip Neri, Mansfield. Since 2012 it has been served from Kirkby-in-Ashfield.

SWADLINCOTE

(Jesus and Mary)
Saints Peter and Paul

Towards the end of the nineteenth century, local Catholics began to gather together to recite the Rosary in the Spread Eagle public house in Newhall. This was the origin of the parish now known as Swadlincote. In 1884 Fr. Hubert de Burgh, chaplain to Lady Loudoun of Willesley Hall near Measham, began to say Mass in a private house in Parliament Street for the Catholic population of the new mining village of Newhall. Towards the end of the 1880s, Lady Loudoun erected in Newhall a school-chapel, dedicated to St. Edward, and provided money to build a house for the priest. The school-chapel was opened by Bishop Bagshawe in 1896. The buildings remained the property of Lady Loudoun until her death in 1915, when they were handed over to the diocese.

Fr. Maurice Parmentier, parish priest from 1903 to 1927, realising that Newhall was no longer the principal centre of population in the parish, decided to move to Swadlincote; this happened in 1921. With a view to building a new church to replace the old school-chapel at Newhall, he collected money assiduously, especially from his friends in Belgium, his native country. In the meantime, the congregation worshipped in a temporary church dedicated to Jesus and Mary. Bishop Dunn was pleased, when he visited Swadlincote in September 1922, with the splendid progress that had been made at Boardman's Hill, where the foundations of the proposed new church had been laid for quite a long time, but it was not contemplated commencing the building of the church for some time "owing to certain financial arrangements". The church was made of two former army huts, which were erected and later clad with brick by men of the parish. This was replaced in 1958 by the present church dedicated to Saints Peter and Paul and opened by Bishop Ellis on 29 June on one of the very few sunny days in the wettest June for fifty-five years! On this occasion, a tangible link with the past was provided by the organ from the old church – which men of the parish hauled up on ropes into the choir loft!

On 14 April 1978 the church was consecrated by Bishop McGuinness.

The presbytery was extended and a social club erected in the 1970s. A Calvary within a brick shelter of Gothic design, which is said to date from the 1850s, stands set back from the presbytery Its origin is obscure, but it seems that it was on the site by 1918 when it was dedicated as a war memorial.

The parish primary school which - in 1898 for example - had one hundred and forty pupils, continued to be housed in the old school-chapel in Newhall until 1972 when it was replaced by the present school on Newhall Road.

SWADLINCOTE - *Convent*

A convent of the **Sisters of Mercy** was founded from Derby in 1955 when the Sisters took over the running of St. Edward's School. They continued to do so until 1988 when they were replaced by lay staff. The convent closed in 1990.

SYSTON

The Divine Infant of Prague

Three attempts have been made to establish the Church in Syston. The first was in 1899, when Fr. Laurence Hendricks, a former Carthusian, who also had charge of the chapel at Barrow-on-Soar, came to reside at Syston and opened a Mass centre. In the following year he moved to Melton Mowbray, but continued, until 1901, to come over to say Mass on a weekday.

After a closure of twenty years, the Rosminian Fr. John Keating began to say Mass on one Sunday a month at No 5 Lower Church Street. This Mass centre lasted from 1921 to 1924.

In 1939 the Rosminians of Ratcliffe again began a weekly Mass - this time in the Assembly Rooms, Leicester Road. During the Second World War, the congregation was swelled by both American servicemen (based at East Goscote) and Italian Prisoners of War (their camp was near Thurmaston). In the mid-1940s the Assembly Rooms were destroyed by fire and Fr. Denis Horgan obtained permission to build a temporary church on the present site in Broad Street. During the clearing-up after the fire in the Assembly Rooms, a broken statue of the Divine Infant of Prague was found among the debris. According to one account, Fr. Horgan was so amazed at this discovery that he decided to dedicate the church to Our Lord under this title. He may not have been aware that the church and/or Mission had been given this title half a century earlier. According to this other account, Fr. Hendricks set up a shrine to the Divine Infant of Prague in each of the Missions in which he had served. Be that as it may, Fr. Horgan collected funds vigorously, and erected a church the building of which with mostly voluntary labour and materials salvaged from bomb sites in the vicinity is a noteworthy example of community enterprise. The marble altar is of nineteenth century character and was presumably brought from another church. The carved oak doors are of some interest, and come from a dismantled Protestant church. The new church was opened in 1948. The building has been considerably enlarged since then. Syston became an independent parish in 1964, a year after it began to be served by diocesan clergy.

Barrow-on-Soar was begun from Loughborough. A church was built by voluntary labour at Barrow-on-Soar in 1839. Over the years, Barrow has been variously attached to Sileby, then to Birstall and finally in 1972 once again to Sileby. The Barrow church was closed in 1989.

Bishop Ellis Primary School in Thurmaston has the distinction of being the only school in the diocese to be named after a serving bishop. It first admitted pupils – one hundred and twenty of them – in January 1969, but the blessing and official opening by Bishop Ellis himself took place on 8 October of that year. When the school celebrated its Silver Jubilee, numbers had risen to three hundred and twenty-three. In 2017 the number was around three hundred and fifty.

TIDESWELL

The Immaculate Heart of Mary – served from Marple Bridge and New Mills

A considerable nucleus of Catholics had survived in Tideswell to the end of Penal Times. It is known that in 1791, and probably for some years previously, they were able to attend Mass at Whetstone Hall, one and a half miles to the west. When this was sold, around 1830, by the Duke of Norfolk, the congregation took action of its own accord to provide itself with a substitute chapel. It seems that the initiative was taken by one Robert Firth, yeoman. He owned an outbuilding, some 33 feet by 17 feet, and he adapted this for the purpose. It served as a Mass centre from Hathersage. At some date before 1857 this chapel was closed, and it may be surmised that its closure became necessary in 1834, when one of the two priests who had hitherto served Hathersage was withdrawn.

From 1857 Mass was again said in Tideswell, possibly in the old chapel, by the priest of Hathersage. This arrangement continued until 1876, when the ageing Canon Joseph Daniel found the duty beyond his strength and handed over the care of the Mass centre to Buxton. Three years later the drift to the towns so diminished the congregation (there were no Catholics in Tideswell in 1879) that the Mission was closed.

Its revival was due to Bishop Bagshawe's personal interest in the district from which his own forbears had sprung. In 1884 he sent Fr. John J. Hooker to be the first resident priest of Tideswell. Accounts of this new foundation are confused and contradictory, but it seems most probable that the chapel now in use was that of 1830, and that in 1887 Fr. Hooker opened a school in Bagshawe Hall, later transferred to a room in the Rising Sun. The school had a short-lived existence and was closed in 1897.

In this form, the Mission survived until the resignation of Bishop Bagshawe in 1901. His successor, Bishop Brindle, immediately decided that the small congregation did not warrant the services of a resident priest. More than twenty years were to pass before it was possible, once again, to provide Tideswell with a priest of its own. The bungalow behind the church was built as the presbytery in the early twentieth century, but is now in private domestic ownership.

In 1937 the Mission was strengthened by the erection of a church at Chapel-en-le-Frith. It soon became clear, however, that the greater part of the congregation resided around this new church and in 1944 the residence of the priest was moved to Chapel-en-le-Frith, and Tideswell reverted to the status of a chapel-of-ease. It has remained such since that time.

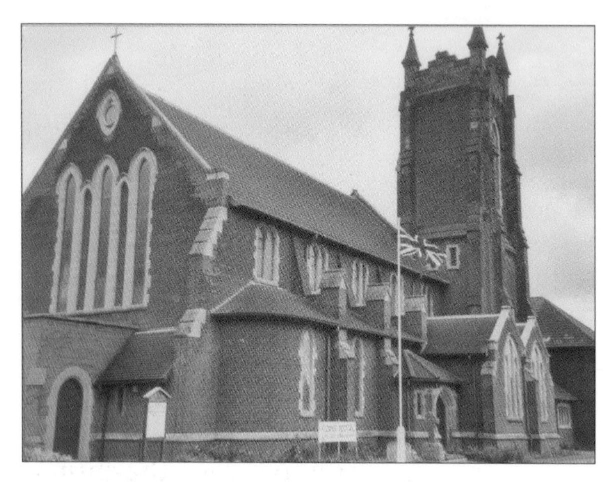

WHITWICK

Holy Cross

The oldest of the Charnwood Forest Missions dates from the pre-Rosminian period when the Cistercians of Mount St. Bernard were exercising an active apostolate in the district. According to one account, the need for a church at Whitwick arose from the presence of Irish labourers engaged in building the first Cistercian monastery. Ambrose de Lisle of Grace Dieu provided the necessary funds for the old church and priest's house, and these consequently remained the private property of the de Lisle family until after 1882.

Bishop Walsh consecrated the first Holy Cross Chapel on 12 October 1837. On the two previous days he had consecrated the domestic chapel at Grace Dieu and the first chapel of the monastery. In 1935, to commemorate the centenary of Gentili's arrival in England, a Lourdes grotto was erected on the site of the old Holy Cross Chapel.

For some considerable time, the Mission suffered from instability. Priests were in short supply. For the first three years it was served from the monastery by Fr. Odilo Woolfrey, whose brother Norbert was at the same time in charge of Loughborough and Barrow-on-Soar, and active at Shepshed. From 1845 to 1848 the Mission was served by Oblates of Mary Immaculate, who were installed also at Grace Dieu during these same years.

Rosminians followed them, but withdrew completely from the Charnwood Forest Missions in 1852.

This period of uncertainty ended with the arrival of Fr. George Bent in 1859. The stability of the parish since that date can be measured by the fact that in the one hundred and twenty years from 1859 it had only six parish priests The Church gained considerable prestige in the early days of the ministry of the Belgian Fr. Angelus Van Paemel (1865-1885). When an epidemic of smallpox broke out, Fr. Van Paemel turned his house into a hospital, and, with the assistance of some Rosminian Sisters from Loughborough, devoted his whole energies to the care of the sick.

The original small chapel at Whitwick was replaced in 1906 by a large new church designed by the architect Ignatius McCarthy, who was also a parishioner. As first built, the church comprised an aisled nave and a sanctuary; the tower was added at a later date. The church was consecrated 3 May 1924. The Lady Chapel contains the original high altar from the 1837 chapel. The east end was reordered in 1987 when the pulpit and altar rails were removed and a new altar installed under the sanctuary arch. The original high altar and stone reredos remain 'in situ'. The stone font, presumably of 1907, now stands in the north transept. The benches appear to be original to the building. Much of the stained-glass in the transept windows dates from the 1950s. A parish hall was built between the church and the school in 1995.

The old church of 1837 was at first also used as a school. This expedient was presumably no longer necessary when, on 2 January 1843, Ambrose de Lisle opened a school, dedicated to St. Aloysius, at the foot of Grace Dieu Rocks, in a locality otherwise known as Turry Log. This apparently served as a mixed school for the whole Mission until sometime after 1888, when the girls were brought into Whitwick, leaving the boys at St. Aloysius'. This new girls' school seems to date in part from the time of Fr. Van Paemel, but became large enough to accommodate all the girls only after Fr. Matthew J. O'Reilly had added to it a row of adjoining cottages. These older establishments were superseded, in 1902 and the following years, by the present buildings adjoining the church. Funds for the erection of the school were provided by Mrs. Haydock of Charnwood Towers, who also paid for the new presbytery, built at this time. The question has often been asked: what makes Catholic schools different? An inspector visiting Holy Cross School in the early 1990s wondered if it might be something to do with religion!

WHITWICK - *Religious Communities*

Cistercians of the Strict Observance (sometimes referred to as Trappists)

Mount Saint Bernard Abbey was founded in 1835 on land provided by Ambrose de Lisle, who was eager to reintroduce monastic life into this country. The small group of monks under Fr. Odilo Woolfrey soon set about cultivating the wild and barren land and the first monastery, designed by William Railton, was opened in 1837.

The sixteenth Earl of Shrewsbury gave a donation for a permanent monastery to be built. Augustus Welby Pugin offered his services for free, and in 1844, the new monastery was opened on the site where it still stands today. In 1848 Mount Saint Bernard was raised to the status of an abbey with the first English abbot since the Reformation, Dom Bernard Palmer.

In 1963 Mount Saint Bernard Abbey made its own foundation in Africa: the Monastery of Our Lady of Bamenda, Cameroon, which is now an independent and flourishing abbey with a community composed mainly of African monks. Fr. Cyprian Tansi, originally a diocesan priest in Nigeria, entered Mount Saint Bernard in 1950 and died in 1964. He was beatified by Pope St. John Paul II in March 1998, the first member of the Diocese of Nottingham to receive this honour.

Rosminian Sisters of Providence

When the new presbytery was erected, the old priest's house was handed over to the Rosminian Sisters of Providence. Their original convent at Whitwick was founded in 1875, but appears to have closed five years later. In reopened in 1888 and closed finally in 1969. During most of the time that the Sisters were in Whitwick they were involved in teaching in the parish school.

Sisters of Charity of St. Paul the Apostle

These Sisters were in Whitwick from 1880 to 1888 during which time they taught in the schools.

WIRKSWORTH

Our Lady and St Teresa of Lisieux – served from Ripley

Wirksworth is a small market-town in the Derbyshire Peak District with a parish church which probably has Anglo-Saxon origins. The area has a long history of lead mining; cotton manufacture started in the late eighteenth century, and the place became an industrial centre during the nineteenth and early twentieth centuries.

Wirksworth can claim to have kept the Faith throughout Penal Times. In 1792 a chapel in the house of a Mr. Cantrell was registered with the Justices of the Peace - and it was in this house belonging to one of his ancestors, that a conventicle of 'Popish recusants' had been detected in 1670.

Nothing more is known of this chapel. The next mention of a Mass centre in the town comes from the years 1840-1850. At this time Mass was said once a month by a priest from Derby. This Mass centre was revived in 1879 by Monsignor Arthur McKenna of St Mary's, Derby who, about the same time, founded the Mission at Matlock. This revival lasted no more than a year.

In 1930 a non-Catholic benefactor gave a "beautiful and picturesque" site large enough for a church and presbytery at Gorsey Bank, to the south-east of the town. Work began on a small stone-built church which was opened on 29 October 1931. In 1976 the sanctuary was reordered by Smith & Roper of Bakewell. The same architects added an extension at the west end in matching style in 1986.

Wirksworth remained a chapel-of-ease of Matlock until 1949. In that year the Benedictines of Belmont Abbey, Herefordshire, took over Alderwasley Hall as a preparatory school, and the Mission at Wirksworth was given into their charge.

When the Benedictines withdrew from the diocese, Wirksworth was looked after by a priest living in the presbytery in Belper. From 1975 to 1989 the priests at the Briars Residential Centre, Crich, served Wirksworth. Since then, although formally part of the Parish of Ripley, it has been looked after by the Parish Priest of Matlock.

WOODHALL SPA

Our Lady and St. Peter

Woodhall Spa came about by accident when, in 1811, a Mr. Parkinson bored a shaft one thousand feet deep in a futile search for coal. He didn't find any coal, but he did discover what, at that time, proved to be the strongest bromoiodine spring in Europe. In the 1830s the Lord of the Manor sank a well and erected the Spa Baths and the Victoria Hotel. Woodhall Spa began to flourish. The London architect, R. Adolphus Came, laid out a planned development in 1887 and subsequently settled in the town and designed many of its buildings. The hotel burned down in 1920, and the Spa Baths finally closed when the well collapsed in 1983.

Fr. Peter Sabela of Grantham opened a Mass centre here in 1895. The first Mass was said on Sunday 16 June of that year, but for the remainder of that season he was able to say Mass only on Tuesday mornings. From the beginning of the following season it was served every Sunday, with a weekday Mass during the rest of the year.

A building site was secured in 1895, and the foundation stone of the present church laid on 2 June 1896. Some of the money necessary for its erection came by legacy from Mr. Thomas Young of Kingerby. The first dedication was to Fr. Sabela's own patron saint – St. Peter. The change to the present lengthier form was made in 1900, when the Mission became independent and was given a resident priest. The church stands in a delightful setting of lawns and mature trees with the detached presbytery built in 1903. The area around Woodhall Spa was a training ground for troops going to Arnhem, so it is probably not surprising that the church was badly damaged by a German bomb. This happened in 1943. The restoration work was carried out by local contractors with considerable help from members of the Parachute Regiment who were stationed near Woodhall Spa at that time. A parish hall was blessed and opened in July 2000.

From 1959 to 1994, the parish was served by members of the

Conventual branch of the Franciscan Order.

At various times chapels-of-ease at Wellingore and Metheringham have been served from Woodhall Spa, but these have subsequently been closed. However, Horncastle is currently (2017) served from Woodhall Spa.

WOODHALL SPA, *Our Lady and St. Peter – Convents*

Sisters of Providence (Ruillé-sur-Loir) had a convent here from 1900 to 1902 when they moved to Lincoln.

Franciscan Tertiary Sisters had a convent from 1912 to 1922.

Religious Congregations in the Diocese of Nottingham

Since its erection in 1850, the Diocese of Nottingham has been served, in various capacities and in a wide variety of locations, by more than fifty Religious Congregations. What follows is a brief and, as far as has been possible, accurate account of these Congregations – their origin, their charism, and the areas of the diocese in which they have worked. Under each of the parishes there is a brief reference to the religious communities who have served there and the work they have done.

Augustinians of the Assumption

Were founded in 1845 by Fr. Emmanuel d'Alzon. They opened the Becket Grammar School for Boys in West Bridgford in 1931 and remained there until 1975 when the Becket was amalgamated with Corpus Christi Secondary School. Among the more notable Assumptionists who served in Nottingham were:

Fr. George Andrew Beck (1904-1978) became, successively, Coadjutor Bishop of Brentwood, Bishop of Brentwood, Bishop of Salford and, finally, Archbishop of Liverpool.

Fr. Roger Killeen (died 1994) after a long career in teaching – at St. Michael's College, Hitchin, and then at the Becket School – in 1976 founded Emmanuel House (named after Emmanuel D'Alzon, the founder of the Assumptionists), Nottingham, as a shelter for the homeless and disadvantaged. Emmanuel House has given this support for more than forty years and continues to do so.

Benedictines

The influence of the Benedictine Order on the life of the Church and on the wider society since its foundation in the sixth century has been enormous. In the Middle Ages, there were roughly twenty Benedictine communities in Lincolnshire alone. All of these and other religious houses were suppressed at the time of the Reformation.

Since the Reformation, Benedictine monks from Ampleforth served the Parish of Barton-on-Humber from 1848 until 1949. In 1949, monks from Belmont Abbey took over the running of St. Benet's Private Preparatory School at Alderwasley, near Matlock. The school was closed and the Benedictines left in the mid-1970s.

Blessed Sacrament Fathers

The Congregation of the Blessed Sacrament was founded in Paris in

1856 by St. Peter Julian Eymard. The aim of this new way of life was to promote the Kingdom of God through the Eucharist. This approach is what made his proposal original.

The Blessed Sacrament Fathers came to the Diocese of Nottingham in 1935 in response to an invitation by Bishop McNulty. In the Braunstone area of Leicester they established the Parish of the Blessed Sacrament, together with a Shrine of the Blessed Sacrament, and a novitiate. Only the parish priest and the assistant priest were involved directly in ministry in the parish. The other priests, brothers and novices maintained the rota of Eucharistic Adoration.

In 1990 the Blessed Sacrament Fathers, who had meanwhile established other houses in Britain, withdrew from Braunstone and the parish was entrusted to the care of diocesan clergy.

Brothers of Mercy

This teaching Congregation was founded in 1839 by Monsignor Victor Scheppers of Malines. At the outbreak of the Second World War in 1939, they bought Stainsby Hall, Smalley, near Heanor in the Parish of Eastwood, and transferred to it a school for boys evacuated from the south of England. In June 1948 a novitiate of the Congregation was also opened in Stainsby Hall. The Brothers of Mercy left the diocese in the mid-1950s.

Carmelites

The Carmelite Order originated with a group of hermits living on Mount Carmel in the Holy Land in the twelfth century. Initially a 'male' Religious Order, by the end of the Middle Ages a female branch had been established. St. Teresa of Avila (1515-1582) reformed both branches of the Order.

A monastery of Discalced Carmelite nuns, whose principal charism is a life of contemplative prayer lived in enclosure, was founded from Notting Hill, London, in Mansfield in 1926. The nuns moved to Ashbourne in 1949, and then left the diocese in 1960.

Cistercians

The Cistercian Order, dating from 1098, is a reformed branch of the Benedictine Order which itself originated in the sixth century. One of the three founders of the Cistercians was an Englishman, St. Stephen Harding, and it was not surprising that soon there were Cistercian monasteries in England. At the time of the dissolution of the religious houses under Henry VIII, there were seventy-six Cistercian monasteries in the British Isles.

In the seventeenth century, the Cistercian Order itself was reformed. This reform was known initially as the 'Trappist' reform, but the term used nowadays is 'Cistercians of the Strict Observance.'

It is to this group that Mount Saint Bernard Abbey, near Coalville, Leicestershire, founded in 1835, belongs. In the early years, partly due to the circumstances of the time, some of the monks were involved in parish work in the neighbourhood of the monastery. But their primary work has always taken place within the monastery, where the monks live a community life in simplicity, silence and solitude. In this way, they have always been a spiritual powerhouse for the diocese and beyond. Like all monasteries following the Rule of St. Benedict, Mount Saint Bernard has a guesthouse to which people come for spiritual guidance and retreats.

Fr. Cyprian Tansi, a Nigerian secular priest, joined Mount Saint Bernard in 1950 and died in Leicester fourteen years later. He was beatified by St. John Paul II in March 1998, the first member of the Diocese of Nottingham to receive this honour.

Corpus Christi Carmelites

Clare Perrins, born in Birmingham in 1875, converted to Catholicism at the age of sixteen. She tried her vocation with various Religious Congregations but felt that God was calling her to find new ways of being at the service of those around her. In Leicester, in 1908, she gathered a small community of like-minded women who engaged in forms of social work that were considered to be very novel at the time. They got involved in various forms of parish ministry such as social and health reform, distress counselling, and prison visiting

Initially connected with the Dominican Order, after a number of years it became clear to Mother Mary Ellerker (as she came to be known), that her community's spirituality was rooted in Carmel, with its blend of prayer and service nourished by the Eucharist. So, the name 'Corpus Christi Carmelite' developed, and in 1927 the Congregation was affiliated to the Carmelite Order. They took as their patroness Saint Thérèse of Lisieux, who had been canonized two years earlier. Inspired by the missionary outlook of Saint Thérèse, and encouraged by clergy who asked for their help, Mother Mary and some of the Sisters crossed the oceans to the Caribbean where they set up houses in Trinidad and Tobago, Saint Vincent, Grenada, Dominica, Saint Lucia, Antigua and Guyana, North America, and Liberia. Mother Mary died in 1949 and, in the Diocese of Port of Spain, the diocesan phase for her beatification was concluded in 2015.

In 1927 the Sisters left Rothley, Leicestershire, where they had run a school for several years. In 1952 they returned to the diocese and, under the auspices of the Nottingham Diocesan Catholic Children's Society, they opened 'Carmel', a home for children aged five to sixteen at Kirby Muxloe near Leicester. This closed in 1993.

The Corpus Christi Carmelites, after serving at various places in the Diocese of Nottingham especially in the Leicester area, finally left the diocese in 2011.

Daughters of Divine Charity

The Congregation of the Daughters of Divine Charity was founded by Mother Franciska Lechner in Austria in 1868. The aim of the Congregation whose motto is 'to do good, give joy and lead all to heaven' is 'to make God's love visible.' Initially the Sisters provided housing for young women coming into the cities to work. Then they began opening schools as well as retirement homes for the poor.

The Daughters of Divine Charity ran St. Mary's Convent School, Long Eaton, for 3 to 16 year old pupils, from 1939 to 1964. The Sisters also worked at Cathedral House from 1968 to 1984, and in St. Joseph's Convent, Chesterfield, from 1937. In 1980 Chesterfield became part of the Hallam Diocese and the Sisters continue their ministry there. They ran 'St. Teresa's Hostel for Business Girls' in St. Peter's Parish, Leicester, from 1949 to 1962.

Daughters of Our Lady of Good Counsel (Vocation Sisters)

Were founded in 1945 by Edna John (Mother Mary Joseph). The first Sisters were under the guidance of the Benedictines, and later they were attached to the Passionists. In 1962 they became a Religious Congregation in their own right. Their purpose was the discernment, fostering, and nurturing of religious and priestly vocations through giving talks, showing films, mounting exhibitions and advising Religious Orders. In the 1960/70s they began their ministry of counselling Religious and clergy.

In 1951 the Vocation Sisters, needing larger premises, bought Hallaton Hall, near Market Harborough, Leicestershire, where they were able to provide accommodation for twelve people considering their vocation in an atmosphere of prayer. They were also able to expand their other ministries, particularly in encouraging and advising Religious in their own search for vocations. They left Hallaton in 1976. From 1962 to 1964, at the invitation of Bishop Ellis, they also took care of Fairfield Hostel for business girls on Fosse Road North, Leicester, which had previously been run by the Daughters of Divine Charity, as well as the house next to the hostel.

The Vocation Sisters moved to Mansfield in 1975 and occupied the convent vacated by the Sisters of Mercy. They left the diocese in 1987.

Dominican Friars

St. Dominic, responding to the needs of his time for preachers who could explain and defend the true faith, founded, in 1216, the Order of Preachers, usually known as 'Dominicans'. From the beginning, Dominican have been drawn to urban centres preaching the Gospel to city-dwellers. They first came to England in 1221, and around 1247 founded a community in Leicester. This, like all other religious houses, was dissolved under Henry VIII in the 1530s.

The Dominicans came back to England in the eighteenth century. In what is now the Diocese of Nottingham, Fr. Matthew Norton OP came to Hinckley in 1765. Dominicans served there from then until 1989. when they handed the parish over to the diocesan clergy. They came to Leicester in 1746. Their Parish of Holy Cross, Leicester, is the mother of all the parishes in the city. In addition to the Parish of Holy Cross, the Dominican Friars serve a Mass centre in the village of Woodhouse in a fourteenth century chapel. They are also responsible for the chaplaincies to two universities, Leicester and De Montfort, and to the Leicester Royal Infirmary.

Dominican Sisters (Stone)

A group of six Dominican Sisters went from Stroud in Gloucestershire to Kentish Town, London, in 1866. Three years later this group became an autonomous community of the Third Order Regular of St Dominic.

In September 1875 the Sisters moved to Leicester, where they opened a small convent school but also taught in parish schools. In 1906 the Sisters moved into the new building of St. Catherine's Nursing Home in Dane Hills. From that time their main apostolate was care and nursing of the elderly. The convent and the chapel were built almost three decades later. In 1929 the Leicester community became part of the Dominican Sisters of the English Congregation of St. Catherine of Siena with its Mother House in Stone in the Archdiocese of Birmingham. In 1992 a small house was purchased near to Holy Cross Priory, Leicester, with the joint purpose of encouraging collaborative pastoral enterprises with the Dominican Friars. The Sisters left Leicester in 2007.

St. Catherine's Nursing Home was closed in 1997. Two Sisters live in a small house in St. Peter's Parish.

Sister Mary Beuno OP, a member of the Congregation of Dominican Sisters of Stone, has been involved in Cotgrave and Keyworth from 1984 to the present.

Dominican Sisters (King William's Town)

The Congregation of the Dominican Sisters of King William's Town was founded in 1877 by Mother Mauritia Tiefenboeck and her companions from Augsburg, Germany. They are called to be a prophetic community of women from many cultures and nationalities. At the core of their identity as Dominicans is the ongoing search for Truth, inspired by the Spirit of Jesus the Christ in whose life and teaching God's Truth has been revealed.

They discover Truth by entering into relationship with God, others and creation.

The Sisters opened a private boarding school in Earl Shilton in 1936. This closed two years later. In March 1933 three Sisters established St. Albert's Convent, Hinckley, where they opened a private independent school. St. Martin's Convent, Stoke Golding, Hinckley, opened in 1948, was closed in 2011. From 1978 to 1989 three Sisters moved to Hinckley where they collaborated as Parish Sisters with the Dominican Friars. They withdrew from Hinckley when the Friars handed over the care of the parish to the diocesan clergy.

Faithful Companions of Jesus

The Foundress of the Faithful Companions of Jesus, Marie Madeleine de Bengy (1781-1858) was born in France on the eve of the French Revolution. Her marriage, in 1804, was cruelly cut short by the death of her husband within a year. Some years later, she received a call from God to found a Religious Congregation whose missionary thrust was to slake the thirst which the marginalised, the outcasts and the neglected children have for dignity, reverence and self-worth. She called this Congregation the 'Faithful Companions of Jesus.'

The only foundation of the Faithful Companions of Jesus in the diocese was at Marple Bridge from 1901 to 1932. There a day and boarding school for girls was attached to the convent.

Franciscan Friars

The first Bishop of Nottingham, Joseph William Hendren, (born in Birmingham in 1791), was a member of the Franciscan Order of which friars from three distinct branches have served in the diocese since its erection in 1850.

The first of these, the Capuchins, a reform of the Observant Franciscans, were ratified as an independent Order in 1528. In 1920, the Capuchin junior seminary was transferred from Oxfordshire to Panton, near Wragby in Lincolnshire. As well as running the seminary, the friars did a lot of pastoral work in the surrounding area. During its time in Panton it was used as a junior seminary also by the diocese, and one of the pupils was William Eric Grasar, ordained for the diocese in 1937. Twenty-five years later, he became Bishop of Shrewsbury and died in 1982. Panton College was closed in 1936 and the Capuchins then left the diocese.

Second were the Friars Minor who, in 1930, took over the Parish of St. Edward on Blue Bell Hill, Nottingham, where they served until 2014, when they handed the parish back to the care of the diocesan clergy.

Third were the Conventuals, usually known as 'Greyfriars' because of the colour of their habit. They served the Parishes of Sleaford, Lincolnshire, 1964 to 1993; Woodhall Spa 1959 to 1994. From Woodhall Spa they looked after Spilsby and Horncastle.

Franciscan Minoresses

This Congregation, originally known as Franciscan Missionary Sisters, was founded by Mother Francis Murphy in London towards the end of the nineteenth century to address various social needs - especially the care of the poor and the dying. The Congregation first came to the Nottingham Diocese in 1897. They continued their original work but then branched out, usually in response to requests from priests or bishops, into teaching and nursing.

The Sisters have served in St. Edward, Nottingham (1897-1903); Beeston (Nottingham); Oakham (1898-1903); Belper (1936-2007); Corby Glen (1900-1901); Skegness (1900-1901); Holy Cross/St. Thomas More, Leicester where, in 1941, they opened St. Francis' Hospital (this closed in 1976.) The Sisters also provided domestic and catering arrangements at St. Hugh's College, Tollerton from 1948 until 1982. Currently the Franciscan Minoresses have convents in Alfreton, Clay Cross and in Melton Mowbray (the Mother House of the Congregation.) It is the only Religious Congregation whose Mother House is in the diocese.

Within the grounds of Saint Clare's Convent, Clay Cross, is a purpose built Franciscan House of Prayer and Solitude, the Portiuncula.

Franciscan Missionaries of St. Joseph

In May 1871 Alice Ingham, a 41-year old Lancashire woman, her stepmother and two friends began community life together. In Franciscan simplicity and apostolic zeal, they worked for the poor, ignorant, sick and dying in the mill town of Rochdale. They earned their living and the resources with which to help the poor, by means of a millinery and confectionary shop on the ground floor of their house on Yorkshire Street, Rochdale.

In 1878 this small group, encouraged in their Franciscan ideals by Fr. Gomair Peeters, OSF, was called by the later Cardinal Herbert Vaughan, then Bishop of Salford, to go to London to the missionary college he had founded to take over the domestic economy of the seminary of St. Joseph's Society. On 8 September 1883 Alice and eleven companions, all professed members of the Third Order Secular, made vows of Poverty, Chastity and Obedience in a new Religious Congregation, now known as the Franciscan Missionaries of St. Joseph.

These Sisters served at Bishop's House, Nottingham, for ten years from 1964.

Franciscan Missionaries of the Sacred Heart

Were in the Cathedral Parish from 1971 to 1980.

Franciscan Sisters of the Holy Ghost

These Sisters conducted a day school for junior boys at Skegness from 1911 to 1918.

Franciscan Tertiary Sisters

These Sisters were at Woodhall Spa between 1912 and 1922.

Holy Ghost Fathers (Spiritans)

The Congregation of the Holy Spirit, a religious missionary institute under the protection of the Immaculate Heart of Mary, was founded in 1703 by Claude Poullart des Places and Francis Libermann.

At the core of the Spiritan vocation is the "apostolic life", the life of love and of holiness lived by Jesus Christ in order to save and sanctify people. Their mission is the evangelisation of the "poor" (Lk 4:18). Therefore, Spiritans go especially: to peoples, groups and individuals who have not yet heard the message of the Gospel or who have scarcely heard it; to those whose needs are the greatest, and to the oppressed. The Spiritan option for the poor involves a solidarity which brings them to share in the world of the marginalized.

The Holy Ghost Fathers, as they are usually known, opened their house of studies at Upton Hall, near Newark in 1945. In 1964, this was transferred to Wellsborough near Market Bosworth, and Upton became the novitiate. The Holy Ghost Fathers left Wellsborough in 1969 and Upton in 1972. In the latter year, the Holy Ghost Fathers took on responsibility for the Parish of Hassop and Bakewell which one of their members still (2017) serves while another Holy Ghost Father serves Our Lady of Good Counsel, Leicester.

Jesuits

In view of their mission as "The Service of Faith and the Promotion of Justice," Jesuits serve as parish priests, chaplains, teachers, academics, writers, doctors, spiritual directors and artists.

Jesuits first came to England in 1580 and worked throughout Penal Times in many parts of the present Diocese of Nottingham, especially in Lincolnshire and Derbyshire. For example, in the seventeenth century they ran a school at Stanley Grange near Ilkeston.

Harlaxton Manor near Grantham was purchased by the Jesuits in 1948, and from 1950 until 1957 and again from 1962 to 1965, it housed the novitiate of the English Jesuit Province. (Harlaxton was unoccupied between 1957 and 1962.)

Although, since the erection of the Diocese of Hallam in 1980, there is no longer any Jesuit involvement in the diocese, the parishes of The Annunciation in Chesterfield, Staveley, Dronfield and Clowne were founded or served by Jesuits. They also founded Mount St. Mary's College, Spinkhill, and Barlborough Hall Preparatory School.

Ladies of Mary

Canon Constant Van Crombrugghe founded the Congregation of the Daughters of Mary and Joseph, also called 'The Ladies of Mary', in Belgium in 1817. Appalled by the famine and misery that raged in Flanders at that time, he began working with Colette De Brandt from Aalst. Together they initiated vocational schools for the poor. In addition to learning lace making, the young women were given a basic Christian education. The Founder insisted on the importance of the Sisters being able to adapt themselves to the specific needs of each time and place. They therefore strove to diversify their teaching so as to form their pupils more effectively and to enable them to live out a significant role in their families and countries. They are an international community of women religious, called to make visible the merciful love of God, in particular by responding to spiritual thirst and to the needs of those to whom society says there is no place.

The Daughters of Mary and Joseph first came to England in 1869. Here they opened a number of schools and, later, Coloma College of Education for the training of teachers. Their only house in the Diocese of Nottingham was at Coalville, where they taught in the school from 1930 to 1945. After the Second Vatican Council Sisters became involved in other ministries including parish work, social work, medicine and retreat work.

Little Company of Mary

The Little Company of Mary was founded in Hyson Green, Nottingham, by Mother Mary Potter in 1877. The Hyson Green house closed in 1922. Although the Sisters nowadays carry out a variety of apostolates, the Foundress's original vision of a group of religious women who, united in spirit with Our Lady on Calvary, would care for the sick, the suffering and the dying, has been maintained to this day. This vision is reflected in, for example, The Sanctuary, established by Sr. Elizabeth Malone in 1987 to care for individuals suffering from the effects of alcoholism and for their families.

In the early years of the Congregation, a number of smaller houses across the diocese were opened in quick succession in order to respond to pastoral needs as envisaged by Bishop Bagshawe. These included: Quorndon, Eastwell, Melton Mowbray (all in Leicestershire) and Osgodby (in Lincolnshire.) All these houses closed after a short period of time since they proved to be incompatible with the aims of the Congregation,

In 1922, when the original house in Hyson Green closed, the Sisters opened a house in West Bridgford where they remained until 1930. In West Bridgford they opened a small nursing home. They then moved to Woodthorpe where they opened what became the Convent Nursing Home and, later, The Convent Hospital. The Sisters withdrew from the hospital in 1998 and closed the convent three years later. From 1981 until 1988, the Sisters were in Bulwell

Currently (2017) members of the Congregation are involved in a variety of ministries in the Nottingham area including Cathedral House and the Mary Potter International Heritage Centre (opened in 2010.)

Mother Mary Potter, who had died in 1913, was declared 'Venerable' in 1988. Nine years later, her remains were brought from Rome and were interred in St. Barnabas' Cathedral.

Loreto Sisters

The Loreto Sisters were founded in 1609 by the Venerable Mary Ward. Her spirituality was rooted in that of St. Ignatius of Loyola, founder of the Jesuits. His Spiritual Exercises are the foundation of the way of life of the Loreto Sisters, a way of life which is dedicated to living the Gospel values and sharing the mission of Christ in the world of today.

The Loreto Sisters came to Nottingham in 1962, when they were asked by Bishop Ellis to run the former St. Catherine's Convent Grammar School previously run by Sisters of Mercy. It was relocated to Aspley and renamed Loreto Grammar School. The Sisters were also involved in the management and/or staffing of other schools in the diocese and in various other ministries. Mary Ward Teacher Training College, run by the Loreto Sisters, was opened in Keyworth in 1968 and closed in 1977.

The Sisters had a convent in Eastwood from 1969 to 2004, and when this closed they left the diocese.

Missionary Sisters of the Holy Rosary

The Missionary Sisters of the Holy Rosary were founded in Killeshandra, Ireland, in 1924 by Bishop Joseph Shanahan, CSSp, Vicar-Apostolic for Southern Nigeria. Their charism was to bring the good news to the poor, especially the women of Nigeria, through education, medical, social and pastoral ministry. Their first mission was to Nigeria and they later spread to several African countries and Latin America.

The Sisters came to the Diocese of Nottingham in July 1976. Based in St. Paul's Parish, Nottingham, the Sisters were engaged in pastoral and social work. They also carried out mission appeals and vocations promotion. The Sisters withdrew from the diocese in August 1990.

Norbertine Sisters (Third Order)

Had a convent in Spalding from 1877 to 1882 and taught in the school during this time.

Poor Clare Colettines

St. Clare of Assisi, close collaborator of St. Francis, gathered around her a group of women who would support the work of the friars by a hidden life of prayer and penance. In the fifteenth century, St. Colette reformed the Poor Clares. In the early years of the twentieth century, a group of Colettines, forced to leave their native France, settled in Lutterworth, where they remained until the mid-1920s. It is to the same branch of the Order that the community in Bulwell, Nottingham, founded from Manchester in the late 1920s, belongs.

Poor Clares of the Immaculate Conception (of Newry)

The spiritual daughters of the Poor Clares who had survived the Cromwellian Wars were able to accept a new challenge in 1830 when they were asked by the Bishop of Dromore to make a foundation in Newry. They were the first Religious Sisters to settle north of the Boyne since 1690. In 1973 this Congregation was renamed the Sisters of St. Clare (to distinguish them from the enclosed Poor Clares). But in their apostolates of education and pastoral care they have continued to serve the Lord with the dedication of their heroic predecessors, having a definite mission to bring the contemplative charism of Clare to the world.

In 1945 Coalville was the first house of this Congregation to be founded in the diocese. It closed in 1990. The other houses were: Gainsborough 1948-1971; Brigg 1953-1989; Leicester St Thomas More 1953-1995; Newark 1953-1995; Cathedral House 1995-2004.

Premonstratensians

The Canons Regular of Prémontré were founded in the early twelfth century by St. Norbert. The order combines the contemplative with the active religious life and in the twelfth century provided a link between the strictly contemplative life of the monks of the preceding ages and the more active life of the friars of the thirteenth century.

Their first foundation in the Diocese of Nottingham was at Crowle, Lincolnshire, in 1872 where they remained until 1982. In 1875 they came to Spalding and, in 1957, to Holbeach; they left both these parishes in 2008.

Presentation Sisters

The Presentation Sisters of the Blessed Virgin Mary were founded on Christmas Eve, 1775. Their foundress Nano Nagle, opened her eyes to the poverty of body and soul and inequity that she saw around her. She responded in the most challenging of circumstances – educating children in secret schools (when Penal Laws forbade the setting-up of schools for Catholics), ministering to the wretched and the dispossessed and sharing everything with them until she had scarcely enough resources for herself. Working at times through illness and often through adversity, Nano gave her 'all' to the poor and needy of Cork. A pioneering Spirit-led woman in every way, Nano had the foresight to set up a Religious Congregation, now known as the Presentation Sisters of the Blessed Virgin Mary, to ensure her legacy.

Since the Congregation's founding, Sisters have worked to secure the breadth of Nano's vision — crossing geographical, political, religious and social frontiers, bringing her vision to life with deeds, embodying her dream through a variety of ministries, especially education, faith and spirituality, social and pastoral, health care and healing. Her vision is captured in the words that she wrote, "If I could be of any service in saving souls in any part of the globe I would willingly do all in my power."

Over more than a century, Presentation Sisters have exercised many ministries in the following parishes: Buxton (1889-2004); All Saints, Glossop (1904-2005); Crowle (1935-1961); Cressbrook (1949-1957); St. Bernadette, Scunthorpe (1951-2002); Stapenhill (1954-1966); St. Alban, Chaddesden (1957-1988); Shirebrook (1958-1981); Bolsover (1981-1986); (Lilybank), Matlock (1962-1990). Currently – 2017 – there are Presentation Sisters in: Matlock, Market Harborough, Warsop, St. Augustine, (Nottingham), St. Mary, (Derby) and St. John Bosco (Leicester).

Religious Sisters of Charity

In 1815 Mary Aikenhead founded, in Dublin, the Religious Sisters of Charity, sometimes referred to as the 'Irish' Sisters of Charity to distinguish them from the 'Daughters of Charity,' who were known as the 'French' Sisters of Charity. Their work included the establishment of schools, hospitals and orphanages for people in need, visiting those in prison. A special emphasis was laid on visiting of the poor, especially the sick in their homes so much so that, in addition to the customary three vows, the Religious Sisters of Charity take a fourth vow specific to the Congregation, 'service of the poor'.

In 1960 the Religious Sisters of Charity came to Boughton in the Parish of St. Joseph, New Ollerton, where they founded a school which was to be the forerunner of St. Joseph's Primary School. The Sisters left Boughton in 1986.

Rosminians

The Institute of Charity was founded in 1828 by Fr Antonio Rosmini. In 1835 three of his followers, also known as Rosminians, came to England. Under its motto "Love fulfils the law", the purpose of the Institute is the holiness of its members through the perfection of charity, and thus it is open, under Providence, to any work in the service of the Church. The Rosminians had a great influence on the development and expansion of the Catholic Church in England in the early nineteenth century. In the Diocese of Nottingham, in addition to pioneering missionary work mainly in Leicestershire, they founded Ratcliffe College in 1847, and its preparatory school, Grace Dieu Manor, in 1933. Currently (2017) Rosminians are working in several parishes in the Leicester area. The Rosmini Centre House of Prayer, near Ratcliffe College, was opened in 2006.

Sacred Heart Fathers

The Congregation of the Priests of the Sacred Heart of Jesus was founded by Fr. Leo John Dehon in 1878 at St. Quentin, France. His principal aim in starting the Congregation was to promote devotion to the Sacred Heart of Jesus and to spread his reign in the hearts of the faithful and in society. Sacred Heart Fathers work in overseas missions, parishes, youth ministry, promoting Eucharistic Adoration etc.

From 1938 until 1949, the Sacred Heart Fathers had a preparatory seminary in Earl Shilton; this closed in 1949. From 1951 until 1972 they were responsible for the Diocesan Travelling Mission which, beginning in Lincolnshire, spread eventually to all counties of the diocese. Their two main bases, both in Lincolnshire, were Market Rasen (1949-2008) and Corby Glen/Bourne/Deeping St. James (1957-1984).

Servants of the Sacred Heart of Jesus

The Servants of the Sacred Heart of Jesus stem from the movement which Fr. Victor Braun set up during the Industrial Revolution in a poor, notorious part of Paris. He organised a few members of his parish to help women who were being trafficked on the streets when they flocked to Paris from Germany looking for work. To ensure this help would continue he formed a new Religious Order, the Servants of the Sacred Heart, who extended their care to orphans, single mothers, and the sick.

At the outbreak of the Franco-Prussian war, the German and Austrian Sisters were expelled from France and formed their own Congregation. Soon after this the English Sisters also separated from the French, forming a new Congregation – The Sisters of the Sacred Hearts of Jesus and Mary – in 1903.

The Sisters are affiliated to the Order of St. Augustine and follow his

Rule of Life, which begins: 'Before all else, live together in harmony, being of one mind and one heart on the way to God.'

In 1875 the Sisters opened a convent in Boston and began teaching in the school. They remained there for two years.

Sisters of Charity of St. Paul (Selly Park)

Genevieve Dupuis (1813-1903) joined the Sisters of Charity of St. Paul in Chartres. She came to England in 1847 to form a community, and to teach children in schools. The initial concern of the Sisters was to provide education for the Catholic poor. Genevieve found that older children were not attending school, so she started night classes for older pupils, thus showing her innovative way to advance further the work of education for the poor.

A woman of great vision and courage, between her arrival in 1847 and her death, Genevieve founded eighty-eight convents in England alone! Six of these were in the Diocese of Nottingham, viz., Boston (where they remained for more than ninety years), Exton, Glossop – All Saints and St. Mary, Hadfield (for nearly 120 years) and Whitwick. Towards the end of the nineteenth century, the Sisters of Charity became an independent Congregation with their Mother House at Selly Park, Birmingham. Over the years, the Sisters became involved in various other apostolates including secondary education and teacher training. The Sisters of the Nativity amalgamated with these Sisters of Charity in 1955. In 1955, the Sisters took over an independent grammar school for girls in St. Joseph's Parish, Leicester, where they remained even after the grammar school was amalgamated with Corpus Christi Secondary Modern School. The Sisters left Leicester in 1992, but remained at St. Mary's, Glossop, where they had been since the 1850s, until 2004.

Sisters of Life

The Sisters of Life had their origins in Sheffield in 1980. In 1983 they moved to the Diocese of Nottingham with the permission of Bishop McGuinness. They were founded to serve small communities of people who wished to dedicate their lives to God by vows of simplicity, listening obedience and community life. They wished to share their faith and life with the people in their parish and local community.

The Sisters of Life do not dedicate themselves to a particular work but use their talents and abilities where they can, believing that their most important calling is 'to be'; they aim to be known primarily for what they are rather than what they do.

Sisters of Mercy

The Sisters of Mercy were founded in Dublin in 1831 by Catherine

McAuley for the relief and instruction of the poor, particularly poor women and girls. This Congregation spread rapidly to all English-speaking parts of the world.

The first group of Sisters of Mercy came to Nottingham in 1844 and, two years later, moved to the purpose-built convent adjacent to the cathedral. From Nottingham, a branch house was opened in Mansfield in 1877 where the Sisters remained until 1974 when, due to, among other things, shortage of personnel, they returned to their Nottingham house. During the one hundred and fifty years they spent in Nottingham, the Sisters of Mercy were involved in a number of areas of pastoral work not least in primary and secondary education. St. Mary's School, St. Joseph's Preparatory School and St. Catherine's Grammar School were some examples. St. Catherine's Care and Nursing Home opened in the Nottingham convent in 1991, but with the increasing demands of government regulations on care homes, it closed eight years later. The Nottingham Convent of Mercy closed in 1999.

The Sisters of Mercy came to Derby, where they established themselves in St. Mary's Parish, in 1849. In that parish, in addition to the main convent on Bridge Gate, they have several outposts including St. Philomena's Convent; Beechwood; Mount Carmel Care Home.

The Sisters have also been involved in education at various levels. From Bridge Gate, the houses have been opened as follows: Belper (1857-1860); Carlton (1882-1889); Derby, St. Joseph (1899-1923); Alvaston (1952-1996); Swadlincote (1955- 1991). St. Mary's Nursing Home, Ednaston, was opened in 1948, but following a review of current ministries by the Institute Trustees, the decision was made to close the Home completely in November 2016.

Sisters of Mercy came from New Ross, County Wexford to Gainsborough and staffed the primary school which was opened in 1877. They subsequently added a secondary school for girls. The Sisters of Mercy left Gainsborough before 1890.

Sisters of Nazareth

In 1851 Victoire Larmenier, a member of the Little Sisters of the Poor in Rennes, France, was sent to England. Six years later, she founded the first Nazareth House, in Hammersmith, London. In 1864 Cardinal Wiseman established the Hammersmith Sisters as a distinct (from the Little Sisters of the Poor) religious community under the title 'Sisters of Nazareth.' Their aim is to share the love of God through their ministries of care and education and their openness to respond to the needs of the times. With this in view, they look after older people in nursing and residential homes – their main focus internationally - and in care villages, where they provide flexible support for assisted living. The Sisters also care for children and young people of all ages, and exercise other ministries according to the needs of the local area. The Nottingham house of this Congregation was opened in 1876 on Woodborough Road. A couple of years later the Sisters moved to Priory Street, Lenton. There the Sisters provided a home for over two hundred deprived children and old people. They also cared for many clergy of the diocese and for two of the recent bishops.

In the early 1980s as social circumstances changed, Nazareth House ceased to provide services for children. In the ensuing years, successive regulation and the demands for increasing standards of care for the elderly meant that the buildings could not be adequately modernised in an economic fashion. These factors, coupled with a declining number of vocations to the religious life, led to the decision by the Sisters of Nazareth to close many of their houses. Nottingham was one of these. After more than one hundred and twenty-five years of service to the people of Nottingham during which one hundred and fifty-eight Sisters of Nazareth had cared for 2,225 children and 1,472 elderly people, the Sisters of Nazareth left Nottingham in 2002.

Sisters of Providence (Immaculate Conception)

Served as Parish Sisters in Holbeach from 1994 until 2011.

Sisters of Providence (Rosminian)

The Rosminian Sisters of Providence of the Institute of Charity were founded in Italy in 1832.

Their Founder, Blessed Antonio Rosmini, based the spirituality of the Institute on complete trust in God's Providence coupled with an awareness of dependence on the grace of Christ and an acute consciousness of the need for justice, purification and holiness. If the members of the Institute live according to these principles, they will be transformed in love as they try to discern and carry out God's Will.

In 1843 two Italian Sisters left their Mother House in Piedmont for Loughborough to form the nucleus of the first convent of the Congregation in England. The following year, the first English postulants joined the Institute. Not long after their arrival in this country, the Sisters began to teach in the parish school. In 1850 they moved to a purpose-built convent in Park Road, where they were to remain for almost one hundred and sixty years. In due course, the Sisters established a boarding school, a school for the poor and an Industrial school for young women.

As the number of Sisters continued to increase, small communities were established in many places throughout the British Isles. In the Diocese of Nottingham, there were – in addition to the original convent in

Loughborough – Rosminian communities in Whitwick, Shepshed, Brigg, and Leicester. These smaller houses have since closed, but the Loughborough convent remains.

Sisters of Providence (Ruillé-sur-Loir)

This Congregation was founded in France in 1806 in order to teach children and to care for the sick. Their charism is: " .. to become 'providence' especially towards the weak and the poor." The Sisters came to Woodhall Spa in 1900 but moved to Lincoln two years later where they opened a school. In 1983, due in part to a lack of vocations and the increasing age of the community, the school was sold to and administered by the Parents' Association under the name of St. Joseph's School, with some involvement and help from the Sisters for a while. In 2014 the Sisters moved to Our Lady of Lincoln Parish, where they continue to exercise various ministries.

Sisters of St. Clotilde

Antoinette Desfontaines had been, prior to the French Revolution, a member of a contemplative Congregation dedicated to the adoration of the Sacred Heart of Jesus in the Blessed Sacrament. In 1821, being convinced of the pressing need of a community of Religious Sisters dedicated to the education of girls, she founded the Sisters of St. Clotilde.

The first convent of this Congregation in England dates from 1903. Sisters of St. Clotilde served at Cathedral House from 1991 to 1994.

Sisters of St. Dorotea de Cenno (Italian)

came to serve the Italian community in the Nottingham area in the early 1980s, and remained there for some years.

Sisters of St. Dorothy (Portuguese)

Saint Paula Frassinetti, the Foundress of the Sisters of Saint Dorothy, was born in Genoa in 1809. Her mother died when she was quite young, and, at the age of nineteen, she went to live with her brother who was a priest. She helped her brother with many of the duties in his parish, but she saw a great need for better education of the poor children of the area. In 1834 she and six other women formed a small community called the "Daughters of Holy Faith". They later came to be known as the "Sisters of St. Dorothy." They founded a community in Rome in 1841 and, from there, founded other communities in Italy and beyond – for example, in Brazil and in Portugal.

The Foundress died in 1882 and was canonised in 1984. Among the advice she gave to her Sisters was: "Be burning flames that inflame with

God's love all those you come in contact with."

The only house of this Congregation in the diocese was at Coalville, whither they came from Portugal sometime after 1910, probably as a result of anti-religious laws promulgated by the First Republic. They left Coalville in 1930.

Sisters of St. Francis

In response to the 1987 Synod of Bishops on "The Vocation and Mission of the Laity", Bishop James McGuinness asked Sr. Kathleen Harmon and Sr. Christiane Champalbert to train laypeople to become effective witnesses to Christ in an increasingly secularised society. This was to be done through programmes of 'formation', by which term was meant a development of understanding of the Catholic Faith as well as the practical action which should flow from this. With this in view, the two Sisters set up the McGuinness Centre in Bulwell. (This was officially opened in May 1988.) A new building adjacent to the bungalow was built and opened in 1993. Bishop McGuinness gave them the name of Sisters of St. Francis. Sr. Kathleen died in 2011; Sr. Christiane continues to train people in counselling.

Sisters of St. Joseph of Peace

The Congregation of the Sisters of St. Joseph of Peace was founded in Nottingham in 1884 by Margaret Anna Cusack, known as Mother Clare. Their purpose was and is to promote the peace of the Church both by word and work. "The very name Sisters of Peace will, it is hoped, inspire a desire for peace and a love for it." The Sisters of St. Joseph of Peace continue a rich heritage devoted to promoting social justice as a way to peace. From the beginning, they have been involved in ministries of social service, education and health care, working directly with the poor and sick, providing housing and care for women, orphans and blind children and adults, and, as need arose, established schools and hospitals. Examples of their varied apostolate, in addition to teaching and serving as Parish Sisters, have been: St. Anthony's Orphanage in Grimsby, the Mother and Babies Home at Borrowash and St. Hugh's Nursing Home in Cleethorpes.

The very first house of the Congregation, opened in the year of their foundation, was in Grimsby. Subsequently their houses in the diocese have been as follows. Nottingham: Blue Bell Hill 1884-1898; Elm Avenue 1898-1910; Mapperley Road 1910-1975; Lucknow Avenue 1975-2000; Hyson Green 1983 – 1988 and then from 2002; West Bridgford 1976 -2013; Wollaton from 2000. Barton-upon-Humber: 1889 -1990. Borrowash: 1946 -1976.
Cleethorpes: St Hugh's Nursing Home 1937 – 2001; Corpus Christi Parish from 2001. Colston Bassett: 1951- 1961. Grantham: 1898-1901. Grimsby: Heneage Road 1884-1980; Abbey Road 1980- 2006; St Anthony's Orphanage

1899 -1957; Harbour Place from 1996. Hadfield: 1978-1985. Hassop: 1888-1889. Leicester: Sacred Heart Parish 1934 – 1959; St. Joseph's Parish from 1961. Sleaford: 1895 -1901. Oadby: from 2016. Since 1945, the Provincial House has been at Rearsby in Leicestershire.

Sisters of the Assumption

The Sisters of the Assumption were founded in Paris in 1839 by Marie Eugenie Milleret. Their aim was to combine a monastic way of life with the education of girls running boarding and day schools. Shortly after the Second World War, they opened Maria Assumpta Training College, Kensington, and closed in 1978. Currently (2017) there are about one thousand Sisters working in more than thirty countries. From 1946 until 1952 they were in Exton but then moved to Hengrave Hall, Suffolk.

Sisters of the Cross and Passion

The Congregation of the Sisters of the Cross and Passion (originally known as Sisters of the Holy Family) was founded, in 1852, by Elizabeth Prout. From 1864 they have been known as Sisters of the Cross and Passion of Our Lord Jesus Christ.

The original aim of the Congregation was to provide contemplative religious life for those women who wanted to be contemplative religious but could not afford a dowry and did not wish to be laysisters.

Central to the charism of the Congregation is the personal and communitarian call to understand and to participate in the Passion of Jesus and to grow in solidarity with the crucified of the world, sharing with them their conviction of the power of the Cross.

In 1889 a convent of this Congregation was established at Corby Glen, Lincolnshire, where the Sisters taught in the school. The convent closed in 1899.

Sisters of the Holy Family of Nazareth

The Congregation of the Holy Family of Nazareth was founded in Rome in 1875 by Frances Siedliska, a Polish noblewoman, who later became known as Blessed Mary of Jesus the Good Shepherd. From Rome the Congregation spread quickly.

The Sisters of the Holy Family of Nazareth are an international Apostolic Congregation. In the tradition of their Foundress, Blessed Mary of Jesus the Good Shepherd, they focus on the life of the Holy Family of Nazareth which urges them to centre all on God, as did Jesus, Mary and Joseph at Nazareth. From this incarnational stance, they approach all creation with respect and awe. All people are seen as children of God, and their ministries in thirteen countries enable them to find the face of God in a great diversity of cultures and life experiences.

The Sisters of the Holy Family of Nazareth served at the cathedral from 1984 to 1990. There they made a home for the clergy and assisted in many other aspects of the life of the cathedral.

Sisters of the Nativity

were founded in France in 1818. Their first house in the Diocese of Nottingham, opened in 1906, was at Market Harborough. The boarding school they established there offered "to young ladies for the study of the purest French accent, the same advantages as in Paris, as well as fluent conversation and special lessons in French Literature".

The Sisters of the Nativity in 1918 opened both a secondary school for girls and a private elementary school on the Glenfield Road in St. Peter's Parish, Leicester. These schools were closed in 1939 when the Sisters moved to Evington Hall in what was then Sacred Heart Parish but later became part of St. Joseph's Parish.

The Sisters of the Nativity amalgamated with the Sisters of Charity of St. Paul (Selly Park) in 1955.

Sisters of the Poor Child Jesus

Sisters of the Poor Child Jesus, founded in Aachen, Germany, in 1844 for the care and education of children, especially those in need, came from Semplveld (where their Foundress, Clara Fey, is buried) to open a secondary school for girls in 1930. Their first convent was St. Peter's Presbytery, Grimsby. They took possession of it in August 1930. In 1933 the school and convent moved to new premises, but both were closed in 1939.

Society of the Holy Child Jesus

Cornelia Connelly founded the Society of the Holy Child Jesus in Derby in 1846. Her aim in doing so was: "To rejoice in God's presence and to help people believe that God lives and acts in them and in our world." The Sisters remained in Derby for only two years and then moved to St Leonards-on-Sea, Sussex, secured for them by Cardinal Wiseman.

Ursulines

came to the diocese when religious communities were expelled from France at the beginning of the twentieth century. Here they established a convent and high school at Welham House, Spilsby, where they remained from 1904 to 1908.

Xaverian Brothers

were in Deeping St. James intermittently in the 1940s and 1950s until 1956 when they left the diocese.

Some Saints and other holy people connected with the Diocese of Nottingham

Fr. A. Pateman

A brief sketch of the lives of some of the canonised or beatified men and women who, over the centuries, have had connections – by birth, residence or death - with the present Diocese of Nottingham. These are listed here according to the date on which they are commemorated in the calendar.

There follows a list (pp: 327) giving, in summary form and in alphabetical order, their real or potential connection with a particular area or parish of the diocese.

12 January **Saint Aelred** [1110 – 1167]
As abbot between 1147 – 1167 of the Cistercian monastery of Rievaulx in Yorkshire, Aelred presided over a community of more than six hundred. It is said that all his monks considered him their best friend. He undoubtedly had a great gift for friendship, and he taught in his treatise 'On Spiritual Friendship' that friendship is both a great grace in itself and an important pathway to God.

Before he became Abbot of Rievaulx, Aelred was, for four years, Abbot of Revesby in Lincolnshire, in what is now our Woodhall Spa parish. He was one of the three sons of a Saxon priest, and brought up in the court of David, King of Scotland, leaving there at the age of twenty-four to join the community of Rievaulx.

The monastic historian Dom David Knowles stated that "No other English monk of the twelfth century so lingers in the memory."

20 January **Blessed Cyprian Tansi** [1903 – 1964]
Father Cyprian came to England with a reputation for sanctity, and the initiative for his beatification came entirely from Nigeria. When it became clear that Father Cyprian might be canonized, Nigeria wanted his relics, and his body was exhumed from the monastery graveyard at Mount St. Bernard in 1986.

Blessed Cyprian was born Michael Iwene, a member of the Igbo tribe, baptised after beginning to attend a Catholic school, worked as a teacher for six years, and was ordained priest in 1937 for the Onitsha archdiocese, serving in four parishes: Nnewi, Dunukofia, Akpu/Ajalli and Agulari. As a priest, he lived a very poor and strict life, making him a problem to his colleagues but very popular with his people.

There were as yet no monasteries of contemplatives in Nigeria. Fr Michael developed an interest in the religious life, and his archbishop sent him to Mt. St. Bernard in 1950 intending that he should be part of a team returning to his home area to introduce the monastic life, but this never came about – the daughter monastery being founded instead in Cameroon in 1963.

On becoming a monk, Fr. Michael took the name 'Cyprian' after the great third century African bishop and martyr. Fr. Cyprian died in Leicester Royal Infirmary on 20 January 1964. He was beatified in Nigeria by Pope John Paul II in March 1998.

"Onye afuro na enuigwe, si aguyi na" ("Count no one saved, until he is found in heaven"). (Saying of Blessed Cyprian remembered by Archbishop Stephen Ezeanya).

24 January **Blessed William Ireland** [1636 – 1679]
Born in 1636 into a Lincolnshire family which supported the Royalist cause in the early part of the seventeenth century, William Ireland (alias Ironmonger) entered the Society of Jesus in 1655. Bishop Challoner tells us that William had "the character of a man of extraordinary piety and regularity, and a wonderful evenness of mind in all events." Ordained in 1667, William was sent to England ten years later. He was captured soon afterwards in the early stages of the Oates' Plot. He was condemned to death on a (false) charge of having been a party to a plot to kill King Charles II. On 24 January 1679, Father Ireland and a layman John Grove were taken from Newgate Prison to Tyburn. On the way there, they were pelted and abused by the mob. Father Ireland professed his innocence of the crime attributed to him and said: "As for all our enemies, we earnestly desire that God would pardon them again and again; for we pardon them heartily, from the bottom of our hearts; and I beseech all good people to pray for us and with us." He was then hung, drawn and quartered – the usual sentence for people convicted of treason.

3 February **Saint Werburga,** Abbess [c. 700]
Traditionally the daughter of Wulfhere, King of Mercia, and his wife Ermengilda . After her father's death, Werburga became a nun at Ely under St. Etheldreda [Audrey]. King Ethelred of Mercia, Werburgha's uncle, recalled her to his kingdom and gave her charge of some convents in the Midlands. These included Threekingham, Lincolnshire, where she died. She was buried at Hanbury, and her relics were translated to Chester, where, in the Cathedral, they were a centre of pilgrimage till the Reformation. She remains the patroness of the city of Chester.

4 February **Saint Gilbert of Sempringham** [c.1085 – 1189]
Gilbert is particularly associated with the present Parish of Bourne in South Lincolnshire, having been born in neighbouring Sempringham of an Anglo-Norman father and Anglo-Saxon mother. His father did not send him for training as a knight, but to the University of Paris. When his father died, he opened a religious house by the village church.

This was in response to a request expressed by some young women of the locality for a deeper religious formation. He looked for supervision from the Cistercians, but was turned down as he envisaged and founded joint religious houses of monks and nuns [nine] and Canons only [four, mostly in Lincolnshire and Yorkshire]. The nuns followed the Rule of Saint Benedict and the Canons that of St Augustine. Gilbert also founded orphanages and leper hospitals. He died at the age of about 105, and was canonized in 1202.

The Gilbertines were the only monastic Order founded in England and since there were no houses elsewhere, with the dissolution of the monasteries, they completely disappeared.

The memory of Saint Gilbert is preserved by a group of men and women, called the Oblates of Saint Gilbert, who try to live their lives close to Christ, following the example of Saint Gilbert. Information about them can be found in our diocesan yearbooks under 'Secular Institutes and Secular Orders.' The Oblates are under the spiritual care of monks of Mount Saint Bernard Abbey. The remains of the Mother House in Sempringham, though consisting of only the footings, are worth a visit.

20 February **Blessed Thomas Pormort** [c.1560 – 1592]
Thomas was also known as Meres, Whitegive and Pryce. He was born at Little Limber, a village seven miles north of Caistor about 1560. He was brought up in the Established Church, and there is a tradition that John Whitgift, a native of Grimsby and later Archbishop of Canterbury, was his godfather. It may have been for this reason that he used 'Whitgift' or 'Whitgive' as one of his aliases.

He entered Trinity College, Cambridge, in the autumn of 1575. The place and circumstances of his entry into full communion with the Catholic Church are not known. He arrived at the English College in Rheims in January 1581, and in the English College in Rome in May of the same year. He was ordained priest in the Basilica of St John Lateran in August 1587.

For a couple of years he was in the service of a Welsh bishop in the Kingdom of Naples. In April 1590 he was in Milan, where he acted as Prefect of Studies in the Swiss College. Writing from Milan to the Rector of the Venerable English College, Rome, Thomas says that he would like to study for a doctorate but can't afford to do so. In his letter, he adds a comment to the effect that, in Milan, no one pays any attention to you unless you have a doctorate! Then he decided to return to England and, at the end of 1590 he was in London, disguised as a servant. All his work in England seems to have been in the London area.

A chance street meeting with an apostate priest, William Tedder, led to his arrest, but he escaped. Recaptured in September 1591, he was put in the Bridewell Prison and taken to the house of Richard Topcliffe, one of the cruellest persecutors of Catholics. Thomas was tried with John Barwis, a haberdasher friend, on 18 February 1592.

Two days later the execution took place on a scaffold erected in St Paul's Churchyard, opposite the house of John Barwis, who had recanted. Topcliffe, still inflamed by Thomas' revelation of his boasts, during the torture, of his (Topcliffe's) familiarity with the Queen, made him 'to stand in his shirt almost two hours on the ladder' on this cold winter afternoon, till he was turned off the ladder, drawn and quartered.

27 February **Blessed Mark Barkworth** [1572-1601]
Mark Barkworth, alias Lambert, was born at Searby, Lincolnshire, four miles south-east of Brigg, in 1572. At the age of 22 he became a Catholic. He went to Rheims and subsequently to Valladolid [1596-99] where he was ordained. In 1601 he was professed as a Benedictine monk.

Soon after his return to England he was arrested and sent for trial at the Old Bailey. "He received the sentence of death," (Bishop Challoner writes), "with a joyful and smiling countenance, and making the sign of the cross, began a hymn of joy, and then gave thanks to the judge." He was hanged, drawn and quartered at Tyburn on 27 February 1601 with the Jesuit Fr. Robert Filcock and Saint Anne Line.

11 April **Saint Guthlac** [c. 673-714]
'May be considered as the earliest saint of our diocese' and 'England's most popular pre-Conquest hermit saint after Cuthbert.'

Guthlac was born about 673 into the royal family of the Mercian tribe of Guthlacingas. At fifteen he became a soldier, and after nine successful years 'he gave up warfare to be a monk at Repton.' He was rather unpopular at first because of his total abstinence from intoxicating drink!

About 701 he moved to the solitary life on an island in the fens of Crowland, where he apparently made his cell in a barrow which had been excavated by treasure hunters, and lived in the style of the Desert Fathers. In 714 he foresaw his death, and his burial was attended by his sister, Pega, an hermit at Peakirk ['Pega's church'], and several of his disciples. A year later the grave was opened, the body found incorrupt, and the cult began. It soon embraced the King of Mercia and the Archbishop of Canterbury and became general. A monastery, which developed into the great Abbey of Crowland, was built near the site of Guthlac's cell and his relics were translated in 1136 and 1196 – possibly twice because the first arrangement was not adequate to the numbers of pilgrims.

The magnificent late twelfth century Guthlac Roll in the British Museum shows his life in eighteen roundels which are cartoons for stained glass windows. Don't miss crowlandabbey.org.uk/guthlac-roll/

4 May **Saint John Houghton** [1487-1535]

John Houghton was born into a family of Essex gentry, studied Law at Christ's College, Cambridge, during the Chancellorship of St. John Fisher and become a diocesan priest. He entered the London Charterhouse in 1516. In 1531, he was elected Prior of Beauvale, but several months later, he returned to London as Prior of that house. Shortly after the passing of the Act of Supremacy, 1 February 1535, he was visited by Robert Lawrence, Prior of Beauvale, and Augustine Webster, Prior of Axholme. Refusing to take the Oath of Supremacy, they were arrested, taken to the Tower of London, tried and found guilty of treason and sentenced to death.

As they were being tied, in their habits, to the hurdles and led away, singing, Saint Thomas More looked out of his cell window and said to his daughter Margaret, 'Lo, dost thou not see, Meg, that these blessed fathers be now going to their deaths as cheerfully as bridegrooms to their marriage.' They were hanged, drawn and quartered at Tyburn, with Blessed John Haile and Saint Richard Reynolds. As the executioner began to grope for his heart, John Houghton was heard to say, 'Good Jesus, what will you do with my heart?' Later ten more members of the London community who also refused to conform were confined in Newgate Prison and starved to death.

4 May **Saint Robert Lawrence** [died 1535]

Robert Lawrence entered the London Charterhouse and soon after his profession was made Prior of Beauvale in Nottinghamshire. The ruins of Beauvale are still visible today, and are the object of an annual pilgrimage on his feastday.

With Augustine Webster, he accompanied John Houghton in his attempt to make a personal appeal to Thomas Cromwell, the king's chief secretary. They were not heard, but instead committed to the Tower of London. In the interrogation by the Royal Commissioners which followed, 'Robert Lawrence says that there is one Catholic Church of which the Bishop of Rome is the head; therefore, he cannot believe that the king is supreme head of the Church.'

4 May **Saint Augustine Webster** [died 1535]
There were nine Charterhouses in England, and Augustine Webster joined the one at Sheen, on the banks of the Thames. Later he became Prior of the Charterhouse on the Isle of Axholme in Lincolnshire.

In his response to the Commissioners 'Augustine Webster says that he cannot take the king to be supreme head of the Church, but him that is by the doctors of the Church taken as head of the Church, that is, the Bishop of Rome, as Ambrose, Jerome, Augustine affirm, and is made at the Council of Basle.'

At the trial of John Houghton, Robert Lawrence and Augustine Webster, the jury refused to bring in a guilty verdict, but on the following day Cromwell so intimidated them that they gave in and a sentence of death was passed.

Wearing their habits, they were dragged on hurdles through the mud of Newgate Street and Holborn to Tyburn. The other two were forced to watch John Houghton being butchered but, undaunted, they preached to the people, telling them to obey the king in all that was not against the honour of God and his Church. As they entered the cart, each was offered a free pardon if they would renounce the Pope.

1 June **Saint Wistan** [died 850]
Little is known of Wistan, sometimes spelt 'Wystan', personally. Son of Wigmund and Elfleda of Mercia, and grandson of King Wiglaf, he was elected king in 840, but preferred to see his mother rule as regent. He was murdered at a place called Wistanstow, probably Wistow in Leicestershire, while attempting to prevent his cousin Behrtric from seizing power by marrying Elfleda, now the Queen Regent. Wystan considered that such a marriage would be incestuous. His body was buried in the royal crypt in Repton with those of his father and grandfather.

In 1019, Alfwaerd, Abbot of Evesham, asked King Cnut to give him Wystan's relics. From then on, Evesham was the centre of the cult.

17 June **Saint Botulph** [died 680]
Some say that the place name, Boston, Lincolnshire, is a corruption of Botulphston, the place where Botulph began to build his monastery in 654, but others say that the foundation was more likely made in Suffolk, at Iken. The church was later destroyed by the Danes, but his relics were rescued. Originally intended for Thorney Abbey, they were finally distributed between Thorney, Ely, Bury St Edmund's and Westminster. Many English churches were dedicated to him, but his cult was confined to his native country and little is known of his personality. Saint Botulph was described by Saint Ceolfrid as a man of "remarkable life and learning."

19 June **Blessed Thomas Woodhouse SJ** [died 1573]
Ordained priest in Mary Tudor's time, he was Rector of Stubton, Lincolnshire for less than a year. In 1560, he became a private tutor in Wales.

He was arrested while celebrating Mass and committed to the Fleet Prison on 14 May 1561. He famously sent the prison washerwoman to Lord Burghley's house with a letter, begging him to be reconciled and to persuade Elizabeth to submit to the Pope.

Put into solitary confinement, he wrote 'divers papers persuading men to the true faith and obedience, tied them to stones and flung them into the street.'

He was hung, drawn and quartered at Tyburn on 19 June 1573. He had become a Jesuit in prison.

20 June **Blessed Anthony Turner SJ** [c. 1628-1679]
Born about 1628, Anthony Turner was a native of Little Dalby near Melton Mowbray, Leicestershire. A convert to Catholicism, he joined the Society of Jesuit in 1653. After studies at Watten and Liège culminating in his ordination to the priesthood, he returned to England where he laboured on the mission for about eighteen years. In June 1679, along with four other Jesuits, Anthony Turner was arrested in the context of the Titus Oates Plot. They were executed at Tyburn. This was part of Anthony's prayer on the scaffold:

> 'O God, who hast created me to a supernatural end, to serve thee in this life by grace, and to enjoy thee in the next by glory, be pleased to grant, by the merits of thy bitter death and passion, that after this wretched life shall be ended, I may not fail of a full enjoyment of thee my last end and sovereign good. I humbly beg pardon for all the sins I have committed against thy divine majesty, since the first instant I came to the use of reason to this very time. I am heartily sorry, from the bottom of my heart, for having offended thee, so good, so powerful, so wise and so just a God, and purpose, by the help of thy grace, never more to offend thee, my good God, whom I love above all things.
>
> O sweet Jesus, who hast suffered a most painful and ignominious death upon the cross for our salvation, apply, I beseech thee, unto me the merits of thy sacred passion, and sanctify unto me these sufferings of mine, which I humbly accept of for thy sake, in union of the sufferings of thy sacred majesty, and in punishment and satisfaction of my sins.
>
> O my dear Saviour and Redeemer, I return thee immortal thanks for all thou hast pleased to do for me in the whole course of my life; and now in the hour of my death, with a firm belief of all the things thou

hast revealed, and a steadfast hope of obtaining everlasting bliss, I cheerfully cast myself into the arms of thy mercy, whose arms were stretched upon the cross for my redemption. Sweet Jesus, receive my spirit.'

5 July **Blessed Richard Yaxley** [c1560 – 1589]

Richard Yaxley, alias Tankard, was martyred at Oxford with Fr. George Nichols and two laymen, Thomas Belson and Humphrey Pritchard. He had been born about 1560 in Boston, Lincolnshire, and was one of twelve children of William and Rose [formerly Langton].

He entered the English College, Rheims, in August 1582 and was ordained priest on 21 September 1585 in Rheims Cathedral. Early in the next year he set out to preach the gospel in England. It seems likely that the time until his arrest was spent in missionary work around Oxford.

In April or May1589 the pursuivants, acting on information supplied by a spy, swooped on the Catherine Wheel Inn in Oxford, where Richard Yaxley and another priest, George Nichols, were lodging with Thomas Belson, a former student in Rheims. Vestments were found and all three were arrested along with Humphrey Pritchard, the barman.

They were sent to Sir Francis Walsingham, Secretary to the Privy Council, and housed in the Bridewell Prison in London. On 25 May Richard Yaxley was sent to Richard Topcliffe in the Tower of London and 'every day put upon the rack.' Then all four were sent back to Oxford to stand trial. The two priests were condemned to be hung, drawn and quartered and the two laymen sentenced to death by hanging for aiding and abetting them.

7 July **Blessed Roger Dickenson** [died 1591]

According to Bishop Challoner, Roger Dickenson was born in Lincolnshire and baptised in Lincoln. After training at Rheims he was ordained there in April 1583. On returning to England, he laboured for some years in the Winchester area devoting particular attention to the poor and to prisoners. Bishop Challoner tells us that he was captured in Winchester and put under guard with a view to being taken to London for trial. "But his guards having over drank themselves, he escaped from them in the night." He was captured a second time and was taken to London where he was tortured, and was then returned to Winchester for trial. Condemned to death, he was martyred on 7 July, 1591 at Winchester along with an elderly layman named Ralph Milner.

July **Blessed Thomas Hunt** [c. 1574-1600]

Born in Norfolk about 1574, and also known as Edmund Canfield, although his real name was Thomas Benstead. Nothing is known about his family or about his early life. In May 1572 Thomas entered the English College, Valladolid, but remained there only for a short time after which he was sent to the recently opened English College in Seville. (It is for this reason that both Valladolid and Seville count him as their first martyr and his portrait still hangs in the English College, Valladolid.)

Soon after his return to England he was arrested and imprisoned in Wisbech Castle, 'a concentration camp for priests', but in March 1600 he escaped with five other priests. Helped by Fr. Garnett, the Jesuit Superior, he returned in May to Lincolnshire with Fr. Sprott. They put up in the Saracen's Head Inn, Lincoln, but were unfortunate enough to arrive at a time when highwaymen were being sought, and a search of the two priests' belongings was sufficient for them to be sent for trial as priests. One of the judges, Sir John Glanville, bullied the jury into passing guilty verdicts, and they were executed the next day. Contrary to the usual practice, both martyrs were allowed to hang until they were dead before being cut down, disembowelled and quartered. The reason given by a contemporary source is that 'the people and even the magistrates had compassion on them and were very edified by the constancy they showed in dying; all recognised that they died without blame and solely for conscience' sake and for the profession of the Catholic religion.'

July **Blessed Thomas Sprott** [c. 1571-1600]

Since we know that when he was arrested in 1596, this martyr was twenty-five, he is probably the 'Thomas, son of Christopher Sprote,' who was baptised in Kendal Parish Church on 20 May 1571. He was trained for the priesthood in the English College, Douai, and ordained in 1596.

Thomas was captured in May of the same year in the Low Countries and arrived in Bridewell Prison on 8 July. From there he escaped one night with nine other priests and laymen. He was one of those who supported the establishment of the Jesuits' first prefecture, in England, in 1598.

We know nothing certain until he was arrested in Lincoln along with Thomas Hunt. But it is not impossible that he may have worked at Twigmoor Hall, a well-known hideout for Catholics some twenty-five miles north of Lincoln and not far from Brigg and Scunthorpe.

Thomas Sprott was martyred in Lincoln with Thomas Hunt in July 1600.

16 July **Venerable John Lion** [died 1599]

He was a layman, and the details of his martyrdom, known up to the eighteenth century, have been lost. He was martyred at Oakham. His story has been tentatively reconstructed as follows:

John Lion was a recusant yeoman with three hundred acres of freehold land, possibly in North Luffenham. He was probably confined in the prison which once stood in Gaol Street. He was indicted at the summer assizes of 1599, and tried and condemned to death in the hall of the Old Norman Castle – now the County Hall - dragged through the streets on a hurdle and put to death outside Oakham on 16 July 1599 opposite what is still known as the Swooning Bridge on the Manton/Uppingham Road. Cut down before he was dead, he was disembowelled and his heart cut out. His last words were, 'Lord, have mercy on them.' It is said that the bystanders were so struck by his constancy that they dipped their handkerchiefs in his blood and said that he was a true martyr.

24 July **Blessed Nicholas Garlick** [c1555 – 1588]

Nicholas Garlick was born at Dinting near Glossop. According to one account, his father was a well-to-do farmer. Having received a good education, Nicholas went up to Oxford but remained there for not more than six months since he could not, in conscience, take an oath acknowledging the supremacy of the Queen in religious matters. (This was a prerequisite for taking a university degree.) Returning to Derbyshire, he kept a free school in Tideswell for a number of years. Three of his pupils became priests. One of them, Blessed Christopher Buxton, was martyred in Canterbury a few months after his master.

Nicholas trained for the priesthood in Rheims and was ordained priest in March 1582. He came back to England in 1583. In the next year he was arrested in London, imprisoned and banished. Although he knew a second capture would not be so leniently treated, after two days in Rheims he set off back to England. In September 1586, we are told that was labouring "with diligence in Hampshire and Dorsetshire." In March 1588, he was working in Derbyshire. He was arrested along with Blessed Robert Ludlam at Padley Hall, near Grindleford, Derbyshire, in July 1588. The two of them together with Blessed Richard Simpson were hung, drawn and quartered in Derby on 24 July 1588.

24 July **Blessed Robert Ludlam** [c. 1551-1588]

Robert Ludlam was born near Sheffield, studied at the English College in Rheims and returned to the mission in 1582. He was captured almost by accident with Nicholas Garlick at Padley Manor, taken for trial in Derby and there executed with him. Previously he had worked well in several counties without ever being spotted by an informer.

When on the ladder, he raised his eyes to heaven 'and with a smiling countenance,' says and eyewitness, 'as if he had seen some heavenly vision, he uttered these his last words: 'Come, blessed of my Father.'

24 July **Blessed Richard Simpson** [c. 1550-1588]
Born at Wells, near Ripon, he had become an Anglican minister. On his conversion he went to study at Douai. He was already in Derby Gaol and wavering when Fathers Garlick and Ludlam were brought in. They gave him courage and he shared their martyrdom which took place at the north end of St. Mary's Bridge.
One onlooker wrote:

When Garlick did the ladder kiss,
And Sympson after hie
Methought that there St. Andrw was
Desirous for to die.

When Ludlam looked smilingly
And joyful did remain,
It seemed St. Stephen was standing by
For to be stoned again.

And what if Sympson seemed to yield
For doubt and dread to die,
He rose again and won the field
And died more constantly.

His watching, fast and shirt of hair,
His speech and death and all
Do record give, do witness bear,
He wailed his former fall.

7 July **Blessed Robert Sutton** [c1545 – 1588]
For several years before his conversion to Catholicism, Robert Sutton was Vicar of Lutterworth in Leicestershire. He had three brothers younger than himself, two of whom became priests. One of these, William, who later drowned on a voyage to Spain, persuaded Robert to be reconciled to Rome. Father John Gerard gives a dramatic description of Robert's departure from Lutterworth. He writes that, after gathering his parishioners together and begging their pardon for having led them into error, he got down from the pulpit, removed his clerical gown under which he was wearing travelling clothes. Then he and his younger brother Abraham mounted the horses which a servant had got ready for them outside the churchyard and made for London and Belgium.

Abraham and Robert headed for the English College, Douai, where – after studies lasting less than a year – they were ordained to the priesthood in 1578 and very soon afterwards set out for England.

Robert, described as "a very reverend learned man [who] at his arraignment disputed very stoutly and learnedly" ministered in Staffordshire for nine years before being arrested in Stafford, probably on 18 July 1588, and condemned. John Gerard tells us he 'went cheerfully and boldly towards his end,' having in his own words 'received greater consolation than I deserved' in his prayer the previous evening. His fellow prisoners described his cell as filled with light. On the scaffold he 'made a fine discourse of the candle we receive in baptism and in the hour of death.'

After his particularly barbaric execution on 27 July 1588, some of the parts of his dismembered body were retrieved. One of these parts, a thumb, was given by Robert's Jesuit brother, Abraham, to Fr John Gerard. This relic was venerated at Stonyhurst College, Lancashire, until 1987 when, on the occasion of the beatification of Robert Sutton, the Jesuits very kindly donated the thumb to the Catholic Parish of Lutterworth where it is now kept.

6 August **Saint Hardulph**

On a promontory left by a large stone quarry, the Church of St Hardulph stands above the village of Breedon-on-the-Hill in Leicestershire. The church contains some of the finest Anglo-Saxon stone carvings in England.

By the side of the River Trent not far away is the 'Anchor cave,' used according the life of St Modwen, by a St Hardulph as a hermitage. Were there two Hardulphs, or just one?

Many scholars think the seventh century Hardulph was King Eardwulf of Northumbria.

22 August **Blessed Richard Kirkman** [died 1582]

A native of Yorkshire, Richard Kirkman's association with our diocese appears to be that he worked in Scrivelsby in Lincolnshire, from the house of Robert Dymoke who died in prison for the Catholic Faith two years before him. Fr. Kirkman had left Scrivelsby when the Dymokes were indicted for recusancy, and was arrested in Wakefield. A chalice was found on him, and he was condemned the next day at the York Assizes.

After being condemned to death, and being angrily branded by one of the justices as a Papist and a traitor, Richard calmly replied that they might just as well accuse the apostles in like fashion since they taught the same doctrine as he (Richard) was teaching and did the same things for which he was being condemned! On receiving his sentence, Richard sang *'Te Deum laudamus'* in a loud voice. He suffered with Blessed William Lacey at the Knavesmire outside the walls of York. On the way to the gallows they had confessed and absolved one another on the hurdle. Like many martyrs before and since, Richard went to his death cheerfully.

28 August **Blessed Hugh More** [c. 1563-1588]
Born in Grantham into a Protestant family, Hugh began to study at one of the Inns of Court. At some point during that time he was reconciled to the Catholic Church. This was not an easy decision for Hugh since his father thereupon disinherited him. As a consequence of his conversion, Hugh abandoned what could have been a promising career in law and, in 1585, left his native country to pursue his vocation to the priesthood in the English College at Rheims. In 1587, bad health forced him to return to England. Although he had not been ordained, he was automatically liable to the same penalties in English law as a priest merely for living in a seminary.

Hugh was arrested and imprisoned soon after his arrival in England, and came to trial at the Old Bailey on 26 August 1588. Hugh's family were more than disgusted with him. His father, who by this time had become Member of Parliament for Grantham, is said to have hated him. Hugh was hanged at Lincoln's Inn Fields on 30 August. He cannot have been more than twenty-five years of age.

In September 1966, a secondary school dedicated to its local martyr was opened in Grantham. When the school celebrated its twenty-first birthday, the hope was expressed that this celebration would launch the school into its next twenty-one years. Despite the fact that there was a question mark about the future of the school, the staff and pupils of the Blessed Hugh More School decided to commemorate the four hundredth anniversary of the execution in 1588 of their Patron, with a play 'They Climb Heaven' written by Fr. Jonathan Cotton. Regrettably, the school – built originally for 150 pupils – was closed in July 1989 since which time there has been no provision for Catholic secondary education in the Grantham area.

9 September **Blessed George Douglas** [died 1587]
A Scot, George Douglas was the son of John, an Edinburgh burgess, a member of Clan Angus. After the accession of Elizabeth I, George went abroad, to be heard of next as a Latin schoolmaster in North Luffenham in Rutland. After about six years he left Rutland and went abroad again, trained for the priesthood and was ordained in the Cathedral church of Notre Dame in Paris in 1574. He went to Flanders and was again a schoolmaster.

Intending to return to Scotland, he travelled to Dover where he obtained a passport from the mayor. It was stolen, so when he was stopped at a checkpoint in Glaston, Rutland, he was taken for interrogation in the nearby village of Wing. It seems he was released.

Something similar happened in Ripon the following year, 1585, although his detention lasted longer. He emerged as a teacher of the prison warden's children, a local JP. But soon he was brought to an underground cell in York prison, before trial, probably at the Lent Assizes of 1587. He was charged with the treasonable offence of 'persuading to popery.'

His execution, at York on 9 September 1587, was carried out with even greater barbarity than usual.

1 October **Blessed Robert Widmerpool** [c. 1560 1588]

Born at Widmerpool, Nottinghamshire, about 1560, he went up to Oxford when he was eighteen. Like several other martyrs, he appears not to have graduated, perhaps because he would have had to take the Oath of Supremacy.

Robert became tutor to the sons of Henry Percy, Earl of Northumberland. This was to lead to his death since he was charged, in particular, with having introduced a priest into the household of the Countess of Northumberland. After his arrest he was imprisoned with Fathers Robert Wilcox, Christopher Buxton and Edward Campion.

On 1 October 1588 he was led out with the three priests to Oaten Hill, Canterbury. Bishop Challoner tells us that: 'At the place of execution with great affection [Robert] kissed both the ladder and the rope as the instruments of his martyrdom; and having now the rope about his neck, began to speak to the people giving God most hearty thanks "for bringing him to so great a glory as that of dying for his faith and truth in the same place where the glorious martyr St. Thomas of Canterbury had shed his blood for the honour of his divine majesty."

Some of the people at these words cried out, "Away, away with the traitor"; but he, not moved at all with their clamours, looking around him and commending himself to the prayers of the Catholics, was flung off the ladder, and so happily exchanged this life for immortality.'

Like the three priests, Robert was hung, drawn and quartered.

1 October **Blessed Christopher Buxton** [1562-1588]

Born in 1562 in Derbyshire, he attended Buxton Grammar School, where he was a pupil of Blessed Nicholas Garlick. It is very possible that he decided to become a Catholic, and later a priest, because of the influence of his teacher. At least two others of Nicholas Garlick's pupils did.

Christopher arrived in Rheims in 1581 to begin his training, which he completed in Rome, where he was ordained in St. John Lateran on 28 October 1586. Arriving in England in the autumn of 1587, he worked for only two months before he was captured and committed to the Marshalsea Prison.

Along with the priests Edward Campion (not to be confused with Saint Edmund Campion) and Robert Wilcox, and the layman Robert Widmerpool, he was led to execution on Oaten Hill, Canterbury. Fr. Wilcox was thirty, Fr. Campion, thirty-six, Robert Widmerpool probably twenty-eight and Christopher Buxton, twenty-six. He was offered his life if he would conform but answered that 'if he had a hundred lives he would willingly surrender them all in defence of his faith.'

1 October **Blessed Edward James** [c.1559-1588]
Born at Beeston (or Breaston) probably in 1559, Edward attended the grammar school in Derby from where he went to St. John's College, Oxford. Like many of the other martyrs he did not graduate since this would have required him to take the Oath of Supremacy. He was timid by nature and short in height. After Oxford, he went to London where a Catholic layman persuaded him to train for the priesthood. Arriving at Rheims in the autumn of 1579, he spent less than a year there before entering the Venerable English College, Rome, where he completed his training and was ordained priest in October 1583.

Along with several others he was arrested almost immediately after his arrival in England in the spring of 1586, even before they had time to disembark from the ship which had brought them from France. 'They did not have the chance to celebrate one Mass in their home country, or hear any Confessions, or preach a single sermon.'

Edward is described as 'a very mild and virtuous man much given to meditation, and had in the same so great consolation that sometimes he could not refrain but express the same by outward signs.'

Edward James was one of four priests who were brought to trial at Chichester on 30 September 1588. There were no acquittals in Tudor treason trials, and they were condemned to be hanged, drawn and quartered. The hideous execution took place the following day. Edward had shown some signs of weakness, so he was forced to watch while his companion, Fr. Ralph Crockett, was butchered. The authorities hoped that this would cause Edward to falter and renounce his Catholic faith. He did not.

5 October **Blessed Robert Sutton** [died 1588]
He was a layman, not to be confused with the priest Robert Sutton [27 July 1588]. This Robert Sutton was born at Kegworth, Leicestershire, and brought up as a Protestant, though his parents may have been Catholics. After graduating from university, he became a teacher somewhere in London, where he met a Fr. Blythe who was working in the Newgate area. It was he who received Robert into the Catholic Church. The news of his conversion got out, and he was taken to prison, where he spent some considerable time.

His formal examination probably took place in August 1588 in the aftermath of the Spanish Armada. The evidence against him was that 'he had been shriven of one Mr. Blythe an old priest in Newgate.'

On 5 October 1588, he was taken from prison to the gallows at Clerkenwell.

5 October **Blessed William Hartley** [c.1551-1588]

A native of Derbyshire where he was born – possibly at Wilne – in 1551 - or 1557. Another source states that he was born in Nottinghamshire. He studied at Oxford and is said to have been a man of great learning, which may explain why he was ordained within a year of his arrival in Rheims in August 1579.

After a year's work in England, involved – it seems – with the printing and distribution of Catholic literature from a secret press, he was captured at Stonor with several others in August 1581 and sent to the Tower of London. After his examination, he was transferred to the Marshalsea Prison.

Brought to trial at the beginning of 1584 on a charge of having plotted to depose the Queen, he was condemned to be executed, but the sentence was commuted to banishment. After a year in Rheims, he came back, was caught again and hanged but not drawn and quartered (the usual punishment for being a Catholic priest) at Clerkenwell, London, on 5 October 1588.

One source, quoted by Bishop Challoner, tells us that his mother was present and that she 'rejoiced exceedingly that she had brought forth a son to glorify God by such a death.'

10 October **Saint Paulinus** [died 644]

Like St. Augustine, Paulinus was a monk of St. Andrew's monastery on the Coelian Hill in Rome. He was sent with Mellitus and Justus to Canterbury in 601 as part of the 'second wave' of Gregory the Great's mission to England. Considerably later, when the Kentish princess Ethelburga, daughter of Ethelbert, went north to become the bride of Edwin, King of Northumbria, Paulinus, newly consecrated as the first Bishop of York, went with her. Bede says that on one occasion in York, Paulinus spent thirty-eight days baptising. Among those he baptised was the future St. Hilda of Whitby. King Edwin was baptised in a wooden church in York in 627.

Paulinus also baptised, with James his deacon, at Littleborough in Retford parish to the north-west of the tidal Trent, possibly as many as three thousand people. Littleborough is the only town in Nottinghamshire which has been continuously inhabited since the first century AD and it sprang up because this is the place where a Roman road from Lincoln to Doncaster crossed the river by means of a causeway which could be used at low tide. This was the principal crossing of the River Trent. In 1066 King Harold crossed here twice with his army, on his way to Stamford Bridge and to Hastings.

Paulinus is said to have founded the church in Southwell, and to have built a stone church in Lincoln, though no trace of it has been found.

But when Edwin of Northumbria died in 632, the atmosphere changed for a while and Paulinus went back south, with Ethelburga and her children. He became Bishop of Rochester, and spent the rest of his life in Kent.

17 November **Saint Hugh of Lincoln** [c1140 – 1200]

The reliability and fullness of detail of the 'Great Life', written by Hugh's secretary, Adam of Eynsham, are said to be almost unsurpassed in medieval hagiography.

Hugh had been born about 1140 in Avalon in imperial Burgundy. His mother died in childbirth, and he was brought up by his father, and then by the Canons Regular, whom he joined. Then he discovered that his real vocation was to the Carthusians, probably the toughest order in the western Church.

In 1172 Hugh was very reluctantly constrained by Henry II to be the effective founding father of a new Carthusian house in Witham in Somerset, one of three religious houses Henry had undertaken to create. This was in commutation of taking the Crusaders' cross as a penance for his part in the murder of Thomas a Becket.

Only one Carthusian monk has ever been a bishop in England, and Hugh spent the happiest month of each year back in his beloved monastery at Witham. Here he lived in all simplicity as a monk of the house who took his turn in the ordinary community duties in choir and it was his special delight to wash the dishes.

Henry II and Baldwin of Canterbury forced the Cathedral chapter of Lincoln to elect him bishop, although the canons dreaded his reputation for austerity. Hugh refused to accept the validity of the election, on various grounds, including the following: 'You have the right to elect your own bishop, since you will have to put up with his personality and authority'. A second, free election therefore took place in the chapter house. The monk of the Chartreuse became bishop of what was at the time the most populous diocese in England, stretching from Humber to Trent, from Leicester to Hertford. He was consecrated on 21 September, 1186, in the infirmary chapel of St. Catherine at Westminster Abbey.

His diocese stretched from the Humber to the Thames. Hugh was always in the saddle, showing great pastoral concern for his people, particularly in burying deceased paupers. Sometimes he was so lost in contemplation that his horse had to be led. He was unusual in dismounting to administer confirmation. He kissed lepers, not to heal them, but – he said - so that they

might heal him. He dispersed anti-Jewish mobs in Lincoln, Stamford and Northampton. His worst expletive seems to have been: 'Holy nut!'
He knew Henry and his two royal sons well, and showed great courage in standing up to them. Involved as a justice in many of the great disputes of the day, he showed the spirit of a peacemaker in them all.

Hugh never spoke or understood the Midland dialect of early English, but the ordinary people flocked to him.

He knew Gilbert of Sempringham, and promoted his cause, which led to Gilbert's canonization in 1202.

Lincoln Cathedral, which had been practically destroyed by the great earthquake of Palm Sunday, 1185, and particularly the Angel Choir, are Hugh's most obvious monument. He carried the hod himself to prosecute the work.

Hugh died in London on 16 November 1200 after Vespers. He was returning from a pilgrimage to the Grande Chartreuse. He breathed his last lying on a cross of ashes which had been prepared beside his bed in the way made famous by St. Martin of Tours. He had often said, 'it would be very hard for us if we were never allowed to die.' He was buried in Lincoln Cathedral, his coffin carried through the muddy streets of the city by the Kings of England and Scotland. Hugh was canonized in 1220. Edward I was present in 1280 when his relics were moved to the shrine in the Angel choir.

Hugh had the reputation of being the most learned religious of his time in England. He revived the famous Lincoln schools, which at the time rivalled Oxford's.

He could complete any Bible sentence which someone else started.

John of Leicester said of him: 'The bishops' stave, the model monk, patron of scholars, hammer of kings, e'en such was Hugh'

Richard the Lionheart said, 'If all bishops were like this one, no king would dare to lift up his head against them.'

At the Council of Oxford in 1197, Hugh successfully resisted Richard's attempts to create a standing army, the first step on a path that led to the Magna Charta.

The Bishop of Salisbury's goods were confiscated, but no one dared touch Hugh's.

The writer John Ruskin described Saint Hugh as 'The most beautiful sacerdotal figure known to me in history'.

Among his sayings are:

'How wretched are those who dread anything except to offend so great a friend!

'How much to be pitied are they who esteem anything else sweet, or desire anything except to cleave lovingly to such a lover, and lovingly obey him. To my mind nothing can seem hard to a man who has through meditation experienced his sweetness, and sweetly digested it in the depths of his heart'

Saint Hugh is the Secondary Patron of our diocese.

1 December **Saint Ralph Sherwin** [1550-1581]

Ralph Sherwin was the first of more than forty martyrs from the Venerable English College in Rome. Born at Rodsley, near Ashbourne, Derbyshire, about 1550, he was brought up a Protestant and educated at Exeter College, Oxford. In 1575 he became a Catholic and went first to Douai and then in 1577 to Rome. His name is the first in the College register. When the students were required to affirm the Missionary Oath, that they were willing to be sent on the English mission, he did so and added, 'today rather than tomorrow' ['potius hodie quam cras'].

In 1580, after three months' work in London, he was captured while he was preaching and committed to the Marshalsea Prison. Transferred to the Tower after a month, he was alternately tortured on the rack and thrown out into the December snow. All without answering any questions. And after a year in the Tower he was brought to trial with Edmund Campion and thirteen others in Westminster Hall. In a letter to his uncle, John Woodward, he wrote, 'Innocency is my only comfort against all the forged villainy which is fathered on my fellow priests and me.'

Two days before his death, meeting Campion in the Tower grounds, he looked up at the sun and exclaimed: 'Ah, Father Campion, I shall soon be above yonder fellow.'

He died at Tyburn with Edmund Campion and Alexander Briant, at the age of thirty-one. His last words were 'Jesus, Jesus, Jesus, be to me a Jesus.' Saint Ralph Sherwin was one of the forty martyrs canonised by Pope Paul VI in 1970. Six years later, the Sherwin Society was established in Ashbourne, and a diocesan pilgrimage in St. Ralph's honour to Rodsley, which is part of the Ashbourne parish, takes place each June.

10 December **Saint Eustace White** [c. 1560-1591]

Eustace White, a secular priest, was born at Louth in Lincolnshire about 1560 and brought up a Protestant. When he converted to the Catholic Faith, his father, an earnest Protestant, put a solemn curse on him. But he did well at Douai, Rheims and finally at the Venerable English College, Rome, where he was ordained in 1588.

Returning to England, he laboured in the west country for three years. Captured near Blandford, he was sent to the Bridewell Prison in London. His hands closely manacled, he lay on straw for forty-six days. Denied food and clothing, he was severely tortured seven times by Richard Topcliffe.

'Lord, more pain if thou pleasest, and more patience' was his only response. He was hung, drawn and quartered at Tyburn on 10 December 1591. He was cut down alive from the noose, but as he rose to his feet he was tripped and two men stood on either arm to facilitate the execution.

10 December **Blessed Thomas Plumtree** [died 1570]
Born somewhere in the vast Lincoln diocese, he matriculated at Corpus Christi, Oxford, in 1543 and graduated BA in 1546. That same year he was made Rector of Stubton, between Newark and Grantham. But he resigned his living under Elizabeth and became master of a school in Lincoln. He was chief chaplain to the army of the Earls of Northumberland and Westmorland in what was called the Rising of the North and on a number of occasions celebrated Mass for them in Ripon and then in Durham. But the Rising failed. Thomas Plumtree was among those arrested. He was imprisoned, firstly in Carlisle and, soon afterwards, in Durham.

On 4 January 1571, he was led out to the market place in Durham. There he was offered his life if he would agree to renounce his Catholic Faith. Upon his refusal to do so, he was hung, drawn and quartered. Ten days later, his remains were buried in a cemetery on the site of the present marketplace. Several days after Thomas' death, the French Ambassador described him as "a well-respected and good living man of high intelligence."

Surname	Firstname	Saint etc.	Status	Connection	County	Parish or area - current
Aelred		St.	Abbot	worked	Lincs.	Woodhall Spa
Barkworth	Mark	Bl.	Martyr	born	Lincs.	Brigg
Botulph		St.	Hermit	worked	Lincs.	Boston
Buxton	Christopher	Bl.	Martyr	born	Derbys.	Marple Bridge
Dickenson	Roger	Bl.	Martyr	born	Lincs.	Lincoln
Garlick	Nicholas	Bl.	Martyr	born/martyred	Derbys.	Glossop
Gilbert		St.	Abbot	worked	Lincs.	Bourne
Guthlac		St.	Hermit	worked	Lincs.	Spalding
Hardulph		St.	Hermit	worked	Derbys.	Melbourne
Hartley	William	Bl.	Martyr	born	Derbys.	?
Houghton	John	St.	Martyr	worked	Notts.	Eastwood
Hugh		St.	Bishop	worked	Lincs.	diocese
Hunt	Thomas	Bl.	Martyr	martyred	Lincs.	Lincoln
Ireland	William	Bl.	Martyr	born	Lincs.	Bardney
James	Edward	Bl.	Martyr	born	Derbys.	Long Eaton
Kirkman	Richard	Bl.	Martyr	worked	Lincs.	Woodhall Spa
Lawrence	Robert	St.	Martyr	worked	Notts.	Eastwood
Lion	John	Ven.	Martyr	martyred	Rutland	Oakham

Surname	Firstname	Saint etc.	Status	Connection	County	Parish or area - current
Ludlam	Robert	Bl.	Martyr	born/martyred	Derbys.	Ashbourne
More	Hugh	Bl.	Martyr	born	Lincs.	Grantham
Paulinus		St.	Bishop	worked	Lincs.	Lincs.
Plumtree	Thomas	Bl.	Martyr	worked	Lincs.	Grantham
Pormort	Thomas	Bl.	Martyr	born	Lincs.	Grimsby/Immingham
Sherwin	Ralph	St.	Martyr	born	Derbys.	Ashbourne
Simpson	Richard	Bl.	Martyr	martyred	Derbys.	Derby St. Mary
Sprott	Thomas	Bl.	Martyr	martyred	Lincs.	Lincoln
Sutton	Robert	Bl.	Martyr	born	Leics.	Melbourne/East Leake
Sutton	Robert	Bl.	Martyr	worked	Leics.	Lutterworth
Tansi	Cyprian	Bl.	Monk	worked	Leics.	Whitwick
Turner	Anthony	Bl.	Martyr	born	Leics.	Melton Mowbray
Webster	Augustine	St.	Martyr	worked	Lincs.	Scunthorpe
Werburga		St.	Abbess	worked	Lincs.	Bourne
White	Eustce	St.	Martyr	born	Lincs.	Louth
Widmerpool	Robert	Bl.	Martyr	born	Notts.	East Leake
Woodhouse	Thomas	Bl.	Martyr	worked	Lincs.	Lincs.
Wystan		St.	Martyr	died	Derbys.	Swadlincote
Yaxley	Richard	Bl.	Martyr	born	Lincs.	Boston

Saint Hugh's College Tollerton

Canon B. Needham

Appointed bishop in 1944, with the ending of war and after consultation, Bishop Ellis took the brave decision to set about founding a college where boys could be helped in their journey towards becoming priests. Tollerton Hall was on the market. It had been requisitioned by the army during the war and some work needed to be done to make it suitable. It was not until September 1948 that it began life as St. Hugh's College, named after St. Hugh of Lincoln, secondary patron of the diocese. With an intake of twenty-six students, the college was staffed by five priests, Fathers Gryce, Sweeney and Swaby from the diocese and Father Winstone from Westminster and Father Higham from Liverpool. Domestic needs were beautifully catered for by the Franciscan Sisters Minoress from Melton Mowbray. The boys were drawn from all parts of our extensive diocese, and indeed from other dioceses, so it needed to be a boarding college. In those pioneering days, the tone was set for it to be a happy and caring community. The college rapidly became a focal point for the diocese, particularly as the Summer Fête drew support from all the parishes and large crowds attended. An outstanding diocesan occasion was the celebration of Mass to mark the Marian Year in 1954, and for many years the college was the venue for the diocesan clergy retreat.

Although it began as what is called a minor seminary, over the years the student numbers increased as the college also accepted boys who had no thought of a vocation to the priesthood. Bishop Ellis remarked that this was a good thing since he had always envisaged a college where catholic boys could be prepared for various careers, but where particular care might be given to those who felt in some way to be called to the priesthood.

Circumstances led the diocese to decide it was no longer possible to maintain the college, so it was closed and the property sold in 1986. Many items had been specially commissioned for the college when it was first opened and these were distributed around the diocese : the statue of St. Hugh found a place in the Cathedral: the statue of Our Lady, 'Virgo Fidelis', went to Saints Peter and Paul Church in Lincoln: the tabernacle, sanctuary lamp, crucifixes and altar candles were given to various parishes.

In his final report to the Governors, the Rector was able to state that, beginning with the first ordinations in 1960, a total of forty boys who had passed through St. Hugh's College had now become priests, the majority of them working in our diocese. It would seem to be a worthy legacy.

The Briars Residential Centre

Canon M. Bell

In the mid-1960s, there was much activity in this country to provide recreational facilities for young people, particularly to those in the 14 to 18 age group. This was as a result of Lady Albemarles's Report on "The Training of Part-Time Youth Leaders."

A National College was established in Leicester for the training of youth leaders. A Catholic Youth Service Council, based in London, emerged as the Catholic voice in the development of a partnership between local authorities and voluntary youth services. The Department of Education and Science and local education departments were looking for help from the voluntary bodies such as the Churches, and were offering considerable practical help in many ways.

For a number of years, during Easter Week, there had been retreats for teenage boys at Mount Saint Mary's College, Spinkhill, (at that time in the Diocese of Nottingham); these retreats were often attended by more than one hundred participants from all over the diocese.

It was from events such as these that the hope for a more formal service for the young people of the diocese began to develop. At this time, in many parishes, youth clubs, Young Christian Worker groups, etc., were being set up to care for our young people.

Bishop Ellis saw the problems affecting the diocese. He said that our young people had to have the opportunity of not merely enjoying themselves with one another but also of taking part in an apostolate to other young people. So he started the Nottingham Diocesan Youth Service.

By the mid-1960s there was a central group of people with area committees doing great work, and local training and other youth activities were being organised, often in partnership with local authorities.

There had to be more! The Diocesan Youth Committee agreed that residential work with young people had an important part to play in the training and formation of young people as the People of God. Therefore, early in 1965, the Committee decided that it would give priority to finding premises for, and the setting-up of, a residential centre for young people somewhere in the diocese.

It seemed an impossible dream – places were visited and turned down. There seemed to be all kinds of obstacles – not least lack of finance! Then suddenly there was a sign of hope: the Department of Education and Science had helped with finance for the purchase of Castlerigg Manor in the Diocese of Lancaster as a residential centre for young people.

Work began to convince the Department of Education and Science of the need in the Diocese of Nottingham. The Department had to be assured that suitable premises were or would be available and, above all, that the venture would not fail. Until all this was done, it was not possible to settle on a property – at the time there did not seem to be anything either available or suitable within the confines of the diocese.

Then, quite out of the blue, in October 1967, Mr. and Mrs. Ronald Heymans, who were running a Quaker Vegetarian Guest House at Crich, decided to retire. They put the house on the market, and from then on things moved fairly quickly – what Father Paul Klee called "the adventure of faith" was on its way. The house was purchased – at a cost of £30,000 (in 2017, a little over £380,000.)

After several months of preparation and a great deal of alteration to make the house suitable for accommodating young people and fulfilling its purpose, it threw open its doors and began its work. There was accommodation for forty people in single, two, three and (one) four-bedded rooms. There was a washbasin in each bedroom; the problem of communal washing facilities as customarily found in many residential centres such as youth hostels did not arise.

The Official Opening took place on 17 April 1970. At the time, this was described as "an event of great importance that merits the description of 'a milestone' in the progress and development of the Catholic Youth Service in this diocese and the country as a whole."

The Opening Ceremony began with the Blessing of the Centre by Bishop Ellis and concluded with the praying of the prayer for the peace of Christ on the house, staff and young people using it, by granting them the strength to serve him faithfully.

Then came the Official Opening by the Secretary of State for Education and Science, the Right Honourable Edward Short MP, who, in his speech, said that "he found it particularly relevant and pleasing for him, at this time to have been invited to open this Residential Centre, because it gave him at first hand the opportunity to see what the Church was doing in the field of youth service."

Bishop Ellis, in his response, made special mention of the financial grant of £16,812 (£182,000 in 2017) and the support of the Department of Education and Science not only for this venture but for what was given to the Catholic Church in the whole field of education.

Father David Caine wrote in the 1971 edition of the Nottingham Diocesan Yearbook: "The Briars anticipates the recommendations of 'Youth and Community Work in the 1970s', a document presented to the Government by the Youth Service Development Council and published in October 1969. Paragraph 256 of this document affirms that 'residential experience is valuable to all young people providing that priority is given to facilitate developing personal relationships and for creating face-to-face situations.' It is the aim of The Briars to provide just these facilities for the youngsters of the diocese and to make the specifically Catholic contribution to youth work that is an essential part of the Christian vocation of all Catholics."

The Briars was years ahead of its time; it was the second such centre in the country! While youth service has changed beyond all recognition, it is still the Cinderella of education.

The Briars came into its own, and over the years it has gone from strength to strength. Long may it continue to cater for the needs of young people who, in the words of the slogan for Pope John Paul II's visit to Britain in 1982, are "the Church of today and the hope of tomorrow."

SPANNED – 1976-2016

Fr. F. Daly

SPANNED (Supporting People with Additional Needs in the Nottingham Diocese) came into being in March 1976, when life for people with limiting or disabling conditions was very different from what it is today. It would be a year before the first Minister for Disabled People was appointed and the notion of 'access' to places, facilities and services would become part of our thinking. People with learning difficulties were officially classified as "sub-normal", which seems unimaginable and those in wheelchairs faced a life of not being able to get out and about as they can do relatively easily now. It was truly a very different time in society but also in the church. Any notion of 'inclusion' was not even on the horizon and these people and their families became objects of patronising pity rather than being taken seriously as 'persons' who had something unique to 'contribute' to our life and faith. SPANNED, as it is now called, set about redressing this imbalance, which should never have been part of the living and Mission of the church communities.

Six groups for people in different parts of the diocese were formed with the great help of religious communities who opened their hearts and homes to us and our work, meeting regularly, and great efforts were made initially to support people with disabilities and their families, then to 'include' them in the life of the Church and finally to 'listen' to them, having offered them the opportunity to 'proclaim' the gospel of Jesus to us in such an inventive and new way. There had already been 'associations' for people with disabilities, especially in regard to pilgrimages to Lourdes, in existence in ours and many other dioceses, and work had taken place in other parts of the country to include and 'form' them in the ways of the Lord, particularly in Westminster, Liverpool and Bristol, but SPANNED was truly unique. We wrote our own programmes of work and formation, took groups out into parishes on Sundays, offered facilities for day care and respite support, and reached out to church and society alike in new and unprecedented ways SPANNED was responsible for inventing the first 'Faith and Light' Celebration in Spinkhill, Sheffield, in August 1978 and on that same occasion pioneering the use of mime and music for people with learning difficulties to interpret and 'proclaim' the Word of God in a totally new way. This work reached its pinnacle in July 2000 with the Millennium presentation of the life of Our Lord, danced to the music of "Riverdance" by a cast of 169 people in the Assembly Rooms, Derby with 800 awe-struck people present. A similar milestone was attained in October 2016, with the presentation of "The Balm of Mercy", a musical specially written to the music of Andrew Lloyd Webber for Pope Francis' "Year of Mercy" with 80 people from SPANNED performing with a choir of 40 others on two unforgettable evenings in Hinckley and the Albert Hall, Nottingham. SPANNED played a leading role in the inception and organisation of the Trent Walk, and overnight sponsored walk of 7.5, 13.5 and 26.5miles which took place in aid of charities working with disabled people on 10 occasions over 18 years from 1981 and raised in excess of £300,000 in so doing. Thousands of pounds have also been raised for many charities through our projects of work and drama, so that we have been and remain an 'outreach' group from the very start of our existence. The work has expanded to include a facility for the deaf and hard of hearing and an umbrella for the catechetical and pastoral care of the travelling communities, and our quarterly publication is second only to the diocesan Year Book in its longevity within the Nottingham Diocese. For the past ten years we have undertaken a project of work each year determined often by the request of the bishops of our country in highlighting certain aspects of our faith and these have been engaging, amusing and memorable. Two residential communities, set up by the then leader of the Loreto Thursday Club in Nottingham and his family, have been in existence for 30 years and we are very proud of the care and concern they have offered so generously and beautifully to their residents who have enjoyed much fuller and more active lives than they might have had otherwise. While we are so proud of what has been achieved, we are mindful of the challenges that lie ahead. For many of our friends, age has brought extra problems in the form of dementia and its associated conditions. This demands great care and sensitivity and has opened up a whole new area for us in our work. There remains also the need to protect and promote the lives of those who may be born with a so-called 'limiting' condition and the desire to create some form of 'perfect' society by eliminating them before birth, as has already happened to many people with certain disabling conditions such as hydrocephalus and spina bifida, or to save the cost of their care in order to meet governmental fiscal targets. This is a chilling but very real prospect, whereby we will be valued in simply 'functional' terms for what we can do and earn rather than for what we can 'contribute' and be. This nightmare scenario must simply not be allowed to happen or our elderly, disabled and vulnerable people will simply cease to be when they have become a 'drain' on financial resources and cannot 'produce' meaningful income for themselves or others. This was never the world that Our Lord intended, and the need to live and proclaim his gospel of truth and love has never been more urgent. Hence the work of SPANNED, so often the flagship of inclusion and contribution in the past, is still vitally important for the future of the Church and indeed of the world itself.

Nottingham Pilgrims Community:
September 1989 – August 2007
Canon J. Cotton

The Nottingham Pilgrims Community was a fruit of the Decade of Evangelisation called for by the Catholic Church, which was the ten years of preparation leading up to the third millennium. For thirteen years it was based in part of the former Presentation Convent School in Matlock, Derbyshire and then, as there were no buildings in the Diocese made available, it moved outside the Diocese to the Convent building in the village of Monks Kirby, near Rugby in the Archdiocese of Birmingham.

The Pilgrims was started by Fr. Jonathan Cotton, a priest of the Diocese of Nottingham, and Sister Angela Murphy, a Presentation Sister. This joint leadership reflected a shared project between the Diocese and the Presentation Sisters. The Pilgrims offered a gap year experience for young people in their late teens and twenties. At first the group supported Vocations Ministry in the Diocese but during the first year it soon became apparent the young people they encountered needed to be evangelised before they could hear the calling to priesthood and religious life.

Consequently, the volunteers were trained to be part of a Youth Mission Team, trained in youth evangelism, as well as receiving personal formation through a discipleship training, learning how to live together in a Catholic Community, sharing daily house duties, prayer times and leisure activities. When sufficient numbers of Volunteers were recruited a second Service Team was run, evangelising through care work and practical social projects in the local community. Youth with a Mission, the Sion Community and members of the Charismatic Renewal Movement were regular contributors to the formation programme of the Pilgrims.

Eventually, The Pilgrims adopted the KE KA KO School of Evangelisation from the Rome based charismatic Community 'Koinonia Giovanni Batista.' This School radically developed their own formation and was offered to Catholics in their formation as evangelists in their parishes, homes and work places. Members of The Pilgrims summed up their way of life by a Covenant Commitment, which all members signed after their initial eight weeks training.

At its height, each year The Pilgrims were sharing the Gospel with and calling to conversion over five thousand young people, as well as challenging many older people to be evangelised and evangelising through the Courses on their School of Evangelisation. As well as individual parish courses, two national summer camps of a variety of the Courses from the School of Evangelisation were held for over eighty people, encouraging them to integrate the experience gained of evangelisation in these summer camps into their home life, schools and work places.

They were invited to open a Ramsgate Pilgrims group by some of the monks at Ramsgate Monastery, Kent. This lasted four years. For a couple of years the Presentation Sisters offered their Convent in Scunthorpe for a House of Prayer. Some longer term members lived briefly in a Student House while they pursued tertiary studies in London in order to develop the evangelisation work of The Pilgrims. Others went to The Diocese of Livingstone in Zambia over two summers to explore the possibility of opening a House there.

Sixty-five Volunteers passed through The Pilgrims with some staying on beyond the first year to help train the new intake of Volunteers. Some felt called to pursue the possibility of a long term core community, staying in The Pilgrims for up to eleven years in order to achieve this. In the end, this proved an unachievable dream.

Over the years, as well as the single young people in the community, three married couples joined The Pilgrims for short periods at different times. A number of people found their marriage partner from among their fellow volunteers. As a result, six marriages were celebrated at different times. Some others found their marriage partners as a result of contacts made during their stay in The Pilgrims. Two members went on to be ordained as Diocesan Priests, and three others became Religious, two as Benedictine Nuns and one as a Franciscan Brother. Two volunteers were received into full communion with the Catholic Church during their time in The Pilgrims. On leaving The Pilgrims, most people entered into service orientated professions: teaching, nursing, police force, probation service, youth work and care work of various descriptions, many playing quiet but prominent roles in their local parishes, neighbourhoods and beyond.

The basic outreach was centred round the proclamation of the *Kerygma,* or the heart of the Gospel message, seeking to call individuals to conversion to Jesus Christ and active membership of the Church. This is sometimes called *first proclamation of the Gospel,* an experience not just for new Christians but also for those already Baptised but not yet evangelised, meaning not fully alive in their relationship with Jesus Christ and living as vibrant members of the Church family.

Canon Jonathan Cotton wrote a book in May 2014 called *Evangelising the Baptised* which was based on the basic approach adopted by The Nottingham Pilgrims Community. [ISBN 978 1 903623 81 7. Published by *What's Your Story,* Luton, Bedfordshire, LU4 9HG, and available from www.goodnewsbooks.net

Nottingham Priests Together
Canon A. Dolan

Early in 1993 a young priest of the diocese felt in need of help in resolving certain issues affecting his life and ministry. He was directed towards Sister Madeleine Campion, a trained counsellor and member of the Sisters of Saint Joseph of Peace. From talking things through with her, he learned how to look, in an honest and constructive way, at the issues; and his joy in being able to do so was so great that he told a few other priests.

As a result, half a dozen priests asked Sister Madeleine, in the early autumn of 1993, if she would give them some help in developing basic skills of self-communication. She gladly agreed to do so and, with the consent of her Provincial, guided this small group through an initial training period of ten weeks.

After this period, the six priests decided to meet together on a regular basis and, by sharing openly with each other in complete confidentiality their joys and their fears, they hoped to be able to support one another and thus to grow as persons, Christians and priests.

This was a tremendous step for them since it does not come easily to most diocesan priests to talk freely even with one another about things that really concern them – their frailties, their temptations, their loneliness. They feel that they have to put on a brave face even with their priestly colleagues. In some cases, they do this for so long that they crack up or, at best, remained stunted in their personal growth.

Then the original six decided that here was something which could be offered to other priests. So they sent a circular to all the priests of the diocese inviting any who were interested in meeting together for personal growth and sharing, to write to one of them for further information. As a result of this letter, a second group began its ten-week basic training; and then there was a third group, and so on. Currently (2017) there are five groups of between six and eight members each. They meet separately usually once a fortnight for two hours. In these meetings, each one reports briefly on what has been happening in his personal life since the previous meeting, and then the group works through a programme of exercises in personal growth.

In November 2013 the groups – who adopted the collective name 'Nottingham Priests Together' - suffered a great loss with the death of Sister Madeleine, who had been their great inspiration and support from the very beginning. However, her spirit lives on, and NPT continues to be a great source of strength and enrichment to many priests of the diocese and, through them, to the people they serve.

The Permanent Diaconate

Rev. Deacon John Wilford

The offices of bishop, priest and deacon emerged together in the early Church. References can be found in the First Letter to Timothy (1Tim.3:8-13) and in the Didache. For many centuries, from St. Stephen and St. Lawrence to St. Francis of Assisi, permanent deacons exercised a ministry of charity, preaching, and administration. But by the time of St Francis, social changes had led to the gradual disappearance of their distinctive ministries. New monastic orders were providing charity and care, while diaconal liturgical roles could be assumed by priests (often vested as deacons) or by acolytes and other clerks. After the First Vatican Council, as times continued to change, notable theologians began to call for the restoration of a permanent diaconate. Among them were Cardinal Leo Joseph Suenens and Karl Rahner. The result was a determination by the Second Vatican Council 'to restore the diaconate as a proper and permanent rank of the hierarchy' (*Lumen Gentium*). In June 1967 Pope Paul VI issued an Apostolic Letter '*Sacrum Diaconatus Ordinem*' and recommended that individual bishops might reintroduce the permanent diaconate as they saw fit within their own dioceses.

Initially, neither Bishop Ellis nor Bishop McGuinness felt able to implement this. There were few guidelines. It was not until 1981 that Bishop McGuinness ordained his first deacon, Peter Skoyles, later attached to the Parish of Whitwick. Peter's role was ground-breaking. He was listed in the Diocesan Year Book under 'Foreign Priests' and not acknowledged in his own parish directory. He was joined by a second deacon, David Thompson, attached to the Parish of Mickleover, again, not acknowledged in his parish directory. David moved out of the diocese in 1992 and Peter in 1996, but during their time, great strides were being taken. In 1988 Bishop McGuinness appointed Fr. Peter Dooling, who had previously been Vice-Rector of the English College, Valladolid, as his first Diocesan Director of the Permanent Diaconate.

In the 1989 Diocesan Year Book, Fr. Dooling set out his commitment to establish a suitable training course for candidates. He offered a plan for a three-year intensive course of studies to prepare suitable selected candidates for diaconal ordination and ministry. They would be taught by a team of academically and spiritually well-qualified clergy. By 1990 that team was in place, led by Fr. Michael Tutcher, Chaplain to Loughborough

University, and Fr. Philip O'Dowd, soon to be Chaplain to Nottingham University. They were able to call upon experts in any specialist subjects, like Canon Law and Liturgy. The course was to be held at Rearsby Convent near Leicester.

The first four deacons to 'graduate' from this course were ordained in 1993, Dr. Mike Baker a college lecturer, Peter Brogan a fireman, Bill Hutchinson a magistrate, and John Tear a Trade Union General Secretary. These were followed in 1997 by nine similarly diverse new deacons, ten more in 2001, ten in 2006, and nine in 2009/10. At this point, however, due to deteriorating health, Frs. O'Dowd and Tutcher had to retire and the course was moved to Maryvale and then to Oscott College, the Seminary of the Archdiocese of Birmingham. From these, three deacons were ordained in 2012/13, five in 2014 and seven in 2016. To date, some 52 deacons have served in the diocese, with well over forty still active. Bishop Malcolm enthusiastically supported the programme, and in 2016 Bishop Patrick issued a comprehensive 'Handbook for the Permanent Diaconate' with revised guidelines, clarifications, and norms for all concerned. There are currently eight candidates in training and many more prospective candidates investigating and applying. The permanent diaconate is now well-established, and men from the widest professional and academic backgrounds are contributing enormously to the ministry of the Diocese of Nottingham.

Extraordinary Ministers of Holy Communion in The Diocese of Nottingham

Fr. M. Eastwood

When lay ministry of Holy Communion was introduced universally in 1973, those called by the Church to this ministry were designated "Extra-ordinary Ministers of Holy Communion". The Latin word was translated into English as "extraordinary" — not to everyone's satisfaction. The purpose was to distinguish the "ordinary" ministry by priests, deacons and acolytes from that now entrusted in "extraordinary" situations to the laity. The comMissioned ministers were, in fact, extra to the "ordinary" ministers. Gradually, however, these lay ministers of the Eucharist became known in our country as "Special Ministers of the Eucharist" or "Eucharistic Ministers".

In 1973 Bishop James McGuinness asked Monsignor Martin Cummins to organise the selection and formation of suitable candidates for comMissioning as Extraordinary Ministers to serve various parishes in the diocese. Accordingly, Monsignor Cummins formed a training team of priests and invited the parish priests of those parishes which most needed Eucharistic Ministers to nominate suitable candidates. The first formation weekends took place in 1978, as a result of which 141 people were comMissioned by the bishop. Formation weekends are normally held at The Briars Youth Centre, Crich.

In the early years, the formation weekends were led entirely by priests; but now they are led by priests and laypeople who make up the Diocesan Formation Team. Over the years, the weekend has developed to provide both spiritual and practical formation, including prayer, learning, practice and fellowship. Spiritually, it focuses on the Mass, Confession, silent prayer, the Prayer of the Church (Divine Office) and reflection. Practically, it focuses on distributing Holy Communion during Mass, taking Holy Communion to the sick and housebound, Exposition of the Blessed Sacrament and Eucharistic Adoration, Celebration of Word and Holy Communion. There is also an introduction to correct terminology, and preparation for Commissioning. The formation weekends are conducted keeping in step with the latest means of technology. Between 80 and 100 people are now commissioned by the bishop each year in St Barnabas' Cathedral. By December 2016, a total of 4052 people had been comMissioned since this ministry was introduced in the diocese.

Extraordinary Ministers in the Diocese of Nottingham wear a scapular when exercising their ministry in church or when ministering to the sick and housebound. This helps to remind them of the privilege that is theirs, and it helps when visiting the sick and housebound to emphasise the sacramental nature of the visit.

Each year commissioned Extraordinary Ministers are expected to attend a day of renewal. The bishop attends the renewal day for each county on a rota basis.

The Commission consists of the bishop as president, chairman and vice-chairman (both appointed by the bishop), secretary, treasurer, director of training, director of aftercare, and three members from each county area. The Commission is responsible for formation, keeping a register of Extraordinary Ministers, renewal days, aftercare, study days, retreats, consultations, newsletter, book of remembrance.

From time to time, study days are arranged either to bring currently active ministers up to date on development since they were comMissioned or to expand on their formation.

In recent years retreat days have been arranged for the members of the Commission and the training team and their spouses, on an annual basis.

A series of consultations has taken place with the priests of the diocese. An inter-diocesan consultation took place in 1998, and a follow-up consultation in 1999. At the latter consultation, the National Liturgical Office was represented as were sixteen of the twenty-two dioceses of England and Wales.

A newsletter is produced in the early part of each year. This gives early notification of renewal days as well as useful information and articles on current developments and contact names and addresses. It also lists ministers who had died in the previous year.

In 2003 a Mass was celebrated to mark the twenty-fifth anniversary of the introduction of the Extraordinary Ministry of Holy Communion in the diocese, and a Mass to mark the fortieth anniversary is planned for 2018.

The Development Of Chaplaincies

Canon A. Dolan

From time immemorial, as a normal part of their ministry, priests have been involved in 'chaplaincy'. As well as providing services to convents, this has included visiting hospitals, prisons and other institutions. But such work was usually carried out by the clergy and Religious Sisters.

However, recent decades have witnessed an extension of such ministries to the laity. Among these ministries must be mentioned chaplaincies to:

universities
schools
hospitals, nursing homes, care homes and prisons
the Travelling Community
East Midlands Airport.

'From Every Race, Language, People and Nation'

Canon E. Jarosz

From its beginning, the Christian Church has constantly been enriched by people of different races and cultures, each of which has made a distinctive contribution to its life and Mission. In the nineteenth and early twentieth centuries, the influence of immigrants from Ireland on the Catholic Church in Britain was enormous. Without them, and including the Irish priests and Religious, the story of the Catholic Church in England, not least in our diocese, would have been very different. In the years that followed the Second World War immigrants from many parts of Europe had a similar effect. More recent times have seen the arrival on our shores, not least in the Diocese of Nottingham, of people from Africa, Asia, and Latin America, as well as further immigration from mainland Europe, and these people have renewed our Church.

One of the largest immigrant communities in the diocese at the present time is from Poland. The origins of this community are to be found in the aftermath of the Second World War. The post war settlement between the victorious allies resulted in a shifting of Poland's borders westwards. Poland gained some land from Germany, but lost considerably more land to the USSR. In addition, the USSR claimed the whole of the new post-war Poland as part of its 'sphere of influence'. Most of the Polish soldiers and airmen and their families who found themselves in the UK at the end of the war decided to remain and to continue to campaign for a fully independent Poland in whatever way they could, whilst beginning the process of building lives, careers, and families here. An agreement was reached between Cardinal Griffin, the then Archbishop of Westminster, and Cardinal Hlond, the then Primate of the Polish Catholic Hierarchy, to permit the Vicar Delegate of the Polish Catholic Mission based in London to appoint priests to care for the spiritual and pastoral needs of the emerging Polish communities in other parts of England and Wales. In our diocese, Polish communities were established in Nottingham, Leicester, Derby, Mansfield, Melton Mowbray, and Scunthorpe with all but the last of these communities eventually acquiring their own church premises.

There were further new arrivals from Poland during the second half of the twentieth century but in general the communities gradually declined as the older members passed to their eternal reward and their children and grandchildren gradually integrated into the life of the local community. However the accession of Poland into the European Union in 2004 and the consequent opening up of the UK labour market saw a dramatic change with many new immigrants arriving from Poland to seek a better life for themselves and their families. This has led to a major revival in all the existing Polish communities and the establishment of new communities in South Lincolnshire.

Another significant immigrant community in the diocese originates from Italy. Many Italians came from Italy in the 1950s and 60s to work in industry - for example, on the steel works in Scunthorpe. Italian priests also came to our diocese to minister to these people and their families in their own language. Rather than having their own churches the priests would make arrangements with local clergy to use diocesan churches. Immigration from Italy had largely stopped by the 1970s and the later decades of the twentieth century saw a gradual process of integration and assimilation so that the number of Italian chaplains is now much reduced.

A further community that has had a presence in the diocese are the

Ukrainians. They are distinctive by the fact that they are part of a Catholic Community that has its own rite which adds to the diversity of the Catholic life of the Diocese. More recent years have seen the arrival of many Catholic immigrants from the southern Indian state of Kerala who use the Syro- Malabar Rite which further enriches the diversity of the liturgical life of the diocese.

Other communities worthy of note include the Goan community from India and East Africa many of whom came to the Leicester area in the 1960s and 70s, people from the Philippines who are found in many parts of the Diocese, and immigrants from many African countries including Nigeria, Zimbabwe, Zambia, and Guinea Bissau.

A tour around our diocese in 2017 would reveal a rich variety of cultures and languages amongst our Catholic congregations. People understandably want to maintain the languages and traditions of their homelands, but they are also usually happy to share their riches with others recognising that this is for the benefit of us all. We are truly 'from every race, language, people, and nation' but one Church united in the praise of God and the service of all the human family.

Pilgrimages within the Diocese

Canon A. Dolan

The notion and practice of pilgrimage cut across most cultures, epochs and religions. Fundamental to the idea of pilgrimage is that one leaves one's surroundings and journeys to a place which is perceived to be sacred due to the presence of a divine or otherwise very special being or of something connected with it.

Since the erection of the Diocese of Nottingham, individuals and groups have gone on pilgrimages to many places, but – for reasons of space – we will confine ourselves to the principal places of pilgrimage within the diocese.

DALE

The oldest of our intra-diocesan pilgrimages, now discontinued, is that to Dale Abbey.

A house of the Premonstratensian Order founded at the end of the twelfth century, Dale is in the Parish of Ilkeston. Canon Philip James McCarthy, parish priest there from 1887 to 1908, initiated a pilgrimage to Dale in honour of Our Lady. This may, or may not, have been a revival of a pre-Reformation pilgrimage. Whatever the case, a shrine to Our Lady of Dale was erected in Ilkeston church in 1889. Two years later, on 18 May 1891, Bishop Bagshawe celebrated Pontifical High Mass in the ruins of Dale Abbey. The altar stone used on that occasion is in the Lady Chapel of the present church at Ilkeston.

From 1891 pilgrimages to Dale Abbey became an annual event and attracted pilgrims from all over the country. A society called "The Roll Call Union of Honour of Our Lady of Dale" was formed. It had an international membership of many thousands. In its heyday, the Dale pilgrimage drew many hundreds of people some of whom would walk in procession from

Ilkeston. There were no pilgrimages from before the Second World War until 1953 when, on 21 June, some five to six hundred pilgrims, including "several nuns from Derby, Matlock and Nottingham", 'walked in procession through the quiet and secluded village (of Dale Abbey)... to the abbey ruins". On this occasion, the preacher, Father Felim Colwell, was a Premonstratensian, the first member of his Order to preach at Dale since the dissolution of the abbey in 1538.

After 1953 pilgrimages to Dale took place intermittently. In 1984 there was what was described as an "Ecumenical Folk Mass" at which the singing was accompanied by guitars and torrential rain! The pilgrimage two years later, attended by some 150 people, was 'Very well organized. The atmosphere was marvellous, and so was the weather". In 1987 nearly all those who went to Dale Abbey on 13 September were from Ilkeston parish; and it was noted, 'We need better publicity in future". There have been no pilgrimages to Dale since that date.

PADLEY

The first pilgrimage to Padley in North Derbyshire where Blessed Robert Ludlam and Blessed Nicholas Garlick were arrested in July 1588, and whence they were taken to Derby there to be hanged, drawn and quartered later that month, along with Blessed Richard Simpson, took place in July 1898. It was organized by the Guild of Ransom.

When the old gatehouse, now known as Padley Chapel, was purchased by the Diocese of Nottingham after a lot of persistent hard work by Monsignor Charles Payne, there began a series of pilgrimages which resulted in Padley becoming perhaps the best-loved and almost certainly the best-known shrine in the diocese.

On 13 July 1933 Monsignor Payne celebrated the first Mass at Padley since the Reformation. Later that same morning, Bishop McNulty sang Pontifical High Mass using a chalice which had also been used by the Jesuit martyr, St Edmund Campion. In the afternoon, "two thousand people walked in the heavy rain from Grindleford Station along the winding road to the Chapel."

For almost half a century the Padley Pilgrimage was an important annual event in the calendar of the Nottingham Diocese. Shortly after its creation in 1980 the Diocese of Hallam took over responsibility for this shrine. Since then, although the annual pilgrimage is organised by both dioceses, Nottingham's interest in Nicholas Garlick and Robert Ludlam seems to have waned somewhat.

Is it too fanciful to suggest that by concentrating on Derby, the place where the two Padley martyrs, together with Blessed Richard Simpson, gave their last testimony for Christ and his Church, this interest might be revived?

BEAUVALE

Two of the first martyrs of the English Reformation, Saints John Houghton and Robert Lawrence, had been Priors of the Carthusian monastery of Beauvale near Eastwood. Founded in 1343, Beauvale was one of nine Charterhouses in England at the time of the Reformation.

The site of the monastery was excavated in 1908, but not much of the monastic buildings is now visible.

Although the Beauvale Society was not founded until 1978, the first diocesan pilgrimage to Beauvale took place in May 1936 in the aftermath of the beatification of the two Priors the previous year. They were canonized as part of the group of Forty Martyrs of England and Wales in 1970. In 1936 also, a small chapel in honour of the Beauvale martyrs was dedicated in the Church of Our Lady of Good Counsel at Eastwood.

Pilgrimages to Beauvale seem to have continued without interruption since 1936. In 1940 the altar stone of the church, which for a long time had been used as a stand for buckets beneath the farmyard pump, was restored to its original use and was placed in the altar of the Martyrs' Chapel at Eastwood.

Although the 1940 pilgrimage was blessed with beautiful weather, but this has not been a distinguishing feature of pilgrimages in honour of the Carthusian martyrs. In 1984, for example, "the weather was foul - it poured". In 1985 "it bucketed with rain, so the preacher shortened his sermon". Which was just as well since most of the congregation were in the open air! It was only the clergy and the musicians who had the benefit of a canvas covering. The following year, "there were a couple of heavy showers"; but in 1987 "for once, the weather was good". And in 1989, it was "too hot".

It is good to be able to report that neither sun nor rain has been able to burn up or dampen diocesan devotion to two of the first martyrs of the Reformation. Neighbouring landowners have always been supportive and helpful in connection with the Beauvale pilgrimage, and Mr. & Mrs. T. Whyte, the current owners of the land on which the visible part of the ruins is situated, have developed the site and generously opened it up to visitors.

RODSLEY

St. Ralph Sherwin, born about 1550 at Rodsley in the present Catholic Parish of All Saints, Ashbourne, trained for the priesthood at the Venerable English College, Rome. After a short priestly ministry in England he was hanged, drawn and quartered at Tyburn on 1 December 1581, thus becoming the first alumnus of the Venerabile to die for his faith. Although there may have been a trickle of devotion to him in his native diocese, no doubt the main impetus leading to his canonization in 1970 as one of the Forty Martyrs of England and Wales, came from his old college.

To promote devotion to St. Ralph in the place of his birth, the Sherwin Society was founded in Ashbourne in 1971. Five years later, on a chilly Tuesday evening, Bishop McGuinness, accompanied by his predecessor, Bishop Ellis, unveiled and blessed a plaque mounted on a barn wall in Rodsley.

The bishop urged that Rodsley "should become a place of pilgrimage where the faithful could gather at certain times to honour the memory of the noble young priest who was born here and to renew within themselves that faith which he had upheld so steadfastly."

After a plea like that, it was not surprising that the Sherwin Society, ably assisted by the Knights of St Columba, should have organized, on 23 June 1977, the first of a continuous series of annual pilgrimages to Rodsley. The pilgrimage usually take place on a Sunday in June.

Starting at the crossroads where the plaque is sited, the pilgrims go in procession to the field where, thanks to the unfailing courtesy of the previous owners of the land, Mr. and Mrs. Glover, and of the present owner, Mass is celebrated. And it never rains at Rodsley - at least not during the Mass!

MELWOOD

The most recent of our intra-diocesan pilgrimages began in 1981, when Canon John Newsham was Parish Priest of Holy Souls, Scunthorpe. In that year, Monsignor Peter O'Dowd, Vicar General, led a procession from Crowle to Low Melwood Farm near Epworth in the Isle of Axholme. There, on the site of the Charterhouse of the Visitation of St. Mary, Mass was celebrated in honour of St. Augustine Webster, Prior of this monastery and fellow-martyr of Saints John Houghton and Robert Lawrence.

There are no longer any remains of the monastery to be seen. But the site itself is of great importance since, even in Saxon times, a chapel dedicated to Our Lady of the Wood stood there and was a place of pilgrimage right up to the Reformation.

In 1396, Thomas de Mowbray, Earl of Nottingham, founded a Carthusian monastery on the spot. After the martyrdom of its Prior, Axholme did not survive very long. It was, in fact, the first of the Carthusian houses in England to be suppressed.

But after a lapse of many centuries, Melwood has once again become a place of prayer; and it provides an opportunity for renewal in the faith of our ancestors with whom we are linked in the Communion of Saints.

In more recent years, although not organised as 'official' diocesan pilgrimages, individuals and groups have come and continue to come to Mount Saint Bernard Abbey, near Coalville, Leicestershire, to honour a former member of that community, the Nigerian Fr Cyprian Tansi, who was beatified in 1998, and to St. Barnabas' Cathedral, the last resting place of the Venerable Mary Potter, Foundress of the Little Company of Mary.

The author of The Imitation of Christ wrote: "It is not always those who are travelling about who grow in sanctity". One might paraphrase the original Latin as "too many pilgrimages can damage your spiritual health"! Yet to go on pilgrimage is in a way to act out the life of what the Second Vatican Council described as the "Pilgrim Church", journeying through this world on its way to heaven, the place where God dwells. And that can't be a bad thing!

The Diocesan Travelling Mission

Fr. P. McBrien

The Sacred Heart Fathers from February 1951 until 1972 were responsible for the Diocesan Travelling Mission which, beginning in Lincolnshire, spread eventually to all counties of the diocese. Their two main bases, both in Lincolnshire, were Market Rasen (1949-2008) and Corby Glen/Bourne/Deeping St. James (1957-1984). During the Second World War the clergy established a number of Mass centres as in rural areas people were unable to travel to Mass due to the rationing of petrol. Once the emergency conditions were lifted most of these were soon discontinued, but from this sense of taking Mass to the people persisted with the Diocesan Travelling Mission. Bishop Ellis made a great gesture to get the Mission going by giving the episcopal Daimler for Father Daniel Rafferty SCJ to use. However the petrol consumption of the car proved to be excessive for the distances he was soon covering and a more economical 10 cwt van was in use within a year. All the equipment, sacred vessels and vestments were second-hand to begin with, but the Mission worked slowly to build up more worthy replacements over the years.

Looking at the list compiled from the Nottingham Diocesan Yearbooks from 1952 to 1973 the spread of the Mission is quite commendable. It is interesting to note that only two Missions were established in Derbyshire; the distance from the Sacred Heart Fathers' parish bases is one reason, and another would be that Derbyshire already had a considerable network of Mass centres run from local parishes. Indeed, a few of the Missions would themselves be taken on as Mass centres under the care of the local parish, Immingham would become an independent parish and the centre of the Port Chaplaincy as a result of the growth of the docks and container terminal on the Humber estuary.

The end of the Diocesan Travelling Mission is not recorded in the Yearbook. In the 1973 edition the surviving ten Missions are in their places in the parish directory, the following year all are gone. The D.T.M. no longer appears, and all the names are gone. It was a time perhaps when people were finding their own transport and the growth of new parishes with new churches was more attractive places to worship than some of the venues the Diocesan Travelling Mission had used.

Lincolnshire	**Mission**	**Opened**	**Closed**
	Aisthorpe (The Old Rectory)	1952	1953
	Alford (The George Inn)	1952	1956
	Ancaster (The Butcher's Arms)	1954	1963
	Ashby Puerorum (Green's)	1952	1953
	Barkston (Village Hall)	1952	1962
	Billingborough	1958	1963
	Boothby Pagnell	1957	1962
	Burton-on-Stather (Thomas's)	1952	1956
	Byard's Leap (Gilboy's)	1953	1955
	Caythorpe (Templeway House)	1952	1954
	Claypole (Henley's, Cleveland Cottage)	1953	1972
	Crowland (Bank House)	1952	1970
	Dunholme (Pollard's)	1952	1954
	Fiskerton (Power's, Moorlands)	1952	1954
	Folkingham (Foster's)	1953	1954
	Glentworth (Kenny's, Grange Cottage)	1953	1955
	Grainthorpe	1961	1972
	Hamborough/Harbrough? (Stella Maris)	1952	1954
	Haxey	1956	1957
	Hogsthorpe (Barry's)	1953	1954
	Holton-le-Clay	1955	1966
	Horbling (Village Hall)	1954	1957
	Huttofs (Trufull, School House)	1953	1954
	mmingham (Cadet Hall)	1952	1952
	Ingham	1957	
	Kexby (Pulford's)	1952	1958
	Little Bytham	1958	1962
	Leadenham (Vickery's, High House East)	1953	
	Marsh Chapel (The Sycamore)	1953	1955
	Moorby (The Camp)	1952	1953
	Nettleham	1961	1965
	New Holland (Reading Room)	1952	1953
	North Coates (RAF)	1954	
	Owston Ferry	1955	1963
	Rippingale	1957	
	Ruskington	1956	1967
	Saltfleet (Laurence's)	1954	
	South Witham	1959	
	Stickney (The Hollies)	1952	1966
	Stragglethorpe (The Hall)	1953	1955

Mission	Opened	Closed
Sutterton (Dr. Coffey's)	1952	1962
Swineshead (LEAC Hostel)	1952	1954
Syston (The Old Hall)	1953	1954
Tongue End (Mrs Moon's)	1952	1954
Wainfleet All Saints (Nurse Jackson's)	1953	1962
Willoughton (Lawler's)	1952	1972
Wilton	1967	1972
Winteringham (Harrison's)	1952	1972
Winterton (Crawford's)	1952	1957

Leicestershire

Mission	Opened	Closed
Anstey	1956	1966
Billesdon	1956	1972
Bottesford (Rutland Café)	1952	1972
Broughton Astley	1956	1958
Buckminster (United Steel Hostel)	1952	1962
Burrough-on-the-Hill (Feeney's)	1954	1955
Castle Bytham (Di Marco's)	1952	1953
Claybrook	1956	1960
Cosby	1956	
Eastwell (Holy Family Church)	1953	1972
Knossington (Whalebones House)	1953	1957
Long Clawson (Dr... Cuddigan's)	1952	1955
Old Dalby (The Army Camp)	1952	1953
Redmile (NUS Camp)	1954	
Stathern (LEAC Hostel)	1952	1955
Waltham-on-the-Wolds (Maloney's)	1952	1954
Woolsthorpe by Belvoir (Village Hall)	1952	1953

Nottinghamshire

Mission	Opened	Closed
Askham (Lea Cottage)	1953	1954
Barston (Village Hall)	1969	1972
Burton Joyce	1959	1962
Carlton-onTrent	1967	1972
Clayworth	1958	1963
Collingham	1956	1972
Dr...akeholes (The Swan Hotel)	1953	1956
Mission (Notts Crop Dr...i Hostel)	1952	1953
Misterton, (Village Hall)	1952	1957
Norwell (Cafferkey's)	1953	1956
Shelton	1955	
Sutton-on-Trent (Flannagan's, The Elms)	1953	1966
Woodbeck (Blackburn's)	1954	1963

Rutland

Mission	Opened	Closed
Allexton, (The Lodge)	1953	1955
Cold Overton (Priddon's Manor Farm)	1953	
Uppingham (Rutland Cinema)	1953	1972

Derbyshire

Mission	Opened	Closed
Ambergate	1959	1966
Walton-on-Trent	1959	1962

Churches, Chapels-of-Ease and Mass Centres

Alderwasley Hall, Derbyshire
1949: Benedictine Preparatory School in Wirksworth Parish. Closed in 1974.

Alford, Lincolnshire
1958: chapel-of-ease served from Mablethorpe. Closed in 1988.

Allexton Hall, near Uppingham, Leicestershire
1903; domestic chapel served mainly from the cathedral. Closed in 1908.

Anstey, Leicestershire
1981; served from St. Patrick's, Leicester. Closed in 1991.

Aston-on-Trent, Derbyshire
pre-1950: Mental Hospital served from Melbourne. Closed in 1967.

Bakewell, Derbyshire, English Martyrs
1890: chapel-of-ease served from Hassop; a former Nonconformist Chapel purchased for Catholic use.

Bardney, Lincolnshire, St. Francis
1944: chapel-of-ease served from various parishes in Central Lincolnshire, most recently from Lincoln St. Hugh.

Barrow-on-Soar, Leicestershire, St Alban
1839: chapel-of-ease after being a parish was later served from Birstall and then Sileby. Closed in 1989.

Barwell, near Hinckley, Leicestershire, YMCA Hall
c.1940: Mass centre served from Earl Shilton. Closed in 1947.

Belton, Rutland
1941: Mass centre served from Oakham. Closed in 1957.

Billesdon, Leicestershire
1945: Mass centre served from St. Joseph's, Leicester. Closed in 1957.

Bilsthorpe, Nottinghamshire
1958: Mass centre served from Southwell. Closed in 1991.

Bingham, Nottinghamshire
1964: Mass centre served from Radcliffe-on-Trent, first using parish church then Methodist church.

Birdholme, Derbyshire
1852: Mass centre in succession to Wingerworth Hall; served from Spinkhill. Closed in 1858.

Blidworth, Nottinghamshire
1942: Mass centre served from Mansfield. Closed in 1960.

Bolsover, Derbyshire, St. Bernadette
1903/1944: chapel-of-ease served from Shirebrook/Langwith Junction.

Borrowash, Derbyshire, Diocesan Rescue Society
1949: convent chapel. Closed in 1959.

Borrowash, Derbyshire, St. Hugh
1959: chapel-of-ease served from Chaddesden until it became a parish in 1972.

Bourne, Lincolnshire, (Sacred Heart and) St. Gilbert
1924: chapel-of-ease served from Corby Glen until it became the parish church in 1976.

Bramcote, Nottinghamshire, St. Gregory
1957: chapel-of-ease served from Stapleford. Closed in 1999.

Broadbottom (Gamesley), Derbyshire, Immaculate Conception
1894/1915: chapel-of-ease served from Hadfield.

Broughton, Lincolnshire
1980: Mass centre served from Brigg. Closed in 1983.

Broughton Astley, Leicestershire
1958: Mass centre served from Blessed Sacrament, Leicester. Closed in 1959.

Burbage, Leicestershire
1943: chapel-of-ease served from Hinckley, initially at The Croft; in 1947 moved to The Bull's Head. Closed in 1988.

Burgh-le-Marsh, Lincolnshire
1952: Mass centre served from Skegness. Closed in 1959.

Burton Joyce, Nottinghamshire
1940: Mass centre served from Sacred Heart, Carlton. Closed in 1945.

Burton-on-Trent (Winshill), Staffordshire, Our Lady of the Most Holy Rosary
1970: chapel-of-ease served from Stapenhill, Burton-on-Trent.

Butterley Grange, near Ripley, Derbyshire
1904: semi-public chapel of the Wright family, served from the Cathedral until 1920, and then from Alfreton. Closed in 1927.

Caistor, Lincolnshire, St. Thomas More
1876: chapel-of-ease served from Osgodby and later Market Rasen.

Calow, Derbyshire, (The White Hart)
1933 to 1945, then in the Parish Church Hall from 1966; Mass centre served from The Annunciation, Chesterfield. Closed in 1972.

Calverton, Nottinghamshire, St. Anthony
1953: chapel-of-ease, initially served from Good Shepherd, Woodthorpe, but subsequently from Southwell.

Castle Donington, Leicestershire, St. John Fisher (1928)
Church of the Risen Lord (1992): chapel-of-ease served from Melbourne.

Centre Parcs, Nottinghamshire
1988: holiday village chapel, served from Sutton-in-Ashfield (1988-93);
New Ollerton (1993-2001); Newark (2002). Catholic Services ceased in 2002.

Chapel St. Leonards, Lincolnshire
1952: Mass centre served from Mablethorpe. Closed in 1965.

Chinley, Derbyshire
1951: Mass centre served from Chapel-en-le-Frith. Closed in 1991.

Church Langton, near Market Harborough, Leicestershire
1961: Mass centre served from Market Harborough. Closed in 1962.

Clay Cross, Derbyshire, St. Patrick & St. Bridget
1861: Mass centre served from either Ilkeston or Chesterfield until 1875 when it became a parish until 1925, but became dependent as chapel-of-ease to Alfreton its former chapel-of-ease.

Coleby Hall, Lincolnshire
1884: domestic chapel of the Tempest family served from Wellingore until 1890 then St. Hugh's, Lincoln. Closed in 1917.

Colston Bassett, Nottinghamshire
1834: (Colston Bassett Hall) Mission/chapel-of-ease served from various centres. Closed in 1918.
1951: Baby Home of the Diocese Rescue Society (later the Catholic Children's Society). Closed in 1961.

Corby Glen, Lincolnshire, Our Lady of Mount Carmel
1976: after a long time as a parish, became a chapel-of-ease served initially from Bourne, then (in 1984) from Grantham until it was closed in 2012.

Cosby, Leicestershire
1956: Mass centre served from St. Mary's, South Wigston. Closed in 1959.

Cotgrave, Nottinghamshire, Our Lady of Grace
1973: chapel-of-ease initially along with Tollerton served from Keyworth. Divided from Keyworth later 2005 to be served from Holy Spirit, West Bridgford.

Cressbrook Hall, Derbyshire
1948: Novitiate Chapel of the Presentation Sisters with chaplain. Closed in 1957.

Cresswell, Derbyshire, Christ the King
1916: served from Spinkhill. Closed in 1974.

Cromford, Derbyshire, (The Greyhound Hotel)
1952: Mass centre served from Matlock. Closed in 1967.

Deeping St. James, Lincolnshire, Our Lady of Lincoln and St. Guthlac
After a history as a Mass centre from 1879 and from 1919 until 1956 the Xaverian Brothers had a presence in the locality; became a chapel-of-ease in 1958 served from Corby Glen, and then in 1976 from Bourne.

Derby, Chaddesden, St. Alban
1943: chapel-of-ease served from St. Mary's, Derby until 1954 when it became a separate parish.

Derby, Chellaston, St. Ralph Sherwin
1948 to 1951 Mass centre in the Rose & Crown; 1951 to1965 at the New Inn; 1965-

1977 in Old People's Hall, Maple Drive. In 1976 chapel-of-ease was started, initially served from St. George's Derby and in 1977 served from Holy Spirit, Sinfin. Separated from Sinfin in 2000 and then served from English Martyrs, Alvaston.

Derby, Mickleover, Our Lady of Lourdes
1958 chapel-of-ease served from St. Joseph's, Derby, until 1961 when it became a separate parish.

Derwent, Derbyshire, St. Henry
1877 chapel-of-ease served from Sheffield until1878, then with private chaplain until 1912, when served from Bamford until 1944. Closed in 1944 when the village was submerged by the waters of Ladybower Reservoir.

Doe Lea, Hardwick Hall, Derbyshire
1946 Mass centre served from Holy Family, Chesterfield. Originally for the Polish Camp, then in 1947 it became a miners' hostel, and served Catholics in the area until it closed in 1956.

Duffield, Derbyshire, St. Margaret Clitherow
1954 chapel-of-ease served from Belper; new church built 1981/2.

Earlesfield, Grantham, Lincolnshire, Church of the Epiphany
1976 Mass centre served from St. Mary the Immaculate, Grantham. Closed in 1981.

East Leake, Leicestershire, Our Lady of the Angels
1953 chapel-of-ease served from St. Mary's, Loughborough until it became a separate parish in 1966.

Eastwell, Leicestershire, Holy Family
1720 Mission in East Leicestershire initially in Eastwell Hall, home of the Eyre family. A new chapel was built in 1798 with a resident priest until 1884. From that date until 1904 served from various places. A priest lived there until 1928. It was served from various places, notably Melton Mowbray until it was taken over by the Diocesan Travelling Mission from 1953. Closed in 1973.

Ednaston Hall, near Brailsford, Derbyshire
1949: chapel of St. Mary's Nursing Home run by the Sisters of Mercy, at times having a resident chaplain, at other times being served from Ashbourne until 2016 when it closed.

Ellistown, near Coalville, Leicestershire, St. Thomas More
1948: a Mass centre established from Coalville; and a chapel-of-ease built in 1954. Closed in 1970.

Elsham Hall, near Brigg, Lincolnshire
1933: domestic chapel of the Elwes family (sometimes with a resident chaplain) served from Panton until 1936 and from Brigg until 1949. Closed in 1976.

Exton, Rutland, St. Thomas of Canterbury
1867: domestic chapel of the Earls of Gainsborough, original residence of priest serving Oakham until 1964; then served from Oakham.

Fillingham, near Market Rasen, Lincolnshire
1950 Mass centre served from Market Rasen. Closed in 1955.

Grace Dieu, Leicestershire
1899/1908 domestic chapel, later preparatory school for Ratcliffe College. Served by Rosminian Fathers.

Grassmoor, Derbyshire
1933 Mass centre served from Chesterfield (from the Annunciation until 1942, then from the new Parish of Holy Family), Mission later moved to Holmewood when the premises at the Sportsman Inn were no longer available; closed in 1943.

Great Easton, near Market Harborough, Leicestershire
1865: domestic chapel served "occasionally" from Stamford. Closed in 1874.

Grimsby, Scartho, Lincolnshire, St. John Fisher
1951: chapel-of-ease served from St. Mary's, Grimsby. Closed in 2017.

Grimsby, Nunsthorpe, Lincolnshire
1951; Mass centre served initially St. Mary's and later from St. Peter's, Grimsby. Closed in 1964.

Grimsby, Lincolnshire, St. Peter
1981: former parish church reopened as chapel-of-ease served from St. Pius X. Closed in 2008.

Grimsby, Lincolnshire, St. Pius X
1958: chapel-of-ease served from St. Peter's until 1972 when it became a parish church. Closed in 2017.

Hainton, Lincolnshire, St. Francis
1836 chapel-of-ease served from Market Rasen.

Halfway, Derbyshire
1923: Mass centre served from Spinkhill. Closed in 1937.
Hallaton Hall, near Market Harborough, Leicestershire
1876 Mass centre served from Market Harborough. Closed in 1877. From 1951 until 1967 chapel of the Daughters of Our Lady of Good Counsel (Vocation Sisters).

Hanthorpe Hall, near Bourne, Lincolnshire
1902: Domestic Chapel. Closed in 1903.

Harlaxton Manor, near Grantham, Lincolnshire
1950: chapel of the Jesuit Novitiate House. Closed in 1965.

Hathern, Leicestershire, St. Aloysius
1899: Mass centre established, 1908: chapel-of-ease served from Shepshed. Closed in 2003.

Hathern, Leicestershire, Knightthorpe Hostel
1949: Mass centre served from Loughborough, St. Mary. Closed in 1952.

Heanor, Derbyshire, Our Lady of Good Counsel / then 1938 Sacred Heart
1928: chapel-of-ease served from Eastwood, Nottinghamshire. Closed in 2004.

Hemswell, near Market Rasen, Lincolnshire
1954: Mass centre served from Market Rasen. Closed in 1984.

Hinckley, Leicestershire, Port House
1943: Mass centre prior to founding of Sacred Heart chapel-of-ease, served from St. Peter's, Hinckley. Closed in 1952

Hinckley, Leicestershire, Sacred Heart
1951: chapel-of-ease served from St. Peter's, Hinckley. Closed in 1988.

Hinckley, Lindley Estate, Leicestershire
1949: Mass centre served from St. Peter's, Hinckley. Closed in 1956.

Holmewood, Derbyshire
1943: Mass centre served from Holy Family, Chesterfield. Closed in 1956.

Holton Holgate, near Spilsby, Lincolnshire
1897: residence of priest for Spilsby. Closed in 1900.

Horncastle, Lincolnshire
1905: Mass centre served initially from Spilsby; from 1954 served from Woodhall Spa.

Husbands Bosworth, Leicestershire
1763: Domestic Chapel in the home of the Turville family; present church built in 1875; since 1941 served from Market Harborough.

Immingham, Lincolnshire, Our Lady Star of the Sea
1956: chapel-of-ease served from St. Peter's/St. Pius X, Grimsby until 1969 when it became a separate parish. It was then merged with St. Pius X in 2013, and then became a constituent part of the new Parish of The Most Holy and Undivided Trinity (Grimsby, Immingham and Cleethorpes) in 2017.

Jacksdale, Nottinghamshire
1951: Mass centre served from Alfreton. Closed in 1960.

Keadby, near Crowle, Lincolnshire
1951: Mass centre for McAlpine construction camp; served from Crowle. Closed in 1994.

Keelby, near Immingham, Lincolnshire
1981: Mass centre served from Immingham. Closed in 1991.

Kegworth, Nottinghamshire
1968: Mass centre served from Shepshed. Closed in 1991.

Keyworth, Nottinghamshire, St. Margaret Clitherow
1962: chapel-of-ease served from West Bridgford for a year, then from Radcliffe-on-Trent until it was merged with Cotgrave to form a parish with Tollerton in 1973. Divided from Cotgrave into two parishes to be served from East Leake in 2011.

Kibworth, Leicestershire
1935: Mass centre served from Market Harborough. Closed in 1956.

Kirby Muxloe/Leicester Forest East, Leicestershire
1952: Chapel of Corpus Christi Carmelite Sisters' 'Carmel' Home. Closed in 1993. Mass centre in St. Andrew's Anglican church served initially from St. Peter's, Leicester and then from Blessed Sacrament. Finally closed in 2007.

Kirkby-in-Ashfield (East Kirkby), Nottinghamshire, St. Joseph /All Souls
1923: chapel-of-ease served from St. Philip Neri, Mansfield, until it became an

independent parish in 1972.
Kirton-in-Lindsey, Lincolnshire, Army barracks
1961 Mass centre served from Market Rasen, and then from Brigg. Closed in 1989.
Leicester, St. Patrick
1854 Mission served by Dominicans from Holy Cross, Leicester, and then by secular clergy from 1894. From 1922 until it closed in 1940 it was served from Our Lady of Good Counsel, Leicester.
1958 new chapel-of-ease served from Our Lady of Good Counsel, Leicester, until 1961 when it became a separate parish.

Leicester, New Parks, Mother of God
1952 chapel-of-ease served from St. Peter's, Leicester until 1960 when it became a separate parish.

Leicester, Eyres Monsell, St. John Bosco
1936: chapel-of-ease served from St. Edward's, Aylestone, Leicester, until 1958 when it became a separate parish. Now served from St. Mary's, South Wigston.

Leicester, Nether Hall, Rosary Church
1958: chapel-of-ease served from St. Joseph's, Leicester.

Leicester, Wakerley Road, St. Margaret Mary
1966: chapel-of-ease served from Sacred Heart, Leicester, until sold to Polish Catholic Mission in 1990, still used for Sunday Mass by arrangement.

Lincoln, Our Lady of Lincoln
1933: served from St. Hugh's, Lincoln until 1943 when it became a separate parish.

Lincoln, Boultham, Saints Peter & Paul
1944: served from St. Hugh's, Lincoln until 1968 when it became a separate parish.

Lindley Hall, Leicestershire
1883: Domestic Chapel in the home of the Eyre family served from Hinckley. Closed in 1917.

Long Bennington, Lincolnshire
1882 to 1887; 1899: Mass centre served from Grantham. Closed about 1901.

Loughborough, Shelthorpe, Leicestershire, Sacred Heart
1956: chapel-of-ease served from St. Mary's, Loughborough, until 1963 when it became a separate parish.

Lowdham, Nottinghamshire
1945: Mass centre served from Carlton. Closed in 1967.

Lowdham Grange, Nottinghamshire
1961: Mass centre served from Carlton. Closed in 1979.

Luddington, Lincolnshire, St. Joseph and St. Dympna
1876: chapel-of-ease served from Crowle.

Mablethorpe, Lincolnshire, St. Joseph
1906: chapel-of-ease served from Louth until 1956 when it became a separate parish.

Mansfield, Forest Town, Nottinghamshire, St. Patrick
1956: chapel-of-ease served from St. Philip Neri, Mansfield, until 1958 when it became a separate parish.

Mansfield Woodhouse, Nottinghamshire, St. Charles Borromeo
1958: chapel-of-ease served from St. Philip Neri, Mansfield, until merged with St. Theresa, Market Warsop in 1974 to create a new parish until 1992. Then it was once again divided and returned to St. Philip Neri, Mansfield. Closed in 1993.

Manton, Rutland
1941: weekday Mass centre served from Oakham. Closed in 1943.

Market Bosworth, Leicestershire, Our Lady and St. Gregory
1931: chapel-of-ease served from Earl Shilton.

Market Warsop, Nottinghamshire, St. Theresa
1942: chapel-of-ease served from Shirebrook until it merged with Mansfield Woodhouse in 1974 to form a new parish. In 1992 it was given back to Shirebrook; 2003 served from St. Philip Neri, Mansfield. In 2012. it was given back to Shirebrook yet again. In 2017, the parish was given into the care of the clergy of St.. Philip Neri, Mansfield.

Marsh Lane, Derbyshire
1923: Mass centre served from Spinkhill. Closed in 1952.
Melton Mowbray, Leicestershire, St. Peter
1965: chapel-of-ease served from St. John's, Melton Mowbray.

Metheringham, Lincolnshire
1958: Mass centre served from Woodhall Spa. Closed in 1988.

Mount St. Bernard, Whitwick, Leicestershire, Abbey of Our Lady and St. Bernard
1835: Monastic church; open to the public.
Mount St. Mary's College, Spinkhill, Derbyshire
1842: school run by the Society of Jesus; open to the public.

Nanpantan, Leicestershire
1954: Mass centre served from St. Mary, Loughborough. Closed in 1955.

Narborough, Leicestershire, St. Pius X
1946: chapel-of-ease served from Blessed Sacrament, Braunstone, Leicester; became a separate parish in 1965.

Nettleham, Lincolnshire
1987: Mass centre served from Our Lady of Lincoln, Lincoln. Closed in 1989.

New Brumby, Scunthorpe, Lincolnshire
1939: Mass centre served from Holy Souls, Scunthorpe. Closed in 1952.

Nocton Hall, Lincolnshire
1875: Domestic chapel of the Marquis of Ripon. Closed in 1889.

Nottingham, Arnold, St. Gilbert
1967: chapel-of-ease served from Good Shepherd, Woodthorpe. Closed in 2001.

Nottingham, Bilborough, St. Hugh of Lincoln
1952: chapel-of-ease served from St. Teresa, Aspley, until 1968 when it became a separate parish.

Nottingham, Clifton
1939: chapel-of-ease served from West Bridgford until 1956 when it became a separate parish.

Nottingham, Sneinton, St. Bernadette
1934: chapel-of-ease served from St. Patrick's then from Sacred Heart, Carlton. Closed in 2017.

Nottingham, Sneinton, St. Christopher
2017: Mass centre using local Anglican parish church after the closure of St. Bernadette's.

Nottingham, Wollaton, St. Thomas More
1941: chapel-of-ease served from St. Paul's, Lenton until 1977 when it became a separate parish.

Oadby, Leicestershire, Immaculate Conception
1940: chapel-of-ease served from Holy Cross until 1947; then from St. Mary, South Wigston, until 1961 when it became a separate parish.

Offcote Hurst, Derbyshire
1951: Carmelite Convent Chapel served from Ashbourne. Closed in 1960.

Osgodby, near Market Rasen, Lincolnshire, Our Lady and St. Joseph
1793: chapel-of-ease served from Market Rasen.

Osgathorpe, Leicestershire
1840: Mass centre served from Grace Dieu then Loughborough Closed in 1845

Ossington, (Agricultural Centre), Nottinghamshire
1948: Mass centre served from Newark. Closed in 1951.

Panton, East Barkwith, Lincolnshire, St. Lawrence
1918: chapel of Capuchin Junior Seminary. Closed in 1936. Later served by the Sacred Heart Fathers. Closed in 1954.

Quorndon, Leicestershire, St. Agnes
1880: Chapel of the Little Company of Mary. Closed in 1888.

Radcliffe-on-Trent, Nottinghamshire, English Martyrs/St. Anne's
1938: chapel-of-ease served from West Bridgford until 1963 when it became a separate parish.

Rainworth, Nottinghamshire, St. George's
1960: chapel-of-ease served from St. Patrick, Forest Town, Mansfield.

Ranby Hall, Nottinghamshire
1903: Domestic chapel. Closed in 1905.

Ratcliffe College, Leicestershire
1844: college chapel served by the Institute of Charity (Rosminians)

Ravenshead, Nottinghamshire
1976: Mass centre served from Kirkby-in-Ashfield. Closed in 1991.

Repton, Derbyshire
1953: Mass centre served from Swadlincote. Closed in 1988.

Riddings, Derbyshire
1860: Mass centre served from Ilkeston. Closed in 1862.

Ripley, Derbyshire, St. Joseph
1930: chapel-of-ease served from Belper until 1952 when became a separate parish.

Rothley, Leicestershire, Sacred Heart
1921: chapel-of-ease served by Rosminians from various centres, from 1941 those at Birstall.

Ruddington, Nottinghamshire
1939: chapel-of-ease served from West Bridgford and 1956 from Corpus Christi, Clifton. Closed in 1967.

Ruskington, Lincolnshire
1968: chapel-of-ease served from Sleaford. Closed in 1982.

Sapcote, Leicestershire
1977: Mass centre served from St. Peter's, Hinckley. Closed in 1988.

Scunthorpe, Ashby, Lincolnshire, St. Bernadette's
1939: chapel-of-ease served from Holy Souls, Scunthorpe until 1950 when it became a separate parish.

Santon Camp & Lysaghts Camp, Scunthorpe, Lincolnshire
1949: several Mass centres at steelworks' hostels; served from Holy Souls, Scunthorpe. Closed in 1956.

Selston, Derbyshire
1981: Mass centre served from Alfreton. Closed in 1989.

Sharnford, Leicestershire
1959: Mass centre served from St. Peter, Hinckley. Closed in 1963.

Skegness, Lincolnshire, Sacred Heart
1877: Mission served from Boston/Sleaford until 1896 when it became a separate parish.

Smalley, Stainsby Hall, Derbyshire
1939: domestic chapel of the Brothers of Mercy. Closed in 1957.

Southwell, Nottinghamshire, Our Lady of Victories
1951: chapel-of-ease served from Holy Trinity Newark until 1962 when it became a separate parish.

Spilsby, Lincolnshire, Our Lady and the English Martyrs
1961: chapel-of-ease served from Woodhall Spa then from 2004 by Skegness.

Spondon, Derbyshire
1917 to 1922, 1944 to 1948, 1952: Mass centre served from St. Mary, Derby, at the British Celanese Works. Finally closed in 1959.

Stanford Hall, Leicestershire
1962: Domestic Chapel served from Lutterworth. Closed in 1977.

Staunton Hall, Nottinghamshire
1899: Domestic chapel of the Cafferata family. Closed in the early years of the twentieth century.

Staunton Harold, Derbyshire, Cheshire Home/Sue Ryder Palliative Care Home
1962: Mass centre served from Melbourne. Closed in 1975.

Stoke Golding, Leicestershire, St. Martin's
1949: chapel of St. Martin's School served from St. Peter, Hinckley. Closed in 2015.

Sutton Bridge, Lincolnshire
1957: chapel-of-ease served from Holbeach. Closed in 1984.

Sutton Scarsdale, Derbyshire
1882: Domestic Chapel with chaplain. Closed in 1888.

Sutton-in-Ashfield, Nottinghamshire, St. Joseph the Worker
1931: chapel-of-ease served from St. Philip Neri, Mansfield until 1957 when it became a separate parish.

Syston, Leicestershire, Divine Infant of Prague
1889 to 1901 (served from Barrow); 1921 to 1924; 1939 served from Ratcliffe; 1943 then Birstall until 1963 when it became a separate parish.

Tibshelf, Derbyshire
1957: Mass centre served from Alfreton. Closed in 1960.

Tideswell, High Peak, Derbyshire, Immaculate Heart of Mary
c.1830: Mission served from Hathersage; 1884 served by a resident priest from time to time but changed status to chapel-of-ease served from Chapel-en-le-Frith in 1944.??

Tixover Grange, Rutland
1917: Mass centre served from Stamford. Closed in 1923.

Tolethorpe Hall, Lincolnshire
1879: Domestic chapel of the Eaton family. Closed in 1909.

Tollerton, Nottinghamshire, St. Hugh's College
1948: Diocesan Junior Seminary chapel. Closed in 1986.

Tuxford, Nottinghamshire
1948: Mass centre (weekday) served from New Ollerton. Closed in 1951.

Ullesthorpe, Leicestershire
1961: Mass centre served from Lutterworth. Closed in 1975.

Uppingham, Rutland
1914/5; 1923 to 1929; 1943 to 1945; Mass centre served from Oakham and for a period by the Diocesan Travelling Mission. Closed in 1982.

Upton Hall, near Southwell, Nottinghamshire
1945: Chapel of Holy Ghost Fathers' Novitiate. Closed in 1972.

Wainfleet, near Skegness, Lincolnshire
1955: chapel-of-ease served from Skegness. Closed in 1966.

Wellingore Hall, Lincolnshire, St. Augustine
1874: Domestic Chapel of the Neville family; with chaplains until 1917, after which it was served from various parishes. Closed in 1999.

Wellsborough, Leicestershire
1965: Chapel of Holy Ghost Fathers' College. Closed in 1969.

Welton, Lincolnshire
1992: Mass centre served from Our Lady, Lincoln. Closed in 1993.

Weston-on-Trent, Derbyshire
1948: Mass centre served from Melbourne. Closed in 1950.

Whaley Bridge, Derbyshire, St. Joseph
1897: Mass centre served from New Mills. Closed in 1918.

Whissendine, Rutland
1942: weekday Mass centre served from Oakham. Closed in 1945.

Whittington/New Whittington, Derbyshire, St. Patrick
1884: chapel-of-ease served from Staveley. Closed in 1977.

Wickenby, Lincolnshire
Mass centre served at one time from Market Rasen but now closed.

Wigston Magna, Leicestershire
1956: Catechetical centre (no Mass) served from South Wigston Closed in 1960.

Willesley Hall, near Measham, Leicestershire
1881: Domestic chapel of the Loudon family served from Ashby. Closed in 1900.

Willington, Derbyshire
1955: Hostel at the power station Mass centre served from St. George, Derby. Closed in 1963.

Wingerworth, Derbyshire
1839: Domestic Chapel of the Hunloke family served from Spinkhill. Closed in 1852; 1948 Mass centre served from Holy Family, Chesterfield. Closed in 1953.

Winster, Derbyshire
c.1896: Mass centre served from Matlock. Date of closure unknown.

Wirksworth, Derbyshire, Our Lady & St. Teresa of Lisieux
1839 to 1850: Mass centre served from Derby; 1930 new church served from Matlock until 1949; then served from Alderwasley Hall, Derbyshire, until 1974; later chapel-of-ease served from Crich/Ripley/Matlock.

Witham Hall, Bourne, Lincolnshire
1904: domestic chapel served by Stamford from 1909. Closed in 1924.

Woodhouse Eaves, Leicestershire
1953: Mass centre in the village institute hall, then in Anglican parish church; served

initially from St. Mary's Loughborough, then Loughborough University Chaplaincy and latterly from Holy Cross, Leicester.

RAF and other Military Stations

RAF Binbrook, Lincolnshire
Mass centre served from Market Rasen. Closed in 1988.

Chilwell, Nottinghamshire
1951: Army barracks, Mass centre. Closed by 1981.

RAF Coddington, Lincolnshire
1977: Mass centre. Closed in 1988.

RAF Coningsby, Lincolnshire
1953: Mass centre served for some time by Woodhall Spa.

RAF Cottesmore, Rutland
Mass centre. Closed in 2007.

RAF Cranwell, Lincolnshire RAF College
Mass centre usually with a resident chaplain, although in recent years served from elsewhere outside the diocese.

RAF Digby, Lincolnshire
1957: Mass centre served from RAF Cranwell.

RAF Edith Weston, Rutland
1959: Mass centre served from RAF Cottesmore. Closed in 1980.

RAF Manby, Lincolnshire
1953: Flying School Mass centre served from Louth. Closed in 1974.

RAF Newton, Nottinghamshire
c.1988 Mass centre served originally from St. Edward, Nottingham, then in 1988 from St. Barnabas Cathedral, Nottingham. Closed in 1989.

RAF Nocton, Lincolnshire
Mass centre served from RAF Cranwell. Closed in 1989.

RAF North Luffenham, Rutland
Mass centre served from St. Joseph, Oakham. Closed in 1989.

RAF Scampton, Lincolnshire
1957: Mass centre usually with chaplain. Closed in 1994.
RAF Swinderby, Lincolnshire
1957: Mass centre. Closed in 1993.

RAF Waddington, Lincolnshire
1957: Mass centre

Chapels now in the Diocese of Hallam

Barlborough Hall, Derbyshire
1938: Preparatory School to Mount St. Mary's, Jesuit

Beighton, Derbyshire, Christ the King
1923: Mass centre; briefly had parish status 1955 to 1957 otherwise served from Spinkhill

Bradwell, Newburgh Hall, Derbyshire
1951: Mass centre served from Bamford.

Brimington, Sutton Lodge, Derbyshire
1921: Domestic Chapel/Mass centre served from Staveley. Closed in 1953; used as presbytery after this date.

Chesterfield, Newbold, Derbyshire, St. Hugh
1953: chapel-of-ease served from The Annunciation, Chesterfield, until 1964 when it became a separate parish.

Clowne, Derbyshire, The Sacred Heart and Our Lady of Victories
1901: Mass centre served from Spinkhill. The new church was built in 1952 and served by diocesan clergy from 1967.

Dronfield, Derbyshire, Holy Spirit
1943: Mass centre at the White Swan; in 1949, a Non-Conformist Chapel was bought for Catholic use, served from Woodseats, Sheffield, until it became a separate parish in 1961.
Eckington, Derbyshire, The Annunciation
1923: served from Spinkhill.

Gleadless, South Yorkshire, St. Anthony
1971: chapel-of-ease served from Hackenthorpe.